Dictionary of Forensic Ps

REFERENCE

Dictionary of Forensic Psychology

Edited by

Graham J. Towl, David P. Farrington, David A. Crighton and Gareth Hughes

WILLAN
PUBLISHING

BP45

Published by

Willan Publishing
Culmcott House
Mill Street, Uffculme
Cullompton, Devon
EX15 3AT, UK
Tel: +44(0)1884 840337
Fax: +44(0)1884 840251
e-mail: info@willanpublishing.co.uk
website: www.willanpublishing.co.uk

Published simultaneously in the USA and Canada by

Willan Publishing
c/o ISBS, 920 NE 58th Ave, Suite 300,
Portland, Oregon 97213-3786, USA
Tel: +001(0)503 287 3093
Fax: +001(0)503 280 8832
e-mail: info@isbs.com
website: www.isbs.com

First published 2008

ISBN 978-1-84392-295-7 paperback
      978-1-84392-296-4 hardback

British Library Cataloguing-in-Publication Data

A catalogue record for this book is available from the British Library

Project managed by Deer Park Productions, Tavistock, Devon
Typeset by Pantek Arts Ltd, Maidstone, Kent
Printed and bound by TJ International Padstow, Cornwall

2/25/10

Dedication

This book is dedicated to the memory of Mark Harris. Mark was a contributor to this Dictionary and was Director of Quality for the Parole Board for England and Wales at the time of his untimely death. He had formerly been a Cropwood Fellow at the University of Cambridge Institute of Criminology and was Head of Quality and Standards with Victim Support, as well as being an Assistant Chief Probation Officer in the London Probation Service. Mark will be greatly missed by his many friends and colleagues in the criminal and civil justice systems.

Contents

List of entries

Addictive behaviours
Adversarial system
Anger
Anger and aggression assessment
Animal cruelty
Applied psychology
Approved premises
Attachment theory

Biological factors in crime
Boot camps
British Crime Survey (BCS)
British Psychological Society (BPS)
Bullying in prisons

Cambridge Framework for Risk
   Assessment (CAMRA)
Care Programme Approach (CPA)
Chartered psychologists
Children and Family Court Advisory
   and Support Service (CAFCASS)
Child witnesses
Clinical psychology
Cognitive interviews
Community punishments
Court duty officers (CDOs)
Courts
Criminal careers
Criminal justice system
Criminal responsibility
Criminology
Crown Prosecution Service (CPS)

Detecting deception
Developmental disabilities in adults
Diagnosis of mental disorder
Double jeopardy
Dyslexia and specific learning disabilities

Educational psychology
Every Child Matters
Evidence-based practice (EBP)
Expert testimony
Eyewitness testimony

False confessions
Family factors
Family violence
Forensic psychiatry
Forensic psychology

Group work

Health Professions Council (HPC)
Health psychology
High secure hospitals
HM Inspectorate of Prisons
HM Prison Service
Homelessness and crime
Hostage negotiation
Human rights

Intellectual assessment
Intelligence, impulsivity and empathy
Investigative psychology

Jury decision-making
Juvenile delinquency

Legal profession

Medium secure units (MSUs)
Mental disorder interventions
Meta-analysis
Moral reasoning
Motivational interviewing (MI)

List of contributors

Derval Ambrose, Kids Company.
Dr Jo Bailey, HM Prison Service and University of East Anglia.
Dr Judi Bamford, Kirklees Metropolitan Council.
Amy Beck, London Probation Service.
Graham Beck, HM Prison Service.
S. George Blom-Cooper, Bedford Row Chambers, London.
Dr Jo Borrill, University of Westminster.
Dr P.A. Botha, Partnerships in Care.
Karen Brady, HM Prison Service.
Douglas Brown, British Psychological Society.
Professor Jennifer Brown, University of Surrey.
Professor Kevin D. Browne, University of Liverpool.
Dr Ros Burnett, University of Oxford.
Kay Cahill, Hassockfield Secure Training Centre.
Dr Colin Campbell, Institute of Psychiatry, King's College London.
Jenny Cann, Ministry of Justice.
Professor David Canter, University of Liverpool.
Sara Casado, Sussex Partnerships NHS Trust.
Professor David A. Crighton, Ministry of Justice and London Metropolitan University.
Patricia M. Crittenden, Family Relations Institute, Florida.
Professor Graham Davies, University of Leicester.
Dr Jason Davies, Abertawe Bro Morgannwg University NHS Trust.
Paul Devonshire, Private Practice.
Angela Donaghy, Hassockfield Secure Training Centre.
Dr Michael Doyle, Edenfield Centre and University of Manchester.
Dr Simon Easton, University of Portsmouth.
Dr Graham John Evans, Lincoln Partnership NHS Trust.
Professor David P. Farrington, University of Cambridge.
Martin Fisher, HM Prison Service, Thames Valley and Hampshire.
John Flatley, Home Office.
Dawn Flemming, Department of Health.
Julia Fossi, HM Inspectorate of Prisons.
Matthew Gaskell, HM Prison Service.
Professor John Geddes, University of Oxford.
Bryan Gibson, Barrister.
Professor Finlay Graham, Kolvin Unit and University of Northumbria.
Professor Don Grubin, University of Newcastle upon Tyne.
Professor John Gunn, Institute of Psychiatry, King's College London.

Gemma Harper, Ministry of Justice.
Mark Harris, Parole Board for England and Wales.
Professor Carol Hedderman, University of Leicester.
Professor Sheilagh Hodgins, Institute of Psychiatry, King's College London.
Deborah Hudspith, Home Office.
Dr Gareth Hughes, University of Cambridge.
Dr Carol A. Ireland, Mersey Care NHS Trust and University of Central Lancashire.
Dr Jane L. Ireland, Mersey NHS Trust and University of Central Lancashire.
Dr Darrick Jolliffe, University of Leicester.
Mark Jones, National Policing Improvement Agency.
Professor Andreas Kapardis, University of Cyprus.
Jacqui Karn, Nacro.
Peter Kind, HM Prison Service.
Dr Caroline Logan, Mersey Care NHS Trust.
Susan Lord, National Probation Service.
Professor Friedrich Lösel, University of Cambridge.
Beverley Love, Home Office.
Dr Ruth Mann, HM Prison Service.
Dr Samantha Mann, University of Portsmouth.
Kevin McCormac, Sentencing Guidelines Secretariat.
Professor James McGuire, University of Liverpool.
Dr Sarah Milne, BLISS (the Premature Babies Charity).
Dr Catrin Morrissey, Nottinghamshire Healthcare NHS Trust.
Dr Adrian Needs, University of Portsmouth.
Professor Raymond W. Novaco, University of California, Irvine.
Dr Margaret O'Rourke, University College Cork.
Dr James Ost, University of Portsmouth.
Madeleine Oswald, Family Court Advisory Service.
Kate Painter, University of Cambridge.
Dr Emma J. Palmer, University of Leicester.
Dr Julie Parker, Partnerships in Care.
Sharon Pearson, Hassockfield Secure Training Centre.
Marie Petersen, University of Cambridge.
Professor David Pilgrim, University of Central Lancashire.
Graham Powell, Private Practice.
Professor Adrian Raine, University of Pennsylvania.
Professor Peter Raynor, University of Swansea.
Dr Michael Rice, University of Cambridge.
Dr Graeme Richardson, Kolvin Unit and University of Northumbria.
Neil Ryrie, University of Nottingham.
Robert A. Schug, University of Southern California.
Dr Lorraine Sheridan, Heriot Watt University.
Michael Spurr, HM Prison Service.
Nigel Stone, University of East Anglia.
Tania Tancred, Kent Probation Service.
Professor John L. Taylor, Northumbria NHS Trust and University of Northumbria.

Professor Brian A. Thomas-Peter, Birmingham and Solihull Mental Health NHS Trust and University of Birmingham.

Professor Graham J. Towl, Ministry of Justice and Universities of Birmingham and Portsmouth.

Jackie Walton, Barnardo's Chilston Project.

Phil Wilmott, Nottinghamshire Healthcare NHS Trust.

Professor Anne Worrall, University of Keele.

The above list of contributors shows the position they held at the time of writing their entry.

Table of cases

Acknowledgements

We are first and foremost grateful to all the individuals who contributed to this first edition of the *Dictionary of Forensic Psychology*, not just for their valued work but also for their forbearance with the complex production process that goes with any dictionary. We are also grateful to friends and colleagues both at the Ministry of Justice and University of Cambridge Institute of Criminology for their specialist advice on specific entries.

We are grateful to the institute for hosting the planning meetings for this project. We also wish to record formally our thanks to the Librarian and staff at the institute and also the Librarian and staff at the Home Office library in Westminster.

Finally our special thanks go to Marie Davies who co-ordinated and project managed the work of collating so many authors with such efficiency and patience.

Graham J. Towl, David P. Farrington, David A. Crighton and Gareth Hughes
London and Cambridge, 2008

Acknowledgements

Introduction and overview

THE BEGINNING OF THE FORENSIC PSYCHOLOGY PROFESSION IN THE UK

On 27 May 1977 at the Plastics and Rubber Institute in Hobart Place, London, the first Division of Criminological and Legal Psychology (DCLP) meeting was held in order to elect the first committee. The first formal DCLP committee meeting was then held at the Institute of Criminology, Cambridge, on 5 July 1977. Much work had been undertaken in the two-year period immediately prior to the launch of the new division in the British Psychological Society (BPS) (Farrington 1999). As a number of officers of the division in the years that followed would attest, negotiations with the BPS can be very hard work, and decisions often tend to be reached only over significant periods of time. It is a tribute to those who undertook this initial groundwork that they showed evident tenacity in their task. The forensic psychology landscape then looked very different from how it looks now in the early stages of the twenty-first century. Perhaps much of the mood of this period can be captured with the following quotation: 'Embattled, criticised, derided psychologists needed to band together for social support against the advancing enemy, preferably within the protective umbrella of the large, established BPS, to defend and promote their view of what was methodologically sound (i.e. scientific) research' (Farrington 1999: 24).

In terms of the official reasons for the setting up of the division, five were set out: first, to give evidence on behalf of the BPS to the government; secondly, to promote 'legal and criminological psychology' as a distinct area of study; thirdly, to provide a forum for professional discussion; fourthly, to establish a code of ethics for forensic psychologists; and, fifthly, to make the public and public bodies more aware of the work undertaken in the forensic field (Farrington 1999: 22–3).

The above brief introductory observations are intended to give the reader a flavour of the birth of the professional organization of forensic psychology in the UK. It was, it is fair to say, a fraught birth, and more challenges were to follow. In putting together this Dictionary, it is important to appreciate the impact of this brief history, particularly in terms of how the professional landscape has developed so far and is poised to develop in the future. Aside from the specific internal professional developments, given that the context of much of the work is in public services, the broader political changes over the period of development of the division also warrant some consideration (Towl 2004).

THE EARLY YEARS OF THE DIVISION

Financial problems featured as a recurrent problem in the early years of the division. This restricted, but by no means prevented, professional progress.

Achievements in these early years included the provision of a number of publications, including an irregularly produced newsletter for members. There was also the setting up of the first MSc in Applied Criminological Psychology at Birkbeck College, University of London. Barry McGurk, a psychologist working in the Prison Service at that time, was largely instrumental in this development. This helped to put the status of psychologists working in prisons on more of a professional footing that would contribute to a growing parity with clinical colleagues working in the health sector. The MSc ran for about a decade, with the first students graduating in 1989. The first DCLP annual conference was held in January 1991 at the University of Kent. In 1993, Monica Lloyd and I took over from James McGuire as editors of the historically struggling *DCLP Newsletter*. Four issues later (in July 1994), the newsletter metamorphosed into *Forensic Update*, which blossomed under subsequent editorial teams and remains a key communication tool and not insubstantial organ of the division.

Within the broader BPS there was the advent of chartership in the late 1980s. This reflected a professional aim of the BPS, which was to put the regulation of applied psychologists on a firmer legal footing (Towl 2004). In the early 1990s the division's membership continued to grow steadily until the late 1990s, when the growth rate increased markedly into the first few years of the following century. David Crighton, as membership chair, worked exceptionally effectively during this period to ensure the efficient administration of a bureaucratic system that had not been designed to deal with such a volume of applications. It was, of course, recognized at the time that this was a desirable problem for the division to have.

Twenty years after the launch of the division, one of its key aims to produce specialist ethical guidance was fulfilled by a diligent working group I was privileged to chair (BPS 1997). In terms of division membership, the sales of divisional publications and conference participation rates, the turn of the century was indeed a golden period. The crucial way in which the notion of 'chartership' impacted on psychologists working in prisons was that, as a group, they began to refer to themselves as 'chartered forensic psychologists'. Indeed, the term 'forensic psychology' itself was increasingly being used more broadly (which contributed to the renaming of the *DCLP Newsletter* as *Forensic Update*). These factors culminated in a vote of the membership, with the DCLP committee of the day, chaired by myself, advocating a change of name to the 'Division of Forensic Psychology'. The membership responded with the highest turnout recorded for a vote in the division, and a thumping majority (88 per cent) voted in favour of the change (Towl 1999).

THE DIVISION OF FORENSIC PSYCHOLOGY IN THE TWENTY-FIRST CENTURY

At the turn of the century the forensic psychology field was booming (Farrington 2003a). Membership of the Division of Forensic Psychology had never been so high, and the degree of involvement of members had increased very markedly indeed. Public sector prisons were recruiting qualified and trainee psychologists at unprecedented levels. Although the first MSc course in Applied Criminological Psychology had been terminated by Birkbeck College towards the end of the twentieth century, it provided a useful exemplar of what was possible for future courses, which mushroomed in the late 1990s and early 2000s.

There is a real sense of privilege about the current base from which the thriving Division of Forensic Psychology can now operate. There are some exciting opportunities ahead. For example, the advent of the statutory regulation of forensic psychologists through the Health Professions Council will have a significant and positive potential impact on the role of the BPS. This will perhaps serve to put a sharper focus on the division in terms of its fitness for purpose as a body involved with the development of professional standards. Also, the continued challenges in establishing a practical but rigorous process for the educational and professional journey undertaken by trainees en route to qualification will benefit from being administratively simplified while maintaining appropriately rigorous standards of practice. It is essential to address such issues actively if the profession is to continue to thrive. This is also an important ethical responsibility for those of us who have been fortunate to have qualified in this tremendously stimulating and growing field.

Having given an outline of some key developments in the professional history of forensic psychology in the UK, it is timely to consider briefly some of the broader changes in public services that set the context for much of our work as forensic psychologists, finishing with a focus on the future of forensic psychology in the UK.

THE PUBLIC SERVICE CONTEXT

Since the Second World War, successive governments have attempted, with varying degrees of success, to improve the efficiency of the Civil Service in terms of both central and local government policies and practices. Particularly perhaps during the last quarter of the twentieth century and into the early twenty-first century, there has been a public sector reform mantra that, crudely put, has asserted that the public sector needs to be more like the private sector in its organization. The underlying claim made is that this will result in improved efficiencies, including better 'customer services'. The merits, demerits and limitations of such an approach to public service delivery have been an area of much discussion and debate. These changes have occurred across sectors to encompass universities, prisons and health services, including hospitals, schools and social services. But what is the relevance of this to forensic psychology and forensic psychologists? In some ways the impacts on forensic psychologists are easier to identify, but the impacts on forensic psychology are no less important, particularly in terms of how the discipline has developed in the UK (Towl 2004).

One of the tools of this 'new' approach to the management and organization of public services has been a renewed focus on the measurement of activities. Psychologically based interventions in prisons, such as a structured set of group-work-based interventions aimed at reducing the risk of participants reoffending, are routinely measured in terms of 'completions'. The term 'completion' merely reflects the presence of an individual for the duration of a particular intervention. It gives no information about his or her suitability for the particular intervention nor about the extent to which the given intervention is matched to the needs of the prison population, nor about the effectiveness of the intervention (Crighton and Towl 2008). Indeed, the advent of what have become called 'accredited offending behaviour programmes' was in part feasible because of their high degree of fit with the prevailing confidence in measurement and manualization as a more systematic way of organizing such public services. This is important in a fuller understanding of the proliferation of manual-based approaches because such developments, in policy and practice, are seldom merely the product of the emerging research evidence, although, of course, this will play a part too.

The growth of such psychologically based interventions contributed to the increased rate of recruitment of psychologists in prisons. Indeed, throughout this particular period of growth the terms 'psychology' and 'psychologist' were often conflated – the manuals were psychologically based but did not need psychologists to facilitate the 'programmes'. There were also fallacious claims of 'shortages' of staff to undertake such work. It is true that there was a limited rate of growth that the infrastructure of fully qualified forensic psychologists could support, but it was not always necessary to have psychologists running psychologically based interventions.

Around the year 2000 some were arguing that there would be an exodus of psychologists from prisons to the Probation Service. This argument was based, it seemed, on a mistaken belief that the Probation Service would pay staff higher salaries. This missed, however, a fundamental point that both the Prison and Probation Services were subject to significant financial pressures and that neither organization would be incentivized to compete on salaries. It is in fact disappointing that more psychologists have not been employed by a wide range of probation services and community-based service providers.

Over this period there was a growth in the number of psychologists working in secure hospitals and forensic mental health services. Refreshingly, the previous professional isolation between forensic and clinical psychologists began to thaw, with more forensic psychologists being appointed in the National Health Service (NHS) and with more clinical psychologists engaging in forensic work. One major benefit of NHS-based work in comparison with the Prison Service has long been a much greater receptivity to research involvement. Another is that, increasingly, NHS-based psychologists have contributed to improving mental health 'in-reach' services in prisons. Given the high levels of mental and physical health problems seen in prisoners, these are tremendously welcome developments.

A knowledge of the broader political and managerial context of public services is also helpful in understanding what is, or is not, likely to happen in terms of pay and conditions and funded training arrangements. Difficult decisions often have to be made regarding the appropriate levels of remuneration, and sometimes such decisions are traded off against the number of potential posts in both health and criminal justice. This has a resonance with some of the substantial practical challenges that were around at the time of the division's birth. The advantage enjoyed at the moment, however, in forensic psychology is that there is a much better developed infrastructure and, of course, there is the considerable benefit of a much more numerically enhanced profession.

ABOUT THIS BOOK

This Dictionary has been made possible because of the increased size of the professional community of forensic psychologists and because of the expansion of interest, research and practice in the discipline. We thus owe a significant debt of gratitude to those who have contributed, often in their own time, to the division's work over the years. These people are too numerous to attempt to mention but, needless to say, there is no doubt about their contributions. Such work continues to be carried out on behalf of present and future forensic psychologists.

In compiling this Dictionary, one of the pleasures has been a reminder of the growing strength, both in terms of breadth and depth, of the discipline as the entries have come in. It is this very diversity that bodes well for the profession's future. It is the diversity and depth of the profession, however, that need to be passed on to the future cohorts of forensic psychologists and forensic practitioners more generally. In particular, there will be a need to work closely with the Health Professionals Council in its statutory regulation of practitioner psychologists while developing and building on the base of forensic psychology. This will mean drawing on a range of psychological perspectives.

The entries in this Dictionary reflect a range of perspectives, and my fellow editors and I have taken an approach of inclusivity. As an editorial team we have endeavoured to capture, as fully as feasible, a range of voices in the discipline. We have also tried to cover the range of areas of knowledge needed by trainees in their quest to become fully qualified practitioners. But we hope and believe that this Dictionary will be of potential interest to a much broader range of readers than trainee forensic psychologists. Applied psychologists from many areas – including, for example, educational and clinical psychology – should find this Dictionary of interest and of growing relevance to their practice. With most of the entries we were in the fortunate position of having a range of potential contributors. We hope that we have chosen wisely but, of course, we understand that a number of others could equally have been able to provide such entries and will perhaps have the opportunity to contribute to future editions of the Dictionary. The profession of forensic psychology moves on, and we hope we have included a sufficient range of entries of interest for the full range of prospective readers. Above all, we hope that this Dictionary proves to be a useful and enjoyable read.

Graham J. Towl

ADDICTIVE BEHAVIOURS

> Addiction can be defined as a process whereby a behaviour becomes the major focus of a person's life, functioning both to produce pleasure and to avoid discomfort. Addiction is characterized by a continuation of the behaviour, despite significant harm to the individual and others and despite difficulty in reducing or stopping when the individual tries to.

People can be addicted to drugs and alcohol, but there are also behavioural addictions (e.g. gambling). Forensic psychologists are most interested in offenders with alcohol and drug problems, while crime itself can share many similarities to an addictive pattern of behaviour. Psychologists view addictions as determined by multiple factors relating to the person, the cultural context and the addictive behaviour, as these develop across the lifespan.

Prevalence and the substance-use crime link

Drug and alcohol problems are highly over-represented in offender populations, and research strongly indicates that these problems are among the top-ranked criminogenic factors. Consistent with findings in North America, data from UK high-security prisons confirm that almost 80 per cent of prisoners evidence problematic substance use. In terms of the substance use and crime link, a number of studies indicate that more than 50 per cent of offenders openly acknowledge that substance use was somehow involved in the criminal activity that led to their present term of imprisonment. The UK's National Treatment Outcome Research Study (NTORS) found that 664 clients (60 per cent of the sample) had committed more than 70,000 separate crimes in the three months prior to treatment.

Substance use is linked to the whole spectrum of offending behaviours, from high-volume acquisitive crime (such as shoplifting and burglary) to more 'serious' offences (such as drug importation, armed robbery, sexual offending and murder). The way these are linked is complex, and there is a wide variation in the nature of the relationship.

Assessment

Substance-using offenders are a heterogeneous group, with research clearly demonstrating that they differ in terms of their use patterns, risk of reoffending (both static and dynamic), other 'needs' (e.g. mental disorders, personality disorders and psychopathy), link to crime and motivation to change. The data rejects the traditional idea of a 'one size fits all' approach to treatment, which remains commonplace.

Assessment and interventions, therefore, should follow the principles of risk, need and responsivity in order adequately to differentiate between individuals on key dimensions and to enable the psychologist to 'match' the need with the treatment of the appropriate range, intensity, duration and flexibility. As a minimum, assessment must:

1. identify the nature and extent of the substance-use problem and criminal behaviour;
2. identify the relationship between substance use and crime; and
3. guide clinical decision-making in the development of an appropriate and individualized treatment plan with the person.

Rather than label an individual as an 'addict' or not, it is more useful to assess drug and alcohol use on a continuum of problem severity. Those with a low-severity problem do require formal intervention – brief intervention and counselling may address their needs. Individuals with more substantial to severe problems require intensive intervention services, structured maintenance and follow-up in order to modify their behaviour. For this latter group, substance use has major detrimental effects on virtually all aspects of their lives (e.g. health, social activities, interpersonal relationships and work) and is strongly linked to past, present and future criminal behaviour. These are the offenders most likely to have coexisting mental health problems, to have high levels of psychopathy, to have a personality disorder and to be 'career criminals'. A forensic psychologist has an important, but not exclusive, role to play in addressing these concerns. These offenders require the full gamut of specialists in the criminal justice system to reduce the risk they pose and to address their multiple needs. Too often many of these needs are not met, to the detriment of the individual and society.

Treatment

Why someone should continue with a behaviour that is evidently self-destructive has led to advances in motivational work for substance users. Substance-abusing offenders are often 'stuck' between competing motivations, which prevents them from moving in the direction of change. Motivational interviewing is a promising and common precursor to more intensive treatment for offenders with substance-abuse problems.

Treatment programmes for substance-using offenders are dominated by two types of treatment. The first is residential in-prison treatment called 'therapeutic communities', where all participants live together in a hierarchically organized structure. New residents are assigned to work teams with the lowest status but can move up the strata (including better work positions, privileges and living accommodation) as they demonstrate increased competency and emotional growth. Group treatment typically conforms to the '12-step' model of treatment and involves 'positive persuasion' to change behaviour and confrontation by peer groups whenever values or rules are breached. On the other hand, peers are also used to provide constructive feedback, affirmation, instruction and suggestions for changing behaviour and attitudes, and they assist the participant in recalling painful childhood memories. There is usually a wide range of support services on offer, with staff from a variety of disciplines.

The second type of programme is cognitive-behavioural treatment (CBT), which comes in a range of durations (depending on need) and which is based on social cognitive theory. CBT is commonly non-residential in that the offender goes to his or her group treatment programme and then back into his or her 'normal' prison location where he or she is likely to mix with offenders who are not engaged in treatment and where there is an increased risk of drug and alcohol supply and accompanying peer pressure. This method of treatment typically identifies the relapse risk factors associated with using and offending, before equipping the participant with a rich array of cognitive and behavioural skills and self-management strategies to protect against the behaviour reoccurring. CBT should help the offender lead a more meaningful life and should support desistance from offending.

Effectiveness

The Correctional Drug Abuse Treatment Effectiveness (CDATE) project reported a meta-analysis of 68 methodologically acceptable behavioural and cognitive-behavioural programmes with over 10,000 participants. Overall, there was a positive mean effect size of 0.12, with separate analyses revealing that the 23 evaluations of behavioural programmes (i.e. without the cognitive element) produced a mean effect size of 0.07, and that the mean effect size of 44 cognitive-behavioural programmes was 0.14. Although these effect sizes are only modest, what is clear is that focusing on cognitions enhances the effectiveness of interventions.

Evaluation of CBT programmes in Canadian Corrections has demonstrated a good treatment effect compared with matched controls, with a particularly strong impact on violent reoffending. Research in the USA and in high-security prisons in the UK also demonstrates that substance-abuse treatment can positively impact on institutional behaviour. Questions remain, however, regarding which approaches work best for different types of offenders and at what point treatment is most advantageous.

Matthew Gaskell

Related entries

Homelessness and crime; Motivational interviewing (MI); Substance abuse/misuse.

Key texts and sources

Lipton, D.S., Pearson, F.S., Cleland, C.M. and Yee, D. (2002a) 'The effects of therapeutic communities and milieu therapy on recidivism', in J. McGuire (ed.) *Offender Rehabilitation and Treatment: Effective Programmes and Policies to Reduce Re-offending.* Chichester: Wiley.

Lipton, D.S., Pearson, F.S., Cleland, C.M. and Yee, D. (2002b) 'The effectiveness of cognitive-behavioural treatment methods on offender recidivism', in J. McGuire (ed.) *Offender Rehabilitation and Treatment: Effective Programmes and Policies to Reduce Re-offending.* Chichester: Wiley.

McMurran, M. (2000) 'Offenders with drink and drug problems', in C.R. Hollin (ed.) *Handbook of Offender Assessment and Treatment.* Chichester: Wiley.

Porporino, F.J., Robinson, D., Millson, B. and Weekes, J.R. (2002) 'An outcome evaluation of prison-based treatment programming for substance users', *Substance Use and Misuse,* 37: 1047–77.

Weekes, J.R., Moser, A.E. and Langevin, C.M. (1998) 'Assessing substance-abusing offenders for treatment', in E.J. Latessa (ed.) *What Works: Strategic Solutions – the International Community Corrections Association Examines Substance Abuse.* Arlington, VA: Kirby Lithographic Company.

ADVERSARIAL SYSTEM

The adversarial system is the process of law that relies on two or more opposing sides seeking to resolve issues before an independent tribunal or court.

The adversarial system of law, generally adopted in common law countries such as the UK, relies on the skill of advocates representing their parties' positions and not on a neutral party – usually the judge or group of judges – trying to ascertain the truth of the case from the parties, as in an inquisitorial system.

The adversarial system is not a search for the truth. It relies on the party bringing the case to prove their allegation. In the criminal courts, the prosecution – generally acting on behalf of the state – has the burden of proving that the defendant is guilty as charged. In the civil courts, it is the party who is making the claim that their interests have been wronged by the defendant that bears the burden of proving their allegation. To establish a case in the criminal courts, the prosecution's case must meet the standard of proof of 'beyond reasonable doubt'. A claimant in the civil courts need only establish his or her case on the lower standard of the 'balance of probabilities' (i.e. that it is more likely than not that the event occurred in order to prove his or her claim).

The adversarial process requires there to be a tribunal of fact (charged with deciding the factual issues) and a tribunal of law (which ensures that the correct law is applied to the proceedings). In the lower criminal courts, such as the magistrates' courts, the presiding district judge or lay panel fulfils both roles – applying the correct law and deciding the outcome of the case. In the higher criminal courts (for example, the Crown courts), a judge concerns him or herself with the law, while a jury of laymen and women decides the facts at trial. In the civil courts, judges decide the law and the issues of dispute. There is only a limited use for jury trials in the civil courts, usually in the cases of defamation proceedings.

The presiding judge or panel must be impartial and is present to ensure fairness. The judge or panel has control over what evidence may be admissible in the proceedings and has powers to exclude anything that is irrelevant or prejudicial to the fairness of the proceedings. This extends to assessing whether expert evidence is necessary; who is eligible to be called as an expert witness; and upon which issues they may provide expert opinion.

The party bringing the case must present evidence that substantiates their claim. This may be in the form of live testimony or documents from lay or expert witnesses, or may include real objects. The defendant is then given the opportunity to cross-examine or inspect any witness or evidence presented against him or her. The defendant may then adduce evidence in support of his or her position, which is accordingly subject to cross-examination or inspection by the party bringing the case. The party defending has no burden to adduce evidence, as it is the party bringing the action that must prove their case.

S. George Blom-Cooper

Related entries

Courts; Legal profession.

Key texts and sources

Archbold (ed. J. Richardson) (2006) *Criminal Pleading, Evidence and Practice.* London: Sweet & Maxwell (4-266 to 4-307, 8-36 to 8-51, 9-1 to 9-16 and 10-61 to 10-71).

The Civil Procedure Rules (2006: Part 35) can be found at http://www.justice.gov.uk/civil/procrules_fin/index.htm.

ANGER

Anger is a negatively toned emotion, subjectively experienced as an aroused state of antagonism towards someone or something perceived to be the source of an aversive event. Anger is distinguished from hostility, which is an attitudinal disposition, and from aggression, which is behaviour intended to cause psychological or physical harm to someone or to a surrogate target.

Anger is triggered or provoked situationally by events that are perceived to constitute deliberate harm-doing by an instigator towards oneself or towards those to whom one is endeared. Provocations usually take the form of insults, unfair treatments or intended thwartings. Anger is prototypically experienced as a justified response to some 'wrong' that has been done, designated as caused by personal, stable and controllable aspects of another's behaviour. Although situationally triggered by acute, proximal occurrences, anger is often primed by personal or group schemas and is influenced by contextual conditions affecting the cognitive, arousal and behavioural systems that comprise anger reactions. Anger activation is centrally linked to threat perceptions and survival responding. Perceived malevolence is a common form of anger-inducing appraisal.

As a normal human emotion, anger has considerable adaptive value. In the face of adversity, it can mobilize psychological resources, energize behaviours for corrective action and facilitate perseverance. Anger serves as a guardian to self-esteem, operates as a means of communicating negative sentiment, potentiates the ability to redress grievances and boosts determination to overcome obstacles to happiness and aspirations. Despite such adaptive functions, anger also has maladaptive effects on personal and social well-being. Generally, strong physiological arousal impairs information processing and lessens the cognitive control of behaviour. As heightened physiological arousal is a core component of anger, people are not cognitively proficient when they become angry. Also, because anger activation is accompanied by aggressive impulses, anger can motivate harm towards others which, in turn, can produce undesirable consequences for the angered person, from direct retaliation, loss of supportive relationships, or social censure.

Anger is inherently a disposition to respond aggressively, but aggression is not an automatic consequence of anger, being regulated by inhibitory control mechanisms. Physical constraints, expectations of punishment or retaliation, empathy, consideration of the consequences and prosocial values operate as regulatory controls. While the experience of anger creates a readiness to respond with aggression, that disposition may be otherwise directed, suppressed or reconstituted.

An important anger-aggression dynamic is the escalation of provocation, involving reciprocally heightened antagonism in an interpersonal exchange. Anger-elicited aggression may evoke further anger in response, progressively generating justification for retaliation. Anger arousal provides the energy and justification for aggressive script enactment. Justification is a core theme for anger and aggression, being rooted in ancient religious texts, classical mythologies about deities and historical accounts of the behaviour of ancient rulers. Correspondingly, anger and physical aggression are often viewed as applying a legitimate punitive response for transgression or as ways of correcting injustice.

Anger occurs in conjunction with many psychiatrically classified disorders, including a variety of impulse control dysfunctions, mood disorders, personality disorders and forms of schizophrenia, especially paranoid. The activation of anger is also recognized as a feature of clinical disorders that result from trauma, such as dissociative disorders, brain damage syndromes and, especially, post-traumatic stress disorder. Anger also appears in mental state disturbances produced by general medical conditions, such as dementia, substance-abuse disorders and neurological dysfunctions resulting from perinatal difficulties.

Among psychiatric patients, anger has been found to predict physical aggression by psychiatric hospital patients (prior to admission) both in the hospital and in the community after discharge. In hospital, anger and aggression incur a great cost, not only in terms of direct care-staff injuries but also for their adverse effects on the treatment milieu.

Anger assessment presents challenges for forensic practitioners. Because it is often embedded with other distressed emotions and has a symbolic significance associated with both badness and madness, accessing anger is not straightforward. In forensic arenas, anger assessment is subject to reactivity as a threat to validity. Reactivity pertains to responses obtained that are reactions by the person to his or her inferences about the test situation, rather than to the explicit elements of the testing – i.e. the person is inclined to produce anger reports in anticipation of what those test responses will mean to some audience. People in forensic or other custodial settings have a tendency to 'mask' anger, as they are unlikely to perceive gain in disclosing it.

In general, anger assessment should be undertaken with multiple measures, seeking triangulation across different instruments, modes of assessment (e.g. interviews, psychometrics, staff-ratings, records data) and time points. The factors likely to induce reactivity (such as juxtaposition with stressful events, potential disapproval, loss of privileges or increased detention) should be minimized. The scores for a particular person are most meaningful in relation to a comparable population. Repeat testing is also advisable because a person's previous scores provide a reference frame. Finally, high-anger self-report scores are generally less ambiguous than low scores.

For the treatment of anger problems, cognitive-behavioural therapy (CBT) approaches have been effective with a wide range of clinical populations. CBT approaches seek to modify cognitive structures and the way a person processes information about social situations. They emphasize self-monitoring, cognitive flexibility in appraising situations, physiological arousal control and the learning of prosocial values and social skills. Therapist-guided progressive exposure to provocation scenarios, therapist modelling, client rehearsal of effective coping and relapse prevention planning are part of the CBT approach.

Raymond W. Novaco

Related entries

Anger and aggression assessment; Family violence; Violence risk assessment.

Key texts and sources

Averill, J.R. (1982) *Anger and Aggression: An Essay on Emotion.* New York, NY: Springer-Verlag.

Doyle, M. and Dolan, M. (2006) 'Evaluating the validity of anger regulation problems, interpersonal style, and disturbed mental state for predicting inpatient violence', *Behavioural Sciences and the Law*, 24: 783–98.

Eckhardt, C., Norlander, B. and Deffenbacher, J. (2004) 'The assessment of anger and hostility: a critical review', *Aggression and Violent Behavior*, 9: 17–43.

Novaco, R.W. (2007) 'Anger dysregulation: its assessment and treatment', in T.A. Cavell and K.T. Malcolm (eds) *Anger, Aggression, and Interventions for Interpersonal Violence.* Mahwah, NJ: Erlbaum.

Novaco, R.W. and Taylor, J.L. (2004) 'Assessment of anger and aggression in male offenders with developmental disabilities', *Psychological Assessment*, 16: 42–50.

ANGER AND AGGRESSION ASSESSMENT

Anger and aggression are primarily a bio-psychosocial concept where biological, affective, cognitive and contextual variables all contribute either to emotional state (short term) or to personality trait (long term).

Anger, hostility and aggression are ubiquitous facets of human experience that have been attended by much research. A large part of the research literature investigating anger has a health psychology focus in which anger is associated with cardiovascular disease and cancer. However, an awareness of its importance in the area of mental health, particularly where it is implicated with assaultative behaviours and aggression, began in the 1990s (e.g. Gould *et al.* 1996; Novaco 2000).

The most widely used tests in mental health clinical practice are currently the State Trait Anger Expression Inventory STAXI (Spielberger *et al.* 1983) and the Novaco Anger Scale and Provocation Inventory (NAS-PI) (Novaco 2003). Many specialists in the assessment and treatment of anger have developed their own assessment systems, such as, for example, the RAMAS Anger Assessment Profile (RAAP) (O'Rourke and Hammond 2000).

The STAXI measures two fundamental aspects of anger: 1) the experience of anger and 2) the expression of anger. The experience of anger can be understood in the context of state – subjective feelings that vary from irritability to intense rage – and trait anger, which refers to a disposition to perceive situations as annoying and to respond to these situations by more frequent expressions of state anger. A third component of the STAXI is the degree to which people attempt to control their expression of anger (anger control).

The NAS-PI is composed of two parts: the Novaco Anger Scale (60 items), which assesses how an individual experiences anger; and the Provocation Inventory (25 items), which identifies the kinds of situations that induce anger in particular individuals. The NAS-PI produces the following scores: 1) total NAS score (cognitive, arousal, behaviour and anger regulation) and 2) PI score (disrespectful treatment, unfairness, frustration, annoying traits of others and irritation).

The RAAP was developed from a clinical anger management programme known as 'Keep Your Cool'. The RAAP aims to provide a profile of individual anger problems in order to enable practitioners to plan targets for intervention and change. Within the framework's specified physiological, behavioural and psychological domains, six component facets are identified that are pertinent to a clinical understanding of anger. A further three facets are identified that predispose the individual's experience of anger, and a facet concerning the consequence of anger is also identified. A feedback mechanism is conceived in which consequences may modify the predisposing facets.

The RAAP contains 10 scales: 1) duration; 2) expression; 3) provocation; 4) somatic tension ; 5) irritability/sensitivity; 6) anger control; 7) consequences; 8) abuse and assault; 9) victimization; and 10) attitude.

Margaret O'Rourke

Related entries

Anger; Multi-modal methods of assessment; Violence risk assessment.

Key texts and sources

Gould, R.A., Ball, S., Kaspi, S.P., Otto, M.W., Pollack, M.H., Shekhar, A. and Fava, M. (1996) 'Prevalence and correlates of anger attacks: a two site study', *Journal of Affective Disorders*, 39: 31–8.

Novaco, R.W. (2000) 'Anger', in A.E. Kazdin (ed.) *Encyclopedia of Psychology*. Washington, DC: American Psychological Association and Oxford University Press.

Novaco, R.W. (2003) *The Novaco Anger Scale and Provocation Inventory (NAS-PI)*. Los Angeles, CA: Western Psychological Services.

O'Rourke, M. and Hammond, S. (2000) *RAMAS Anger Assessment Profile: Professional Manual*. London: RAMAS Foundation (available online at www.ramas.co.uk).

Spielberger, C.D., Jacobs, G.A., Russell, S. and Crane, R.S. (1983) 'Assessment of anger: the State-Trait Anger Scale', in J.N. Butcher and C.D. Spielberger (eds) *Advances in Personality Assessment. Vol. 2.* Hillsdale, NJ: Erlbaum.

ANIMAL CRUELTY

Animal cruelty is a behaviour carried out intentionally to hurt or torture an animal, which may cause its death. It is a cruel act that causes pain and suffering to the animal.

In recent years it has become widely accepted that cruelty to animals can be an indicator of many other forms of violence, including child abuse, domestic violence and elder abuse. This is well documented, but has only recently received academic attention. Cruelty to animals is a complex matter, and defining it can be difficult because of vast cultural differences.

What can commonly be shared and agreed is that animal cruelty is a cruel behaviour carried out intentionally to hurt or torture an animal, which may cause its death – a cruel act that causes pain and suffering to the animal. Cruelty ranges from intentionally teasing, hurting, pushing, kicking, slapping, drowning, shooting and other violent acts with the use of weapons, to deliberate passive neglect and hoarding that could kill the animal.

Cruelty to animals is a serious matter that should not be ignored, mainly because of its link to other serious forms of violence. For example, studies suggest that children who are cruel to animals tend to be violent to people later in life. A famous UK case concerns Mary Bell, an 11-year-old girl who strangled two children aged 3 and 4. Bell had a history of strangling cats and pigeons but no one ever paid attention to the warning signs in her violent behaviour towards animals. Likewise, case histories of serial killers and mass murderers suggest that many were cruel to animals in their childhood.

Furthermore, it is argued that cruelty to animals tends to be associated with domestic violence, child abuse and elder abuse, which are referred to as the circles of violence. It is therefore seen as a significant indicator that children or juveniles are at high risk of becoming perpetrators of violence in society – they will continue with cruelty when they are grown up. These key factors need special attention: the link of abuse should not be ignored.

When analysing serious interpersonal violence the key factors that contribute to the violent offending behaviour are investigated, especially the progression from juvenile delinquency to adult violence. Existing literature suggests that the diagnosis of conduct disorder can be a strong indicator of serious young adult violence. Nevertheless, it was not until 1987 that physical cruelty to animals was added to the list of symptoms for the diagnosis of conduct disorder (CD) in the American Psychiatric Association's third revised edition of the *Diagnostic and Statistical Manual of Mental*

Disorders (DSM-IIIR). It has been suggested that animal cruelty may be exhibited by 25 per cent of CD children and that animal cruelty may be the earliest detectable symptom of CD. CD as a major indicator of anti-social behaviour and of cruelty to animals deserves more attention from researchers and mental health professionals.

The early assessment of animal cruelty is important for the detection of delinquent behaviour and for the prevention of further violence. Since early intervention is critical in the prevention and reduction of aggression and violence, researchers and other professionals are encouraged to recognize that animal cruelty is a significant problem and public health issue that should receive primary attention.

Marie Petersen

Related entries

Family violence; Juvenile delinquency.

Key texts and sources

Ascione, F.R. and Arkow, P. (1999) *Child Abuse, Domestic Violence and Animal Abuse: Linking the Circles of Compassion for Prevention and Intervention.* West Lafayette, IN: Purdue University Press.

Petersen, M.L. and Farrington, D.P. (2007) 'Cruelty to animals' and Violence to People? *Victims and Offenders*, 2: 21–43.

Wilson, P. and Norris, G. (2003) 'Relationship between criminal behaviour and mental illness in young adults: conduct disorder, cruelty to animals and young adult serious violence', *Psychiatry, Psychology and Law*, 10: 239–43.

APPLIED PSYCHOLOGY

Applied psychology is the use of psychological knowledge (models, findings and methods) to assess, understand and address issues and problems encountered in a range of real-life settings.

The psychological knowledge drawn upon by applied psychologists initially derives from their study of the various branches of the discipline, including psychobiology (learning, motivation, emotion, perception, motor control), cognitive psychology (perceptual analysis, attention, memory, language, thinking and reasoning), developmental psychology (cognitive development, communication, social relationships), social psychology (attitudes, attribution, social interaction, social and group processes), personality (motives, self and identity, personality types and structure, abilities) and research methods (e.g. surveys, experiments and qualitative analysis). Increasingly there are also fields of applied research that feed directly into applied practice – for example, the development of assessment and diagnostic tools that become available through the major test publishers and controlled studies of intervention techniques, published in the specialist applied journals, that help extend and improve professional skills.

The application of such knowledge begins with the investigation of the real-life problems that are faced by individuals, groups of people or organizations composed of people. For example, when working with individuals there will be an analysis of three loosely coupled systems that cover their behaviour, their cognitions and beliefs and their physiological experience (what they feel). When working with groups there will often be an analysis of membership rules, initiation processes, conformity pressures, identity, rewards and sanctions, and patterns of within-group interaction. Working with organizations may include an analysis of workforce and management skills, channels of communication and their use, power structures and processes, reward structures, the capacity for managing change and growth, and issues of leadership and governance.

Following the investigation of the problem is a psychological formulation, which will describe the issues and their facets, will explain how problems or issues have arisen, and will explain how problems have been maintained or neglected rather than solved or addressed. Formulation may concern problems with the individual (e.g. excessive displays of temper), with groups (e.g. poor cohesion and unsupportive interaction between group members) or with an organization (e.g. a high rate of staff turnover or difficulty in responding constructively to evolving challenges).

From the formulation will flow the intervention (i.e. a strategy to achieve a solution or at least to find a way forward), which is evidence based and which follows directly from the scientific understanding of aetiological and maintenance factors. Since the same problem may arise for different reasons, problems may be tackled in a range of ways appropriate to the precise aetiological circumstances. One person may lose his or her temper because of a history of head injury and reduced behavioural control; another may have grown up in an environment in which anger was seen as an appropriate form of self-assertion; another may be under extreme pressure and so the slightest thing has a last-straw effect; and yet another may not understand the feelings of others and may not realize the impact his or her anger is having. Similarly, one group may lack cohesion because of shortcomings in the selection process that allows the admission of unsuitable people, whereas another group may lack cohesion because of the lack of any team-building strategy. One organization may not respond effectively to challenges because senior managers lack the necessary skills, whereas in another poor decision-making procedures reduce the likelihood of appropriate or prompt policy revision.

It follows that applied psychologists can work at different levels in their field. Some will work at the level of the individual – for example with a school child, with an offender, with someone with a mental health problem, with a sportsperson who is failing to achieve or with someone who feels he or she has never reached his or her full potential. Some will work with groups – perhaps services users in a residential facility, a football team or a sales force. Others will work with organizations, including policy and strategy development for health and service institutions, or with business and commercial enterprises in both the profit and not-for-profit sectors. Some applied psychologists will also become involved at the highest level with government policy – for example, how government addresses such issues as road safety, smoking, substance abuse or health-related dietary concerns (such as the amount of fat and salt in food products).

In the UK, professional applied psychologists have at least three years' postgraduate integrated training in theory and practice, usually at the doctoral level, which confers upon them eligibility for chartered psychologist status (CPsychol) with the British Psychological Society (BPS). Within the BPS there are different divisions that represent the various fields of professional activity – i.e. clinical psychology, counselling psychology, health psychology, forensic psychology, neuropsychology, sports and exercise psychology, educational psychology and occupational psychology. The situation in the USA is somewhat different in that applied psychologists are licensed by state boards, but, again, the national body, the American Psychological Association (APA), has a range of divisions similar to that found in the UK. However, there are more divisions in the USA and some are quite specialized, such as public services psychologists, consumer psychologists and population and environmental psychologists. The BPS and APA provide information about where each type of applied psychologist works, who employs them, what they do, whom their clients are, whom they work with, how they are trained and for how long, where vacancies are advertised and what pay can be expected.

Whatever the precise nature of the work of the applied psychologist, neither his or her knowledge base nor work environment is static. Therefore in each of the applied fields there is a constant revision and fine tuning of the definitions of core competencies, of training routes to professional status, of policies and methods of service delivery, of procedures for professional regulation and revalidation, and of the requirements for mandatory continuing professional development.

Graham Powell

Related entries

British Psychological Society (BPS); Chartered psychologists; Health Professions Council.

Key texts and sources

Davey, G., Albery, I.P., Chandler, C., Field, A., Jones, D., Messer, D., Moore, S. and Sterling, C. (2004) *Complete Psychology*. London: Hodder & Stoughton.

See also the websites of the American Psychological Association (**www.apa.org/about/divisions** and **www.apa.org/science/nonacad_careers**) and the British Psychological Society (**www.bps.org.uk/ careers**).

APPROVED PREMISES

Approved premises, formerly known as proba-tion and/or bail hostels, represent controlled accommodation for offenders under the supervision of the Probation Service.

Approved premises represent both a public pro-tection measure and a resettlement function for the offender. They provide a higher degree of supervision than would be achieved in other, less secure, forms of accommodation. The majority of approved premises are owned and managed by the National Probation Service for England and Wales, with a small number being managed by voluntary sector providers.

Approved premises can accommodate offenders with a wide range of offending histo-ries. They are available for both men and women who are under supervision in the com-munity. There are currently 104 approved premises across England and Wales. In total they provide approximately 2,300 bed spaces. Residents must pay rent from their wages or benefits. The vast majority of residents are placed in approved premises by the courts, on community orders or on bail, or by the Parole Board on licence. Probation staff conduct rele-vant risk assessment procedures before agreeing admission.

Approved premises provide a structured regime that residents are obliged to follow, and 24-hour supervision from trained staff is in place. Residents are required to comply with the conditions of their order or licence and the con-ditions of residence (or house rules). House rules set out the standards of behaviour expected of residents, 'forbidding them [the res-idents] to act in such a way as to cause disruption to neighbours and the immediate community, or to bring the premises into disre-pute' (Home Office approved premises web page). Breaches of the conditions of residence can lead to an eviction, a return to court or an immediate recall to prison. In addition, breach of licence will result in recall to prison.

As part of the enhanced supervision provided by approved premises, a number of protective and restrictive measures can be put in place. The public protection measures that approved prem-ises facilitate include the following:

- *Security measures*: stringent internal and external security measures are in place, including CCTV coverage, alarmed exits and restricted window openings.
- *Tagging*: there are electronic-monitoring facili-ties for residents subject to electronic tagging.
- *Resident monitoring*: the daily monitoring and recording of incoming mail. Residents also undergo the routine observation and recording of their behaviour.
- *Curfew periods*: a standard minimum curfew (from 11 p.m. to 6 a.m.) exists in all approved premises. Extended curfew periods can also be imposed.
- *Drug testing*: there is provision for on-site drug testing where residents are suspected of, or have a known history of, illegal sub-stance misuse.
- *Exclusion zones and/or contact restrictions*: some offenders are prohibited from entering certain geographical areas as part of their probation order or licence and/or from hav-ing contact with named individuals, such as victims of their crime.
- *Police*: the joint management of offenders means regular liaison with, and visits to, approved premises by the police.
- *Room searches*: anything found in a room that is illegal or not permitted, such as drugs, would result in a sanction (such as recall to prison) and could also lead to police action.

Derval Ambrose

Related entries

National Probation Service (NPS).

Key texts and sources

See the Home Office's web page on approved premises (http://www.probation.homeoffice.gov.uk/files/pdf/Approved%20Premises%20FAQ.pdf).

ATTACHMENT THEORY

Attachment theory is a theory of individual differences in self-protective behaviour. There are several versions of attachment theory, all derived from the work of John Bowlby (1969/82, 1973, 1980) and Mary Ainsworth (Ainsworth *et al.* 1978). The version that is most attuned to forensic issues is the Dynamic-Maturational Model (DMM) of attachment and adaptation. Crucial to the importance of the DMM to forensic issues is its status as a meta-theory that combines the contributions of other theories, as opposed to competing with them.

The key issues in attachment theory, and in the Dynamic-Maturational Model (DMM) of attachment and adaptation (Crittenden 2002, 2006b) in particular, that are relevant to forensic psychology are as follows.

Danger

The DMM addresses not only individual differences in early attachment but also – and especially – differences in adaptation in adolescence and adulthood that endanger the self (usually a mental health issue) or others (usually a forensic issue). Needless to say, offenders are identified by their threat to others but, in addition, they experience high rates of psychological disorder, bullying and attack in prison, self-injury and suicide. Thus, the central issue in attachment – protection from danger – is crucial to forensic cases.

Development

Attachment theory (and the DMM in particular) addresses the process by which developmental history, in interaction with maturation, produces adult variation in adaptation. Offenders – especially violent and sexual offenders – are thought to have experienced exposure to a wide variety of dangerous conditions during infancy, childhood and adolescence. Attachment theory posits that each infant and child learns what is dangerous and how to protect the self from experienced dangers. Children also learn how probable danger is. When a young child has been repeatedly exposed to serious danger that could not be predicted, prevented or deflected, the child usually becomes warily attentive to the signal of threat and primed to respond self-protectively to any such signals. The overestimation of threat and excessively aggressive responses typify violent offenders and may reflect an adaptation to their early developmental experience. If so, there are implications both for the treatment of known offenders and for prevention among endangered children and their families.

Points of particular concern are the types of danger to which children are exposed, the developmental timing of exposure and the sorts of support available to them. In the case of violent offenders, it is probable that several different types of threat were experienced in a sequential and age-salient manner. Further, it is likely that the children were not protected or comforted by their parents and, moreover, that their parents were often the source of danger, especially when they were very young. For example, early child abuse by the parent might have been followed in the school years by bullying at school and shaming at home, and these, in turn, were followed in adolescence by gang-based danger. Finally, there is probably a variety of such developmental pathways, each leading to somewhat different outcomes in adulthood.

Information processing

Experience affects behaviour through information processing that occurs in the brain. The DMM consists of both patterns of behaviour (i.e. self-protective strategies – see below) and patterns of processing information. Key to understanding information processing are evolved neurological structures that function to increase survival and experientially derived changes in how those structures are used by individuals. Experience with danger is proposed to be among the most potent sources of influence on the development of individual differences in information processing.

Two aspects of sensory stimulation are thought to be processed differently through the brain, each leading to different sources of information regarding the safety of the self. 'Cognition' is information based on the temporal order of the stimulation, whereas 'affect' is information based on the intensity of stimulation. These two transformations of sensory stimulation lead to separate representations of the environment. The maturation of the brain, in the context of experience, modifies cognition and affect, leading to omitted, distorted and falsified forms of information. It is proposed that people who behave dangerously perceive danger more than other people; omit, distort or falsify the information they communicate to others (thinking that doing so will protect themselves); and vary in whether affect or cognition is treated preferentially (i.e. some threatened individuals rely on cognitive information and omit affect from processing, and vice versa). These transformations are the basis for behaviour.

Self-protective strategies

The DMM describes a set of self-protective strategies that result from relying predominately on cognitive contingencies (Type A) or affective feeling (Type C) or both (Type B). Further, within these three clusters (A, B and C) are many variations. The more the information used to construct the strategy is distorted (from true to distorted to false), the higher the numeral used to identify the strategy. For example, A1-2 (emotional distance from a cool but protective parent) uses almost entirely true cognitive information, whereas A3 (compulsive care-giving of a neglectful parent) uses distorted information and A7 (delusional idealization of a dangerous parent) uses false information. Among Type C strategies, C1-2 (mildly threatening and disarming to an unpredictable but caring parent) uses almost entirely true affect, whereas C5-6 (obsessed with revenge and rescue from a dangerously deceptive parent) uses distorted information and C7-8 (menacing and paranoid with life-threatening and dangerous parents) uses false information. Although there are no published empirical papers at present, the higher numerals appear clinically to be found more often among offenders and to be found only in individuals who are unsafe (to themselves and others) and who are living independently.

Adaptation

Attachment is a theory about how humans adapt to dangerous circumstances and how that early adaptation might lead to dangerously maladaptive behaviour later, especially under safe circumstances. The connection between the theory and the life experience for offenders is that individuals who have grown up with danger are likely to develop deceptive, aggressive and/or inappropriately self-comforting strategies for coping with threat; to recreate around themselves the sort of dangerous environment with which they are familiar; and, if offered safe circumstances, to misconstrue them as having hidden threats, which then elicits the maladaptive self-protective strategy. The point is that sometimes learning to survive dangerous circumstances in the short term can make it difficult to live in safety for the long term. Both information processing and learned behaviour may need to change before such individuals can live safely in safe contexts.

Implications for forensic work

The DMM approach to attachment has three primary implications for forensic work. First, if information processing underlies behaviour and if the ABC strategies reflect differences in how information is processed, then treatment for individuals with different A or C strategies might need to be different. Indeed, administering the wrong treatment (i.e. one suited to the opposite strategy) might be harmful. Secondly, to know what psychological and behavioural strategy an individual is using, one needs expert assessments (just as one does for other psycho-logical constructs – e.g. IQ, psychiatric diagnosis). These assessments are structured, replicable, have published validity data and require training and authorization to use. Expert opinion, based on private observation, is neither reliable nor valid and should not be used. Thirdly, because the treatment of serious offenders is not very effective, because much suffering is caused by violent behaviour and because the problems are incurred through a developmental process, attention should be turned to prevention in high-risk (i.e. endangered) populations.

What isn't known

Useful as attachment theory appears to be for forensic work, the validating studies for this population have not yet been done. Such studies, carried out with methodological rigour, should be undertaken.

Patricia M. Crittenden

Related entries

Criminal careers; Family factors.

Key texts and sources

Crittenden, P.M. (1999) 'Danger and development: the organization of self-protective strategies', in J.I. Vondra and D. Barnett (eds) *Atypical Attachment in Infancy and Early Childhood among Children at Developmental Risk. Monographs of the Society for Research on Child Development.* Ann Arbor, MI: Society for Research on Child Development.

Crittenden, P.M. (2002) 'Attachment theory, information processing, and psychiatric disorder', *World Journal of Psychiatry*, 1: 72–5.

Crittenden, P.M. (2006a) 'A dynamic-maturational model of attachment', *Australian and New Zealand Journal of Family Therapy*, 27: 105–15.

Crittenden, P.M. (2006b) 'Why do inadequate parents do what they do?', in O. Mayseless (ed.) *Parenting Representations: Theory, Research, and Clinical Implications.* Cambridge: Cambridge University Press.

B

BIOLOGICAL FACTORS IN CRIME

Biological factors in crime refer to a range of historical concepts used to account for crime, including physical stigmata, atavism, biological inheritance, mental deficiency, somatotypes and genetic syndromes. They also refer to current, more advanced biological notions, including behavioural genetics, evolutionary psychology, neuroscience, reward dominance and prefrontal dysfunction theories, that suggest a biological component in the explanation of crime.

Criminality, like all human behaviour, is highly dependent on complex biological processes and mechanisms, acting in concert with a vast array of environmental influences. Rooted in the work of early positivist criminologists, the acceptance of biological causations of criminal behaviour has traditionally been met with moral suspicion and reticence, and research findings have gone largely ignored by criminologists and sociologists. Biological concepts central to earlier criminological theories (physical stigmata, atavism, biological inheritance, mental deficiency, somatotypes and XYY syndrome) have given way to more advanced and refined themes in recent perspectives (behavioural genetics, evolutionary psychology, neuroscience, reward dominance and prefrontal dysfunction theories) – all suggesting a biological component in the explanation of crime.

The genetic transmission of crime is considered by many researchers to be evidence that supports its biological basis. Though there is no known 'criminal gene' *per se*, some genes contribute to traits (low empathy, low IQ, aggression, impulsivity) that increase the proba-

bility of criminal behaviour, either alone or when combined with the right environments. Data from studies have demonstrated that identical twins – who share 100 per cent of their genetic material – are more concordant for criminality than fraternal twins (who share only half their genes). Studies examining the adopted-away children of criminal parents have also demonstrated a genetic basis to criminal behaviour. According to evolutionary psychologists, some criminal tendencies may in fact represent advantageous and adaptive strategies that have contributed to reproductive success.

Hundreds of studies over the past several decades have examined the psychophysiological basis of anti-sociality, criminality, delinquency and psychopathy (a personality disorder often associated with crime). The strongest finding from these studies is low physiological arousal, suggesting that anti-social individuals are chronically under-aroused. Traditional psychophysiological measures of arousal include heart rate, skin conductance (sweat gland) activity and electroencephalogram (EEG – reflecting electrical activity of the brain) measured during a 'resting' state. Low resting heart rate is considered the best replicated biological correlate of anti-social behaviour, while skin conductance and EEG under arousal have also been identified in scores of other studies of violent and anti-social persons. Two theoretical interpretations of low arousal are fearlessness theory (low levels of arousal are markers of low levels of fear) and stimulation-seeking theory (low arousal represents an unpleasant physiological state whereby anti-socials seek stimulation in the form of criminal behaviour to increase their arousal levels back to an optimal or normal level). Both may be complementary rather than competing theories.

Malformed or malfunctioning regions in the brain have been implicated in criminal behaviour. Brain-imaging studies indicate that violent offenders have structural and functional deficits to the frontal lobe (behind the forehead) and the temporal lobe (near the ears). Recent reviews of the literature converge on the conclusion that the brain region most likely to be compromised in anti-social, violent populations is the prefrontal cortex (a frontal lobe subregion occupying approximately one third of the entire cerebrum). Reduced prefrontal functioning can result in an inability to control aggressive feelings and impulses from the deeper, more emotional and primitive areas of the brain. Prefrontal damage also encourages risk-taking, irresponsibility, rule-breaking, emotional and aggressive outbursts, and argumentative behaviour that can also predispose to violent criminal acts.

Patients who have suffered damage to both grey and white matter in the prefrontal region of the brain may acquire an anti-social, psychopathic-like personality. A famous example is the nineteenth-century case of Phineus Gage, a responsible, well liked American railroad worker whose personality became markedly anti-social after he suffered the passage of an iron rod through his skull in an accidental explosion, effectively destroying a portion of his prefrontal cortex. Studies using positron emission tomography (PET), which measures the metabolic activity of different brain regions, have shown significantly poorer prefrontal functioning in murderers when compared with normal persons. Magnetic resonance imaging (MRI) studies have shown reduced prefrontal grey matter volume in individuals with anti-social personality disorder (a psychiatric disorder strongly associated with criminal behaviour). Neuropsychological studies have also demonstrated that anti-social individuals perform poorly on tests thought to measure frontal functioning.

Additional brain regions have been implicated in criminal behaviour. For example, PET studies indicate that the brains of murderers are also characterized by deficits in such key areas as the left angular gyrus and corpus callosum. The left angular gyrus plays a key role in integrating information from the temporal (side of head), parietal (top and back of head) and occipital (very back of head) lobes, and has been associated with reading and arithmetic. Impairments in these functions could lead to school failure, occupational failure and, consequently, a criminal career. The corpus callosum provides communication between the two brain hemispheres and has been linked to inappropriate emotional expression and a lack of long-term planning. Furthermore, the limbic system (a 'claw'-shaped network of smaller structures located towards the centre of the brain and important in emotional responses, drive-related behaviour and memory) has been associated with violent and aggressive impulses. Two limbic structures, the hippocampus and amygdala, have demonstrated functional impairments in studies of violent individuals. It has been suggested that, for psychopaths, amygdala dysfunction reduces both responsiveness to the sadness and fear of potential victims and the ability to learn stimulus-reinforcement associations crucial for moral socialization.

Researchers have examined other biological factors that may play a role in crime. Birth complications such as anoxia (getting too little oxygen), forceps delivery and pre-eclampsia (hypertension leading to anoxia) are thought to contribute to brain damage and have been related to later conduct disorder, delinquency, impulsive crime and adult violence. This is especially true when birth complications co-occur with social risk factors for violence, such as maternal rejection of the child. Additionally, minor physical anomalies have been associated with pregnancy complications and are thought to reflect foetal maldevelopment (including brain maldevelopment) towards the end of the first trimester of pregnancy. These anomalies (low-seated ears, adherent ear lobes, furrowed tongue, curved fifth finger, single transverse palmar crease, gaps between the first and second toes, unusually long third toes and fine hair), though not stigmatizing, have been found to characterize pre-adult anti-social behaviour and temperament.

Nutritional factors that have demonstrated effects on human behaviour in general have shown relationships to aggression and crime.

For example, hypoglycemia (low blood sugar) has been claimed to be linked to impaired brain function and violent crime. Lower cholesterol levels and vitamin (B3, B6 and C), mineral (iron and zinc) and protein deficiencies have also shown relationships with various forms of anti-social behaviour. Children with poor nutrition early in life have been found to develop anti-social and aggressive behaviour in late childhood and late adolescence, independent of social risk factors. Furthermore, environmental pollutants (i.e. heavy metals such as lead and manganese that have neurotoxic effects) have been implicated as biological factors in crime.

Hormonal influences on criminal behaviour have also been examined. Abnormal levels of male sex hormones (androgens), such as testosterone, have been shown to produce aggressive behaviour, and cortisol, a hormone thought to index arousal of the hypothalamus, pituitary and adrenal glands (the HPA axis), may play a role in mediating anti-social, violent and criminal behaviour. While normal individuals who are aroused or stressed show an increase in cortisol levels, anti-social individuals demonstrate lower cortisol levels (thought to represent under-arousal and fearlessness). Some biological research has also claimed a controversial link between premenstrual syndrome and aggression in females, but this requires replication.

Neurotransmitters – chemicals stored in the synaptic vesicles of communicating nerve cell axons – form the basis to the transmission of information throughout the brain. Biological research indicates that reduced serotonin and norepinephrine levels appear to be related to anti-social behavior, with some initial evidence indicating relationships with other neurotransmitters, such as dopamine, acetylcholine and γ-aminobutric acid (GABA). A new generation of neurogenetic studies is now beginning to identify specific genes (e.g. monoamine oxidase-A) that predispose to adult anti-social behaviour when combined with negative environmental influences, such as child abuse.

The implications for forensic practice include arguments for reduced culpability for criminal acts based on evidence for biological impairments – currently exemplified by the hotly debated use of brain-imaging data to explain the cause of offending in both the guilt and penalty phases of capital cases. Additionally, biological data may be used to prevent biologically based crime-prone individuals from future offending via pre-emptive programming incarceration or institutionalization. To some, this may echo the brutal and repressive state policies (i.e. sterilization and psychosurgery) spawned by the American eugenics movement in the early 1900s. It must be remembered, however, that biology is not destiny and that these changeable biological dispositions towards crime should not be considered apart from important social and environmental influences.

Results from biological research studies on crime must be scrutinized closely before being systematically employed in forensic applications. Many findings are provisional, some are mixed and all require extensive replication before acquiring any legitimate applied forensic value. Biological information from offenders should ultimately be used cautiously by the criminal justice system – and only in combination with other sources of collateral data – when making important decisions in such areas as criminal responsibility and dangerousness.

Robert A. Schug and Adrian Raine

Related entries

Criminal careers; Family factors.

Key texts and sources

Lombroso, C. (2006) *Criminal Man* (trans. M. Gibson and N.H. Rafter). Durham, NC: Duke University Press (originally published in 1876).

Patrick, C.J. (ed.) (2006) *Handbook of Psychopathy*. New York, NY: Guilford Press.

Raine, A. (2002) 'The biological basis of crime', in J.Q. Wilson and J. Petersilia (eds) *Crime: Public Policies for Crime Control*. Oakland, CA: ICS Press.

Silva, J.A. (2007) 'The relevance of neuroscience to forensic psychiatry', *Journal of the American Academy of Psychiatry and the Law*, 35: 6–9.

Walsh, A. and Ellis, L. (2007) *Criminology: An Interdisciplinary Approach*. Thousand Oaks, CA: Sage.

BOOT CAMPS

Boot camps are American shock incarceration regimes for adults and juveniles that emphasize discipline and physical training in a military-style environment. They are generally restricted to non-violent or first-time offenders.

The first two boot camp prisons were introduced in the USA in 1983 and, by 1994, they were established in 36 states. The focus of the early prisons was on creating a military atmosphere, with drilling, discipline, hard labour and intense physical training. Gradually rehabilitative components (such as counselling, education, cognitive and behavioural skills training, and drug treatment) were introduced. Staff and inmates wore military uniforms, and inmates joined the prison in groups as squads or platoons. Inmates' heads were shaved regularly. Boot camps were designed for young non-violent offenders who did not have a previous extensive criminal history. Punishment for misbehaviour was instant and often involved some rigorous physical activity.

In the USA, correctional boot camps exist in federal, state and local juvenile and adult jurisdictions. In juvenile camps less emphasis is placed on hard labour and academic education is mandatory. A recent review of 43 controlled studies in the USA on the effects of boot camps on reoffending produced mixed results (Wilson and MacKenzie 2006). Where desirable effects on recidivism were found it was concluded that these programmes had devoted most time to rehabilitative activities and intensive supervision and care after release. The existing literature suggests that the military elements of boot camps, used in isolation, are ineffective in reducing recidivism.

In 1995, an intensive regime based on the positive aspects of American boot camps was approved in the UK. Entitled 'high intensity training' (HIT), it was based at Thorn Cross Young Offender Institution (YOI). The HIT regime consisted of five phases of five weeks each. The programme included physical exercise, military-style drill, life and social skills, cognitive-behavioural skills and vocational training. During the final stage, young offenders were released on temporary licence from Monday to Friday to undertake work in the community. The aim was to provide young offenders with a permanent job or training opportunity following release. Hence, military elements comprised a minor part of the overall HIT scheme.

Evaluation of the regime was relatively positive, with 35 per cent of young offenders being reconvicted within one year, compared with a prediction of 47 per cent (Farrington *et al.* 2002). In contrast, as many control young offenders were reconvicted (55 per cent) as had been predicted (56 per cent). Moreover, the regime was more successful with medium and high-risk offenders than with low-risk offenders. For those who were reconvicted, the average time between release and reoffending was 228 days for HIT young offenders compared with 177 days for controls – a significant difference.

The Home Secretary at the time, however, considered that there remained a need to establish a more military style of training for young offenders. He was impressed by the quality of the training offered to military service personnel under sentence and wished to test whether a military approach to custody would benefit civilian young offenders and would be effective in reducing offending. Hence the Military Corrective Training Centre (MCTC) was established at Colchester, Essex, and the first young offenders entered the centre in 1997. The regime was unique in that military staff were involved alongside prison staff in dealing with young offenders in a military setting. The regime was far more austere than a normal YOI. It was, in essence, a UK military-style regime and was branded as a 'boot camp' by the media.

Young offenders wore a military uniform with coloured tags signifying which of the three stages they were in. The emphasis was on physical training, fitness and drill, smartness, cleanliness, and room and kit inspections. The idea was that imposed discipline would encourage self discipline and that drill would promote peer pressure and team spirit. There was a successful 'zero tolerance' policy to bullying and drug taking. Life, education and work skills were also significant features of the programme.

Young offenders reported an increase in self-esteem and self-confidence, and improved health, fitness, self-worth, self-control and prosocial attitudes. None the less, the positive changes in the institution did not appear to affect recidivism on release. An analysis based on 66 experimental and 103 control young offenders found that the predicted and actual percentages reconvicted were similar for both. Consequently, the MCTC seemed to have no effect on reconvictions.

The HIT and MCTC regimes were similar in adopting an austere, disciplined, military-style drilling and a demanding physical routine combined with educational, vocational and life-skills training. These two UK experiments support the view that military-style training, unless combined with offending behaviour and aftercare programmes, does not reduce recidivism.

Kate Painter

Related entries

Criminal careers; Juvenile delinquency; What Works.

Key texts and sources

Farrington, D.P., Ditchfield, J., Hancock, G., Howard, P., Jolliffe, D., Livingstone, M. and Painter, K. (2002) *Evaluation of Two Intensive Regimes for Young Offenders. Home Office Research Study 239.* London: Home Office.
Wilson, D.B. and MacKenzie, D.L. (2006) 'Boot camps', in B.C. Welsh and D.P. Farrington (eds) *Preventing Crime: What Works for Children, Offenders, Victims and Places.* Dordrecht: Springer.

BRITISH CRIME SURVEY (BCS)

The British Crime Survey (BCS) is an annual, large-scale government household survey conducted in the UK to capture over 45,000 adults' experiences of crime.

The British Crime Survey (BCS) is one of the largest UK government household surveys, with over 45,000 adults interviewed annually.

The survey is commissioned by the Home Office with sampling and data collection carried out by an external research agency – currently BMRB Social Research. The survey was first conducted in 1982 and included Scotland but has since been restricted to England and Wales. It ran at roughly two-yearly intervals until 2001 when it became a continuous survey.

The BCS is primarily a victimization survey with those interviewed asked about the household's experience of property crimes (e.g. burglary) and personal crimes (e.g. theft from a person) which they themselves have experienced in the 12 months prior to interview. The core victimization questions have remained consistent over time, with respondents asked directly about their experience of crime, irrespective of whether or not they have reported incidents to the police. As such, the BCS provides a record of people's experiences of crime that is unaffected by changes in reporting rates or variations in police recording practices or activity. Thus, for the crime types it covers, the BCS is considered to provide a better measure of level and trends in crime than that available from police-recorded crime figures.

However, the BCS and police recorded figures should be seen as a complementary series that, together, provides a better picture of crime than could be obtained from either series alone, and analyses of the two sources are presented annually in the Home Office statistical bulletin, *Crime in England and Wales.*

The BCS has a random probability sample that is designed to yield nationally representative estimates for two linked populations in England and Wales: private households and adults resident in private households. The BCS is a face-to-face survey in which trained interviewers visit sampled addresses to seek co-operation with those who have been selected for interview. In households with more than one adult resident, just one is randomly selected for interview. The average length of interview is 45 minutes, and the BCS achieves a relatively high response rate for a voluntary sample survey (e.g. 75 per cent in 2005–6).

The content of the BCS extends beyond merely counting criminal incidents, although it is for this estimate that it has become established as a definitive source of information. The survey provides a rich source of data about victims of crime, the circumstances in which incidents occur and the behaviour of offenders in committing crimes. In this way, the survey has provided data to inform crime reduction measures and to gauge their effectiveness. In addition, the BCS is used to collect attitudinal data on a range of crime-related topics. Some of these topics are well established aspects of the BCS, providing a good time-series on issues such as attitudes towards the police and the criminal justice system, anti-social behaviour and the use of illegal drugs. Annual datasets are deposited at the UK Data Archive to enable secondary analysis by academic researchers.

John Flatley

Related entries

Criminology; Victim support.

Key texts and sources

Home Office (2006a) *Crime in England and Wales, 2005/06*. London: Home Office (available online at http://www.homeoffice.gov.uk/rds/pdfs06/hosb1206.pdf).
Home Office (2007a) *Crime in England and Wales, 2005/06. Supplementary Volume 1*. London: Home Office (available online at http://www.homeoffice.gov.uk/rds/pdfs07/hosb0207.pdf).
Home Office (2007b) *Crime in England and Wales, 2005/06. Supplementary Volume 2*. London: Home Office (available online at http://www.homeoffice.gov.uk/rds/pdfs07/hosb1007.pdf).
See also the BCS's website (http://www.homeoffice.gov.uk/rds/bcs1.html).

BRITISH PSYCHOLOGICAL SOCIETY (BPS)

The British Psychological Society (BPS) is the professional body for psychologists in the UK concerned with the development, promotion and application of pure and applied psychology for the public good and with promoting the efficiency and usefulness of its members.

Psychology is the scientific study of people, the mind and behaviour. It is both a thriving academic discipline and a vital professional practice. Psychologists and psychological research have a big impact on all aspects of public life, particularly in such areas as education, health, the economy, industry and social justice.

The British Psychological Society (BPS) is the representative body for psychology and psychologists in the UK. The society was formed in 1901 and now has approximately 45,000 members. By its Royal Charter, granted in 1965, the society is charged with national responsibility for the development, promotion and application of pure and applied psychology for the public good and with promoting the efficiency and usefulness of society members by maintaining a high standard of professional education and knowledge.

The Society's main aims are to:

- encourage the development of psychology as a scientific discipline and an applied profession;
- raise standards of training and practice in the application of psychology; and
- raise public awareness of psychology and increase the influence of psychological practice in society.

Forensic psychology is the specialist area of psychology dealing with forensic matters, such as offending behaviour and its detection, reoffending and its reduction, the administration of justice, aspects of evidence and the work of the courts. Forensic psychologists work in prisons and young offender institutions, youth

treatment centres, health and social service settings, probation services, special hospitals and
regional secure units, and in research and teaching and training in the field at universities.

Sometimes forensic psychologists are called
as expert witnesses, and the BPS maintains an
open access, online database of its members
who are available for this type of work. It also
provides a professional focus for its members
working in the field of forensic psychology
through its Division of Forensic Psychology
(DFP), which is devoted to furthering the development and application of forensic psychology,
specializing in promoting the application of
psychological theories, methods and processes
to the forensic/legal system.

Ensuring that the qualifications and practice
of forensic psychologists are of the highest
order is a major aim of the society and, through
the training committee of the DFP, it is responsible for assessing courses in forensic
psychology for accreditation by the society. The
division is also responsible for the supervised
practice requirements for training to become a
chartered forensic psychologist.

The society supports this drive for excellence through a number of publications and
events. Its main forensic psychology publications are its scientific journal, *Legal and
Criminological Psychology*, the DFP's newsletter, *Forensic Update*, and its occasional papers,
Issues in Forensic Psychology. The DFP also
organizes conferences and seminars on forensic psychology.

Douglas Brown

Related entries

*Applied psychology; Chartered psychologists;
Health Professions Council (HPC).*

Key texts and sources

See the BPS's website (www.bps.org.uk). The online
database of BPS members available for expert
witness work is at http://www.bps.org.uk/bps/e-
services/find-a-psychologist/expertwitness.cfm.

BULLYING IN PRISONS

Bullying is behaviour involving an intentional
physical, psychological or verbal attack, an
imbalance of power or an intent to cause
fear or distress in the absence of provocation
of the bully that occurs more than once.

Attempting to outline a fixed, measurable definition of prison bullying has proven difficult.
Early definitions were based on bullying in
schools and focused on direct behaviours (e.g.
physical, verbal, sexual and theft-related aggression) as opposed to indirect behaviours (e.g.
more subtle behaviours, such as gossiping,
spreading rumours and ostracizing). In 1993
the definitions available were summarized in
one paper, where it was indicated that, in order
for a behaviour to be classed as bullying, it must
contain physical, psychological or verbal attack;
involve an imbalance of power; the victim must
not have provoked the bully; the aggression had
to have occurred more than once; and the bully
must have intended his or her actions specifically to cause fear or distress. Not all these
elements are universally accepted, however, with
each criticized with regards to its application to
prison bullying. Indeed, it could be argued that
the only consensus in relation to defining bullying has been on the difficulties in determining
an agreed definition that can be reliably measured. It has further been argued that current
definitions do not sufficiently account for motivations, with a move in the wider aggression
field to define aggression (e.g. bullying) by its
motivation as opposed to its typology. In an
attempt to encapsulate the difficulties in defining prison bullying, Ireland (2002: 26) offered
the following broader definition of bullying:

*An individual is being bullied when they are
the victim of direct and/or indirect aggression
happening on a weekly basis, by the same perpetrator or different perpetrators. Single
incidences of aggression can be viewed as bullying, particularly where they are severe and
when the individual either believes or fears
that they are at risk of future victimisation by*

the same perpetrator or others. An incident can be considered bullying if the victim believes that they have been aggressed towards, regardless of the actual intention of the bully. It can also be bullying when the imbalance of power between the bully and his/her victim is implied and not immediately evident.

Overview of the area

As an area of academic study, the examination of bullying behaviour among prisoners has had a briefer history in terms of academic interest than the bullying that occurs in other settings. The first study exploring prison bullying was published in 1996, with a marked increase in research since 1999 and with 24 studies published between 1999 and 2006. To date, studies have covered the full remit of the prison population (i.e. adults, young offenders, juveniles, men and women), although of these juveniles and women remain the least researched groups.

With regards to the proportions of bullying that occur among prisoners, estimates are higher than those found in other settings, such as schools. This is largely dependent, however, on the method of data collection employed. If prisoners are asked directly, 'Have you bullied others and/or been bullied?', proportions in relation to perpetration have been as high as 67 per cent in some studies, with an average estimate of 21 per cent. Proportions in relation to victim estimates have reached 57 per cent in some studies, with an average of 23 per cent. Methods such as behavioural checklists (e.g. the Direct and Indirect Prison Behaviour Checklist – DIPC) whereby prisoners are asked to indicate a range of discrete aggressive behaviours they have engaged in or experienced, with the use of the term 'bullying' avoided, have produced higher overall average estimates. Using this method, average proportions for perpetration have reached 52 per cent and, for victimization, 53 per cent. In a more recent study exploring estimates of bullying behaviours over a one-month period, over 80 per cent of prisoners reported at least once incidence of victimization in the previous month, with over 60 per cent reporting perpetration items.

Across the different types of bullying behav-iours reported, indirect aggression has been reported to occur to at least the same extent, if not more frequently, than direct aggression. Indirect aggression is expected to occur in prisons on the basis of two core reasons; 1) that it is an effective method of aggression a perpetrator is likely to be able to employ without being detected by the prison authorities; and 2) that, developmentally, older age groups (i.e. those above the age of 15) will employ indirect aggression to a greater extent due to their increased levels of social skill, with indirect aggression complementing and replacing direct aggression over time and eventually forming part of an individual's aggressive repertoire.

It should not be a surprise, therefore, that prison research has reported increased estimates of indirect bullying in comparison with direct bullying, since prison research has focused primarily on older adolescents (i.e. those over 18) and adults. Interestingly, differences in the nature of bullying among prisoners have been limited to age differences, with no evidence of sex differences.

Prison research has also tended to explore bullying by separating participants into one of four groups: 'pure bullies' (i.e. those who solely report perpetration), 'pure victims' (i.e. those who solely report victimization), 'bully/victims' (i.e. those who report perpetration and victimization) and those 'not involved'. Bully/victims have proven to represent an interesting group on the basis that they tend to be the largest category of perpetrator and victim groups and also since the notion of a 'mutual' perpetrator–victim group is a relatively new finding in bullying and aggression research. Previous research has explored how perpetrators can become victims over time (and vice versa), but not the notion that an individual can be both a perpetrator and a victim simultaneously.

Also of interest in relation to bully/victims has been the consistency across studies in relation to behavioural predictors of membership to this group: bully/victims have consistently been predicted by higher levels of negative (e.g. disruptive) behaviour than the other groups. This finding has held men, women, juvenile, young offender and adult samples. It has been argued that bully/victims display disruptive behaviour in order to secure staff attention, which will then limit the opportunities other prisoners have to bully them, and to raise their status among other prisoners, thus protecting themselves against being seen as vulnerable to future victimization.

There has been a focus in the last five years away from describing the nature and extent of prison bullying towards exploring the methods applied to measure bullying, the different groups involved and the advancement of theory. An interest in the methods used has led to a scaled version of the behavioural checklist used most frequently to measure bullying (i.e. the DIPC). The scaled version accounts for the frequency of behaviours indicative of bullying (i.e. the DIPC-SCALED). Initial analysis with this scaled measure has indicated the presence of 'chronic' groups – namely, those reporting one standard deviation above average levels of victimization and/or perpetration. One fifth of prisoners in one large-scale study were classified into one of these 'chronic' groups (as a perpetrator, victim or both).

Attention to theoretical models has also been a fairly recent development, with theoretical models now in existence to explain why prison bullying occurs (e.g. the interactional model), how victims are likely to respond (e.g. the applied fear response model), the role of information processing (e.g. the applied social information processing model) and the biopsychosocial interactions in bullying. Summarizing the contribution of all these models is not possible here. It is, however, important to highlight two of the core contributions of these models. First is the recognition that bullying will always take place in settings where individuals reside together and that there may be some adaptive element of this behaviour in terms of its potential for protecting individuals from harm. Secondly is the shift in focus away from individual psychopathology to the importance of the environment and an individual's interaction with this. Models such as the interactional model outline the role of both the social and physical environment in promoting bullying, with attention focused on the environmental reinforcements that occur after an act of bullying has taken place. In short, models such as this argue strongly for a move away from 'treating' the individual involved in bullying (either as a bully and/or a victim) in isolation from the environment in which he or she is placed.

Implications for practice

Of the research conducted in this area to date, there are a number of implications that can be drawn and applied to practice. Some of the core implications are as follows:

- The policies and procedures designed to manage bullying should not have the eradication of bullying as an aim, since this is unachievable (prisons that indicate that they have no bullying are simply not measuring the problem accurately). Rather, policies and procedures should have the aim of minimizing bullying as much as possible – the focus should be on promoting 'healthy prison communities'. A healthy community will lead to a reduction in bullying.
- Connected to this, intervention into bullying should include a primary focus on the role of the environment and how this can be managed in such a way as to minimize bullying. Importantly, there should be a shift away from individual psychopathology approaches (i.e. the notion that someone is a victim and/or a bully solely due to something being 'wrong' with him or her) to approaches that account for the social and physical environment.
- There should be an equal focus on the management of indirect methods of bullying, with management strategies serving to raise awareness of this form of aggression and managing it to the same level as direct aggression.
- Differences in the nature of bullying are limited to age. There are no sex differences. Thus, approaches for dealing with bullying should not be different for men and women

prisoners. Rather, approaches should be tailored to the differences evident in the prison environment.

● The majority of prisoners involved in perpetration or victimization will fall into the 'bully/victim' group. Bully/victims should be considered a primary victim group.

Jane L. Ireland

Related entries

Anger; Anger and aggression assessment.

Key texts and sources

Ireland, J.L. (2000) 'Bullying among prisoners: a review of research', *Aggression and Violent Behaviour: A Review Journal,* 5: 201–15.

Ireland, J.L. (2002) *Bullying among Prisoners: Evidence, Research and Intervention Strategies.* Hove: Brunner-Routledge.

Ireland, J.L. (ed.) (2005) *Bullying among Prisoners: Innovations in Theory and Research.* Cullompton: Willan Publishing.

Ireland, J.L. and Ireland, C.A. (2003) 'How do offenders define bullying? A study of adult, young and juvenile male offenders', *Legal and Criminological Psychology,* 8: 159–73.

Olweus, D. (1978) *Aggression in Schools: Bullies and Whipping Boys.* Washington, DC: Hemisphere.

C

CAMBRIDGE FRAMEWORK FOR RISK ASSESSMENT (CAMRA)

The Cambridge Framework for Risk Assessment (CAMRA) is a public domain, structured approach to the assessment of risk involving a sequence of six stages designed to guide practitioners to consider pertinent issues in risk assessment and management.

The Cambridge Framework for Risk Assessment (CAMRA) is a structure that practitioners in forensic settings can apply to the assessment of risk. The CAMRA process involves six stages, each of which requires the practitioner to consider issues pertinent to that stage. CAMRA guides the practitioner through the risk assessment task from specification of the risk behaviour to the development of a plan for monitoring, intervention and review.

In terms of the six stages, CAMRA advocates the following approach:

- *Stage 1*: specification of the criterion variable(s) (the risk behaviour(s)).
- *Stage 2*: specification of predictor variables and exploration and examination (with reference to the evidence base, offence accounts and the accounts of significant others, and the identification of the factors that are likely to predict the occurrence of the risk behaviour within a specified timescale).
- *Stage 3*: identification of factors that are likely to increase and decrease risk of the criterion variable occurring.

- *Stage 4*: estimation of probability and consequences of the criterion variable occurring.
- *Stage 5*: assessment of acceptability of risk of given the consequences of the criterion variable occurring.
- *Stage 6*: specification of appropriate monitoring, intervention and review arrangements.

CAMRA is based on a number of principles that underpin each stage of the model. A key principle of the CAMRA approach is the need for the practitioner to be specific in terms of the risk behaviour(s) that is subject to the assessment and management plan. The model therefore requires the practitioner to specify the behaviour that will be risk assessed and when appropriate to identify the likely victims of this behaviour. The model recognizes that, within an individual case, there may be more than one risk behaviour that requires assessment but advocates that this is recognized at an early stage so that individual assessments for each risk can be completed as part of the process.

The second principle that underpins CAMRA is that of anchoring the risk assessment within the available evidence base. CAMRA asks the practitioner to be familiar with and to refer to the relevant knowledge base when conducting his or her assessment and when making risk predictions. It also encourages the practitioner to consider a range of accounts of the behaviour being assessed as a means of ensuring that the information used is accurate and valid.

Finally, CAMRA identifies that risk may be heightened or reduced as a consequence of the presence or absence of a range of factors. CAMRA therefore asks the practitioner to consider factors that may protect against offending as well as increase risk and requires the practitioner to draw these together with other elements of the assessment to develop a time-bound risk management plan.

Karen Brady

Related entries

Recidivism prediction; Risk assessment; Risk–needs assessment (Level of Service Inventory – LSI).

Key texts and sources

Towl, G.J. and Crighton, D.A. (1996) *The Handbook of Psychology for Forensic Practitioners.* London: Routledge.

Towl, G.J. and Crighton, D.A. (2000) 'Risk assessment and management', in G.J. Towl *et al.* (eds) *Suicide in Prisons.* Leicester: British Psychological Society.

CARE PROGRAMME APPROACH (CPA)

The care programme approach (CPA) is a framework designed to improve the delivery of effective mental health care for people with severe mental health problems, involving systematic arrangments for assessing health and social needs, for the formation of a health and social care plan, for the appointment of a key worker and for a regular review process.

The care programme approach (CPA) was introduced in 1990 to provide a framework for effective mental health care for people with severe mental health problems using secondary mental health services. Its four main elements were as follows:

- Systematic arrangements for assessing the health and social needs of people accepted into specialist mental health services.
- The formation of a care plan that identifies the health and social care required from a variety of providers.

- The appointment of a key worker (care co-ordinator) to keep in close touch with the service user and to monitor and co-ordinate care.
- Regular review and, where necessary, agreed changes to the care plan.

The CPA was reviewed in 2006 through a national, open consultation (Department of Health 2006c) to ensure national policy was more consistently applied. Overall there was support for CPA policy but there was an association between bureaucracy and the CPA. Following the consultation, certain implementation changes were made:

- CPA policy will focus on those with the highest level of need and on the co-ordination of the most complex service response (to meet those needs). Therefore the previous distinction between 'Standard' and 'Enhanced' CPA will be removed and replaced with one level that is focused on a high level of need and a complex service response.
- Everyone who is in contact with secondary mental health services (whether requiring a complex co-ordination of care or a more simple co-ordination of care) should receive services underpinned by the same principles and values – placing the person at the centre of the care/support.
- Key competences have been developed to describe and support the role of the care co-ordinator.
- National training material for the mental health services workforce will be developed for risk, safety and care co-ordination.
- Regulatory bodies, such as the Healthcare Commission, will assess trusts against CPA standards, concentrating on service-user-defined outcomes.

National Health Service trusts are required to meet these policy implementation changes by October 2008.

Dawn Flemming

Related entries

Forensic psychiatry; National Health Service (NHS).

Key texts and sources

Department of Health (1999a) *Effective Care Co-ordination in Mental Health Services: Modernising the Care Programme Approach – a Policy Booklet.* London: Department of Health.

Department of Health (2004a) *The National Service Framework – Five Years On.* London: Department of Health.

Department of Health (2006c) *Reviewing the Care Programme Approach.* London: Department of Health.

See also the website of the Care Programme Approach Association (**www.cpaa.co.uk**). For information on the current review, see **www.nimhe.csip.org.uk/cpa**.

CHARTERED PSYCHOLOGISTS

The title 'chartered psychologist' refers to a practitioner in psychology who has applied to, and been entered on, the Register of Chartered Psychologists maintained by the British Psychological Society.

One key part of the Royal Charter for the British Psychological Society (BPS) sets out a requirement to 'maintain, with such particulars as the Council shall decide, a Register of Chartered Psychologists, consisting of those Members of the Society who have applied for and been granted admission to the Register in accordance with the provisions of the Statutes'.

All psychologists admitted to this register will have successfully completed a first qualification in psychology accredited by the BPS as providing the 'graduate basis for registration', generally by completion of a first degree in psychology, an approved joint degree or a postgraduate conversion course. They will also have undertaken a further period of postgraduate study and supervised training in applied psychology. Psychologists who have joined the Register of Chartered Psychologists voluntarily agree to abide by a professional code of ethics and conduct, making them subject to disciplinary procedures through the BPS. This code allows for issues of professional conduct and fitness to practice to be considered by a disciplinary board, on which non-psychologists make up the majority of members.

In the absence of statutory regulation of psychology, the government, through the Privy Council, agreed to the creation of the Register of Chartered Psychologists and legally protected the title 'chartered psychologist'. This voluntary register came into operation fully from 1990.

The BPS currently comprises a number of divisions representing professional psychology across sub-specialists areas. These are largely based on historical patterns of postgraduate training that developed within specific work settings. There are currently seven divisions providing initial postgraduate training in practitioner psychology (clinical, counselling, educational, forensic, health, occupational and sport and exercise).

Chartered psychologists are professionally accountable through the BPS for their own practice and also for that of others under their professional supervision.

David A. Crighton

Related entries

Applied psychology; British Psychological Society (BPS); Health Professions Council.

Key texts and sources

The BPS's charter is available online at **http://www.bps.org.uk/the-society/ethics-rules-charter-code-of-conduct/charter/full-charter.cfm**. The *Code of Ethics and Conduct* is available online at **http://www.bps.org.uk/document-download-area/document-download$.cfm?file_uuid=5084A882-1143-DFD0-7E6C-F1938A65C242&ext=pdf**.

CHILDREN AND FAMILY COURT ADVISORY AND SUPPORT SERVICE (CAFCASS)

> The Children and Family Court Advisory and Support Service (CAFCASS) is a national non-departmental public body for England, accountable to Parliament through the Department for Children, Schools and Families. Its functions are set out in the Criminal Justice and Court Services Act 2000.

The Children and Family Court Advisory and Support Service (CAFCASS) was set up on 1 April 2001 to bring together the family court services previously provided by the Family Court Welfare Service, the Guardian ad Litem Service and the Children's Division of the Official Solicitor's Office. The role of CAFCASS is, independently, to safeguard and promote the welfare of children in family court proceedings. The legislation that governs this work is the Children Act 1989 and the Children and Adoption Act 2002.

Under the title of family court adviser, CAFCASS officers carry out a number of roles.

Children and family reporter

The children and family reporter becomes involved in private law proceedings when parents are separating or divorcing and there is conflict over issues of residence (previously known as 'custody') or contact (previously known as 'access'). These issues are considered under s. 8 of the Children Act 1989 and may also include specific issues, such as change of surname. The children and family reporter will work towards achieving a solution that is in the child's best interests, and this will sometimes involve providing a report where there are issues of welfare for the court to consider.

Children's guardian

The children's guardian represents the interests of children in public law proceedings, during cases where social services have become involved in order to protect children from abuse or neglect, in contested adoptions and in cases where secure accommodation is being considered. The guardian is appointed as soon as an application is made to the court for an order in respect of a child and has the task of representing the child's wishes and feelings to the court, as well as his or her best interests. The guardian provides an independent overview to the court of the actions taken by the local authority and of the suitability of its plan for the child.

Reporting officer

The reporting officer ensures that parents understand what adoption means for them and their child and whether or not they consent to it.

Guardian ad litem

A guardian *ad litem* is occasionally appointed by the court in cases in private law where parents have not been able to reach agreement and there is a need for a child's rights and interests to be separately represented. In these cases, the guardian *ad litem* instructs a solicitor to represent the child.

CAFCASS will approach the Official Solicitor in cases where the parents are considered to be not capable of giving instructions to a solicitor (for example, if they have severe mental health or learning difficulties).

CAFCASS operates across ten regional areas in England. It has a budget of £107 million. It is run by a management board and corporate directors. The Chief Executive is supported by a Corporate Decisions Group, a Children's Rights Director, regional directors and other senior managers.

Madeleine Oswald

Related entries

Courts; Social Services; Victim support

Key texts and sources

See the CAFCASS website (http://www.cafcass.gov.uk).

CHILD WITNESSES

'Child witness' refers to any child who is a victim of, or observes as a spectator, an event, and who subsequently furnishes a report for any investigation or trial. In England and Wales, the term 'child' refers to any person up to the age of 17 years.

Traditionally, lawyers have been sceptical of the likely reliability and accuracy of children as witnesses. In the 1980s, increasing concern over the plight of child victims of sexual and physical abuse whose abusers went unpunished because of the inadmissibility of children's evidence led to a revival in research interest in their competency. Research demonstrated that children's recall of experienced events – both created for experiments or taken from their own lives – was often highly accurate, and this in turn informed changes to the law in England and Wales to remove prohibitions on children's evidence and to facilitate the giving of that evidence at trial. The Criminal Justice Act 1988 introduced closed-circuit television (the 'live link') to enable children to give their evidence from outside the courtroom and so to obviate the need to confront the accused or enter the court itself – two aspects of the trial process that research had highlighted as major stressors for young witnesses.

The Criminal Justice Act 1991 permitted the use of prior video-recorded interviews conducted by a trained police officer or social worker as a substitute for the child's live examination in chief at trial. The main advantage of this innovation was seen as an opportunity to capture a 'fresh' account from the child soon after a complaint had emerged and so to counter the impact of the long delays typically experienced by children prior to trial and the consequent deterioration in memory. The use of trained interviewers was designed to improve the quality and completeness of testimony heard by the court. Research demonstrated that all parties, including child witnesses themselves, appreciated the advantages of these facilities. Today, many child witnesses, including virtually all cases involving complaints of sexual abuse,

have their evidence heard using these procedures, and similar facilities are now available in Scotland.

Two allegations frequently levelled at children concerned their vulnerability to suggestion and readiness to lie. Research in the early 1990s demonstrated the circumstances under which children would – and would not – respond to questions in a suggestive manner. These studies underlined the importance of considering the motivational and social dimensions of children's testimony as well as simply memory. They demonstrated that prior negative stereotypes passed to children by authority figures, combined with repeated interviews involving leading questions, could seriously distort children's narrative accounts of the events they had experienced. Further, repeated questioning about a non-existent event from the child's past, coupled with instructions to imagine the situation concerned, dramatically increased the numbers of children claiming the event had really occurred. Children did not merely accede to such misleading statements, some actively embellished them with spurious detail to the extent that child protection experts were unable to distinguish truthful from suggested accounts.

The problems of suggestibility vary very much between children and across situations. Age is a critical factor: most studies were conducted with children aged between 3 and 6 years and, even in this group, the impact of suggestion declined strongly with age. Other factors known to have a demonstrable influence on suggestibility include prior familiarity and knowledge about the event; event plausibility (a child can be convinced he or she was lost in a shopping precinct aged 5, but not that he or she received a rectal enema at the same age); and the strength of any pre-existing memory trace (the shorter the exposure, the longer the delay between a witnessed event and subsequent questioning, the greater the vulnerability to suggestion). Children clearly vary in their degree of suggestibility, but the precise factors underlying such individual differences are poorly understood. Social factors, such as the strength of parent–child attachment, appear as important as intellectual development in predicting suggestible responding.

As regards deliberate lying, research confirms that deception is learnt early: children as young as 3 years of age can demonstrate such behaviour. The ability to tell plausible lies appears to be a by-product of the development of the theory of mind: a growing understanding of how events are perceived from another individual's perspective. The ability to detect lying in children is inversely related to age, and people who themselves have children are better lie detectors than those who do not. There are no physical signs that are invariably associated with lying. Symptoms such as nervousness and speech disruption are indicative of stress, which can be caused by factors other than deliberate deception. Like adults, children can, on occasion, make false allegations of sexual or physical abuse. Content-based credibility analysis is a technique developed for the German courts to assess the credibility of statements made by children. However, the reliability of the technique and its vulnerability to coaching remain under question.

These findings underline the importance of early and appropriate interviewing procedures with children. Examination of miscarriages of justice caused by children's unfounded allegations has demonstrated that faulty interviewing practice is a principal cause. Effective interviewing demands that interviewers reduce the social distance between themselves and the child in order to minimize suggestive responding and that, as far as possible, the child should tell his or her own story rather than interviewers imposing their own perception of events and seeking confirmation from the child through a series of leading or coercive questions.

Social distance can be reduced by building rapport with the child through discussion of matters of interest to the child before broaching sensitive matters. Research using actual interview protocols has shown that a well conducted rapport session increases the reliability and accuracy of evidence elicited from a child. As regards questioning style, an initial request to the child to provide his or her own free account, followed by the use of open-ended questions to expand upon and clarify key issues

('Tell me what he was wearing'), has been shown to lead to the most complete and accurate accounts from child complainants of abuse. While the use of leading questions ('He was wearing jeans, wasn't he?') has an adverse impact on children's evidential accuracy, the use of closed ('Was he wearing trousers or jeans?') or even specific questions ('What colour were his trousers?') can also be a source of suggestive responding when questions refer to non-existent events or features.

A number of protocols have been developed that aim to minimize suggestibility in the child witness interview. The official guidance for England and Wales is *Achieving Best Evidence in Criminal Proceedings: Guidance for Vulnerable or Intimidated Witnesses, including Children* (Home Office 2002). This recommends an interview embodying four phases: rapport, free narrative, questioning and closure (the last designed to ensure that the child leaves the interview in as positive a frame of mind as possible). Analysis of the content of actual investigative interviews shows that the majority contain all four phases. While the proportion of leading questions is small (as low as one per interview), interviewers show a reluctance to use open-ended questions (just 6 per cent in one study), the remainder being closed or specific. Further research is required into training interviewers to adopt and then maintain good interviewing practice, and into interviewing minority ethnic people, very young children and learning disabled children to avoid a 'one size fits all' approach.

As regard implications for practice, suggestibility is countered by the emphasis on early interviewing and the video recording of all questions and answers. The use of open-ended questions should ensure that what the court hears is in the child's own words. At trial, the availability of the live link and videotaped interviews should lead to more and better prepared young witnesses coming to court. However, as many as 76 per cent of cases involving allegations by children are discontinued prior to trial, and video technology has so far had no appreciable impact on conviction rates. Despite much recent research and consequent legal changes, child witnesses still face an uphill struggle to have their voice heard in court.

Graham Davies

Related entries

Cognitive interviews; Expert testimony; Eyewitness testimony.

Key texts and sources

Ceci, S.J., Crossman, A.M., Scullin, M., Gilstrap, L. and Huffman, M.L. (2002) 'Children's suggestibility research: implications for the courtroom and the forensic interview', in H.L. Westcott *et al.* (eds) *Children's Testimony: A Handbook of Psychological Research and Forensic Practice.* Chichester: Wiley.

Home Office (2002) *Achieving Best Evidence in Criminal Proceedings: Guidance for Vulnerable or Intimidated Witnesses, including Children.* London: Home Office Communications Directorate (available online at **http://www.cps.gov.uk/publications/prosecution/bestevidencevol1.html**).

Powell, M., Fisher, R. and Wright, M. (2005) 'Investigative interviewing', in N. Brewer and K.D. Williams (eds) *Psychology and Law: An Empirical Perspective.* New York, NY: Guilford Press.

Vrij, A. (2002) 'Deception in children: a literature review and implications for children's testimony', in H.L. Westcott *et al.* (eds) *Children's Testimony: A Handbook of Psychological Research and Forensic Practice.* Chichester: Wiley.

Westcott, H.L. (2006) 'Child witness testimony: what do we know and where are we going?', *Child and Family Law Quarterly*, 18: 175–90.

CLINICAL PSYCHOLOGY

The term 'clinical psychology' was introduced in 1907 by the American psychologist, Lightner Witmer (1867–1956), who distinguished it from other uses of psychology as the study of individuals, by observation or experimentation, with the intention of promoting change.

The themes in the above are evident in almost every subsequent definition of clinical psychology, the modern American Psychological Association definition being a good example:

The field of Clinical Psychology integrates science, theory, and practice to understand, predict, and alleviate maladjustment, disability, and discomfort as well as to promote human adaptation, adjustment, and personal development. Clinical Psychology focuses on the intellectual, emotional, biological, psychological, social, and behavioral aspects of human functioning across the life span, in varying cultures, and at all socioeconomic levels.

(www.apa.org).

Psychology is applied by many people in the helping professions, often using intuitive techniques, interpersonal sensitivity and skills or basic counselling techniques. A more sophisticated use involves circumscribed psychological activities, such as behaviour modification, problem-focused cognitive therapy and other problem-focused, manualized interventions. Clinical psychologists are equipped by their training with the generic skills that allow them to adapt the application of psychology to clinical problems and populations, in contrast to some other professions that focus on a therapeutic technique or circumscribed population. Some, if not most, clinical psychologists specialize, but they generally acquire this specialist competence in post-doctoral experience and training.

Clinical psychology has been described as:

[a] 'specialist psychological intervention, in circumstances where there are deep-rooted underlying influences, or which call on the discretionary capacity to draw on a multiple theoretical base, to devise an individually tailored strategy for a complicated presenting problem. Flexibility to adapt and combine approaches is the key to competence at this level, which comes from a broad, thorough and sophisticated understanding of the various psychological theories. Clinical psychologists are the only profession that operates at this level. It is the skills required for this level of intervention, entailing flexible and generic knowledge and application of psychology, which distinguishes clinical psychologists from other disciplines.

(adapted from Management Advisory Service to the NHS 1989).

These themes continue in a recent benchmarking exercise seeking to define clinical psychology in the National Health Service:

> *Clinical psychologists are more than psychological therapists. While many do practise psychotherapy at a high level this is not a skill distinct to clinical psychologists, nor should it be. The background and training of clinical psychologists is rooted in the science of psychology, and clinical psychology is one of the applications of psychological science to help address human problems. The ability to design and carry out innovative applied research is a skill developed to a doctoral level in training and is important for the development and delivery of evidence-based practice ... One of the contributions made by clinical psychologists is the development and testing of new interventions and activities, based on psychological theory. Thus practice feeds and draws on research and theory that in turn influences practice*

(BPS 2005)

Brian A. Thomas-Peter

Related entries

Applied psychology; Chartered psychologists; Health Professions Council (HPC); National Health Service (NHS).

Key texts and sources

BPS (2005) *Subject Benchmarks for Applied Psychology*. Leicester: BPS.
See also the websites of the American Psychology Association (www.apa.org) and the BPS (www.bps.org.uk/careers/society_qual/clinical.cfm).

COGNITIVE INTERVIEWS

The cognitive interview is a systematic way of eliciting the maximum amount of relevant information from an eyewitness/interviewee.

The cognitive interview was developed by Fisher and Geiselman and aims to overcome some of the problems associated with inaccurate eye-witness testimonies. The developers suggest that it is most appropriate to use with co-operative eye-witnesses and in cases where the majority of evidence will come from eyewitness accounts and there is a dearth of physical evidence (Fisher and Geiselman 1992).

The cognitive interview relies heavily on research in the field of cognitive psychology but also uses ideas and approaches from other disciplines and areas. Two dimensions of knowledge have been identified by cognitive psychologists. One dimension concerns process aspects, such as procedural and declarative knowledge, and the other dimension concerns organizational aspects, such as semantic and episodic knowledge (Moody *et al.* 1998). The cognitive interview is directed at episodic knowledge. Episodic knowledge is the memory of events that have already happened and, by its very definition, is experiential in nature. It is organized by time and location and is perceptual in its description (Benjafield 1992).

The cognitive interview focuses on memory and communication. The interviewer employs the five principles of memory retrieval to aid the interviewee to retrieve stored information. The five principles are as follows:

1. *Context recreation*: recall is enhanced by recreating the event stimuli (physical and psychological). This may involve prompting the interviewee to recall both the physical and emotional surroundings of the event.
2. *Focused retrieval*: distractions deteriorate the memory retrieval process. Therefore, intrusions are minimalized and techniques such as the interviewee closing his or her eyes may be applied.
3. *Extensive retrieval*: recall is improved by increasing the number of retrieval attempts. The interviewer may therefore encourage multiple attempts to recall the event.
4. *Varied retrieval*: recall may be activated by different probes. The interviewer may explore recall in different ways, such as asking the interviewee to recall events in reverse order or from the perspective of a third party.

5. *Multiple representations*: events may be stored and recalled in two forms (episodic and thematic). The interviewee may be encouraged to explore such themes as details that are unusual, and they may be prompted to apply multiple senses (sound, touch, etc.) (adapted from Moody *et al.* 1998: 84).

The second aspect of the cognitive interview is communication. The interviewer needs to be an effective listener, and the interview should enhance communication, enabling the interviewee to formulate a complete and useful response (Fisher and Geiselman 1992).

There are a number of studies suggesting the effectiveness of the cognitive interview approach. For example, a study conducted with the Miami Police Department (Fisher *et al.* 1989) found that experienced detectives elicited 47 per cent more information after receiving training on the cognitive interview than prior to the training. In addition, a study conducted in Britain (George 1991) reported that detectives elicited 55 per cent more information post-training in the cognitive interview.

Derval Ambrose

Related entries

Detecting deception.

Key texts and sources

Benjafield, J. (1992) *Cognition*. Englewood Cliffs, NJ: Prentice Hall.

Fisher, R.P. and Geiselman, R.E. (1992) *Memory Enhancing Techniques for Investigative Interviewing: The Cognitive Interview*. Springfield, IL: Charles C. Thomas.

Moody, J.W., Blanton, J.E. and Cheney, P.H. (1998) 'A theoretically grounded approach to assist memory recall during information requirements determination', *Journal of Management Information Systems*, 15: 79–98.

COMMUNITY PUNISHMENTS

Community punishments are sentences, imposed on offenders by criminal courts, that do not involve imprisonment. These include various forms of reprimand, financial penalties, supervision, monitoring, treatment and unpaid work. They are sometimes referred to as 'non-custodial' sentences or 'alternatives to prison'.

Although community punishments vary around the world, it is possible to classify them in three ways: self-regulatory, financial and supervisory. Self-regulatory penalties involve some form of public admonition or reprimand that is assumed to be sufficiently shaming of itself to deter the offender from further law-breaking. In England and Wales, the most common of such penalties is the conditional discharge. Financial penalties are of two kinds: fines are both retributive and deterrent in purpose and are generally paid to the central administration of a criminal justice system; and compensation is paid (through the courts) to the victim of a crime and is intended to provide reparation.

Supervisory sentences are imposed when the courts believe that the offender is unable to stop committing crimes without support or surveillance, and they may contain one or more of three elements: rehabilitation (through hostel residence, education, therapeutic programmes and/or mental health or substance misuse treatment), reparation (through unpaid work or specified activities) and incapacitation (through curfews, electronic monitoring and/or prohibition from certain activities). Some community punishments have long histories while others have been introduced more recently. In England and Wales, the origins of probation (the main form of supervision) can be traced back to the nineteenth century, whereas community service (unpaid work) was introduced in the 1970s and electronic monitoring in the 1980s.

Expansion in the use of supervisory sentences since the 1970s has been due to the desire of governments to be seen to be finding less expensive, but equally demanding, alternatives to imprisonment. In reality, such expansion has been an accompaniment, rather than an alternative, to a rising prison population. Community punishments have many advantages over imprisonment. They allow offenders to retain family, work and social ties while, at the same time, giving them the opportunity to repair the damage they have done to the community and to resolve the personal and social problems that may have led to their offending. They enable the offender to avoid the stigma of imprisonment and the risk of becoming embedded in a criminal culture as a result of constant association with other criminals in prison. Community punishments are also less costly to administer than imprisonment.

Despite these advantages, community punishments have an 'image' problem. Although many more offenders receive some form of community sentence than are imprisoned, penal debates and policies focus overwhelmingly on prisons and neglect other forms of punishment. The public and media perceive that community sentences are but a poor substitute for the 'real punishment' of prison. Viewed as 'soft options', community punishments are often represented in policy documents as weak and undemanding 'let offs' that do not command public confidence. There is, therefore, a constant search among advocates of community punishments to include ever more demanding conditions that distinguish 'intermediate sentences' (as they have been called) from traditional welfare-oriented supervision.

The nature of probation intervention has changed in the past 20–30 years. Personal counselling, based on psychotherapeutic approaches, has been replaced by cognitive-behavioural programmes, based on social learning theory. Rather than attempting to change the whole personality or circumstances of an offender, cognitive-behavioural programmes focus on specific unacceptable behaviours and seek to modify these by correcting distortions in the way offenders think about their crime. Offenders are required to accept full responsibility for their actions (instead of blaming the victim or their circumstances), to empathize with the victim of their offences and to expand their repertoire of responses to those situations that previously triggered a criminal response. Programmes cover a range of specific problem behaviours, such as thinking skills, anger management, substance misuse and sex offending. Many programmes are now delivered by psychologists working alongside probation officers.

These programmes collectively form the 'What Works' agenda. The etymology of this phrase lies in a famously pessimistic (and later retracted) remark made in 1974 by a criminologist called Robert Martinson to the effect that 'nothing works' in penal interventions. The disillusion that followed this conclusion (supported by research findings at the time) led to a loss of confidence in probation that lasted until the early 1990s when the 'discovery' of cognitive-behavioural programmes led to a renewed interest in rehabilitation. The phrase 'What Works' (and the related concept of evidence-based practice) caught the imagination of politicians and professionals and now dominates community punishments in the English-speaking world. Evaluation research in the 1990s gave cause for cautious optimism in respect of the effectiveness of such programmes in reducing reoffending, but critics have argued more recently that enthusiasm for the cognitive-behavioural approach should not result in the neglect of other provision, such as basic literacy skills and social skills. Nor should the wider social problems that may lead people into crime be overlooked.

Since 2004, the National Offender Management Service of England and Wales has brought the Prison Service and the Probation Service closer in an attempt to provide 'end-to-end offender management'. Increasingly, offenders are being subjected to punishments that involved time spent in prison and in the community. This presents a new set of challenges to those professionals who work with offenders in the community and who have to balance the need to protect the public against the desire to prevent what is now known as the 'revolving door' of short-term imprisonment and supervision failure.

Anne Worrall

Related entries

National Probation Service (NPS); Nothing Works; What Works.

Key texts and sources

Bottoms, A., Rex, S. and Robinson, G. (eds) (2004) *Alternatives to Prison: Options for an Insecure Society*. Cullompton: Willan Publishing.

Mair, G. (ed.) (2004) *What Matters in Probation?* Cullompton: Willan Publishing.

McGuire, J. (2002) *Offender Rehabilitation and Treatment: Effective Programmes and Policies to Reduce Reoffending. Wiley Series in Forensic Clinical Psychology*. Chichester: Wiley.

Raynor, P. and Robinson, G. (2005) *Rehabilitation, Crime and Justice*. London: Palgrave Macmillan.

Worrall, A. and Hoy, C. (2005) *Punishment in the Community: Managing Offenders, Making Choices*. Cullompton: Willan Publishing.

COURT DUTY OFFICERS (CDOs)

Court duty officers (CDOs) are employed by the National Probation Service and can be located in either magistrates' courts or in Crown courts. They are the public face of probation in the court and also act as an interface for offender managers (previously named probation officers and Probation Service officers) working in probation in the community.

Court duty officers (CDOs) working in magistrates' courts are usually Probation Service officers, while Crown courts tend to have multigrade teams of both probation officers and Probation Service officers. Probation officers are also deployed at both Crown and magistrates' courts specifically to write reports.

It is important to note that the 'fine tunings' on the role of the CDO will vary from court to court as well between areas, depending on what the judiciary require from staff employed as CDOs. For example, the remit of the court of appeal will be significantly different from that of a Crown court, which in turn will have a different remit and workload from a local magistrates' court. There is no national agreement on the deployment of CDOs.

Key knowledge

CDOs must be familiar with legislation in so far as it relates to sentences supervised by the Probation Service and must have a knowledge of national and local probation policies and resources. They must ensure that they keep themselves updated with changes in legislation.

Key tasks prior to sentence

The CDO is responsible for checking whether offenders being processed through the court are known to probation and, if so, for advising on relevant issues, such as risk and response to supervision. In addition the CDO is responsible for starting the process of notification of a 'serious further offence' (SFO) if the offender has been charged with a further offence that falls within the SFO criteria.

If a defendant pleads guilty or is found guilty the CDOs will, if requested, arrange for the completion of a 'pre-sentence report'. There are currently three different types of pre-sentence report, and the CDO can advise the court of the most appropriate. These reports are standard delivery reports (SDRs) fast delivery reports (FDRs) and oral reports. FDRs and oral reports can be delivered on the same day.

CDOs may be required to provide FDRs and oral reports direct to the court. Some may also provide SDRs dependent on the local court arrangements. If a CDO is completing a report, he or she will arrange to interview the defendant to report on offending-related issues and to propose a suitable sentence. CDOs completing reports are also required to undertake a risk assessment using the Offender Assessment System (OASys), which is a tool assessing risk of harm and risk of reoffending. When an SDR is prepared, a full OASys assessment is completed. This is undertaken to aid sentencing and future offender management. Providing court reports is usually organized as a discrete task, separate from other court duty tasks that require the CDO's presence in court. CDOs may be asked to clarify information contained in court reports.

The aim of all reports is to aid sentencers in considering what sentences may be suitable. If it is stated, the CDO will advise the field offender manager of the sentencer's view on the purposes of sentencing (e.g. punishment or public protection) and will indicate the seriousness of the offence. In addition, the CDO may have to liaise with other professions, such as mental health specialists, solicitors and barristers, in progressing the case through court. If possible, the CDO will interview the offender after sentence to explain the sentence. The CDO liaises with colleagues in field teams, completes sentence notifications and, if a community sentence is passed, provides reporting instructions to the offender.

CDOs liaise direct with local prisons if there is any concern that an individual may be at risk of harming him or herself. This is to ensure that the individual is effectively monitored when received into custody. CDOs also have the role of notifying victim liaison officers (VLOs) – who are also employed by the National Probation Service – of any cases that fit the statutory requirements for the VLO to make contact with the victim. If a community sentence (such as a drug treatment and testing order or community order with a drug rehabilitation requirement) is passed, these generally involve regular progress reviews at court. CDOs may be required to present review reports to the court, to answer any questions that the court may have and to feed relevant information back to the field officer.

Amy Beck

Related entries

Courts; National Probation Service (NPS).

Key texts and sources

The *Probation Bench Handbook* is available online at http://www.probation.homeoffice.gov.uk/files/pdf/Probation%20Bench%20Handbook%202nd%20Edition%202007.pdf.

COURTS

The terms 'courts' refers to places where justice is administered in the form of a judicial tribunal constituted for the hearing and determination of legal cases.

Courts in the UK are divided into national systems, which cover England and Wales, Northern Ireland and Scotland. All courts in the UK are subject to European law and the jurisdiction of the European courts. The courts system is divided into criminal and civil courts. Military law in administered by a parallel system of courts martial structured along similar lines to criminal courts in England, Wales and Northern Ireland.

England, Wales and Northern Ireland

County courts

County courts deal with civil cases. They can deal with a wide range of cases, including landlord and tenant disputes, consumer disputes, personal injury claims, undefended divorce cases (in some county courts), some domestic violence cases (but these may also be heard in the magistrates' court), race and sex discrimination cases, debt problems and employment problems.

Magistrates' courts

Magistrates' courts deal with criminal and some civil cases, and cases are dealt with by lay magistrates or a district judge. Magistrates' courts deal with criminal offences where the defendant is not entitled to trial by jury, known as summary offences. Summary offences involve a maximum penalty of six months' imprisonment and/or a fine of up to £2,000. Magistrates also deal with offences where the defendant can choose trial by jury but decides to have his or her case heard in the magistrates' court. If the defendant chooses trial by jury, the case will be passed on to the Crown court.

Magistrates can deal with a limited number of civil cases, including some civil debts, licences for public houses and clubs, some matrimonial problems and the welfare of children (for example, local authority care or supervision orders, adoption proceedings and residence orders).

Youth courts

Youth courts deal with young people who have committed criminal offences and who are aged between 10 and 17. The youth court is part of the magistrates' court, and up to three specially trained magistrates hear the case. For young people charged with very serious offences (offences which, for an adult, are punishable with 14 years' imprisonment or more), the youth court can commit them for trial at the Crown court.

Crown court

The Crown court deals with the more serious criminal offences that will be tried by judge and jury, appeals from the magistrates' court that are dealt with by a judge and at least two magistrates, and convictions in the magistrates' court that are referred to the Crown court for sentencing. The Crown court has more severe powers to fine and imprison than in the magistrates' court.

High court

The high court deals with civil cases and hears appeals. It also has the power to review the actions of individuals or organizations to make sure they have acted legally and justly. The high court has three divisions: the Family Division, the Queen's Bench Division and the Chancery Division.

The Family Division deals with complex defended divorce cases, wardship, adoption, domestic violence and related family matters. It also deals with appeals from magistrates' and county courts in matrimonial cases and with the affairs of people who are mentally ill. It can also deal with simple probate matters. The Queen's Bench Division deals with large and/or complex claims for compensation. It also deals with a limited number of appeals from magistrates' courts or Crown courts, as well as reviewing the actions of organizations to see whether they have acted legally, and with libel and slander actions. The Chancery Division deals with a range of areas of financial and related law, including trusts, contested wills, bankruptcy, mortgages, charities and contested revenue (usually income tax) cases.

The high court can be used for a case if the value of the claim is over £15,000. In some circumstances, a case over £15,000 can be remitted to the county court and, similarly, a case under the value of £15,000 may be transferred to the high court from the county court.

Court of appeal

The court of appeal deals with civil and criminal appeals. Civil appeals from the high court and the county court are dealt with, as well as those from the Employment Appeal Tribunal and the Lands Tribunal. Criminal appeals include appeals against convictions in the Crown court and points of law referred by the Attorney General following acquittal in the Crown court or where the sentence imposed may have been unduly lenient.

House of Lords

The Lords deal mainly with appeals from the court of appeal, or direct from the high court, where the case involves a point of law or general public importance. Appeals are mostly about civil cases, although the Lords do deal with some criminal appeals.

Scotland

District courts

The district courts are managed individually by each local authority in Scotland. They are broadly analogous to magistrates' courts. The district court deals only with summary criminal matters. There are also certain offences (such as assaults resulting in a broken bone) that cannot be heard in the district court but must go to the sheriff court. In district courts a lay justice of the peace sits with a legally qualified clerk and, in some areas justices sit in threes. A legally qualified stipendiary magistrate may sit at the district courts in Glasgow and he or she enjoys greater powers.

Sheriff courts

The sheriff courts are managed by the Scottish Court Service. They are an intermediate level of court between district courts and the High Court of Justiciary. They have greater powers and deal with a wider range of work than district courts. They have both criminal and civil jurisdictions.

Court of Session

The Court of Session is Scotland's supreme civil court and sits in Parliament House in Edinburgh as a court of first instance and a court of appeal. An appeal lies to the House of Lords. The court is divided into the Outer House and the Inner House. The Outer House consists of 24 lords ordinary sitting alone or, in certain cases, with a civil jury. They hear cases at first instance on a wide range of civil matters, including cases based on delict (tort) and contract, commercial cases and judicial review. The judges generally cover a wide spectrum of work.

The Inner House is, in essence, the appeal court, though it accepts a small range of first-instance cases. It is divided into the First and the Second Divisions, of equal authority. Each division is made up of five judges, but the quorum is three. An Extra Division of three judges may sit to address additional work. The divisions hear cases on appeal from the Outer House, the sheriff court and certain tribunals and other bodies. On occasion, if a case is particularly important or difficult, or if it is necessary to overrule a previous binding authority, a larger court of five or more judges may be convened.

High Court of Justiciary

The High Court of Justiciary is Scotland's supreme criminal court. It has jurisdiction over the whole of Scotland and over all crimes, unless its jurisdiction is excluded by statute. When sitting as a trial court (i.e. as a court of 'first instance'), it sits in cities and larger towns throughout Scotland. Both Edinburgh and Glasgow have permanent high-court buildings. Throughout the rest of the country the high court sits in the local sheriff court building. When exercising its appellate jurisdiction it sits only in Edinburgh. The only further appeal possible is to the Privy Council of the House of Lords, as provided for by Schedule 6 of the Scotland Act 1998.

The high court is presided over by the Lord Justice General and the Lord Justice Clerk. They usually sit as chairpersons in the courts of criminal appeal. In practice the high court, when sitting as a court of first instance, deals with the most serious crimes, such as murder, rape, culpable homicide, armed robbery, drug trafficking and serious sexual offences, particularly those involving children. Cases are presided over by a single judge and are tried by a jury of 15 men and women.

When sitting as an appellate court, the court consists of at least three judges when hearing appeals against conviction and two when hearing sentence appeals, although more judges may sit when the court is dealing with exceptionally difficult cases or those where important matters of law may be considered.

Europe

Court of First Instance

The Court of First Instance is based in Luxembourg. A case can be taken to this court if European Community law has not been implemented properly by a national government, or if there is confusion over its interpretation or if it has been ignored. A case that is lost at the Court of First Instance may be able to be appealed at the European Court of Justice.

European Court of Justice

The European Court of Justice advises on the interpretation of European Community law and takes action against infringements. It examines the validity of acts of the European Community institutions and clarifies European Community law by making preliminary rulings. It also hears appeals against decisions made by the Court of First Instance.

European Court of Human Rights

The European Court of Human Rights deals with cases in which a person thinks his or her human rights have been contravened and for which there is no legal remedy in the national legal system.

David A. Crighton

Related entries

Adversarial system; Legal profession.

Key texts and sources

See the websites of Her Majesty's Court Service (**http://www.hmcourts-service.gov.uk/**), the Northern Ireland Courts Service (**http://www.courtsni.gov.uk/**) and the Scottish Courts Service (**http://www.scotcourts.gov.uk/**).

CRIMINAL CAREERS

A criminal career is basically a sequence of offences committed at different ages. It has a beginning (onset), an end (desistance) and a career length in between (duration). Only a certain proportion of each birth cohort (prevalence) commits offences and has a criminal career, and a small fraction of offenders (the chronics) commit a large fraction of all offences.

During their careers, offenders commit crimes at a certain rate (frequency) while they are at risk of offending in the community (e.g. not incarcerated, abroad or incapacitated by illness). For offenders who commit several offences, it is possible to investigate to what extent they specialize in certain types of crimes and to what extent the seriousness of their offending escalates over time.

Offending is typically measured using either official records or self-reports. Most is known about crimes committed by lower-class males living in urban areas. In order to study the development of offending and criminal careers, longitudinal (follow-up) research is needed in which persons are interviewed repeatedly from childhood to adulthood. For example, in the Cambridge Study in Delinquent Development (Farrington *et al.* 2006), about 400 south London males were followed up from the age of 8 to the age of 48. Most knowledge about criminal careers is based on arrests or convictions. This is because studies of the development of criminal careers require exact information about the timing of offences, which is available in official records but not usually in self-reports.

Prevalence

The cumulative prevalence of arrests and convictions of males is surprisingly high. In the Cambridge study, 40 per cent of London males were convicted for criminal offences up to the age of 40, when these were restricted to offences normally recorded in the Criminal Record Office. Similarly, a longitudinal follow-up of a 1953 English birth cohort in official records by the Home Office found that 33 per cent of males and 9 per cent of females were convicted of 'standard list' offences up to the age of 45.

Offending typically increases to a peak in the teenage years and then decreases. In the Cambridge study, the peak age for the prevalence of convictions was at 17. The median age of conviction for most types of offences (burglary, robbery, theft of and from vehicles, shoplifting) was 17, while it was 20 for violence and 21 for fraud. In national English data analysed by Roger Tarling, the peak age varied from 14 for shoplifting to 20 for fraud/forgery and drug offences.

Individual offending frequency

Much research has been concerned to estimate the individual offending frequency (the rate at which offenders commit offences) during criminal careers. In calculating the individual offending frequency and other criminal career features such as onset, duration and desistance, a major problem is to estimate when careers really begin and when they really end. Roger Tarling assumed that careers began at the age of criminal responsibility (10 in England and Wales) and ended on the date of the last conviction. On this assumption, male offenders in the 1953 birth cohort had a conviction rate of 0.5 per year (one every 2 years), while the corresponding figure for female offenders was 0.3 per year (one every 3.3 years). However, it is important to 'scale up' from convictions to the true number of offences committed. In the Cambridge study, convicted offenders self-reported 22 times as many offences as they had convictions.

If periods of acceleration or deceleration in the individual offending frequency could be identified, and if the predictors of acceleration or deceleration could be established, these could have important implications for theory and policy. There are many life events or conditions that might lead to an increase in individual offending frequency. For example, in the Cambridge study, London males committed offences at a higher rate during periods of unemployment than during periods of employment. This difference was restricted to offences involving material gain, suggesting that unemployment caused a lack of money, which in turn caused an increase in offending to obtain money.

Onset

Criminal career research on onset using official records generally shows a peak age of onset between 13 and 16. In the Cambridge study, the peak age of onset was at 14, and 5 per cent of the males were first convicted at that age. The best childhood predictors of an early versus a later onset of offending were rarely spending leisure time with the father, high troublesomeness, authoritarian parents and high psychomotor impulsivity.

The main childhood risk factors for the early onset of offending before the age of 20 are well known: individual factors (e.g. low intelligence, low school attainment, hyperactivity, impulsiveness, risk-taking, low empathy, anti-social and aggressive behaviour), family factors (e.g. poor parental supervision, harsh discipline, child physical abuse, inconsistent discipline, a cold parental attitude and child neglect, low involvement of parents with children, parental conflict, broken families, criminal parents, delinquent

siblings), socio-economic factors (e.g. low family income, large family size, poor housing), peer factors (e.g. delinquent peers, peer rejection, low popularity), school factors (e.g. attending a high delinquency-rate school) and neighbourhood factors (e.g. living in a deprived, high-crime neighbourhood) (see Juvenile deliquency).

In the Cambridge study, the average age of the first conviction was 19. The males first convicted at the earliest ages (10–13) tended to become the most persistent offenders, committing an average of nine offences leading to convictions in an average criminal career lasting 13 years up to the age of 50. While it is clear that an early age of onset foreshadows a long criminal career, aggregate results may hide different types of offenders. For example, Terrie Moffitt distinguished between 'life-course persistent' offenders, who had an early onset and a long criminal career, and 'adolescence limited' offenders, who started later and had a short criminal career.

Desistance

The true age of desistance from offending can only be determined with certainty after offenders die. In the Cambridge study up to the age of 50, the average age of the last conviction was 28. Since the average age of the first conviction was 19, the average length of the recorded criminal career was nine years, with an average of 4.5 convictions per offender during this time period.

In the Philadelphia cohort study, Marvin Wolfgang showed how the probability of reoffending (persistence as opposed to desistance) increased after each successive offence. This probability was .54 after the first offence, .65 after the second and .72 after the third, and it reached an asymptote of .80 after six or more arrests. Similarly, Home Office analyses of national English data for males born in 1953 showed that the probability of persistence increased from .45 after the first conviction to .83 after the seventh. The corresponding probabilities for females were from .22 to .78.

Several projects have explicitly investigated why offenders desist. For example, in the Cambridge study, getting married and moving out of London both fostered desistance. In their follow-up of 500 Boston delinquents, Robert Sampson and John Laub identified job stability and marital attachment in adulthood as crucial factors in desistance. Some policy implications of desistance research are that ex-offenders should be helped to settle down in stable marital relationships and in stable jobs, and helped to break away from their criminal associates.

Chronic offenders

In the Philadelphia cohort study, Marvin Wolfgang showed that 6 per cent of the males (18 per cent of the offenders) accounted for half (52 per cent) of all the juvenile arrests, and these 6 per cent were labelled the 'chronic offenders'. The chronics accounted for even higher percentages of serious offences: 69 per cent of all aggravated assaults, 71 per cent of homicides, 73 per cent of forcible rapes and 82 per cent of robberies. Other researchers have largely replicated these results. For example, in the Cambridge study, about 7 per cent of the males (and 17 per cent of the offenders) accounted for about half of all the convictions up to the age of 50. Home Office research suggests that about 100,000 'prolific' offenders in England and Wales commit about half of all offences each year.

The key question is to what extent the chronic offenders can be predicted in advance, and whether they differ prospectively from the non-chronic offenders in their individual offending frequency. This was investigated in the Cambridge study using a seven-point scale based on variables measured at the age of 8–10, reflecting child anti-social behaviour, family economic deprivation, convicted parents, low intelligence and poor parental child-rearing behaviour. Of 55 boys scoring 4 or more, 15 became chronic offenders up to the age of 25 (out of 23 chronics altogether), 22 others were convicted, and only 18 were not convicted. Hence, it was concluded that most of the chronics could have been predicted in advance on the basis of information available at the age of 10.

Duration

There has been less research on the duration of criminal careers. National figures for English males born in 1953 and followed up to the age of 39 showed that the average duration of criminal careers was 10 years (excluding one-time offenders, who had zero duration). The corresponding average duration for females was 6 years.

Another important concept is the residual length of a criminal career at any given point in time. Blumstein *et al.* (1988) estimated this in the USA and found that it increased to a peak between the ages of 30 and 40. One area where knowledge about residual career length is important is in estimating the incapacitative effects of imprisonment. If the average time served exceeds the residual career length, people would be imprisoned beyond the point at which they would have stopped offending anyway. Hence, valuable prison space would be wasted by incarcerating those who would in any case have desisted from offending.

Continuity

Generally, there is significant continuity between offending in one age range and offending in another. In the Cambridge study, nearly three quarters (73 per cent) of those convicted as juveniles at the age of 10–16 were reconvicted at the age of 17–24, in comparison with only 16 per cent of those not convicted as juveniles. Nearly half (45 per cent) of those convicted as juveniles were reconvicted at the age of 25–32, in comparison with only 8 per cent of those not convicted as juveniles. Furthermore, this continuity over time did not merely reflect continuity in police reaction to crime. For 10 specified offences, the significant continuity between offending in one age range and offending in a later age range held for self-reports as well as for official convictions.

Specialization

In the Cambridge study, offenders were predominantly versatile rather than specialized.

About one third of the convicted males up to the age of 32 ($n = 50$) were convicted of violence (assault, robbery or threatening behaviour). They committed a total of 85 violent offences (an average of 1.7 each), but they also committed 263 non-violent offences (an average of 5.3 each). Only 7 of the 50 violent offenders had no convictions for non-violent offences. A model was tested that assumed that violent offences occurred at random in criminal careers. Since the data fitted this model, it was concluded that there was little indication that offenders specialized in violence. Furthermore, violent offenders and non-violent but persistent offenders were similar in childhood, adolescent and adult features. Hence, violent offenders are difficult to distinguish from frequent offenders.

Implications for practice

Criminal career research has many policy implications (Piquero *et al.* 2007). First, offending can be prevented by targeting key risk factors. Parent training and general parent education can improve parenting skills, cognitive-behavioural skills training can reduce impulsiveness and can increase empathy, and preschool intellectual enrichment programmes can improve school success. Secondly, it is important to identify chronic offenders at an early stage and to devise special programmes for them. Thirdly, it is important to take account of residual career length in setting the length of prison sentences, because it is futile to incarcerate people after they would have stopped offending anyway. Fourthly, the versatility of offenders means that it does not make much sense to have specific programmes for violent offenders. Since criminal career research shows that violent offenders are essentially frequent offenders, programmes to prevent violent offending should target frequent or chronic offenders. Fifthly, desistance can be fostered by programmes that help offenders to settle down with a steady job and a steady partner.

David P. Farrington

Related entries

Juvenile delinquency; Recidivism prediction; Reconviction studies.

Key texts and sources

Blumstein, A., Cohen, J., Roth, J.A. and Visher, C.A. (1988) *Criminal Careers and 'Career Criminals'* (2 vols). Washington, DC: National Academy Press.

Farrington, D.P. (1997) 'Human development and criminal careers', in M. Maguire *et al.* (eds) *The Oxford Handbook of Criminology* (2nd edn). Oxford: Oxford University Press.

Farrington, D.P. et al. (2006) *Criminal Careers up to Age 50 and Life Success up to Age 48: New Findings from the Cambridge Study in Delinquent Development. Home Office Research Study* 299. London: Home Office (available online at **www.homeoffice.gov.uk/rds**).

Piquero, A.R., Farrington, D.P. and Blumstein, A. (2007) *Key Issues in Criminal Career Research: New Analyses of the Cambridge Study in Delinquent Development.* Cambridge: Cambridge University Press.

CRIMINAL JUSTICE SYSTEM

The criminal justice system of England and Wales is one of the major public services. It is used for the purpose of social control, the prevention of crime, the enforcement of laws and the adminsitration of justice. The criminal justice system includes such agencies as the police, the courts, the Prison Service, the Crown Prosecution Service and the National Probation Service. These agencies work together to deliver the criminal justice process.

The stated aim of the government of England and Wales is to deliver justice for all, by convicting and punishing those guilty of crimes and by trying to prevent them from reoffending while protecting the law-abiding public. The government is responsible for detecting crime and for bringing offenders to justice, and for carrying out the orders of the courts (such as collecting fines and supervising community and custodial punishment). The work of the agencies involved in the criminal justice system is overseen by three government departments: the Home Office, the Attorney General's Office and the Ministry of Justice.

The Home Office is principally concerned with the protection of the public. This involves the detection and prevention of crime through its oversight of the Police Service, which monitors and detains suspects. The Ministry of Justice is the department that controls the legislative agenda for crime control by proposing what should constitute criminal behaviour and through its sentencing proposals for particular offences. The Ministry of Justice also oversees the National Offender Management Service (NOMS) for the punishment and rehabilitation of offenders.

The Attorney General, assisted by the Solicitor General, is the chief legal adviser to the government. They are responsible for ensuring the rule of law is upheld. The Attorney General is responsible to Parliament for the Crown Prosecution Service, the Serious Fraud Office, the Revenue and Customs Prosecutions Office, the Treasury Solicitor's Department and the Director of Public Prosecutions in Northern Ireland. The Attorney General has an overarching responsibility for the management of criminal cases.

The Ministry of Justice is responsible for operating the court system and for improving the justice sytem. Its responsibilities extend to ensuring that fundamental constitutional rights are preserved for those interacting with the criminal justice system. This includes catering for the needs of victims, witnesses and the accused.

Forensic psychologists play a key role in the profiling of offenders on behalf of crime-investigating authorities. They are particularly involved in assessing the risk of reoffending and in working to manage or reduce the risk to the public via NOMS. They may also be called upon to act as expert witnesses in court.

S. George Blom-Cooper

Related entries

Adversarial system; Courts; Victim Support.

Key texts and sources

Davies, M., Croall, H. and Tyrer, J. (2005) *Criminal Justice: An Introduction to the Criminal Justice System of England and Wales* (3rd edn). Harlow: Longman.

See also the following websites: www.cjsonline.gov.uk; http://www.cjsonline.gov.uk/the_cjs/departments_of_the_cjs/office_of_the_attorney_general/index.html; http://www.homeoffice.gov.uk/; and http://www.justice.gov.uk/.

CRIMINAL RESPONSIBILITY

> Criminal responsibility encompasses the circumstances, events or situations as a result of which someone can be called to account under the criminal law. These circumstances, events or situations automatically connote either penal sanctions (punishment) or alternatives to these sanctions (such as a police caution or diversion from prosecution).

Criminal responsibility applies only where a crime is committed (or in some instances planned or in preparation) so that it is essential, first, to understand the nature of crime itself and the legal, philosophical and conceptual issues surrounding crime. Such responsibility applies in the absence of any special or general defences, subject to an offence being established by law in a criminal court having regard to the presumption of innocence and the burden of proof (or, in the case of a caution, an admission of responsibility to the police).

Criminal responsibility has various dimensions. It may connote, or be interlinked with the following:

- 'Criminal capacity' – the idea that only people above the 'age of criminal responsibility' can be guilty of a crime, currently in England and Wales 10 years of age.
- Issues of mental capacity in that an accused person must not have been 1) insane or otherwise mentally incapable of crime; or 2) of such a state of mind at the time of a given offence that any essential *mens rea* (criminal intent) in the definition of that offence was not present.
- Issues of physical capacity that may negate the particular criminal act. Although rare in practice, in one notorious miscarriage of justice case it was established that the 'offender' was sexually incapable. Similarly there was once a statutory rule that boys under 14 years of age were incapable of rape.

In other senses, 'criminal responsibility' leads to considerations of the following:

- Pure law in relation to given crimes, such as burglary, theft, criminal damage and murder in terms of their individual definitions and ingredients.
- On whom and when responsibility may be cast in a given context, as where there is: 1) a conspiracy, incitement or an attempt to commit an offence (known as inchoate offences); 2) mass disorder/mass disobedience of the criminal law; 3) organized crime; 4) forms of secondary responsibility, such as vicarious, parental or corporate responsibility; or 5) someone employing an innocent agent as a conduit for his or her own actions.
- Accountability, in terms of bringing an offender to justice and/or his or her facing up to what has occurred (taking responsibility).
- The extent to which moral, ethical, religious or similar considerations coincide with, or diverge from, those concerning criminal responsibility.
- Issues of a wider, socio-political nature (the need for the community, offender, victims, citizens and/or criminal justice practitioners to accept responsibility for resolving the harm done by a breach of the criminal law and the idea of the offender 'paying back' for an offence that he or she has committed).

There is a fundamental divide between criminal and civil responsibility, despite the fact that many crimes are also torts (civil wrongs for which purely private remedies can be sought in the civil courts). This affects, for example, rights, procedures, rules, evidence, powers and the way in which citizens are or may be treated by the authorities. The protection afforded by human rights is greater when considering criminal responsibility, and codes, standards and procedures operate at a higher level all round (hence, for example, the requirement in a criminal case for proof beyond reasonable doubt). This schism is well illustrated by the anti-social behaviour order (ASBO) which, despite outward appearances, is civil not criminal in nature (and thus only attracts 'civil responsibility'). The criminal anti-social behaviour order (CRASBO), on the other hand, is defined differently in that a court may *attach* a CRASBO to a

sentence that is criminal in nature. Civil matters do not attract penal sanctions as such – not in the sense of punishment proper (or its criminally based alternatives).

Criticisms have arisen that, because the ASBO may result in criminal proceedings on breach, there has been a short circuiting of the criminal process – the creation of 'potential future criminal responsibility'. Other modern-day instances of 'confusion' over criminal responsibility include the following:

- The growth of non-criminal mechanisms (such as the police caution in place of prosecution but that, none the less, will appear on the 'offender's' criminal record).
- Other forms of diversion from prosecution (such as some drug-referral schemes) and administrative fines (such as those levied by HM Revenue and Customs and a host of other public and regulatory authorities).
- Enhanced police powers to require people to act in a given way or face arrest (and other forms of restriction in the interests of law and order in which the parameters of criminal responsibility have become blurred).
- The rise in fixed penalties and automatic penalties (e.g. for not renewing a vehicle excise licence on time) instead of prosecution.
- Proprietary fines (that are based on a contractual relationship and that are purely civil in nature but are often styled 'penalties' or 'fines').

Historically, the notion of criminal responsibility and of bringing offenders to justice lies at the heart of all discourses on criminal policy, law and order and 'keeping the (Queen's) peace'; at the heart of the creation of punishments (or, in more liberal times, alternative approaches); and of the development of courts, police forces, a criminal justice system and 'corrections' mechanisms to ensure compliance. Since early times the fundamental ideas that have shaped criminal responsibility have often centred on conflicting notions of blame, retribution, reparation, condemnation, deterrence and shame. Some modern developments show a deeper understanding that not all responsibility should fall on the offender, but the prison and its escalating use in England and Wales demonstrate how deep-rooted negative, punitive and blame-oriented views of criminal responsibility still remain in contemporary society.

There is nothing intrinsic or absolute about the nature of criminal responsibility: it arises only in an artificial and technical way when the law declares something to be a criminal offence at any given moment in time, even though many serious offences (such as murder, rape and other forms of violence) would seem to speak for themselves as candidates. Since 1997, the Labour government has created some 3,000 new offences (the precise number of these is impossible to discern) accompanied by novel, wide-ranging, criminal law-making powers on the part of the executive. The rule that everyone is presumed to know the law has become increasingly vacuous, which has caused a dilution in condemnatory attitudes towards some kinds of criminal responsibility – and hence in confidence in criminal processes – because of their hidden quality and because of the fact that criminal responsibility has become an all-pervading or potential hazard for even the most cautious of people. It has been argued that many lesser offences should be recategorized as 'contraventions' which would involve penal sanctions but not criminal responsibility. The trend, however, seems to be in the opposite direction.

Bryan Gibson

Related entries

Criminal careers; Criminal justice system.

Key texts and sources

Devlin, P. (1959) *The Enforcement of Morals* (reprinted as *Morals and the Criminal Law*, ed. R.M. Baird and S.E. Rosenbaum 1988). Loughton: Prometheus Books.

Gibson, B. and Cavadino, P. (2008) *The Criminal Justice System: An Introduction.* Hook: Waterside Press.

Hart, H.L.A. (1963) *Law, Liberty and Morality* (reprinted 1968). Oxford: Oxford University Press.

Ormerod, D. (ed.) (2005) *Smith and Hogan's Criminal Law* (11th edn). London: LexisNexis.

CRIMINOLOGY

> Criminology is the study of crime and criminals.

In its broadest sense, criminology is the study of crime and the criminal (Coleman and Norris 2000). However, there is much debate in the field of criminology regarding the precise nature of the definition. This is in part due to the potentially different interpretations that can be inferred from the terms 'crime' and 'criminal' and a recognition of the altering societal influences on the definition of the terms (Coleman and Norris 2000). For example, what is defined as a crime in one decade may not be in another – the decriminalizing of homosexuality being but one example. In the light of these debates, other potential definitions of criminology could include the following:

- The attempt to describe and analyse the extent, nature and distribution of the various forms of 'crime' and 'offenders'.
- The analysis of the 'causes' of crime, including the development of explanatory and causative theories of crime.
- The study of the development of criminal laws and the various processes of law enforcement and criminal justice.
- The analysis of various forms of policy and practice in punishment, such as analysing the effectiveness of court disposals.
- The investigation of the victims of crime, including the extent, nature and distribution of victimization (adapted from Coleman and Norris 2000: 14).

Garland (1994: 17) defines criminology as 'a specific genre of discourse and inquiry about crime – a genre which has developed in the modern period and which can be distinguished from other ways of talking and thinking about criminal conduct'.

There are other areas that could also be included as being relevant to the study of criminology, and some will have obvious overlaps with other disciplines, such as psychology, victimology and penology. This is perhaps why, traditionally, there has been a trend to describe criminology as a fusion of other disciplines.

Development of criminology

Garland (1994: 18) proposes that modern criminology evolved out of two separate entities – namely, 'the governmental project' and 'the Lombrosian project'. By the government project he is referring to a long series of inquiries focusing on improving the effectiveness and administration of justice. This includes monitoring the patterns of crime and exploring the practices in prisons. The Lombrosian project (see below) is a reflection of the development of an aetiological approach to crime and is premised on a theory that offenders can be empirically differentiated from non-offenders (Garland 1994).

The classical school

The classical school, as it has come to be known, developed from the work of a group of 'Enlightenment' philosophers active in the eighteenth century who argued that 'human problems should be tackled by the application of reason, rather then tradition, religion or superstition' (Coleman and Norris 2000: 17). This took place within a wider social revolution and revolt against regimes. In a criminal justice context the focus was primarily on creating a system in which both the legal system and punishments for crime were more predictable and non-discriminatory (Coleman and Norris 2000).

The classical school of thought regarded humans as rational and self-directed and as having free will. In addition it saw humans as somewhat hedonistic and, as such, an ordered and peaceful state would need well constructed laws and punishments to deter certain behaviour and to encourage peaceful law-abiding living. In addition, it proposed that punishments should be commensurate to the offence in that they should be 'known, fixed and just severe enough to deter' (Coleman and Norris 2000: 19).

The classical school was very influential in the development of the legal and criminal justice systems as we recognize them today. However, this approach has been criticized for being overly simplistic and for being insensitive to the nuances of individuality or individual circumstances and influences (Coleman and Norris 2000).

The moral statisticians

A group of scholars who were to become known as the 'moral statisticians' emerged in the early nineteenth century. Their approach was essentially to adopt a more scientific approach to social phenomena. This move towards the scientific was aided by the publication of national crime statistics in France in 1827 (Coleman and Norris 2000). This publication presented the opportunity to analyse the statistics of crime and, therefore, to comment on the extent and nature of crime and the impact of interventions/punishments.

Adolphe Quetelet, one of the most well-known moral statisticians, conducted in-depth analyses on the statistics and proposed a series of patterns and, as such risk factors for the committal of criminal acts. Quetelet came to the conclusion that the causes of crime were routed in aspects of social organization and that, in order to reduce the likelihood of crime, the government needed to provide legislation to identify and remove these causes as necessary (Coleman and Norris 2000).

The positivist school

In contrast to the classical school and the moral statisticians, the positivist school presupposes that criminal behaviour is caused by internal and external factors beyond the control of the individual. It also adopts a scientific approach to the study of human behaviour and can be divided into three strands; biological, psychological and social positivism.

Cesare Lombroso, an Italian prison doctor in the late nineteenth century, was the most significant contributor to biological positivism and is often regarded as the 'father' of criminology. His work was influenced by earlier theories of phrenology and by Charles Darwin's theory of evolution. Lombroso conducted extensive physiological research with convicted criminals, exploring a number of wide-ranging physiological differences, such as hairline, cheek bones, etc. He concluded that criminals were 'throwbacks' to an earlier stage of human evolution and were indicative of 'atavistic' criminal tendencies. Lombroso's work was heavily criticized in his lifetime and has been largely discredited by professionals. However, the positivist school of thought should be seen in a broader context: Lombroso's legacy was to instigate a strong focus on the 'scientific' and he criticized heavily the earlier classical approach.

An example of psychological positivism is the work of Hans Eysenck, who proposed that psychological or personality factors (such as extraversion and neuroticism) could increase an individual's propensity to commit crime. The work of Emile Durkheim represents a more sociological positivist approach, viewing crime as a societal issue born out of social inequalities (such as the uneven distribution of wealth). What has become known as 'criminology' grew vastly in the wake of the work of Lombroso and his followers. Garland (1985, 1997) suggests that some of the reasons for this growth included the following:

1 The development of various forms of statistical data, such as the kind that had already been exploited by the moral statisticians;

2 The advances in, and increasing prestige, of the discipline of psychiatry;

3 It connected with, and gave scientific respectability to, prejudices and fears about the 'dangerous classes' in the expanding cities;

4 It offered new possibilities for the scientific, expert and seemingly humane regulation of the population for governments and administrators, when existing strategies were seen as failing;

5 The development of the prison in the nineteenth century provided a context within which it could develop as a practical form of knowledge with the individual criminal readily available and 'obvious' object of study (Coleman and Norris 2000: 22).

The British context

Britain had remained notably distant from the early development of the criminological movement, with a large part of the relevant research and theorizing taking part in other parts of Europe, such as France and Italy (Garland 1994). This was due in large part to the British context being more medically orientated. The focus on offenders had been significantly driven by the developing discipline of psychiatry and by specific prison doctors (Coleman and Norris 2000). In addition, in the British context the approach was more focused on mental health issues and the practicalities of prison administration. Thus it was not the prevailing view that those who offended were somehow a distinctive category of individuals, as proposed by Lombroso and others in the emerging field of criminology (Garland 1994). One exception to this predominant tradition in Britain was Goring's *The English Convict*, published in 1913. Goring had conducted a large-scale study using advanced statistical techniques and he concluded that there was a specific 'type' of person who offended – namely, a 'person of poor physique and mental capacity' (Coleman and Norris 2000: 23).

British researchers and practitioners were to become more involved in the period leading up to the First World War when the field of criminology was taking a broader approach and the early proposals of Lombroso had been revised (Coleman and Norris 2000). The research that ensued over the following decades was heavily focused on the nature versus nurture debate, and attempts to measure the extent of criminal behaviour (Coleman and Norris 2000). Researchers continued to seek the causes of crime while maintaining a scientific approach.

Derval Ambrose

Related entries

Criminal justice system.

Key texts and sources

Coleman, C. and Norris, C. (2000) *Introducing Criminology*. Cullompton: Willan Publishing.
Garland, D. (1994) 'Of crimes and criminals: the development of criminology in Britain', in M. Maguire *et al.* (eds) *The Oxford Handbook of Criminology*. Oxford: Oxford University Press.
Goring, C. (1913) *The English Convict*. London: HMSO.

CROWN PROSECUTION SERVICE (CPS)

The Crown Prosecution Service (CPS) was formed in 1985 under the Prosecution of Offences Act of that year as an independent, nationwide service operating through regions or areas and responsible for the prosecution of offences in England and Wales.

Before the formation of the Crown Prosecution Service (CPS) in 1985, prosecutions in magistrates' courts were carried out by solicitors employed locally by individual police forces (either from the private sector or from the police's own prosecuting departments) or, in some instances, prosecutions were conducted by police officers themselves, which had been the regular method from the time of the Bow Street runners. The CPS is now responsible for prosecuting criminal cases investigated by the police in England and Wales.

The early days of the CPS were typified by organizational and management disarray as the fledgling service sought to establish itself alongside the remaining, mostly long-standing, criminal justice agencies and in the face of resource issues. In the 1990s, however, it quickly matured into a viable mechanism, particularly under its then head, Dame Barbara Mills QC, Director of Public Prosecutions (the first woman to take charge of a major criminal justice agency). The Director of Public Prosecutions reports to the Attorney General who, in turn, reports to Parliament. Within the CPS, Crown prosecutors are styled 'chief Crown prosecutor', 'principal Crown prosecutor', 'senior Crown prosecutor' and so on, according to rank. There are also specialisms in the service, such as rape, domestic violence, drugs, fraud (work also undertaken by the Serious Fraud Office, which is a separate agency), organized crime and terrorism. Similarly, there are a number of senior directors (e.g. of policy, of casework).

Crown prosecutors operate under a *Code for Crown Prosecutors* that lays down guidelines, procedures and standards to be applied in individual cases according to their facts and merits

under a continuing process known as 'review' and that contains both general advice and advice relating to particular types of offence. Before a prosecution can take place, the case must 'pass' two tests: the evidential test and the public interest test. The evidential test asks the question: 'Is there evidence sufficient to go before magistrates and/or a jury so that there is a realistic prospect of conviction?'. The public interest test asks: 'Does this particular case merit prosecution?' (i.e. is it in the public's interest to prosecute?). Both tests require an exercise in discretion and are quasi-judicial in nature. They must be applied fairly and consistently.

Special considerations apply to juveniles, and the CPS is particularly concerned with the rights and treatment of victims of crime, now enshrined in a Prosecutor's Pledge (see **www.cps.gov.uk**).

Since the Criminal Justice Act 2003, the decision as to whether to launch a prosecution and to charge a suspect and the nature of that charge is taken by a Crown prosecutor rather than the police in all but the most straightforward or minor cases, or in an emergency. Once begun, each case is reviewed at intervals to ensure that the twin tests mentioned above are still satisfied.

The CPS can take over a private prosecution in order either to prosecute or to discontinue it. On some occasions a private prosecutor has insisted on continuing against the advice or even the wishes of the CPS and, in rare cases, prosecutions have been successful in these circumstances (including one conviction for manslaughter). The process of discontinuance is a regular feature of day-to-day events in the criminal courts, following a review where it has become clear that the tests are no longer satisfied. The decision to discontinue is for the CPS alone – neither the police nor a court can insist on a case proceeding.

The costs of the CPS are borne out of public funds, and there have been suggestions that decisions whether or not to prosecute or to discontinue have, on occasion, been driven by monetary constraints rather than the interests of justice. There have also been criticisms that the CPS can be secretive or lack openness (some 'sensitive' criteria for prosecution decision-making are not published in the ordinary CPS code), and there have also been allegations of government pressure to pursue particular types of offence or not to prosecute. Indicative of the sensitive nature of the prosecution function is the experience of the Serious Fraud Office (again accountable via the Attorney General) concerning a decision not to prosecute BAE Systems following allegations of corruption in relation to defence contracts with Saudi Arabia 'in the national interest', said by the High Court to undermine the Rule of Law.

Crown prosecutors must be solicitors or barristers capable of working on their own in the courtroom. They must therefore be expert in criminal law, evidence and criminal procedure, though not in sentencing, which, in England and Wales, remains the exclusive province of the courts (even if there have been proposals to place an element of responsibility on prosecutors to inform courts of any relevant sentencing law and guidance and to explain why certain cases have been brought). In some instances unduly lenient sentences can be referred by the Director of Public Prosecutions to the Attorney General, and the latter may refer these to the Court of Appeal (known as an Attorney General's reference). Certain lesser matters can be conducted in the magistrates' court by a CPS-designated case worker.

The CPS headquarters are in London and York, and the service operates within a structure that reflects police force areas as part of a co-ordinated criminal justice system 'whereby national policy is delivered locally'.

Bryan Gibson

Related entries

Courts; Criminal justice system; Legal profession.

Key texts and sources

Gibson, B. and Cavadino, P. (2008) *The Criminal Justice System: An Introduction*. Hook: Waterside Press.

Spencer, R.J. (ed.) (1989) *Jackson's Machinery of Justice in England*. Cambridge: Cambridge University Press.

See also the CPS's website (**www.cps.gov.uk**).

D

DETECTING DECEPTION

> Deception is the deliberate act of trying to mislead another.

Deception is a very common event. The general consensus is that people lie, on average, a couple of times a day. Most of these lies are trivial and are designed to oil social situations. They typically go undetected because there is no real need to detect them. Sometimes, even when the deception is not trivial, an observer may not be motivated to discover it, if the truth is likely to be more painful than the not knowing – for example, a parent suspects that his or her child might be committing crimes but would rather avoid facing up to those suspicions than discover if this is really the case and face the decision of having to report his or her child to authorities. However, situations arise where it is definitely in the observer's interest to know if he or she is being lied to by a communicator. The need for lie detectors to identify correctly more serious lies told in forensic situations by suspects, prisoners, and, sometimes, witnesses makes clear the need for effective deception-detection techniques. Such liars are often highly motivated to succeed in their deceit, with much at stake.

Research in detecting deception has consistently revealed that people are not good at detecting lies. Most studies reveal accuracy in the range of 45–60 per cent, with an average of about 57 per cent where 50 per cent accuracy could be expected by flipping a coin. Furthermore, in studies where the lie detection ability of professional lie detectors (e.g. police and customs officers) was tested, little difference has been found between them and laypersons.

In addition to situations such as those mentioned above where people may not be motivated to detect deceit (the ostrich effect), there are other reasons that contribute to this low accuracy.

There is no Pinocchio's nose cue that necessarily betrays a liar. The act of lying in itself is unlikely to result in any particular behaviour but the processes that accompany deceit may do. These include anxiety about getting caught, an urge to control one's behaviour, and an increase in cognitive load from having to invent a plausible lie, deliver it convincingly and monitor the lie receiver to see if it appears to be being believed. Liars do not behave as people expect. Laypersons and professional lie detectors alike expect nervous behaviour in a liar, marked by an inability to maintain eye contact and anxious fidgeting. While a liar may well be nervous, most tend to exhibit behaviour that is more in alignment with an increase in cognitive load than with being nervous, perhaps because this mechanism is overriding in terms of behaviour. Cognitive load results in a reduction in such movements as fidgeting and blinking and increases the number of speech pauses, yet most liars are perfectly able to maintain eye contact. Most lie-detection studies reveal a truth bias – that is, observers are more likely to consider that communicators are telling the truth than lying. One reason for this is probably because people expect a liar to be unable to maintain eye contact and, as long as eye contact is maintained, then the observer assumes the communicator is truthful. Most people are completely unaware of how much body language they typically exhibit and, whereas lots of hand movements, for example, are actually more likely to be associated with truthfulness, observers assume the opposite.

Studies have demonstrated that watching a communicator's non-verbal behaviour, particularly the face, can be so misleading that observers can achieve as high an accuracy (or higher) by listening to the communicator without seeing him or her at all. There is a considerable body of research into the verbal behaviour of liars (e.g. statement validity analysis) that suggests there are consistent differences between deceptive and truthful speech content. For example, liars are more likely to recount a story in chronological order, to include fewer details and so on. Furthermore, by concentrating on the face – a channel we are all practised in using to express what we want to express to others – observers are more likely to miss any potential contradictions or anomalies the liar might let slip.

As mentioned above, people lie regularly, and most of these lies go undetected. Because people therefore tend to assume that most of the deceptive behaviour they encounter is actually truthful, this lack of accurate feedback reinforces their inaccurate veracity judgements. Similarly, professional lie detectors, who often erroneously rate themselves as more competent lie detectors than laypersons, also often do not receive adequate feedback. For example, a customs officer may be aware of each time he correctly identifies a smuggler when he stops and searches such people, but really he has no idea of how many of the people who pass him without their being stopped are also smugglers.

The majority of research into deceptive behaviour is laboratory based. Typically participants, often students, are asked to lie or tell the truth about various issues while being videotaped. Their behaviour is then analysed, and it is these video clips that are shown to observers in deception detection studies. Although researchers endeavour to make their studies reflect real life as much as possible, such experiments lack ecological validity on several counts: the stakes are necessarily low (it is patently unethical to punish participants for an unconvincing performance, though the negative consequences of getting caught in a lie in real life could potentially be very high); the participant need feel no guilt about lying as it has been effectively condoned by the experimenter; in real life, people normally spontaneously choose whether or not to lie, but in such experiments the participant is not lying of his or her own volition (though some experimenters try to overcome this by giving participants the choice of lying or truth telling, but the result is still somewhat contrived); and the participant knows that his or her behaviour will be analysed, which may result in unnatural behaviour in itself. Therefore the task for lie detectors in these studies is rather artificial, which may contribute to the low accuracy often found. To support this assertion, in a series of studies where police officers were asked to make veracity judgements after watching video clips of real-life suspects in their police interviews, accuracy ranged from 60 per cent to 73 per cent. These higher than typically found accuracy rates would suggest that, in a contextually relevant situation, deception detection ability may be higher than laboratory studies would suggest. Unfortunately it has not been possible to compare these accuracy rates with laypersons' due to the sensitive nature of the material (i.e. suspect interviews).

Several mechanical lie-detection devices exist nowadays, though mostly these measure arousal rather than deception because, although deception may result in certain emotions, and hence behaviours, it is not a behaviour in itself. People are commonly confused about this point. Many devices, such as the polygraph, voice stress analyser, thermal activity camera, etc., work on the premise that a liar is nervous. Indeed, a liar may well be nervous, but so may be many truth tellers when there is the possibility that they will not be believed or if accused of doing something they did not do. This is something that such devices do not sufficiently take into account, and the result is often a high incidence of truth tellers judged as lying. The use of fMRI (functional magnetic resonance imaging) is a new development in lie detection and differs from arousal-based techniques in that it reveals that areas of the brain that control withholding information are activated during deception. However, while it is an interesting addition to knowledge of deceptive processes, its use is extremely restrictive, with participants barely able to speak or move while in the machine.

Significant implications for practice

Many professional lie detectors receive no training in deception detection or, if they do, it may hinder rather than help their ability. Many popular police manuals, for example, encourage officers to believe the notion that liars behave nervously. Dispelling such myths can only improve accuracy among professional lie detectors. Furthermore, looking for signs of increased cognitive load in communicators rather than looking for signs of mendacity has improved accuracy in experiments where police officers participated as observers. Increasing the cognitive load in interviewees (truth tellers and liars alike) by asking them to recount a story backwards, increased lie detection ability in police officers from 42 to 60 per cent (Mann *et al.* 2004). Although 60 per cent is not a very high accuracy level, it does represent a significant improvement. Because in most lying situations liars often have to think harder than truth tellers, introducing more mentally taxing interventions during the interview will allow lie detectors to exploit this extra load. This should result in more pronounced differences between liars and truth tellers in terms of displaying signs of cognitive load. Furthermore, focusing on what the communicator says rather than watching him or her while saying it should improve accuracy.

Samantha Mann

Related entries

Cognitive interviews; Polygraphy.

Key texts and sources

Bond, C.F. and DePaulo, B.M. (2006) 'Accuracy of deception judgements', *Personality and Social Psychology Review*, 10: 214–34.

DePaulo, B.M., Kashy, D.A., Kirkendol, S.E., Wyer, M.M. and Epstein, J.A. (1996) 'Lying in everyday life', *Journal of Personality and Social Psychology*, 70: 979–95.

Mann, S., Vrij, A. and Bull, R. (2002) 'Suspects, lies and videotape: an analysis of authentic high-stakes liars', *Law and Human Behavior*, 26: 365–76.

Mann, S., Vrij, A. and Bull, R. (2004) 'Detecting true lies: police officers' ability to detect suspects' lies', *Journal of Applied Psychology*, 89: 137–49.

Vrij, A. (2008) *Detecting Lies and Deceit: Pitfalls and Opportunities.* Chichester: Wiley.

DEVELOPMENTAL DISABILITIES IN ADULTS

The term 'developmental disability' (DD) refers to the definition given in the US Developmental Disabilities Assistance and Bill of Rights Act 2000 and is a broad concept covering the equivalent terms of learning disability, mental retardation and intellectual disability commonly used in the UK, North America and Australia, respectively.

In general terms, 'developmental disability' (DD) means a severe, chronic disability of an individual that: 1) is attributable to a mental or physical impairment or combination of both; 2) is manifested before 22 years of age; 3) is likely to continue indefinitely; and 4) results in substantial functional limitations in three or more areas of major life activity. In addition to intellectual disability, the concept includes other conditions that do not necessarily involve significant sub-average intellectual functioning, such as autism and epilepsy. The definition of DD also focuses on a person's lifelong need for individually planned support and assistance. For these reasons, it is an appropriate term to describe the population served by specialist disability forensic services in the UK and other parts of the world.

Historically, DD has been viewed as a key determinant of offending behaviour. Commentators from the nineteenth century onwards have suggested a causal association between low intelligence and criminality. There is robust evidence supporting a relationship between intellectual functioning (IQ) and offending, with those with lower IQs showing greater rates of offending than those in higher functioning groups. This relationship appears to hold even when socio-economic status is controlled for. However, most of the research in this area has involved participants with IQ scores ranging from low average to high average (80–120 IQ points). Studies that have included participants with significantly low IQs (fewer than 80 IQ points) have found that offending rates for this group are lower than those in the low average group (81–90 IQ points). Thus, it would appear that, when studies are extended to include participants with IQs below 80, the relationship between intellectual functioning and offending is not simple and linear.

Studies in the UK on the prevalence of offending by people with DD yield different rates, depending on the location of the study sample: community DD services, 2–5 per cent; police stations, 0.5–8.6 per cent; prisons (remand), 0–5 per cent; and prisons (convicted), 0.4–0.8 per cent. In addition to study location resulting in sampling bias and filtering effects, other sources of variation of prevalence of offending reported across studies include the inclusion criteria used (particularly if people with borderline intellectual functioning are included or not) and the method used to detect DD (e.g. IQ test vs. clinical interview). The countries in which prevalence studies are conducted can affect reported rates considerably, probably due in large part to the different social and criminal justice policies that are applied. For example, studies of the prevalence of convicted prisoners with DD in prisons in England have reported rates of up to 5 per cent, compared with just under 10 per cent in the USA, and over 28 per cent in Eire. Therefore, despite the long association between intellectual functioning and criminality, and in the absence of well designed studies comparing the prevalence of offending in populations of people with DD with those for non-DD populations, it is not clear that people with DD commit more crime than those without DD. Similarly, there is no good evidence to show that the frequency and nature of offending by people with DD differ from offenders in the general population.

Follow-up studies of offenders with DD have reported recidivism rates of up to 72 per cent. However, as for prevalence studies of offending by people with DD, reported recidivism rates vary a great deal for many of the same reasons, including study methods and procedures, research settings and the definition of recidivism used. Recent research in the USA on 252 offenders with DD subject to a case management community programme found that 25 per cent of programme completers were rearrested

within six months of finishing the programme, compared with 43 per cent of those who dropped out of the programme. There is a dearth of controlled studies comparing recidivism rates for offenders with DD and non-DD offenders but, in another US study, 43 per cent of 79,000 general offenders on probation were rearrested. Based on the limited data available to date it is not clear that recidivism rates for offenders with DD and those for general offenders are very different.

The evidence for the effectiveness of interventions for offending by people with DD is quite limited but has been building steadily over recent years. The treatment of anger and aggression for offenders with DD using cognitive-behavioural therapy approaches is best developed, with a number of small controlled studies showing good outcomes for treatment over wait-list control conditions for participants treated in both community and secure hospital settings. This is an important development because research conducted across three continents, using broadly similar methods, has shown that aggression is a serious issue in the DD population and is the main reason for people with DD being admitted (and readmitted) to institutions, and the primary reason for the prescription of behaviour control groups in this population.

There are no controlled trials of treatment for sex offenders with DD, mainly due to ethical issues of denying those who present serious risks to others potentially beneficial interventions. In a recent review of 19 studies of treatment effectiveness for sex offenders with DD, Courtney and Rose (2004) concluded that the outcomes for psychological interventions appear to be marginally superior to those for drug therapy and service/management interventions. The evidence available, while based on small-scale methodologically weak studies that have yielded variable outcomes, indicates that attitudes towards, and cognitions concerning, sexual offending can be improved. There is some limited evidence that mandated and longer interventions result in lower levels of sexual reoffending in this population.

The research evidence supporting interventions for fire-setters with DD is even more limited. There have been one case study, two small case series and one pre-post intervention outcome study that have provided some encouragement that broadly cognitive-behavioural group-based interventions can help with fire interest and attitudes and emotional problems associated with previous fire-setting behaviour in these clients.

There have been some advances recently in the development and modification of measures designed to assess the risk of violence and sexual aggression in offenders with DD. Established risk measures, such as the Violence Risk Appraisal Guide, HCR-20 and Static-99, have been shown to have good reliability and validity when used with DD offenders in high, medium and low-secure and community settings. Further work has shown that the severity of assessed personality disorder (including psychopathy) in offenders with DD is positively associated with measures of risk of future violence and sexual aggression.

The deinstitutionalization policy of recent years has resulted in significant changes in the design and delivery of services for offenders with DD. Against this background the evidence to support the use of assessment tools and interventions for these clients has been building gradually from a very low baseline. It is not clear if people with DD are over-represented in the offender population, or whether offending is more prevalent among people with DD compared with the general population. However, there is some limited evidence available to guide clinical services and practitioners in developing cognitive-behavioural interventions for people with DD who are angry and violent, are sexually aggressive or who set fires. There has also been some progress in the development of dynamic and actuarial risk assessments to help evaluate clients' progress in therapy and rehabilitation. While there are difficulties in interpreting the findings of recidivism studies involving offenders with DD, early indications are that, as for non-DD offenders, mandated and longer-term interventions result in better outcomes than voluntary and shorter treatments. Further research with this population is required to build on the limited evidence available to improve knowledge and future practice.

John L. Taylor

Related entries

Diagnosis of mental disorder; Dyslexia and specific learning disabilities.

Key texts and sources

Courtney, J. and Rose, J. (2004) 'The effectiveness of treatment for male sex offenders with learning disabilities: a review of the literature', *Journal of Sexual Aggression*, 10: 215–36.

Lindsay, W.R., Hogue, T., Taylor, J.L., Steptoe, L., Mooney, P., O'Brien, G., Johnston, S. and Smith, A.H.W. (in press) 'Risk assessment in offenders with intellectual disability: a comparison across three levels of security', *International Journal of Offender Therapy and Comparative Criminology*.

Lindsay, W.R. and Taylor, J.L. (2005) 'A selective review of research on offenders with developmental disabilities: assessment and treatment', *Clinical Psychology and Psychotherapy*, 12: 201–14.

Lindsay, W.R., Taylor, J.L. and Sturmey, P. (eds) (2004) *Offenders with Developmental Disabilities*. Chichester: Wiley.

Taylor, J.L. (2002) 'A review of assessment and treatment of anger and aggression in offenders with intellectual disability', *Journal of Intellectual Disability Research*, 46 (suppl. 1): 57–73.

DIAGNOSIS OF MENTAL DISORDER

Diagnosis, in medicine, means both the process of identifying a disease by its signs and symptoms and the determining description or name of that disease. The naming and classification of diseases is called 'nosology' (Greek *nosos* = 'disease'). On the historical assumption that mental disorders were the consequence of disease processes, the same approach has been applied in mental health.

A diagnosis, when viewed as a hypothetical construct, has to meet with the usual scientific strictures of validity and reliability. In this it can be said to have served general medicine well, if not psychiatry. Thus a diagnosis must have construct validity (the presenting symptoms and signs always occur together, including common cause or causes – its aetiology) and predictive validity (the natural development or outcome if untreated – the prognosis – is universally the same). It must also have inter-test and inter-tester reliability. The elements of a diagnosis will be constructed from the signs (what the clinician observes in how the patient behaves) and symptoms (what the patient identifies as problematic). Depending on the pattern of these signs and symptoms, a correspondence will be made with a clinically recognized diagnosis. A diagnosis can be named according to:

- the identifying signs and symptoms (in general medicine, hypertension and dyspepsia and, in psychiatry, depressive thoughts and manic behaviour);
- anatomical site (in general medicine, carditis – the heart and ocular degeneration – the eye). It can be said that psychiatry has no anatomically-based diagnoses;
- pathological process (in general medicine, tumour and vascular degeneration, absent in general psychiatry, though present with the dementias); and
- cause or aetiology (lead poisoning and, in psychiatry, drug-induced psychosis and post-traumatic stress disorder).

Diagnosis in psychiatry has yet to reach the sophistication of that in general medicine.

Because of the assumed commonality in pathology of a particular diagnosis, a diagnosis will lead clinicians to prescribe a set of treatments or interventions that are associated with its cure (total removal of the condition), its amelioration (reduction in symptoms) or the prevention of further deterioration. This will also support the predictive validity of a diagnosis.

The appropriateness of this approach in mental health matters is a cause for continuing debate. In the medical model, the diagnosis is seen as the primary phase in the clinical process followed by the formulation, which contains additional relevant information about the patient that needs to be taken into account when treating or managing a condition beyond the presenting 'crisis'. Because of its association with the biological reductionism of the medical model, diagnosis is held with some opprobrium among many psychologists, who have favoured the process of formulation in their clinical assessment without necessarily including a diagnostic label.

When the efficacy of psychiatric treatments came to be addressed in a more scientific manner in the middle of the twentieth century, a major problem was establishing the accurate and consistent definition of patient populations for comparison between sites. The World Health Organization (WHO) promoted a project to systematize medical diagnoses throughout the world. This project included psychiatry, and this resulted in the publication of the *International Classification of Diseases and Related Health Problems* (ICD-10). This was a major advance, and it can be imagined that the result was the product of much politicking between the various schools of thought on the subject. The diagnoses associated with mental disorders are contained in Chapter V, various diagnoses being contained within the following categories:

- *F00–F09*: organic, including symptomatic, mental disorders.
- *F10–F19*: mental and behavioural disorders due to psychoactive substance use.
- *F20–F29*: schizophrenia, schizotypal and delusional disorders.
- *F30–F39*: mood (affective) disorders.
- *F40–F49*: neurotic, stress-related and somatoform disorders.
- *F50–F59*: behavioural syndromes associated with physiological disturbances and physical factors.
- *F60–F69*: disorders of adult personality and behaviour.
- *F70-F79*: mental retardation.
- *F80–F89*: disorders of psychological development.
- *F90–F99*: behavioural and emotional disorders with onset usually occurring in childhood and adolescence.
- *F99*: unspecified mental disorder.

While this system supplied diagnostic categories

that would be internationally recognized, it did not supply operational definitions by which they could be determined and therefore assist inter-rater reliability between clinicians. This issue was addressed by the American Psychiatric Association, which produced *The Diagnostic and Statistical Manual*, its latest edition (2000) being the DSM-IV-TR. This supplies criteria that have to be met if a certain diagnosis is to be applied. In the development of this approach there has been much debate, and it can be said that it is a continuing and evolving process. The ICD-10 and the DSM-IV-TR are the two classificatory systems that are used in general clinical practice and scientific research. Although there are similarities between the two systems, there are also differences.

The DSM-IVTR has over 300 different psychiatric disorders, ranging from 'acute stress disorder' to 'voyeurism'. The presenting clinical problem is organized according to 5 axes:

- *Axis I*: the diagnosis (e.g. depression, schizophrenia) – what can be called 'state variables',
- *Axis II*: developmental disorders (e.g. autism and, according to the North American nomenclature, 'mental retardation') and personality disorders (e.g. 'avoidant' and 'borderline') – what can be called 'trait variables'.
- *Axis III*: physical conditions that play a role in the development, continuance or exacerbation of the Axis I disorder – to alert clinicians that the psychological presentation might be the consequence of some physical disorder.
- *Axis IV*: the severity of psychosocial stressors (e.g. bereavement) that have an impact on Axis I disorder.
- *Axis V*: an evaluation of the individual's present level of functioning in the present and in comparison with the best level within the past year.

The assessment leading to a psychiatric diagnosis is no different from general medicine, although the focus will be more on mental than on physical functioning. This is called the 'mental state examination' (MSE), which explores the cognition (thinking and memory), affect (emotional states) and motivation or 'will' of the patient, since these will be the areas of functioning associated with mental disorders. As a result of the WHO's project, the Present State Examination was developed, together with a computerized version – CATEGO – which guided the questions towards the identification of particular diagnoses. This makes for standardization in the questions that are asked by the interviewing clinician. A similar interview schedule has been developed for the DSM-IV-TR – the Structured Interview for the DSM-IV (SCID-II). As well as for general clinical use, these tools can be used in general epidemiological screening exercises or for the definition of experimental groups in research projects.

In a medico-legal context, the issue of diagnosis is relevant in two respects: 1) who is qualified to give a diagnosis; and 2) what diagnoses are permissible. With regard to (1), since a diagnosis is a medical procedure, it is considered in the UK that only a medical practitioner can give a diagnosis since it is only within his or her professional competence to do so. However, courts do not always maintain this rigid distinction. For example, in North America, all registered psychologists are allowed the restricted act of diagnosis. Although non-medical practitioners might not be able formally to diagnose, they are still in a position to offer opinions about the individual clinical features of a client's functioning, based on their own professional expertise. Thus a clinical psychologist could give evidence about someone's particular symptomatology without having to give a diagnosis – e.g. delusional system, memory, thought disorder. With regard to (2), since there are changes in diagnostic fashion over time, the test of the acceptability of a diagnosis will be on the basis of whether it can be demonstrated that it is, at the present moment, generally accepted within the professional community. An example of this is post-traumatic stress disorder, which has recently achieved official acceptance as a diagnostic category.

Paul Devonshire

Related entries

Developmental disabilities in adults; Forensic psychiatry; Severe Mental Illness (psychosis)

Key texts and sources

American Psychiatric Association (2000) *Diagnostic and Statistical Manual of Mental Disorders* (4th edn). Washington, DC: American Psychiatric Association.

DOUBLE JEOPARDY

Double jeopardy is a long-standing principle of common law that no one should be tried a second time after acquittal. It has been founded in Roman law and common law since the twelfth century. Double jeopardy was initially brought in to protect those who were subject to both canon law and temporal law.

People argued about the medieval right not to be tried twice, as though fraudulently getting off was some sort of game.

(Blunkett cited in the *Guardian* 12 September 2006)

The common law says wrong guilty verdicts can be wrong, but wrong not guilty verdicts cannot be wrong.

(Whitton 2003)

Double jeopardy is the rule that, in the event of someone being prosecuted a second time for the same offence, he or she can claim that he or she has already been acquitted of that offence ('autrefois acquit'), and the court will therefore not let the case proceed. In practice, this rule has the consequence that such second prosecutions are not launched and so do not reach court. The few legal double jeopardy cases that have come before the courts have tended to turn on whether the earlier trial was indeed for the same offence and based on the same facts.

This strict common law rule was first qualified in England by the Criminal Procedure and Investigations Act 1996. This Act allows the prosecution to appeal an acquittal on the grounds that either the witnesses or the jury were intimidated. Following the murder of Stephen Lawrence, the Macpherson Report (1999) suggested that double jeopardy should be reconsidered where 'fresh and viable' new evidence comes to light. Similarly, in 2001, the Law Commission recommended that it should be possible for an acquitted murder suspect to face a second trial – because someone convicted of an offence is able to cite new evidence as grounds for appeal or for review of conviction, it could be said the concept of fresh evidence is already established in the criminal justice system.

The Macpherson recommendations were implemented through the passing of the Criminal Justice Act 2003 (see Part 10 for further details regarding 'retrial of serious offences'). Retrials are now permitted if there is 'new' and 'compelling' evidence. The change refers, however, only to a number of serious offences, including murder, manslaughter, kidnapping, rape, armed robbery and serious drugs crimes. All cases must be approved by the Director of Public Prosecutions, and the court of appeal must agree to quash the original acquittal in order for the case to proceed.

The double jeopardy provisions of the 2003 Act came into force in April 2005. On 11 September 2006, William Dunlop became the first person to be convicted of murder after previously having been acquitted for the same offence. He was tried twice for the murder of Julie Hogg, but two juries failed to reach a verdict and he was formally acquitted in 1991. Some years later, he confessed to the murder and was convicted of perjury. The case was reinvestigated in early 2005, when the new law came into effect. His case was referred to the court of appeal in November 2005 for permission for a new trial to proceed. He was subsequently retried (and lodged a guilty plea) for the murder of Julie Hogg and sentenced to life imprisonment.

Jo Bailey

Related entries

Courts; Crown Prosecution Service (CPS); Legal profession.

Key texts and sources

Macpherson, Sir W. (1999) *The Stephen Lawrence Inquiry: Report of an Inquiry by Sir William Macpherson of Cluny* (Cm 4262-1). London: HMSO.

Whitton, E. (1998) *The Cartel: Lawyers and their Nine Magic Tricks.* Herwick.

See the Office of Public Sector Information's website for the texts of the Criminal Procedures and Investigations Act 1996 (http://www.opsi.gov.uk/acts/acts1996/ukga_19960025_en_1) and the Criminal Justice Act 2003 (http://www.opsi.gov.uk/acts/acts2003/20030044.htm).

DYSLEXIA AND SPECIFIC LEARNING DISABILITIES

'Dyslexia' is a term originally applied to a selective impairment in previously normal reading ability following a cerebro-vascular or other accident. Later, by analogy, it was applied to a difficulty in learning how to read during an otherwise apparently normal course of development; by extension, to any combination of developmental disorders in which reading disability is a component; and, finally, to low reading attainment, irrespective of cause.

The constructs of developmental dyslexia and specific learning disabilities are politically and scientifically controversial, and may remain so during the useful lifetime of this Dictionary. Definitions of developmental dyslexia are thus many and various. Some are strictly phenomenological, being confined to a description of the presenting problem as 'a basic difficulty in learning how to decode print', while others are both phenomenological and aetiological, attributing the difficulty to 'a neuro-developmental disorder with a biological origin and behavioural signs which extend far beyond problems with written language'.

The strictly phenomenological definitions are doubly problematic: when they take measures of reading attainment alone into account, they do not discriminate between dyslexics and ordinary poor readers; when they go beyond reading attainment, they confound impairments in phonological processing with sometimes-occurring co-morbid impairments in social cognition, motor control and executive functioning. The combined phenomenological and aetiological definitions are problematic in a different way: at the level of the individual a biological origin is necessarily conjectural; and it is a residual category when other, known possibilities have been excluded in the course of a differential diagnosis – which is itself controversial.

In our present state of knowledge, difficulty in learning to read might best be defined as 'a multifactorial trait in which basic constitutional (genetic) vulnerabilities (notably in phonological skills) interact with other cognitive skills and environmental factors to produce an increased risk of dyslexia in a continuous way'. This definition breaks new ground in two ways. It incorporates environmental factors, such as emergent literacy in the childhood home and teaching methods in the elementary school, which were previously either disregarded or explicitly excluded, and it acknowledges the multidimensionality of human aptitudes, using insights derived from dynamic systems approaches to the understanding of human development. Such a definition is consistent with a model of developmental psychopathology in which:

the etiology of complex behavioural disorders is multifactorial and involves the interaction of multiple risk and protective factors, which can be either genetic or environmental; risk and protective factors alter the development of cognitive functions necessary for normal development; no single etiological factor is sufficient for a disorder, and few may be necessary; comorbidity among complicated behavioural disorders is to be expected because of shared etiologic and cognitive risk factors; [and] the liability distribution for a given disease is continuous and quantitative rather than discrete and categorical, so that the threshold for having the disorder is somewhat arbitrary.

Diagnosis

There is no standard method for diagnosing developmental dyslexia. More than one method has proved to be unstable for establishing caseness over time in an axiomatically lifelong condition, and all methods produce definitional artefacts. By assessing knowledge and aptitudes, cognitive and behavioural methods disregard the hypothesized distinction between dyslexics and ordinary poor readers. These methods are essential to the teacher but they are uninformative as to causality. However, it is now clear that there is no scientific support for attempts to determine causality by defining dyslexia psychometrically, whether in terms of a discrepancy between reading attainment and a measure of intelligence or in terms of specified groups of WAIS (or WISC) subtests: the 'ACID' profile of subtest scores is not an acid test for dyslexia. An aetiological diagnosis of dyslexia is still, at best, a theory.

Prevalence

Many scholars accept that 'current estimates of the incidence of true reading disabilities are greatly inflated', that most people who are labelled as dyslexic have in fact been misdiagnosed and that the primary cause of their difficulty is more likely to be experiential than it is to be biological. Scholarly caution is especially pertinent when estimates are based on the results of screening (rather than diagnostic) tests in the general population, where false positives may be expected to outnumber true positives several-fold. In this context, the frequently encountered expression 'risk of dyslexia' is properly interpreted as conjectural with respect to the causes of reading difficulties in any individual, particularly when screening test results are interpreted without taking that individual's home and school experiences into account.

A recent (and currently controversial) innovation has been the diagnosis of learning disabilities in terms of response to instruction or response to intervention. When prevalence is determined in this way, it has been found that the proportion of non-responders to a programme of systematic and explicit instruction in phonological skills is typically lower than 3 per cent of a normal population of schoolchildren. Although it would be unsafe to assume that the difficulties of all non-responders are primarily biological, this finding implies an upper limit for the prevalence of serious and protracted difficulties in learning how to decode print.

As for an elevated prevalence rate for dyslexia among offenders, offenders' low literacy levels may be predicted by literacy levels in those members of the general population among whom many offenders grow up, coupled with the low ability levels found in a disproportionate number of serious and persistent offenders, so that little if any variance is left to be explained by dyslexia beyond that accounted for by the base rate. Where reading difficulties are co-morbid with hyperactivity, impulsivity and attentional difficulties, the co-morbidity creates an expectation that the prevalence of low reading attainment will be higher among offenders than it is in the general population. Nevertheless, the association between those behaviours and offending is correlational rather than causal. Taken together, both the base rate to be inferred from response-to-intervention studies and the odds ratios predicting delinquency from low school attainment suggest that, among offenders, the prevalence rate for a specific and persistent learning difficulty – as opposed to low attainment – in reading is unlikely to be greater than 4 or 5 per cent. Among offenders especially, the effects of child abuse and neglect, head injuries and substance abuse may be contributory causes of difficulty in reading.

Implications for practice

In all courts it is now accepted that cognitively impaired or low-literate litigants, defendants and witnesses may require assistance and accommodation in their disabilities at all stages of the legal process and that miscarriages of justice may occur if these courtesies are denied.

However, both the circulation of outdated concepts of dyslexia and the publicity given to contentious claims about its prevalence, diagnosis and remediability increase the likelihood that members of the bench taking 'judicial notice' will misdirect themselves. Moreover, it appears from reported cases that the testimony given by expert witnesses may reflect outdated professional practice among educational psychologists much better than it reflects the state of scientific knowledge at the time of the hearing.

In the civil courts, following the Education Act 1981, claimants at first sought damages against local education authorities for failure to recognize or to make provision for children with special educational needs in literacy or numeracy. By claiming failure to diagnose and to remediate dyslexia specifically, more recent litigants have gone beyond the scientific evidence. From reported cases it appears that the role of co-morbid conditions has been insufficiently examined and that rebuttable assumptions about causality have gone unchallenged. Although the medical analogy of diagnosis is helpful as a metaphor, it is misleading when applied literally to Part II of the Statement of Special Educational Needs, since what the legislation requires is an ascertainment of need, not an ascertainment of cause.

In the criminal courts, it has been suggested that dyslexia might mitigate an offender's blameworthiness. However, this argument is unlikely to succeed with respect to low reading attainment alone. With respect to co-morbid impairments in executive functioning, social cognition or schizotypy, it is possible that a diagnosis that points towards mitigation from one perspective will suggest to the court from a different perspective that an offender might be either more dangerous or more likely to reoffend than an offender without such impairments.

Dyscalculia

Developmental dyscalculia 'is a specific learning disability affecting the normal acquisition of arithmetic skills. Genetic, neurobiologic, and epidemiologic evidence indicates that dyscalculia, like other learning disabilities, is a brain-based disorder. However, poor teaching and environmental deprivation have also been implicated in its etiology'. On a narrower definition, developmental dyscalculia 'appears to be a specific difficulty in understanding basic numerical concepts, especially the concept of numerosity'. Educational interventions for dyscalculia range from the rote learning of arithmetic facts to acquiring strategies for solving arithmetic exercises, but the long-term prognosis of dyscalculia and the role of remediation in its outcome are yet to be determined. As a learning disability with a probable biological cause, dyscalculia is one of a number of possible and by no means mutually exclusive explanations for low attainment in arithmetic.

Michael Rice

Related entries

Developmental disabilities in adults.

Key texts and sources

Butterworth, B. (2005) 'The development of arithmetical abilities', *Journal of Child Psychology and Psychiatry*, 46: 3–18.

Kavale, K.A. and Forness, S.R. (2000) 'What definitions of learning disability say and don't say: a critical analysis', *Journal of Learning Disabilities*, 33: 239–56.

Pennington, B.F. (2006) 'From single to multiple deficit models of developmental disorders', *Cognition*, 101: 385–413.

Rice, M. and Brooks, G. (2004) *Developmental Dyslexia in Adults: A Research Review*. London: National Research and Development Centre for Adult Literacy and Numeracy.

Vellutino, F.R., Fletcher, J.M., Snowling, M.J. and Scanlon, D.M. (2004) 'Specific reading disability (dyslexia): what have we learned in the past four decades?', *Journal of Child Psychology and Psychiatry*, 45: 2–40.

E

EDUCATIONAL PSYCHOLOGY

Educational psychology is the application of psychology to the problems encountered by children and young people in all aspects of education. It aims to 'promote child development and learning through the application of psychology by working with individuals and groups of children, teachers and other adults in schools, families, other LEA officers, health and social services and other agencies' (DfEE 2000).

Educational psychology is a branch of applied psychology given chartered status by the British Psychological Society and therefore subject to the agreed *Ethics and Code of Conduct* (BPS 2006a). The practice of educational psychology promotes an understanding of the influence of organizational ethos and culture, educational curricula, communication systems and management leadership styles on effective outcomes for children and young people.

Educational psychologists were described by Currie (Scottish Executive 2002) as engaging in five core activities: consultation, assessment, intervention, training and research. They use applied scientist-practitioner theoretical models and methods of working where hypotheses focus on interaction and where the contexts and systems within which a child or young person lives are at the centre of establishing effective interventions that bring about change. Engaging in research activities is central to the role, especially where this might improve the effectiveness of interventions for individuals and organizations through evidence-based practice.

Working with schools, behaviour and educational support teams, youth offending teams and a range of other agencies, educational psychologists are often involved in developing effective psychological interventions to raise educational standards generally and specifically for gender and minority groups; in tackling the underachievement of vulnerable groups; in promoting inclusion and reducing exclusion; in supporting behaviour policy development; and in managing organizational change. Intervention and support for children and young people who present and/or experience behavioural, emotional and/or social difficulties are wide ranging, including direct work with individuals or groups, parents, teachers, schools and organizations with a focus on, for example, emotional literacy, anti-bullying, traumatic incidence or bereavement and loss.

The majority of educational psychologists are employed by local authorities and work in children's services but, in addition, they also work in youth justice, in health authorities, in social care departments and organizations within the voluntary sector. Multidisciplinary working lies at the heart of the role of the educational psychologist – through establishing collaborative processes and working within jointly established protocols, educational psychology has a far-reaching impact across a broad range of settings and at many different levels.

Judi Bamford

Related entries

Applied psychology; Chartered psychologists; Health Professions Council (HPC).

Key texts and sources

BPS (2006a) *The British Psychological Society: Ethics and Code of Conduct.* Leicester: BPS (available online at **http://www.bps.org.uk/document-download-area/document-download$.cfm?file_u uid=5084A882-1143-DFD0-7E6C-F1938A65C242&ext=pdf**).

BPS (2006b) *DECP Booklet: Educational and Child Psychologists within Communities.* Leicester: BPS.

DfEE (2000) *Educational Psychology Services (England): Current Role, Good Practice and Future Directions.* London: HMSO.

DfES (2006) *A Review of the Functions and Contribution of Educational Psychologists in England and Wales in the Light of Every Child Matters* (RR792). London: HMSO.

Scottish Executive (2002) *Review of Educational Psychology Services in Scotland.* Edinburgh: Scottish Executive.

EVERY CHILD MATTERS

Every Child Matters is a government report completed after the death of Victoria Climbié, who was murdered at the age of 8 years 3 months by her great aunt and the man they both lived with.

Victoria Climbié was murdered at the age of 8 years 3 months by her great aunt and the man they both lived with in February 2000. She had been subjected to sustained and severe physical abuse and neglect over at least the preceding nine months. Lord Laming's report of the inquiry into events revealed a catalogue of mistakes in the work of social services, health services and the police that resulted in her not being properly protected.

The government's response to the Laming Inquiry report was to publish the green paper, *Every Child Matters* (DfES 2003). This discussion paper, through its subsequent legislation (the Children Act 2004) and stream of associated publications, brought about the most significant changes to strategy and professional practice in relation to children for many years. It became known informally as the 'Every Child Matters agenda' and was intended to bring

about profound change in the ways in which professionals work to produce positive outcomes for children. It has had a significant impact on governance, policy and practice in many fields.

In terms of strategic direction, the Children Act 2004 legislated that all services for children provided by local authorities in England and Wales should be integrated into single departments known as children's trusts or children and young people's services. These would be, in effect, amalgamations and restructurings of the pre-existing local education authority and social services departments. There would be one director of children's services in each local authority.

Every Child Matters sets out five outcomes for children and young people: 'Staying safe'; 'Being healthy'; 'Enjoying and achieving'; 'Making a positive contribution'; and 'Achieving economic well-being'. All actions taken by children's services should be aimed at delivering these outcomes. There are four key themes running through all such work: support for parents and carers; early intervention; information sharing; and training in core skills for all workers. The creation of integrated children's services is intended to yield benefits through the development of shared resources: the pooling of previously separate budgets is intended to rationalize funding streams, allowing for more creative and flexible provision for vulnerable children.

The development of systems to share information about children between agencies is seen as a crucial step in two areas: to safeguard children effectively so that agencies inform each other of concerns and to support parents by ensuring that they do not have to give the same information to a series of different professionals. The use of a 'common assessment framework' is part of this initiative.

The government sees the criminal justice system as having a vital contribution to make in helping secure the five outcomes for young people, with a particular focus on 'Staying safe' and 'Making a positive contribution'. Workers in the criminal justice system, just as others who work with children and young people, will be expected to ensure that their work is aimed at meeting those outcomes.

Neil Ryrie

Related entries

Social services.

Key texts and sources

See the Every Child Matters' website (**http://www. everychildmatters.gov.uk**).

EVIDENCE-BASED PRACTICE (EBP)

Evidence-based practice (EBP) is based on scientifically collected data or information that are analysed and organized to improve understanding of a given area of practice.

The process of evidence-based practice (EBP) involves the pursuit of the answer to a practice based question followed by a critical appraisal of the evidence. The most challenging aspect of EBP is possibly making judgements that draw together the evidence and its application in individual cases. Such professional judgements always need to give primacy to ethical considerations and not just issues of efficacy. The areas subject to investigation cover the full range of areas of activity of professional practice.

Much of the early work on EBP for health workers can be traced back to epidemiological research. An early proponent of what has come to be called EBP was Ernst Codman who, at the beginning of the last century, promulgated his view that physicians should record the results of their interventions and share such practice-based learning. This touches on one of the key aspects of contemporary EBP – that practitioners have an active role to play in the development of effective EBP. Arguably, at its best EBP involves a process of reciprocal iteration between the evidence base and practice. In other words, both may inform each other. In 1972, a UK epidemiologist called for the wide use of EBP among health workers. His studies led to the landmark establishment of the Cochrane Collaboration (www.cochrane.org). This collaboration has played a major role in the advocacy and dissemination of evidence-based approaches to practice. In the UK there has been a steady stream of critical reviews of the literature in some key areas of health practice, including psychological therapies.

Some have erroneously argued that EBP overly relies on randomized control trials. Whereas it may be the case that some have viewed the quality of evidence in an unduly hierarchical manner, research rigour is clearly important. However, a hierarchical approach, uncritically applied, can miss the fundamental point about what constitutes good research for the exploration and examination of particular research questions. What is important is that practitioners need to be aware of the strengths and weaknesses of different research methodologies. Crucially, researchers need to be aware of what is the most appropriate research methodology to contribute to answering research questions on testable theses.

One very important issue is the extent to which EBP is actually practised. In the forensic field, debates about EBP have sometimes been unduly constrained by the so-called, and somewhat limited, 'What Works' literature. It has been persuasively argued that this set of literature tends to be characterized by an overemphasis on meta-analysis and that such research tends to be somewhat narrowly focused on reconvictions as an outcome measure. The lack of sophistication to such analyses can present a very diminished picture of the potential of the much broader EBP context of such work. For example, if a practitioner was concerned with reoffending as an outcome from a given intervention, then a range of measures in addition to reconviction data may be used. It is important to consider such matters because, otherwise, there is the risk of the measures used being insufficiently sensitive to detect potentially real behavioural changes. Some interventions may also have a number of potentially relevant outcomes: in the case of drug misuse interventions, efficacy could be measured with a range of both health and criminal justice-based outcomes. The two are not mutually exclusive.

EBP has a broad range of potential applications in the forensic field. This is perhaps best illustrated by an example. Prisoners tend to have high levels of both physical and mental health needs. In recent years (2001 and 2004b) the UK Department of Health has produced documentation highlighting the potential of evidence-based psychological therapies in addressing many of these needs. Forensic psychologists in prisons in the past decade have tended to be drawn towards working with offenders in experimental, structured, group-work-based interventions designed to reduce the risk of reoffending. This has sometimes been at the expense of evidence-based psychological approaches to address broader mental health and drug misuse problems.

The health needs of prisoners tend to be unmet. Prisoners, as a group, do not tend to engage with, or be engaged very effectively with, health professionals. Forensic psychologists are well placed to begin more effectively to address this gap by applying the evidence in practice. However good the research, if forensic practitioners do not engage with the process of improving outcomes for prisoners, no one will benefit from the research. Psychologists (of whatever applied psychology specialism) have an ethical responsibility to keep up to date with germane evidence-based approaches. In this case the evidence would relate to prisoner needs – especially those that are presently unmet. This is becoming more straightforward with the increasing availability of information on the Internet and a wider recognition among a range of professional groups of the need to keep up to date for their continuing professional development.

As indicated above, there is an increased availability of scientifically collected and analysed knowledge bases that practitioners may draw from in making their judgements about how such evidence may be sensibly applied. EBP is a potentially powerful set of scientifically based approaches that may improve outcomes for some of those with the highest levels of need. Forensic psychologists have a key potential role and ethical responsibility in ensuring that evidence-based approaches are delivered in practice and that, in turn, practitioners contribute further to developing the knowledge base.

Graham J. Towl

Related entries

Nothing Works; Number needed to treat (NNT); What Works.

Key texts and sources

Badenoch, D. and Heneghan, C. (2005) *Evidence-based Medicine Toolkit*. London: BMJ Books.

Glaziou, P., Vandenbroucke, J. and Chalmers, I. (2004) 'Assessing the quality of research', *British Medical Journal*, 328: 39–41.

Haves, R. (2004) 'Introduction to evidence-based practices', in C.E. Stout and R. Haves (eds) *Evidence-based Practice: Methods, Models and Tools for Mental Health Professionals*. Hoboken, NJ: Wiley.

Towl, G.J. (ed.) (2006) *Psychological Research in Prisons*. Oxford: Blackwell.

EXPERT TESTIMONY

Expert testimony is the provision of facts and opinions to the court by an individual who is believed to have substantial knowledge of a scientific, technical or professional subject on the basis of specialist training, profession, publication or experience.

The courts have used experts to assist them in dealing with litigation for several hundred years, with a case in 1782 perhaps serving as the root of the modern rules on expert testimony, wherein evidence was accepted from a civil engineer, John Smeaton, in relation to the silting up of Wells harbour in Norfolk.

In the provision of their testimony, expert witnesses are required to offer evidence of both facts and opinion on matters beyond the knowledge and experience of the court. These facts include those the expert has directly observed and those that have been reported to the expert. The opinion expressed should be objective and impartial and is provided with a view to assisting the court in making its decision. As such, expert testimony differs from the evidence given by professional witnesses, who may nevertheless be expert in that they are asked to provide facts only.

Expert testimony may assist the court in making a decision on liability and/or quantum, and is provided by a range of individuals, including physicians and other healthcare specialists, accountants, employment consultants and others, with the more frequent involvement of forensic scientists in criminal cases. In civil cases, expert testimony is provided by way of written reports – experts now attend court in person less frequently than they did in the past. The increasing tendency for civil cases now to be settled out of court springs primarily from the Woolf reforms of 1999, as expressed in the rules for the county court and high court, known as the *Civil Procedure Rules*. These were introduced with the aim of accelerating and simplifying procedures, of reducing the risk of the partisanship of experts and of making litigation less adversarial.

The Woolf reforms endeavoured to address concerns that litigation was often too adversarial when cases were run by the parties rather than the courts, and that the rules were too often ignored or flouted by the parties in the absence of active and consistent enforcement by the courts. As a result, the Civil Procedure Rules, Part 35 (1999) made it clear that the expert's prime duty was to the court, rather than to the person or persons instructing or paying him or her. It also emphasized the expert's duty to provide unbiased opinion on matters within his or her expertise only, giving details of the facts or assumptions on which the opinion is based. In addition, and to emphasize the expected impartiality, the expert is required to identify alternative interpretations of the facts and to inform the court if his or her opinion has changed as a result of reading any other expert's report or, indeed, for any other reason.

It is, perhaps, the promotion of the concept of a single joint expert being called to give evidence to the court, appointed by both parties or, even, potentially by the court, in the Civil Procedure Rules, Part 35 that best illustrates the requirement for impartiality in the provision of expert testimony. The expert is required to address the report to the court and must comment on the likelihood that there may be a range of expert opinions on the matter in hand. The expert must then explain how he or she has come to the opinion he or she holds, in the light of the evidence. The expert is expected to comment on the confidence he or she places on his or her opinion and to identify any factors that might limit the confidence the court can place on the opinion expressed. The opinion, at all times, must be expressed in such a way as to recognize the requirement to restrict comment on matters on which the judge and jury will decide (such as who is to blame and to what degree). Any failure to adhere to the conditions and limitations set can lead to the inadmissibility of the expert testimony.

In all cases, therefore, it remains for the court to decide how much weight or evidential value should be assigned to the expert testimony. The standard of proof will differ according to the setting such that, in civil cases, expert testimony will be assessed in terms of the balance of probabilities. In the criminal courts, the expert testimony will be assessed with regard to the requirement to prove beyond reasonable doubt. In testing and assessing the expert's opinion, the court may deem it sufficient to accept a written report, and/or the expert may be required to give testimony in person, under direct questioning in court.

The refinement of the definition of the role of expert witnesses and of the expectations of the court in relation to expert testimony provided in the Civil Procedure Rules, Part 35 has been followed by the Protocol for the Instruction of Experts to give Evidence in Civil Claims (2005), which endeavoured to provide clarification on various points.

The provision of expert testimony will usually require training above and beyond the skills training, professional education and/or experience gained through familiarity with a subject. An understanding of the procedures relating to the provision of expert testimony in court will help an expert best fulfil his or her role of assisting the court. Experts need to be fully aware of their duties to the court and should be able to undertake those duties competently so as to aid in the administration of justice, while being aware that significant failure in their duty to the court can lead to repercussions at the discretion of the court.

Simon Easton

Related entries

Courts; Eyewitness testimony; Forensic psychology.

Key texts and sources

Blom-Cooper, L. (ed.) (2006) *Experts in the Civil Courts.* Oxford: Expert Witness Institute/Oxford University Press.

Bond, C., Solon, M. and Harper, P. (1997) *The Expert Witness in Court.* Crayford: Shaw & Sons.

Ministry of Justice (1998) *Civil Procedure Rules, Part 35: Experts and Assessors.* London: Ministry of Justice.

Ministry of Justice (2005a) *Criminal Procedure Rules, Part 33: Expert Evidence.* London: Ministry of Justice.

Ministry of Justice (2005b) *Civil Justice Council Protocol for the Instruction of Experts to give Evidence in Civil Claims.* London: Ministry of Justice.

Williams, V. (2007) *Civil Procedure Handbook, 2007/2008* (rev. edn). Oxford: Oxford University Press.

EYEWITNESS TESTIMONY

Eyewitness testimony is the provision of formal evidence on the basis of events experienced by the party providing that evidence.

The testimony of eyewitnesses can be an incredibly powerful form of evidence. Yet, as psychologists have repeatedly shown for over 100 years, it can also be extremely unreliable. The aim of this entry is to provide a brief (and necessarily selective) overview of the findings of psychological research in three areas of eyewitness memory: the effects of suggestive questioning; memories of non-existent films; and memories of childhood events that did not occur.

The effects of suggestive questioning

The psychological study of eyewitness testimony has a long history that can be traced back to the earliest days of discipline. The most influential modern research in this area centres on the work conducted by Elizabeth Loftus. In a seminal paper, Loftus and Palmer (1974) demonstrated how easily subtle changes in question wording could alter details of partici-pants' eyewitness reports. In their first experiment, participants watched seven films of automobile accidents. They were then questioned and asked to give estimates of the speed the cars were travelling. They found that varying just one word of the question – specifically the verb used to describe the speed of the collision – had a significant impact on participants' estimates. Participants who were asked how fast the cars were travelling when they 'smashed' into each other gave significantly higher estimates of speed than participants who were asked how fast the cars were going when they 'hit' each other.

Based on the results of a second experiment, Loftus and Palmer argued that these differences were due to changes in the underlying memory representation of the accident. In this second experiment participants were again shown a film and questioned suggestively about the speed of the cars. The earlier findings regarding suggestive questioning and speed estimates were replicated ('smashed' led to higher estimates of speed than 'hit'). More importantly, however, was the finding that, when questioned one week later, participants in the 'smashed' condition were more likely incorrectly to claim to have seen broken glass at the scene of the accident than those in the 'hit' condition. Thus, these subtle difference in wording led not only to different initial estimates of speed but also to non-existent details of the film being recalled after a one-week delay.

This phenomenon, where participants change details of their memory in line with mis-leading post-event information (PEI), is known as the misinformation effect. The effects have been replicated extensively, although there is ongoing disagreement concerning the exact causes, extent and duration of the effect. Since Loftus and Palmer's paper, numerous experiments have demonstrated that subtle changes in wording can lead participants to report non-existent details of events they have witnessed. In general, peripheral details of a witnessed scene are more vulnerable to the effects of misleading PEI than are central details. However, recent research has shown that participants do, under some circumstances, come to report that they can remember central aspects of events they did not witness.

Memories of non-existent films

On 4 October 1992, an El Al cargo plane crashed into a block of flats in a southern suburb of Amsterdam, killing all four crew and 39 people in the building. There was extensive media coverage of the aftermath of the crash but, critically, no film of the moment of impact. Ten months after the event, Crombag *et al.* asked participants whether they remembered seeing a film of a plane crashing into a block of flats in Amsterdam. Despite the fact that no film of the impact existed, 55 per cent of respondents claimed to have seen such a film and were willing to provide details of how long it was before fire broke out. In a follow-up experiment, Crombag and colleagues found that 66 per cent of participants claimed to have seen the non-existent film. Many were also willing to give detailed information, such as the angle at which the aeroplane hit the building, how long before fire broke out and how long it was before the emergency services arrived.

In contrast to studies of the misinformation effect, it is unlikely that the simple act of asking participants whether they had seen this film (a suggestive question) was sufficient to lead them to remember the non-existent event. Rather, as Crombag and colleagues argued, these responses were probably due to a combination of the participants' imagination, commonsense inference about what 'must have happened' and hearsay evidence obtained from the media. The highly charged and emotional nature of this event may have led participants to combine all these sources of information to create a coherent, yet incorrect, memory of what happened. When questioned ten months later about the existence of a film of the impact, participants may have found it difficult to disentangle which piece of information came from where – referred to in the psychological literature as a source monitoring error. These findings have been replicated several times using different kinds of events, including the car crash in which Diana, Princess of Wales died, the sinking of the *Estonia* ferry and the assassination of the controversial Dutch politician, Pim Fortuyn (for more details, see Smeets *et al.* 2006).

Thus, psychological research has shown that witness memory can be unreliable and that there are a variety of reasons (e.g. suggestive questioning, commonsense inferences, source monitoring errors) why people might falsely claim to have seen something they have not. However, a controversy that swept through North America in the late 1980s and early 1990s meant that psychologists had to devise new methodologies for investigating the fallibility of witness memory. This controversy concerned claims made by adult patients, often years after the event and sometimes after a course of therapy, that they had 'recovered' memories of having been sexually abused as children. The question that psychology could not convincingly answer at that time was whether such memories were likely to be genuine, the product of suggestion or some mix of the two. After 15 years, much controversy and some ingenious experiments, psychologists are now much better placed to answer this question.

Memories of childhood events that did not occur

We now know that, under certain circumstances, participants will claim to have experienced events in their childhood that we are fairly certain did not occur. This was first demonstrated in a case study reported by Loftus and Pickrell. In this case study, a 14-year-old boy (Chris) was asked to recall details over five days regarding four events involving family members. One of the events was false and three of them were true (as verified by the family). Chris was interviewed in the presence of a sibling (who was a confederate of the investigators) about these events. The sibling provided verbal corroboration that all the events (including the false event) had taken place. Over time Chris began to report more about the four events, even rating the false event (becoming lost in a shopping mall as a child) as more likely to have occurred than all but one of the three true events.

Loftus and Pickrell replicated this effect with a larger sample of undergraduate students. In this study participants were asked to complete a booklet concerning four events, the third of which was false (becoming lost in a shopping mall). Parents, who confirmed that their child had never become lost in a shopping mall as a child, also provided details of the real events. Participants were interviewed three times over three weeks and also asked, between interviews, to write down in their booklets anything that came to mind about the events. Loftus and Pickrell found that, after three weeks, 6 out of 24 participants (25 per cent) erroneously believed part or all of the false event. However, as Pezdek *et al.* argued, becoming lost in a shopping mall is a fairly plausible and common event that many people could fairly easily construct a convincing narrative about. Pezdek and colleagues demonstrated that an event that was lower in plausibility (in this case receiving an enema as a child) was less likely to be implanted that the 'lost in the shopping mall' event. Loftus and Pickrell's findings have since been replicated several times, and we now know that at least 25 per cent of participants, when questioned repeatedly about childhood events that did not occur, will nevertheless claim to remember such events. We also know that therapeutic techniques aimed at 'helping' people to remember childhood events (e.g. guided imagery, use of photographs, dream interpretation) can also lead participants to develop false beliefs and memories about those events (for more details, see Ost 2006).

In conclusion, eyewitness testimony is considered powerful and persuasive evidence. Yet, as this very brief and selective overview has shown, there are reasons to be extremely cautious about its reliability. Memory reports can fairly easily become distorted, and these distortions can have serious implications for the legal system. Understanding the circumstances under which these distortions occur will undoubtedly continue to be an ongoing challenge for psychological research.

James Ost

Related entries

Child witnesses; Expert testimony.

Key texts and sources

Loftus, E.F. and Palmer, J.C. (1974) 'Reconstruction of automobile destruction: an example of the interaction between language and memory', *Journal of Verbal Learning and Verbal Behavior*, 13: 585–9.

Ost, J. (2006) 'Recovered memories', in T. Williamson (ed.) *Investigative Interviewing: Rights, Research, Regulation.* Cullompton: Willan Publishing.

Smeets, T., Jelicic, M., Peters, M.J.V., Candel, I., Horselenberg, R. and Merckelbach, H. (2006) '"Of course I remember seeing that film" – how ambiguous questions generate crashing memories', *Applied Cognitive Psychology*, 20: 779–89.

F

FALSE CONFESSIONS

> 'In criminal law, the confession evidence is considered to be the most damaging form of evidence produced at a trial' (Conti 1999). A confession, however, might in fact be false, the accused not having committed the criminal act. The consequences are a miscarriage of justice where the individual is wrongly convicted and delay in and/or the prevention of the detection, arrest and conviction of the real culprit(s).

Methodological difficulties abound in establishing any accurate statistics about the incidence of false confession in the criminal justice system of any jurisdiction. In the UK, at the appeal stage, false confession has been identified as the reason for a wrongful conviction second only to the wrong identification of the suspect (Lloyd-Bostock 1989). In Iceland, 12 per cent of prisoners claimed to have made a false confession (Gudjonsson and Sigurdsson 1994). In the USA, Costanzo and Leo (2007) state that '14 per cent to 25 per cent of known wrongful convictions appear to involve false confessions'.

In the USA, judges came to question the reliability of confessions because of police investigatory methods. As a result of the case of *Miranda* v. *Arizona*, the US Supreme Court limited the prosecution's use of statements made by the defendant while in police custody, unless certain criteria were met. This development was matched in the UK with the Police and Criminal Evidence Act 1984 (PACE), which prescribes police procedures that will furnish admissible evidence in court. This includes the audiotaping of interviews. This makes available to the defence the conditions under which a confession has been obtained, and so the validity and reliability of the confession can become the main plank for the defence.

Kassin (1997) has developed a three-fold typology of false confessions – 'voluntary', 'coerced compliant' and 'coerced internalized' – with McCann (1998) adding a fourth – 'coerced reactive':

- *Voluntary*: 'self-incriminating statement that is purposefully offered in the absence of pressure by the police'. Psychological explanations for this phenomenon include concepts from psychoanalysis – for example, the unconscious compulsion to confess (Reik 1959) – and from social psychology – for example, the need for fame and recognition (Radelet *et al.* 1992) or through altruism.
- *Coerced compliant*: the confession is the result of coercive techniques used by the interviewer (e.g. torture, threats or inducements).
- *Coerced-internalized*: the persuasive techniques are more subtle and psychologically manipulative. Kassin considered this to be the result of two factors:
  - The vulnerability of the individual, whom he described as 'one whose memory is malleable by virtue of his or her youth, interpersonal trust, naiveté, suggestibility, lack of intelligence, stress, fatigue, alcohol or drugs'. The interrogation process has been compared with hypnosis (Wrightman and Kassin 1993).
  - The presentation of false information by the interviewer. Magid (2001) notes that 'virtually all interrogations – or at least all successful interrogations – involve deception' (e.g. expressed misstatements, such as the false existence of evidence and bogus sympathy with the interviewee).

- *Coerced reactive*: the confession is the result of coercion by somebody other than the interviewing police.

In the case of children and juveniles, and of people with learning difficulties, mental illness or brain dysfunction, it is understood that there might be a lack of appreciation of the serious consequences of a confession if the individual is not adequately supported during interviews. The PACE codes of conduct 'provide for an appropriate adult to be called to the police station whenever a juvenile or mentally vulnerable person has been detained in police custody'. It is the police's responsibility to maintain a list of 'appropriate adults', who are drawn from ordinary members of the local community. The decision of 'vulnerability' is made by the investigating police based on their subjective judgement of the suspect rather than on any formal objective tests.

Gudjonsson (1992) has proposed the concept of 'interrogative suggestibility', whereby personality variables, such as Eysenck's neuroticism, predispose individuals to make false confessions. Multiple exposures to unpleasant or traumatic life events (e.g. bullying, the death of a significant other or being a victim of violence) have been associated with the reporting of false confessions (Gudjonsson *et al.* 2007). Adopting Schachter and Singer's (1962) two-factor theory, the false confession arises from a misattribution. Since the interviewee interprets his or her anxiety as guilt, the corollary is that he or she must have committed the act of which he or she is accused. Bem's (1966) self-perception theory postulates that an individual, if persuaded that he or she did something, will then shift his or her self-image to the sort of person who does such things.

The phenomenon of false confession has a long history: the witch-trials of the eighteenth century, in both North America and the UK; the 1930s show trials in the former Soviet Union; and, more recently, in the Korean, Vietnam and Iraq Wars, where the process is referred to as 'brainwashing'. In such contexts, the confessions are used for political propaganda rather than military intelligence. Such information is highly unreliable for military purposes.

False confessions have been conceptualized as the result of individual and/or situational factors. From personal accounts, Schein (1956) identified two types of responders to interrogation – 'co-operators' and 'resistors'. The former were characterized by those who dislike physical or psychological discomfort and/or who have guilt-proneness, while the latter had a capacity to form sound judgements in ambiguous or poorly defined situations. Psychophysiological and psychosocial factors are also involved: night-time arrest, physical beatings, sleep deprivation, physical discomfort (cold and hunger), threats and intimidation. Beck and Godin (1951) similarly identified a significant assault on a person's self-concept as a contributory component of interrogation. Because of ethical considerations in western democracies, it would be difficult to conduct empirical research in this area. The methodology relies on self-report studies of those who have had such experiences, rather than direct observation. It can be said that the techniques of interrogation have developed without any theoretical framework and have relied on the intuition of interrogators and a pragmatic understanding of what works.

Paul Devonshire

Related entries

Developmental disabilities in adults; Polygraphy.

Key texts and sources

Conti, R.P. (1999) 'The psychology of false confessions', *Journal of Credibility Assessment and Witness Psychology*, 2: 14-36.

Gudjonsson, G. (2003) *The Psychology of Interrogations and Confessions: A Handbook.* Chichester: Wiley.

Kassin, S.M. (1997) 'The psychology of confession of evidence', *American Psychologist*, 52: 221-33.

See also the Home Office's policing web page for the PACE codes of practice (http://www.police-homeoffice.gov.uk/operational-policing/powers-pace-codes/pacecodes.html).

FAMILY FACTORS

Many different family factors have been studied as predictors of offending. They can be grouped into six categories (Farrington 2002): criminal and anti-social parents and siblings; large family size; child-rearing methods; abuse or neglect; parental conflict and disrupted families; and other parental features.

In order to investigate family factors as predictors of offending, the best evidence comes from prospective longitudinal surveys of community samples of at least several hundred people. For example, in the Cambridge Study in Delinquent Development (Farrington 2003b), 411 south London males were followed up from the age of 8 to the age of 48, and family factors measured at the age of 8–10 were compared with later convictions and self-reported offending. Another important longitudinal survey is the Pittsburgh Youth Survey, in which 1,517 Pittsburgh boys were followed up from the age of 7–13 to the age of 25–30. (For more details of these studies and of the other studies discussed in this entry, see Farrington and Welsh 2007).

Crime runs in families

Criminal and anti-social parents tend to have delinquent and anti-social children, as shown in the classic longitudinal surveys by Joan McCord in Boston and Lee Robins in St Louis. The most extensive research on the concentration of offending in families was carried out in the Cambridge study. Having a convicted father, mother, brother or sister predicted a boy's own convictions, and all four relatives were independently important as predictors. For example, 63 per cent of boys with convicted fathers were themselves convicted, compared with 30 per cent of the remainder. Same-sex relationships were stronger than opposite-sex relationships, and older siblings were stronger predictors than younger siblings. Only 6 per cent of the families accounted for half of all the convictions of all family members.

Large family size

Large family size (a large number of children in the family) is a relatively strong and highly replicable predictor of delinquency. It was similarly important in the Cambridge and Pittsburgh studies, even though families were on average smaller in Pittsburgh in the 1990s than in London in the 1960s. In the Cambridge study, if a boy had four or more siblings by his tenth birthday, this doubled his risk of being convicted as a juvenile. Large family size predicted self-reported delinquency as well as convictions. It was the most important independent predictor of convictions up to the age of 32 in a logistic regression analysis: 58 per cent of boys from large families were convicted up to this age.

Child-rearing methods

Many different types of child-rearing methods predict a child's delinquency. The most important dimensions of child-rearing are the supervision or monitoring of children, discipline or parental reinforcement, the warmth or coldness of emotional relationships and parental involvement with children.

Parental supervision refers to the degree of monitoring by parents of the child's activities, and their degree of watchfulness or vigilance. Of all these child-rearing methods, poor parental supervision is usually the strongest and most replicable predictor of offending. It typically predicts a doubled risk of delinquency. Many studies show that parents who do not know where their children are when they are out, and parents who let their children roam the streets unsupervised from an early age, tend to have delinquent children. For example, in the classic Cambridge-Somerville study in Boston, Joan McCord found that poor parental supervision in childhood was the best predictor of both violent and property crimes up to the age of 45.

Parental discipline refers to how parents react to a child's behaviour. It is clear that harsh or punitive discipline (involving physical punishment) predicts a child's delinquency. In a follow-up study of nearly 700 Nottingham children, John and Elizabeth Newson found that physical punishment at the ages of 7 and 11 predicted later convictions: 40 per cent of offenders had been smacked or beaten at the age of 11, compared with 14 per cent of non-offenders.

Erratic or inconsistent discipline also predicts delinquency. This can involve either erratic discipline by one parent, sometimes turning a blind eye to bad behaviour and sometimes punishing it severely, or inconsistency between two parents, with one parent being tolerant or indulgent and the other being harshly punitive. It is not clear whether unusually lax discipline predicts delinquency. Just as inappropriate methods of responding to bad behaviour predict delinquency, low parental reinforcement (not praising) of good behaviour is also a predictor.

Cold, rejecting parents tend to have delinquent children, as Joan McCord found almost 30 years ago in the Cambridge-Somerville study. More recently, she concluded that parental warmth could act as a protective factor against the effects of physical punishment. Whereas 51 per cent of boys with cold, physically punishing mothers were convicted in her study, only 21 per cent of boys with warm, physically punishing mothers were convicted, similar to the 23 per cent of boys with warm, non-punitive mothers who were convicted. The father's warmth was also a protective factor against the father's physical punishment.

Child abuse and neglect

Children who are physically abused or neglected tend to become offenders later in life. The most famous study of this was carried out by Cathy Widom in Indianapolis. She used court records to identify over 900 children who had been abused or neglected before the age of 11 and compared these with a control group matched on age, race, gender, school class and place of residence. A 20-year follow-up showed that the children who were abused or neglected were more likely to be arrested as juveniles and as adults than were the controls, and they were more likely to be arrested for juvenile violence. Child abuse predicted later violence after controlling for other predictors, such as gender, ethnicity and age, and predictability was greater for females than for males. Child sexual abuse,

and child physical abuse and neglect, predicted adult arrests for sex crimes.

Parental conflict and disrupted families

Most studies of broken homes have focused on the loss of the father rather than the mother, because the loss of a father is much more common. In general, it has been found that children who are separated from a biological parent are more likely to offend than children from intact families. For example, in the Newcastle Thousand Family Study, Israel Kolvin and his colleagues discovered that boys who experienced divorce or separation in their first five years of life had a doubled risk of conviction up to the age of 32 (53 as opposed to 28 per cent).

Joan McCord in Boston carried out an innovative study of the relationship between homes broken by loss of the biological father and later serious offending by boys. She found that the prevalence of offending was high for boys from broken homes without affectionate mothers (62 per cent) and for those from unbroken homes characterized by parental conflict (52 per cent), irrespective of whether they had affectionate mothers. The prevalence of offending was low for those from unbroken homes without conflict (26 per cent) and – importantly – equally low for boys from broken homes with affectionate mothers (22 per cent). These results suggest that it might not be the broken home that is criminogenic but the parental conflict that often causes it. They also suggest that a loving mother might in some sense be able to compensate for the loss of a father.

Other parental features

Numerous other parental features predict delinquency and anti-social behaviour in children. For example, early child-bearing or teenage pregnancy is a risk factor. Merry Morash and Lila Rucker analysed results from four surveys in the USA and England (including the Cambridge study) and found that teenage mothers were associated with low-income families, welfare support and absent biological fathers, that they used poor child-rearing methods and that their children were characterized by low school attainment and delinquency.

However, the presence of the biological father mitigated many of these adverse factors and generally seemed to have a protective effect.

In the Cambridge and Pittsburgh studies, the age of the mother at her first birth was only a moderate predictor of the boy's later delinquency. In the Cambridge study, for example, 27 per cent of sons of teenage mothers were convicted as juveniles, compared with 18 per cent of the remainder. More detailed analyses in this study showed that teenage mothers who went on to have large numbers of children were especially likely to have convicted children. Of course, it must be remembered that the age of the mother is highly correlated with the age of the father – having a young father may be just as important as having a young mother.

Implications for practice

The main implication for practice is that offending can be reduced by family-based intervention programmes that target key family risk factors, such as poor child-rearing, poor supervision and inconsistent or harsh discipline (Farrington and Welsh 2007). The most important programmes are based on parent management training and home visiting.

Parent management training is greatly influenced by the work of Gerald Patterson. His careful observations of parent–child interaction showed that the parents of anti-social children failed to tell their children how they were expected to behave, failed to monitor their behaviour to ensure that it was desirable and failed to enforce rules promptly and unambiguously with appropriate rewards and penalties. These parents used more punishment (such as scolding, shouting or threatening), but failed to make it contingent on the child's behaviour. Therefore, Patterson trained these parents in effective child-rearing methods – namely, noticing what a child is doing, monitoring behaviour over long periods, clearly stating house rules, making rewards and punishments contingent on behaviour, and negotiating disagreements so that conflicts and crises did not escalate. Parent management training, based on rewarding children for desirable behaviour and punishing them (not physically, but by 'time-out' or sending them to their room or by depriving them of things they want) for undesirable behaviour, has been shown to be effective in numerous evaluations and meta-analyses.

The most important pioneering work on home visiting was carried out by David Olds. His programme was designed with three broad objectives: 1) to improve the outcomes of pregnancy; 2) to improve the quality of care that parents provide to their children; and 3) to improve the women's own personal life-course development (e.g. completing their education, finding work and planning future pregnancies). Women on the programme received home visits from nurses during pregnancy, or both during pregnancy and during the first two years of life of their child. Each visit lasted about one and a quarter hours, and the mothers were visited on average every two weeks. The home visitors gave advice about the pre-natal and post-natal care of the child, about infant development and about the importance of proper nutrition and avoiding smoking, drinking and drug use during pregnancy. Evaluations show that this programme is effective in preventing later delinquency by the children.

David P. Farrington

Related entries

Intelligence, impulsivity and empathy; Juvenile delinquency.

Key texts and sources

Arthur, R. (2007) *Family Life and Youth Offending.* London: Routledge.

Farrington, D.P. (2002) 'Families and crime', in J.Q. Wilson and J. Petersilia (eds) *Crime: Public Policies for Crime Control* (2nd edn). Oakland, CA: Institute for Contemporary Studies Press.

Farrington, D.P. (2003b) 'Key results from the first 40 years of the Cambridge Study in Delinquent Development', in T.P. Thornberry and M.D. Krohn (eds) *Taking Stock of Delinquency: An Overview of Findings from Contemporary Longitudinal Studies.* New York, NY: Kluwer/Plenum.

Farrington, D.P. and Welsh, B.C. (2007) *Saving Children from a Life of Crime: Early Risk Factors and Effective Interventions.* Oxford: Oxford University Press.

Simons, R.L., Simons, L.G. and Wallace, L.E. (2004) *Families, Delinquency and Crime.* Los Angeles, CA: Roxbury.

FAMILY VIOLENCE

Family violence has been defined by the Council of Europe (1986) as 'Any act or omission committed within the framework of the family by one of its members that undermines the life, the bodily or psychological integrity or the liberty of another member of the same family or that seriously harms the development of his or her personality.'

The above definition incorporates all forms of violence involving physical, psychological and/or sexual threats or the use of aggression towards another. It also provides for the treatment or use of persons or property in a way that causes injury and/or forcibly interferes with personal freedom. This may be of an emotional nature (for instance, verbal or non-verbal threats of violence, suicide, destroying pets, punching walls, throwing objects, locking a person in a room) or may involve other aversive treatment (such as withholding money, food and social interaction, or corrupting and exploiting the individual involved).

Violence may occur in any family situation of a married or unmarried couple (including same-sex partners), their relatives, parents and dependants and between any adults and children who live together or continue to have relations resulting from prior cohabitation. However, family or domestic violence is usually categorized into five types: spouse abuse and child abuse (by adults), parent abuse and sibling abuse (by children) and elder abuse (by children as adults).

All types of family violence can be characterized in the same way and dichotomized into 'active' and 'passive' forms (see Table 1). Active violence involves abusive acts where anger is directed towards the victim. Passive violence refers to neglect, where anger is indirect and shown by a lack of concern for the victim and by avoiding anger-provoking interactions. Hence neglect is considered violent in a metaphorical sense in that it does not involve physical force but causes both physical and psychological injury. Victims of family violence are unlikely to be subjected to one form of maltreatment only. For example, sexual abuse and physical abuse are preceded and accompanied by psychological, emotional and material abuse. Once a victim of violence, there is a high chance of becoming involved with violence in future, either as a victim or perpetrator. This has a major impact on forensic practice. For example, court and police records in Australia, the UK and the USA show that approximately 40–42 per cent of murder or manslaughter cases are a consequence of family violence and that a third of the domestic victims are children.

Kevin D. Browne

Table 1 Two-way classification of family violence, with examples of the major forms

Physical violence	Psychological violence	Sexual violence
Active		
Non-accidental injury	Intimidation	Incest
Forced coercion and restraint	Emotional and material abuse	Assault and rape
Passive		
Poor health care	Lack of affection	Failure to protect
Physical neglect	Emotional and material neglect	Prostitution

Source: Browne and Herbert (1997).

Related entries

Anger and aggression assessment; Victim support.

Key texts and sources

Browne, K.D., Hanks, H., Stratton, P. and Hamilton, C.E. (2002) *The Early Prediction and Prevention of Child Abuse: A Handbook.* Chichester: Wiley.

Browne, K.D. and Herbert, M. (1997) *Preventing Family Violence.* Chichester: Wiley.

Dobash, R.E., Dobash, R.P., Cavanagh, K. and Lewis, R. (2000) *Changing Violent Men.* Beverley Hills, CA: Sage.

Pinheiro, P.S. (2006) *World Report on Violence against Children (United Nations Secretary-General's Study on Violence against Children).* New York, NY: United Nations.

World Health Organization (2002) *World Report on Violence and Health.* Geneva: WHO.

FORENSIC PSYCHIATRY

Forensic psychiatry is a medical sub-specialty and a branch of psychiatry. It is a growing sub-specialty in many western countries. As the core issues of forensic psychiatry are concerned with legal matters, the practice and definition of forensic psychiatry will vary from country to country. A simple universal definition is 'that part of psychiatry which deals with patients and problems at the interface of the legal and psychiatric systems.' Such a definition embraces all legal problems, including civil, mental health and criminal issues, etc.

Unlike the universal definition of forensic psychiatry given above, in Britain there is a bias towards the criminal legal system, which enables a slightly more focused and scientific definition for most areas of forensic psychiatry practice: 'the prevention, amelioration and treatment of victimization that is associated with mental disease.' The topic includes further sub-specialties, such as child and adolescent forensic psychiatry, learning disability forensic psychiatry and forensic psychotherapy, which are not dealt with here.

Key skills and knowledge

In British forensic practice, the skills of forensic psychiatry can be delineated as follows:

- The assessment of behavioural abnormalities.
- The writing of reports for courts and lawyers.
- Giving evidence in court.
- Understanding and using security as a means of treatment.
- Specialized community care.
- The treatment of chronic disorders, especially those that exhibit behavioural problems, such as severe psychoses and personality disorders.
- Psychological treatments (particularly psychotherapy) of behaviour disorders.
- The ethical management of people who pose a threat to others.

This list of skills requires a detailed knowledge of mental health law and the criminal justice system, as well as a detailed knowledge of the psychoses, personality disorders, abuses of substances and organic brain syndromes, as a basic minimum. In addition, some unusual psychiatric problems fall into the realm of forensic psychiatric practice (e.g. pseudologica phantastica, jealousy, stalking, etc.)

As society becomes more risk aversive, so various methods of risk assessment are thought to be the province of forensic psychiatry. These embrace sound clinical diagnosis and prognosis as well as specialized psychological tests.

Implications for practice

Forensic psychiatry is very much an interface discipline: its name implies an interface between psychiatry and the legal system, especially working with police officers, probation officers, prison officers and the courts. There is a very considerable overlap between forensic psychiatry and forensic psychology. Close working relationships with nurses and occupational therapists are also absolutely essential.

The range of clinical skills in forensic psychiatry has to cover the full gamut of treatment environments, from high security to other levels of hospital care and to community and outpatient work and environments (such as prisons) where the forensic psychiatrist is but a visitor.

John Gunn

Related entries

Diagnosis of mental disorder; Forensic psychology; Severe Mental illness (psychosis).

Key texts and sources

Gunn, J. and Taylor, P.J. (1993) *Forensic Psychiatry: Clinical, Legal and Ethical Issues.* London: Butterworth-Heinemann.

London Deanery (2007) *Forensic Psychiatry* (available online at **www.londondeanery.ac.uk/ careers/career-guide/forensic-psychiatry**).

Rosner, R. (2003) *Principles and Practice of Forensic Psychiatry* (2nd edn). London: Hodder.

FORENSIC PSYCHOLOGY

Forensic psychology is the application of methods, theories and findings from a wide range of areas within psychology to the contexts and concerns of criminal and civil justice. The settings in which forensic psychologists work include the police, the courts, prisons, secure units and hospitals, probation and other community-based services, and academia.

Much of the work in forensic psychology is directed towards the effective and ethical operation of agencies that are concerned with the prevention, detection, resolution or regulation of conduct that harms or threatens the rights or safety of others. As such, forensic psychologists are engaged with some of the most extreme and pressing problems in society.

An extensive knowledge base is required to support this, and this is reflected in the core curriculum for training courses accredited by the Division of Forensic Psychology of the British Psychological Society (BPS). The curriculum encompasses five main areas (in addition to research), outlined as follows:

- 'The context of practice in forensic psychology' includes psychology and criminal behaviour, the framework of the law and the criminal and civil justice systems, method-

ological issues, and ethical and professional considerations in professional practice.

- 'Applications of psychology to processes in the justice system' is subdivided into investigations, legal process, detention, throughcare and aftercare.

- 'Working with specific client groups encountered in forensic psychology' requires coverage of assessment and intervention with offenders and victims of offences (in both cases including adults and children), and applications and interventions in criminal and civil justice, such as those involving litigants, appellants and individuals seeking arbitration and mediation.

- 'Using and communicating information in forensic psychological practice' concerns approaches to assessment, criteria for professional report production, the giving of expert testimony and consultancy, project management and organizational interventions.

- 'Research methods' addresses processes relevant to the design, conduct and dissemination of research and entails familiarity with a comprehensive range of methodologies, skills and analytical techniques.

This reflection of the field can be further elaborated with reference to the division's characterization of the breadth of experience required for completion of the supervised practice stage of eligibility for chartered status. In addition to the areas indicated above, recognized 'behaviours' of concern include sexual offending, arson, violence and drugs offences; they also include such problem areas as self-injury, psychological trauma and social competence, while extending to the activities of the professional, such as decision-making, profiling in investigations and child protection. 'Characteristics' not only include sex and age but also, for example, mental illness, learning disability and personality disorder. Among the less widely known 'locations' are hostels, family courts, lifer panels and mental health review tribunals. Supervised practice also entails gaining and demonstrating competence in four 'core roles'. These are 'conducting psychological applications and interventions', 'research', 'communicating psychological advice and knowledge to other professionals' and 'training other professionals in psychological skills and knowledge'. A comprehensive picture of the field should include mention of areas of involvement that are more appropriate to the post-qualification stage. Such areas include liaison with professionals at higher levels and crisis negotiation.

It will be apparent that some parts of this body of knowledge and skills relate to the framework of the law and that some relate to the nature and procedures of particular organizations and settings. Some suggest an interface with disciplines with overlapping concerns, such as criminology and penology. Other aspects refer to fundamental competences that are to be found across psychological specialisms and that are adapted from the conclusions of the BPS's project on occupational standards in applied psychology. The influence of other branches of applied psychology may also be detected in numerous task and target areas. For example, interventions and mental disorder have a clinical resonance, and organizational interventions derive essentially from occupational psychology. While forensic psychologists have been at the forefront of innovative research and practice in areas such as intra-group aggression in secure environments, behavioural monitoring in relation to risk assessment and the evaluation of rehabilitation programmes, the knowledge bases that inform numerous areas often have their origins in other areas of the discipline. For example, the development of appropriate practice in interviewing child witnesses owes a great debt to research and theorizing in developmental and cognitive psychology. Social psychologists have highlighted the existence of popular but erroneous assumptions in attempts to detect deception. The list could go on. Forensic psychology is a field where many strands of psychological knowledge converge.

Indeed, there have been commentators who have argued against what they see as the incorrect use of the term 'forensic' and who contend that forensic psychology should not be regarded as a separate field of psychology at all. According to this view it is simply and properly the use of psychology for a function – that of facilitating legal decisions. In terms of etymology, this is correct. The Latin *forensis* refers to the 'forum', the place of judicial and other public business in ancient Rome. Proponents of this view have typically argued for the continued differentiation of 'criminological' and 'legal' psychology (concerned with psychological approaches to crime and the legal system, respectively). These comprised the original and once carefully deliberated title of what is now the Division of Forensic Psychology. Treating language with a degree of elasticity, however redolent of Humpty Dumpty in *Alice in Wonderland*, is not the primary objection. It is, for example, some time since fusiliers carried light flintlock muskets for the purpose of guarding artillery, and even the term 'clinical' in psychology is open to question as a description of the work of many of its practitioners. 'Forensic' is also less cumbersome than a concatenation of the terms it replaced, even if it invites rather misleading comparisons with forensic psychiatry and pathology.

Of greater importance is whether the umbrella term 'forensic psychology' is sustainable in terms of the coherence of the presumed field and whether it is desirable in terms of consequences. To some commentators the breadth of settings, client groups, knowledge and roles alluded to here is excessive, and their attempted integration reflects professional manoeuvring and loose thinking, while leaving the practitioner vulnerable to ethical pitfalls. Certainly, no individual could be an expert in all or even many of the potentially relevant areas. It has also been suggested that implying the contrary through a single adjectival title might be confusing to other professionals, especially those in settings such as the courts who have been accustomed to the traditional use of the term 'forensic'.

Since the BPS title 'chartered forensic psychologist' was adopted in 1993 and the division changed its name in 1999, there has been a massive increase in the employment of forensic psychologists, particularly at the pre-chartership stage. This should, however, be attributed primarily to large injections of funding to support the delivery of accredited group-based rehabilitation programmes rather than to a change of nomenclature. There has also been an increase in the number of publications within what might be regarded as the field, even though the word 'forensic' is not always used. The sense of identity of a specialized area is both reflected and brought into sharper focus by the appearance of standards for training and qualification, and these, along with appropriate infrastructures, are now established though still evolving. However, there are tensions. The expansion in employment, notably in the Prison Service, has been accompanied by a managerialist emphasis on targets and auditing, that in many places has resulted in a shrinkage of roles around those associated with the delivery of manualized, group-based programmes. In the eyes of some practitioners this has undermined opportunities for developing the versatility and synergy that, combined with an in-depth knowledge of contextual issues, previously characterized the field at its best. In secure mental health settings, on the other hand, qualified forensic psychologists have received tangible rewards based on the extent as well as the quality of their contributions.

Such developments demonstrate that, to a large degree, the practice of forensic psychology has been moulded not by formal definition but by how it has been allowed to be practised. A more consistent and proactive evolution may depend on a renewed commitment to the key elements in the 'definition' offered in the opening sentence of this entry. This would reaffirm forensic psychologists as well rounded professionals with a comprehensive range of skills and knowledge as applied psychologists, combined with specialized skills, knowledge and awareness appropriate to meeting the priorities and challenges in their particular work environments.

To illustrate, the aim of programmes in prisons is to influence behaviour: this cannot rest solely on the delivery of programmes. Future developments in a more holistic approach might include a greater willingness to recognize and act on such issues as individual differences; the sequencing of interventions; the limitations of deficit models; the influence of regime, social climate and other potential mediators of outcome; and the optimal functioning of relevant personnel and throughcare. These should be allied throughout to the traditions of careful research and effective working relationships – and to the ability to respond to the occasional emergency.

Adrian Needs

Related entries

Applied psychology; Chartered psychologists; Forensic psychiatry; Health Professions Council (HPC).

Key texts and sources

Arrigo, B. and Shipley, S.L. (2005) *Introduction to Forensic Psychology: Issues and Controversies in Law, Law Enforcement and Corrections* (2nd edn). New York, NY: Elsevier Academic Press.

Blackburn, R. (1996) 'What is forensic psychology?', *Legal and Criminological Psychology*, 1: 3–16.

Needs, A. and Towl, G. (2004) *Applying Psychology to Forensic Practice*. Oxford: BPS/Blackwell.

Otto, R.K. and Heilbrun, K. (2002) 'The practice of forensic psychology: a look to the future in the light of the past', *American Psychologist*, 57: 5–18.

Thomas-Peter, B.A. (2006) 'The modern context of psychology in corrections: influences, limitations and values of "what works"', in G.J. Towl (ed.) *Psychological Research in Prisons*. Oxford: BPS/Blackwell.

GROUP WORK

> Group work is a professional practice that refers to the giving of help or the accomplishment of tasks in a group setting.

There are three main types of group work which may have relevance in forensic settings: information-based groups, psycho-educational groups, and counselling or psychotherapy groups. Examples of information-based groups might include alcohol or drug education programmes or pre-release programmes. Pycho-educational groups tend to be structured and they combine information-giving and psychological approaches to change. They usually include some cognitive-behavioural and skills training programmes (e.g. those focused on emotion management, problem-solving or specific types of offending behaviour). Counselling or psychotherapy groups are likely to be less structured and, in particular, use the group process to facilitate understanding and change. Psychotherapy groups are likely be employed in therapeutic communities but may also form part of the treatment programme in other forensic settings. These three types of group work are, nevertheless, clearly not distinct from one another and can overlap.

Group-work approaches are employed in preference to individual approaches for a number of reasons. First, it is often assumed that they are more cost and time effective and that they enable more patients to be treated (Vinogradov and Yalom, 1994; Morrison 2001).

In fact, there is limited empirical evidence that this is the case. Tucker and Oei (2007) reviewed 36 studies regarding the comparative cost effectiveness and efficacy of group and individual cognitive-behavioural therapy and found mixed results. Secondly, group approaches utilize the impact of processes not accessible in individual work, such as group cohesion, imitative behaviour, interpersonal learning, mutual support and the potential for using group members in the therapeutic process. These non-specific factors have been shown to produce improvements in outcomes (Corey and Corey 2002), but there is little hard empirical evidence that they consistently do so or that their advantages outweigh the disadvantages of group work (Tucker and Oei 2007). Accordingly, forensic practitioners need to weigh up the cost and benefits of group vs. individual treatment in each clinical case.

Catrin Morrissey

Related entries

Nothing Works; Offending behaviour interventions; What Works.

Key texts and sources

Corey, M. and Corey, G. (2002) *Groups: Process and Practice.* Pacific Grove, CA: Brooks/Cole.

Tucker, M. and Oei, T.P.S. (2007) 'Is group more cost effective than individual cognitive behavioural therapy? The evidence is not solid yet', *Behavioural and Cognitive Psychotherapy*, 35: 77–91.

Vinogradov, S. and Yalom, I. (1994) 'Group therapy', in R. Hales *et al.* (eds) *The American Psychiatric Press Textbook of Psychiatry* (2nd edn). Washington, DC: American Psychiatric Press.

HEALTH PROFESSIONS COUNCIL (HPC)

The Health Professions Council (HPC) is a statutory body established to protect the health and well-being of the public. It provides for the statutory regulation of a group of 13 health professions.

The Health Professions Council (HPC) was established under the Health Professions Order 2001, which enabled the statutory registration and regulation of health professions (in 2006, 13 health professions were regulated by the HPC). The HPC is governed by a council made up of 26 members: one representative from each of the professions regulated and 13 lay members, plus a president. There are 13 alternative professional members who may substitute in the absence of the 13 representatives.

Four statutory committees exist to deal with conduct and competence, the health of the professionals registered with the HPC, the investigation of complaints, and the establishment and monitoring of training and education standards. These are chaired by a member of the council and they make recommendations and decisions in consultation with the council.

If a health professional does not meet the standards set by the HPC, action can be taken against him or her, which might include stopping him or her from practising. Anyone unhappy with the treatment he or she has received or who is worried about the behaviour of a health profession registrant can raise their concerns directly with the HPC, which looks at complaints to decide whether it needs to take action or not.

Hearings are usually public but may sometimes be held in private if the panel feels this is in the interests of patient confidentiality or to protect the private life of the registrant concerned. Panels are made up of a chairperson, a registrant partner and a lay member. In hearings of the health committee, or if it is felt to be a factor in a particular case, a registered doctor will also be on the panel. A legal assessor will also be present. These people, however, play no part in the decision-making process but advise the panel. Hearings are as informal as possible, with the HPC solicitor normally opening the hearing by presenting the case and calling HPC witnesses. The registrant or his or her representative may cross-examine the witnesses. The panel may then ask questions. Once the HPC case is complete, the registrant may call witnesses or make statements to the panel. If the panel decides the case is proven, it says it is 'well founded'. The HPC can impose a range of disciplinary sanctions in such cases including the option to 'strike off' registrants.

David A. Crighton

Related entries

Applied psychology; National Health Service (NHS).

Key texts and sources

See the HPC's website (**www.hpc.org.uk**).

HEALTH PSYCHOLOGY

Health psychology is a relatively new discipline in applied psychology. It was conceptualized by Matarazzo in 1980 as the 'aggregate of the specific educational, scientific and professional contribution of the discipline of psychology to the promotion and maintenance of health, the promotion and treatment of illness and related dysfunction' (p. 815).

Health psychology steps away from the idea that health and illness are caused solely by biological factors and centres itself on the bio-psychosocial model of heath and illness, first developed by Engel (1977, 1980). This approach holds that, in addition to biological factors (e.g. viruses and genetics), social (e.g. housing and social norms around a behaviour) and psychological (e.g. individual beliefs and attitudes) factors are also important contributors to health and illness. Health psychology emphasizes the 'psycho' component of the model to explore the psychological factors involved in the causes, progression and consequences of health and illness.

The key areas of research and practice in health psychology include the following:

- Understanding and predicting the beliefs, attitudes and behaviours that promote good health and developing models of health-related behaviours, together with interventions based on these.
- The psychology of disease progression.
- Beliefs about illness and treatments and relationships with caregivers.
- Stress and its impact on health and illness.
- The impact of the perception of control on health and illness.
- The role of psychology in the perception and treatment of pain.
- Quality-of-life perceptions and measurement.

The key areas of health psychology of interest in a forensic setting include understanding behaviours (such as drug and alcohol use, stress and coping); the psychology of health; and understanding stress, illness and sickness absence among Prison and Probation Service staff. Health psychologists can work with individuals, groups, in a consultancy role, in developing programmes and in writing guidelines and policies in any of these areas. Some specific examples are outlined below, but there are many more potential applications.

Models of health-related behaviours, such as the theory of planned behaviour (Ajzen 1985, 1988), have been successfully applied to smoking cessation and drug and alcohol use. The theory proposes that, if an individual has 1) a positive attitude towards the behaviour, such as giving up drugs; 2) a high subjective norm – a belief that others who are important to him or her would like him or her to give up drug taking and the motivation to comply with such wishes; and 3) high perceived behavioural control – the perception of his or her abilities to give up drug taking, – the individual is more likely to form intentions and to go on to changing his or her behaviours. Interventions can address any of the models of predictors of intention and behaviour. Health psychologists (e.g. DiClemente and Prochaska 1985) have identified four stages in changing such behaviours as smoking and drug and alcohol use. These are initiation of change, maintenance, the process of changing behaviour and coping with relapse. An individual's attitudes, perceived subjective norms and behavioural control will vary according to the stage of change he or she is in. Therefore, interventions need to address the specific needs at each stage.

Prisoners often experience very high levels of stress, coupled with low perceptions of control over their situation. It is this combination of high stress and low perceived control that can lead to psychological ill-health and the exacerbation of mental illnesses and self-harm behaviour. High levels of stress and a lack of perceived control at work have also been shown to lead to increased days of sickness absence among Prison

Service staff (Milne 2004). Health psychology has highlighted positive ways of coping with stress, such as seeking social support. The ways of coping with stress have also been linked to personality styles, with some traits more likely to produce maladaptive coping styles (such as using drugs and alcohol or engaging in self-harm) and others more likely to produce adaptive coping styles (such as rationalization, using humour or seeking social support).

Assessments can be used to target interventions to predict individuals with a propensity for maladaptive coping and to promote appropriate adaptive coping responses in accordance with their personalities. Milne (2004) used the COPE scale (Carver et al. 1989) to explore the impact of personality traits on coping styles concerned with perceived stress and sickness absence among Prison Service staff. Negative coping styles, such as denial and self-blame, were found to be associated with high levels of stress and high sickness absence. The use of humour and social support was associated with lower levels of stress and fewer days of sickness absence.

Sarah Milne

Related entries

Applied psychology; Health Professions Council (HPC); National Health Service (NHS).

Key texts and sources

Conner, M. and Norman, P. (2007) *Predicting Health Behaviour* (2nd edn). Buckingham: Open University Press.

Ogden, J. (2004) *Health Psychology: A Textbook* (3rd edn). Buckingham: Open University Press.

Walker, J. (2001) *Control and the Psychology of Health: Theory, Measurement and Application.* Buckingham: Open University Press.

HIGH SECURE HOSPITALS

The National Health Service Act 1977 (s. 4) requires the Secretary of State to provide high secure hospitals for detained mentally disordered patients 'who in his opinion require treatment under conditions of special security on account of their dangerous, violent or criminal propensities'.

There are three high secure hospitals serving England and Wales. These are Ashworth Hospital in Merseyside (est. 1933), Broadmoor Hospital in Berkshire (est. 1863) and Rampton Hospital in Nottinghamshire (est. 1914). High secure hospitals provide in-patient care and treatment in conditions of maximum security for men and women who are deemed to be a grave and immediate danger to themselves and/or to others, under the Mental Health Act 1983.

There are three main criteria to consider before deciding if those referred to a high secure hospital are suitable for admission: 1) the presence or absence of a recognizable mental disorder; 2) liability to detention; and 3) dangerousness.

The people referred may be suffering from a mental disorder or may, in some way be an appropriate focus for psychiatric attention (for example, if they have asked for treatment). To be detainable under the Mental Health Act 1983, a person must be suffering from one of the categories of mental disorder referred to in s. 1 of the Act. These are mental illness, mental impairment, severe mental impairment or psychopathic disorder. If the person suffers from psychopathic disorder or mental impairment, the Act states that he or she is only detainable if treatment is likely to alleviate or prevent a deterioration in his or her condition. The high levels of care and observation provided can only be justified when the highest levels of security are required; a lesser degree of security would not provide a reasonable safeguard to the public. It is an unacceptable infringement of a patient's civil rights to detain him or her in a higher level of security than necessary. The security available is of such a kind and degree to detain patients who, if at large, would present a grave and immediate danger to the public and who could not be safely contained in the security available at a medium secure unit.

In recent years a number of inquiries have had a significant impact on the management and delivery of services in all three high secure hospitals. In 1980 the Boynton Inquiry into Rampton Hospital highlighted the problems of professional and cultural isolation and the focus on containment rather than therapy. The Health Advisory Service made similar comments about Broadmoor in its report of 1988. Ashworth Hospital was subject to two inquiries in the 1990s. The first, chaired by Blom-Cooper in 1992, again highlighted the professional and cultural isolation of high secure hospitals and questioned the need for their continued existence in modern forensic services. The Fallon Inquiry into the personality disorder services at Ashworth (published in 1999) identified serious professional, cultural and managerial deficits, and an independent review of all aspects of physical security at high secure hospitals was recommended, resulting in the Tilt Report (published in 2000).

Since these reports, the three high secure hospitals have faced major changes. However, despite this upheaval they continue to offer an essential service, providing treatment in conditions of security not available elsewhere in the National Health Service (including new services to manage patients with dangerous and severe personality disorders).

Michael Doyle

Related entries

Forensic psychiatry; Medium Secure Units.

Key texts and sources

Blom-Cooper, L., Brown, M., Dolan, R. and Murphy, E. (1992) *Report of the Committee of Inquiry into Complaints about Ashworth Hospital.* London: HMSO.

Department of Health (1994) *Report of the Working Group on High Security and Related Psychiatric Provision* (the Reed Report). London: Department of Health.

Fallon, P., Bluglass, R., Edwards, B. and Daniels, G. (1999) *Report of the Committee of Inquiry into the Personality Disorder Unit, Ashworth Special Hospital. Vol. 1.* London: HMSO.

Tilt, R., Perry, B. and Martin, C. *et al.* (2000) *Report of the Review of Security at the High Security Hospitals.* London: Department of Health.

See also the website of the Dangerous People with Severe Personality Disorder programme (http://www.dspdprogramme.gov.uk/get_flash.php).

HM INSPECTORATE OF PRISONS

HM Inspectorate of Prisons for England and Wales is an independent inspectorate that reports on the conditions for, and the treatment of, those in custody.

HM Inspectorate of Prisons has a statutory responsiblility to inspect all prisons, as well as immigration removal centres and holding facilities on behalf of the Immigration and Nationality Directorate, and it has recently been invited to inspect regularly the Military Corrective Training Centre in Colchester. In addition, HM Chief Inspector of Prisons is invited to inspect prisons in other jurisdictions, such as Northern Ireland, the Channel Islands, the Isle of Man and some other countries.

The role of the inspectorate is to provide independent scrutiny of the conditions for, and treatment of, prisoners and other detainees, promoting the concept of 'healthy prisons' in which staff work effectively to support prisoners and detainees to reduce reoffending or to achieve other agreed outcomes. Independent inspection of places of custody is mandated in the optional protocol to the UN Convention against Torture (December 2003), which came into effect in June 2006: 'The objective of the present Protocol is to establish a system of regular visits undertaken by independent international and national bodies to places where people are deprived of their liberty, in order to prevent torture and other cruel, inhuman or degrading treatment or punishment.'

All inspections are conducted against the inspectorate's published inspection criteria ('expectations'). Expectations draw from and are referenced against international human rights standards and, as such, go beyond Prison Service and National Offender Management Service standards, service-level agreements and private sector contracts. They cover the inspectorate's four tests that provide the cornerstones to 'healthy' custodial environments and that require the safe, respectful and purposeful treatment of offenders in custody and their effective resettlement. All full inspections are carried out in co-operation with the education and healthcare inspectorates.

The inspectorate is interested in outcomes for prisoners, how those outcomes are achieved and how delivery can be improved. There are six key sources of evidence for inspection: observation, prisoner surveys, discussions with prisoners, staff and relevant third parties, and documentation. A mixed method approach to data gathering is used during inspections, employing both qualitative and quantitative methodologies. All findings and judgements are triangulated so that each area inspected is investigated using at least three evidence bases. Triangulation is used to increase the validity of the data gathered and to provide a more coherent and credible narrative of the analysis, as well as to reduce bias and limitations in the methodological approach. As a result, inspections provide a robust, independent, evidence-based assessment of conditions in prisons and of the treatment of prisoners that is recognized both nationally and internationally.

Following each inspection, inspection findings are reported back verbally to the establishment's managers. A summary is produced, with a formal assessment of the establishment's performance (well, reasonably well, not sufficiently well or poorly) against each of the four healthy prison tests. Reports detail lists of recommendations that would ensure that the prison is moving towards what the inspectorate would consider a 'healthy' custodial environment and are published within 16 weeks of inspection. The establishment is then expected to produce an action plan, based on the recommendations made in the report, within three months of publication.

The inspectorate's programme of inspection is based on a mixture of chronology and risk assessments. Full inspections of adult prisons run on a five-year cycle, which includes one full and one follow-up inspection during that period, while juvenile and immigration removal centres operate on a three-year cycle. All unannounced follow-up inspections run on a risk-assessed basis. Establishments deemed high risk are revisited for a full follow-up within 12–36 months of a full inspection to assess progress against previous recommendations, with a particular emphasis on areas of concern. Fresh healthy prison assessments are made, and an inspection report published with a full healthy prison summary. Lower-risk establishments are revisted for a short follow-up 24-36 months after their last full inspection. The previous healthy prison asessments are reassesed and a report published with a shortened healthy prison summary.

The inspectorate details the number of recommendations that are accepted and acheived following each type of inspection in its annual reports. On average, over 90 per cent of recommendations are accepted and over 70 per cent achieved (see HMCIP annual reports). This highlights how seriously establishments consider the inspectorate, as well as showing the impact the inspectorate has on improving the conditions for, and treatment of, those in custody.

Alongside inspections, the inspectorate is involved in carying out thematic work in areas that have, over the course of inspections, been highlighted as causing concern or that are in need of review due to policy or legislative changes. Recent thematics have been conducted on race relations, foreign nationals, older prisoners, extreme custody, prisoners under escort and recalled prisoners. The inspectorate also carries out cross-cutting or joint work with other criminal justice inspectorates.

The inspectorate employs approximately 40 individuals from a variety of different backgrounds: prison governors, probation officers, social workers or those who have worked in youth offending teams; those with a background in immigration law, forensic psychology, criminology or social research; and editors and administrative staff.

Julia Fossi

Related entries

HM Prison Service; National Offender Management Service (NOMS).

Key texts and sources

HM Inspectorate of Prisons (2005a) *Annual Report, 2003–2004.* London: HMSO.

HM Inspectorate of Prisons (2005b) *IRC Expectations: Criteria for Assessing the Conditions for and Treatment of Immigration Detainees.* London: HMSO.

HM Inspectorate of Prisons (2005c) *Juvenile Expectations: Criteria for Assessing the Conditions for and Treatment of Children and Young People in Custody.* London: HMSO.

HM Inspectorate of Prisons (2006a) *Annual Report, 2004–2005.* London: HMSO.

HM Inspectorate of Prisons (2006b) *Expectations: Criteria for Assessing the Conditions in Prisons and the Treatment of Prisoners.* London: HMSO.

See also HM Inspectorate of Prisons' website (**http://inspectorates.homeoffice.gov.uk/hmiprisons/**).

HM PRISON SERVICE

HM Prison Service refers to the system of public sector-managed custodial institutions in England and Wales that exists to hold individuals committed by the courts in a safe environment and thereby to protect the public. Secondly, the Prison Service aims to reduce crime by promoting law-abiding behaviour in prisoners in custody and by providing productive activities that rehabilitate and educate individuals ready for release.

Imprisonment within a government-run institution has always been a part of law enforcement. Removing a person from society is one method of enforcing laws, and it also serves to protect society from that person's offending.

Throughout history, prisons and the reasons for imprisonment have changed, and the conditions in prisons have varied, depending on society's views at the time.

HM Prison Service's role needs to evolve to meet the changing requirements of the criminal justice system and to be consistent with international human rights legislation. The primary purpose of a sentence of imprisonment is to punish the offender and to protect the public by depriving him or her of their liberty. The Prison Service's role is to keep the person in custody to help them make constructive use of his or her time in prison and to help sentenced prisoners not to reoffend.

The modern Prison Service is based on two main purposes: first, to hold individuals committed by the courts in a safe environment and thereby to protect the public; and, secondly, to reduce crime by promoting law-abiding behaviour in custody and by providing productive activities that rehabilitate and educate individuals ready for release. These functions are encapsulated in the Prison Service's statement of purpose:

Her Majesty's Prison Service serves the Public by keeping in custody those committed by the courts.

Our duty is to look after them with humanity and to help them lead law abiding and useful lives in custody and after release.

There are currently over 80,000 individuals in prison custody in England and Wales. These include adult male, young male, adult women and young women offenders. Adult male offenders are classified into one of four security categories: A, B, C or D. These categories define the severity of the individual's crime and the risk posed to the public if he should escape (in descending order). Category A, B and C prisoners are held in 'closed' prisons, whereas Category D prisoners are held in 'open' prisons. Women prisoners and young offenders or juveniles are not categorized in the same way as adult male offenders.

The origins of the modern Prison Service lie in the late eighteenth century when John Howard published a critical review of prison conditions entitled *The State of Prisons.* Prompted by this damning appraisal of British prisons and the decline in transportation to the colonies, the government at the time passed the Penitentiary Act 1779, which made the rehabilitation of criminals a function of all prisons. Since then, governments have continued to consider prisons as the main form of punishment available to the criminal justice system in England and Wales. For many years, local authorities continued to run and own the prisons within their jurisdiction, but this system changed after the Prison Act 1877. This Act brought all prisons into the remit of central government.

The Prison Commission controlled all the prisons in England and Wales until 1963, when the commission was abolished and the prisons became part of the Home Office's agenda. The Prison Service became an executive agency of the Home Office in 1993. Policy and performance targets are set by the Home Secretary, but it is the Prison Service's own management that takes responsibility for determining how best to meet them. The majority of prisons come under the control of the Prison Service, but a provision in the Criminal Justice Act 1991 means that private sector contractors can also manage prisons.

Michael Spurr and Jo Bailey

Related entries

National Offender Management Service (NOMS); National Probation Service (NPS).

> **Key texts and sources**
>
> See HM Prison Service's website (**www.hmprison service.gov.uk**).

HOMELESSNESS AND CRIME

> Homelessness, whether sleeping rough or in temporary, unsuitable accommodation, is reciprocally related to crime in a vicious circle of imprisonment–housing needs–offending.

While homelessness is typically envisioned as living on the streets and sleeping rough on doorsteps or under bridges (primary homeless-ness), legal definitions include people without settled or habitable accommodation (secondary homelessness). This wider definition makes estimates of the scale of homelessness more difficult while, in the case of primary homelessness, it is likely that street counts of visible rough sleepers greatly underestimate the true number. The charity, Shelter, worked with 4,000 street homeless during 2005, and 152,780 homeless households in England were recorded in 2005–06. These figures show a decrease in recent years, but the problem remains substantial. Like offending and criminal careers, street homelessness can be short-lived or episodic, but it may be part of a process whereby individuals become progressively disconnected from mainstream society and entrenched in a subcultural, socially excluded lifestyle.

The relationship between crime and homelessness is complex. In previous centuries, simply being homeless was the crime (vagrants were imprisoned or taken into servitude), and stereotypes still prevail of the homeless as dangerous or as a threat from which the public should be protected. Homelessness is both a cause and effect of offending behaviour, and both have shared background risk factors, including poverty, family breakdown, physical and sexual abuse, school exclusion, mental health problems, and drug and alcohol dependence. Poor housing in a deprived neighbourhood is a well-known criminogenic factor. Research indicates that most of the visible homeless are on the street involuntarily, their plight triggered by violent family arguments, relationship breakdowns, debt or eviction for non-payment.

Homelessness is integrally involved in the 'revolving gate' of short prison sentences, from which ex-offenders are released without statutory support. Several studies have drawn attention to the circular nature of the problems experienced by released prisoners, which catapult them back into prison. Inadequate housing is central in this. The association between imprisonment and homelessness is three-fold: accommodation problems precede and follow prison sentences and they accompany them. That is, according to much publicized Social

Exclusion Unit statistics: 1) one in three prisoners does not have permanent accommodation at the time of his or her sentence; while 2) those leaving prison without suitable accommodation are two or three times more likely to reoffend; and 3) loss of accommodation during a sentence is inevitable when prisoners have no means of continuing to pay their rent. This strong link between unsettled housing and imprisonment is similarly evident in an Australian study, which observed high levels of post-release 'transitoriness' and found that 59 per cent of those who moved twice or more were back in prison within nine months (Baldry *et al.* 2003). This vicious circle appears to be the outcome of a 'progressive stripping away of things that promote social attachment such as stable housing, family and social engagements each time a person is incarcerated' (Baldry *et al.* 2003: ii). Without a settled address and the basic needs it affords, the odds are stacked against obtaining employment. Moreover, the problems are cumulative. Being street homeless attracts the attention of the police and, for those who resort to survival crime, being of 'no fixed abode' decreases the chances of bail or a community sentence.

Living on the streets can lead to a criminal lifestyle. In a much praised study of youth crime and homelessness that integrates several theoretical perspectives (*inter alia* control, strain, life course) into a social capital theory of crime, Hagan and McCarthy (1997) argue that, while background factors are important, a more comprehensive causal understanding of crime committed by the homeless requires the investigation of the foreground experiences of street life that influence offending. Faced with hunger, harsh weather and becoming objects of hate, the new homeless join 'street families' and, under the tutelage of others in their networks, acquire criminal skills and are drawn further into a homeless, criminal subculture. Comparison with the responses to homeless youth in Vancouver and Toronto, in the early 1990s, indicated that aggressive policing and prosecution amplify criminal activity, whereas accommodation and employment opportunities facilitate departure from the streets.

The homeless population are also the victims of crime. Indeed, a number of studies indicate that they are 'more sinned against than sinning'. In a recent survey carried out in London, Oxford and Cambridge (Newburn and Rock 2006), 52 per cent of the 336 homeless interviewees reported that they had been victims of violence in the past year. This contrasts with 4 per cent in the general population. They seldom report such victimization to the police, by whom they feel harassed rather than protected. Further, while abuse and intimidation from members of the public are features of their everyday reality, they perceive themselves as socially invisible and separate from the rest of society. Understanding the interweave of crime and homelessness touches on great criminological debates about the relative influence of personal and structural factors. While homelessness may be viewed as a product of personal crisis or individual failure to accept responsibilities, it can be conceptualized as an outcome of inadequate housing supply and, more generally, as function of social and legal injustices. A study by Carlen (1996) found that many had been victims of serious physical and sexual abuse and, as well as seeking relief in drugs or alcohol, they resorted to the 'survivalist' behaviour of begging, theft and prostitution and received disproportionate punishments as a function of having nowhere to live. What ought to be criminalized, some argue, is the condition of homelessness or, in other words, social policies that neglect to provide vulnerable members of society with adequate housing.

The implications that may be drawn from the research are that punitive crime control strategies in addressing street homelessness are more likely to marginalize further the homeless and increase their involvement in crime, while a way back into mainstream society may best be achieved via welfare assistance and strengths-based approaches (building on the skills of the homeless by providing them with employment). Following several decades in which resettlement services for short-term prisoners were neglected, UK policy in the last five years reflects a recognition of the strategic importance of tackling homelessness in order to break the cycle of 'revolving gate' imprisonment. Among several initiatives, the Reducing Reoffending National Action Plan has accommodation as one of its seven 'pathways' out of offending, while co-ordinated resettlement provision (including housing support) is central to the integration of the Prison and Probation Services into the National Offender Management Service. Included in the same framework, voluntary sector services, such as Nacro, Shelter and Crisis, are prominent in publicizing and meeting the housing needs of ex-prisoners.

More prisoners can now access housing advice while in prison, and their housing needs are more likely to be included in early assessments of their needs. The provision of advice is still patchy, however, and insufficient resources are being given to investigating and following up often complex, unresolved housing issues. When prisoners are sent to prisons that are remotely located from their returning area – especially likely for women prisoners – the receiving prison is unlikely to have links with the appropriate local resettlement services. Homeless prisoners in England still have to demonstrate housing need to their local authorities, many of which reject applications from pre-release prisoners, despite 2002 legislation that includes prisoners among applicants with a priority need for housing. Shelter (2007) notes that this extension of priority need has had little impact: the number of ex-prisoners being accepted as having priority need is falling such that, if present trends continue, numbers will soon fall to the equivalent of one applicant per authority per year. 'Custody plus', (intended to ensure statutory supervision following short prison sentences) has been indefinitely deferred. Hence it remains the case that the majority of releasees will still lack a key worker to support their access to housing and other resources that are so vital to successful integration.

Ros Burnett

Related entries

HM Prison Service; National Probation Service (NPS); Revolving doors.

Key texts and sources

Baldry, E., McDonnell, D., Maplestone, P. and Peeters, M. (2003) *Ex-prisoners and Accommodation: What Bearing do Different Forms of Housing have on Social Reintegration?* Melbourne: Australian Housing and Urban Research Institute (available online at **www.ahuri.edu.au/general/search/**).

Carlen, P. (1996) *Jigsaw: A Political Criminology of Youth Homelessness.* Buckingham: Open University Press.

Hagan, J. and McCarthy, B. (1997) *Mean Streets: Youth Crime and Homelessness.* Cambridge: Cambridge University Press.

Newburn, T. and Rock, P. (2006) *Living in Fear: Violence and Victimisation in the Lives of Single Homeless People.* London: Crisis.

Shelter (2007) *Barred from Housing: A Discussion of the Barriers Faced by Prisoners in Accessing Accommodation on Release.* London: Shelter (available online at **www.shelter.org.uk**).

HOSTAGE NEGOTIATION

Hostages are often taken to force other people or the state to fulfil the hostage-takers' demands. Hostage negotiation tries to defuse such situations by presenting the hostage-takers with problem-solving options that might progress the conflict towards a non-violent resolution.

A hostage incident involves one or more people holding another person or persons against their will for the purpose of forcing the fulfilment of substantive demands on a third party. Typically, hostage-takers make direct or implied threats to harm the hostages if their demands are not met. These demands include things the hostage-takers cannot obtain for themselves, such as money, escape or political or social change. Bargaining techniques can be used in most hostage incidents because the authorities have something the hostage-takers want (e.g. money, transport, alcohol, the power to enforce an action, etc.).

Hostage-takers demonstrate goal-oriented, purposeful behaviour in that the hostages are used as leverage to force people to fulfil the hostage-takers' demands. While the hostages remain at risk, the hostage-takers' primary goal is not to hurt them: the hostage-takers' realize that, by keeping the hostages alive, they may achieve their goal and that, if they harm them, they will change the incident dynamics and increase the likelihood that the authorities will use force to resolve the incident.

Hostage negotiation strategies include stalling for time, lowering the hostage-takers' expectations and reversing the hostage-takers' sense of empowerment and control. Negotiators buy time using delaying tactics and by initiating give-and-take bargaining. This is done to contain the incident and to demonstrate to the hostage-takers that force will be used if necessary.

Hostage-takers initially feel in control and empowered but, as time passes, the negotiation team builds trust and rapport with the hostage-takers and convinces them that they will not accomplish their objective and that they should surrender peacefully. Successful negotiation takes time, and negotiatiors must use active listening skills in order to communicate effectively with the hostage-takers, to defuse the conflict and to work to establishing a level of rapport that allows the negotiators and hostage-takers to explore problem-solving options and to progress towards a non-violent resolution.

Martin Fisher

Related entries

Serious incidents in prisons.

Key texts and sources

Lanceley, F.J. (2003) *On Scene Guide for Crisis Negotiations* (2nd edn). Washington, DC: CRC Press.

HUMAN RIGHTS

The Universal Declaration of Human Rights states that 'Everyone shall be subject only to such limitations as are determined by law solely for the purpose of securing due recognition and respect for the rights and freedoms of others and of meeting the just requirements of morality, public order and the general welfare in a democratic society'.

The suffering and hardship of the Second World War contributed to a number of social changes, including a renewed focus on the importance of human rights. Consequently, the General Assembly of the United Nations published the Universal Declaration of Human Rights in 1948. This was followed by the European Convention on Human Rights (ECHR) in 1958, which exercises its inter-state authority through the European Commission and the European Court of Human Rights. While such conventions and declarations have subsequently been revised and refined, the underlying principles have remained largely intact.

While the UK has always been a signatory to the ECHR, it was not until the Human Rights Act 1998 came into law in October 2000 that UK citizens were afforded full protection under the ECHR. The term 'human rights' is used to cover a wide area of state procedures, policies and law that, prior to the Human Rights Act 1998, would have been referred to as 'civil liberties'. Human rights, however, encompasses those inalienable rights that are considered to exist independently of the political process, whereas civil liberties refers to limits on the government's power that are intended to protect individuals' freedoms.

Human rights have a particular resonance in forensic practice, given the various uses of state power that characterize the criminal justice process. Similarly, those in contact with criminal justice agencies (e.g. offenders and some victims of crime) tend to be economically and socially disadvantaged. There is thus a powerful combination of state power and individual disempowerment that brings human rights issues into sharp focus. Such concerns may perhaps be amplified when those who come into contact with state power are individuals with mental health problems or children and young people.

Prisoners are both socially and economically impoverished. For example, prisoners in the UK lose the right to vote, which means a fundamental part of their citizenship is removed, as well as their liberty. However, those detained or imprisoned by the state are entitled to have their human rights preserved, and it is part of the Chief Inspector of Prisons' remit to ensure the rights of prisoners are observed, whether on remand or sentenced.

The rights afforded by the ECHR are fundamental rights that should apply to all citizens. These rights range from the right to life, to the right not to be enslaved, to the right to respect for one's property. They are divided into three categories:

- First are the absolute rights (including a prohibition on inhuman or degrading treatment or punishment). It is not possible for the state to place restrictions on these rights.
- Secondly are the limited rights (relating to fair trial procedures and the right to liberty). These are qualifiable rights (for example, although the right to liberty is protected, the state is allowed to qualify this right by passing laws to allow for detention on remand or after conviction, for immigration purposes or for mental health reasons).
- Thirdly are the qualified rights. Although these rights are protected by the ECHR, the state can impose restrictions on them where this is necessary for the wider public good.

It has frequently been observed that the way a society treats its most vulnerable members is a measure of its level of civilization. Similarly, the ways forensic psychologists conduct themselves when working simultaneously with some of the most powerful institutions in society and with some of the most vulnerable client groups is a real test of their moral, ethical and professional fibre.

Graham J. Towl

Related entries

Courts; HM Prison Service; Multi-agency public protection arrangements (MAPPAs); Public protection.

Key texts and sources

Andrews, J.A. (ed.) (1982) *Human Rights in Criminal Procedure: A Comparative Study.* The Hague: Martinus Nijhoff.

Kilkelly, V. (1999) *The Child and the European Convention on Human Rights.* Aldershot: Ashgate.

Sharma, A. (2006) *Are Human Rights Western?* Oxford: Oxford University Press.

United Nations (1983) *Human Rights: A Compilation of International Instruments.* New York, NY: United Nations.

INTELLECTUAL ASSESSMENT

> Intellectual assessment examines the cognitive capacity of an individual. A clear and concise definition of this can be challenging because intelligence itself is extremely complex and because efforts continue to be made as to how it is constructed and what it consists of. Traditionally, although not exclusively, intellectual assessment has been used to help identify appropriate educational placements. Its use has been extended to job selection, identifying neuropsychological deficits and identifying appropriate rehabilitation work for such deficits. It has further been used in the sentencing of offenders.

Outside education and job selection, one of the greatest uses of intellectual assessment has been to form part of learning disability assessments, where an individual can present with significant impairments in both his or her intellectual and social functioning. Here, intellectual assessments determine the intellectual capacity of an individual and help to determine if such an individual is functioning at a superior level to others, at a broadly average level or presents with impairments in his or her functioning. In western society this has traditionally been reflected by an individual's IQ (intelligence quotient), with an IQ of below 70 being generally regarded as an intellectual impairment, although an individual would not be regarded as having a learning disability without also presenting with an impairment in his or her social functioning (such as his or her ability to live independently).

Intellectual assessment can form part of a wider neuropsychological assessment that evaluates a wide range of cognitive abilities and that considers the extent of the impairment to a particular skill after brain injury or neurological illness in an attempt to help identify the area of the brain that may have sustained damage.

Knowledge summary

Although there have been many prominent individuals who have developed intelligence tests over the years, they were first invented in 1904 by Dr Alfred Binet. This was in response to a request from the French Minister of Education at the time for a way of distinguishing the gifted, normal and challenged children in the educational system. The aim was to ensure that individual children received an education that was appropriate to their intellectual capabilities. The test Binet developed used a number to rank intelligence – namely, IQ – that could then be used to compare an individual's score with those of the general population.

From these beginnings intelligence tests have developed and progressed, and their use has extended to other domains, such as industrial and occupational assessments. As intelligence tests developed, their use often led, although not always, to detailed guidelines being produced as to their use and limitations.

In general terms, intellectual assessment forms part of cognitive functioning, which can be defined as the information-handling aspect of behaviour (Lezak 1995). This behaviour can be classified into four broad areas: receiving information (selection, acquisition and classification of information); memory and learning (information storage and retrieval); thinking (mental organization and the reorganization of information); and expressive functioning (how information is communicated or acted upon).

One of the most commonly used assessments of general intellectual capacity is the

WAIS III (Wechsler 1997). Although this is currently being updated into the WAIS IV, the WAIS III can provide a full-scale IQ that indicates where an individual falls in his or her intellectual capacity when compared with the general population, ranging from extremely low to intellectual superior capacity. As part of this assessment, the full-scale IQ can be broken down further into performance IQ and verbal IQ. These can then be collapsed into four index scores that provide more meaningful information with regard to an individual's functioning. These index scores give an assessment of verbal and visual abilities, as well as an assessment of processing speed and working memory. The index scores offer a greater depth of information as to an individual's intellectual abilities and, in this sense, should be viewed as more meaningful than simply focusing on performance, verbal and full-scale IQs.

Index scores can offer information about an individual's ability to reason and to express him or herself verbally and about his or her ability to respond to visual symbols and patterns, including novel-based learning through perceptual skills. Index scores also assess an individual's ability to process information given to him or her as well as his or her working memory (sometimes referred to as 'attention'). Working memory is a complex process that includes the ability to hold and manipulate information in the mind, to respond to a problem, to formulate a response or strategy and remain focused on a task, with a good level of concentration.

It is important to consider the limitations of intellectual assessments – for example, cultural and educational biases are not always taken into account. Similarly, such assessments do not always consider abilities outside the traditional, academic, general approach towards intelligence, although this is beginning to change now that other forms of intellectual assessment, such as emotional intelligence, are being recognized. There remains, of course the fundamental difficulty of assessing a construct that, as yet, eludes a clear definition and understanding.

Implications for practice

Providing intellectual assessments are used with a clear rationale and purpose, and with an appreciation as to their limitations, they can provide useful information. It is important to remain mindful, however, that most standard assessments of intelligence do not focus on individuals' more creative and practical aspects, which can be indicative of high functioning and good ability. Further, such assessments do not always take into account other factors that may impact on the assessment, such as cultural or sociological factors. It is also important to recognize that continuing controversy as to what constitutes intelligence and how it is subsequently measured is likely to lead to problems in efforts to evaluate an individual's intelligence. A further implication is the 'Flynn effect' (Flynn 2007): IQ scores increase over time and, thus, the norms become outdated. As yet, the reasons for such increases are unknown, but they do pose questions about the validity of intellectual assessments.

Intellectual assessments, therefore, if used appropriately, have a value, particularly in forensic settings, in engaging with, and maximizing, an individual's abilities. However, failure to explore how an individual functions cognitively or an attempt to assess his or her functioning globally rather than through more refined methods (such as focusing on full-scale IQ scores as opposed to the more specific index scores of the WAIS-III) may lead to a client being measured against unrealistic goals. This could lead to a misinterpretation of the individual's apparent failure to understand the concepts involved as treatment resistance, poor motivation or over-compliance, as opposed to difficulties in intellectual functioning.

Carol A. Ireland

Related entries

Developmental disabilities in adults; Dyslexia and specific learning disabilities; Intelligence, impulsivity and empathy.

Key texts and sources

Flanagan, D.P. and Harrison, P.L. (2005) *Contemporary Intellectual Assessment: Theories, Tests, and Issues.* New York, NY: Guilford Press.

Flynn, J. (2007) *What is Intelligence? Beyond the Flynn Effect.* Cambridge: Cambridge University Press.

Gregory, R.J. (1998) *Foundations of Intellectual Assessment.* Boston, MA: Allyn & Bacon.

Lezak, M. (1995) *Neuropsychological Assessment* (3rd edn). Oxford: Oxford University Press.

Wechsler, D. (1997) *WAIS-III Manual.* New York, NY: Psychological Corporation.

INTELLIGENCE, IMPULSIVITY AND EMPATHY

It is important to distinguish between short-term and long-term individual differences. Both influence the likelihood of a person committing a crime or anti-social act (an individual's criminal potential), but short-term individual differences are those that are transitory and specific to a given situation, such as being under the influence of drugs or alcohol or being frustrated. Long-term individual differences are stable and enduring, and they influence the likelihood of offending or anti-social behaviour over long periods of time and across many different situations. Three long-term individual differences that, it has been proposed, have an influence on offending are intelligence, impulsivity and empathy.

Intelligence

Intelligence is usually defined as one (or a set) of cognitive abilities, such as abstract reasoning, planning, problem-solving and learning from experience. Intelligence is most commonly measured with standardized tests that assess various facets of these abilities, and considerable evidence has accumulated to suggest that those who commit offences score lower on these measures than those who do not. Those who commit more serious (violent) or frequent offences have been found to score particularly low on measures of intelligence. As a rule of thumb, offenders typically score one standard deviation below non-offenders on measures of intelligence.

The nature of the relationship between low intelligence and offending is still debated by researchers. However, the fact that those who self-report offences also have low intelligence suggests that it is not simply the case that less intelligent offenders are more likely to get caught. Some researchers suggest that low intelligence and offending are directly linked – that is, offenders' poor cognitive abilities make it less likely that they will be able to formulate and enact methods of addressing and solving problems that do not involve contravening the law. Other researchers suggest that the relationship between low intelligence and offending is indirect. On this view, low intelligence leads to school failure, which in turn leads to diminished legitimate opportunities for success and an increase in exposure to similarly disenfranchised (delinquent) individuals. Evidence has been presented to support both the direct and indirect relationship between low intelligence and offending and, in reality, low intelligence probably contributes both directly and indirectly to an increased likelihood of offending.

Impulsivity

Impulsivity is one of many terms available in the literature that refers to an inability to control behaviour (others include low self-control, hyperactivity, an inability to delay gratification, risk-taking and not considering the consequences before acting). Not surprisingly given the variation in nomenclature, this construct can also be measured in a multitude of ways, such as self-reports, teacher, parent or peers' reports, psychomotor tasks and observation of behaviour. However, all versions and measurement of this construct suggest that it is related to offending. Furthermore, researchers are generally in agreement that impulsivity is one of the most important factors related to offending, and it has been included as a central feature in some of the most influential theories of crime. The relationship between most measures of impulsivity and serious, violent and frequent offending has been identified as particularly strong.

Almost by definition, impulsivity is proposed to increase the likelihood of offending because offenders act before considering the consequence of their behaviour. This includes consequences to the victim (e.g. the possibilty of material loss) and consequences to themselves (e.g. possibly being apprehended and punished). Some researchers have suggested that the influence of impulsivity may be greater among those who live in deprived neighbourhoods. The concept of impulsivity also shares some similarity with intelligence (e.g. ability to consider abstract concepts, such as the future consequences of action), and some researchers have suggested that both concepts reflect underlying deficits in executive brain functioning.

Empathy

Empathy refers to the ability to experience the emotions of another person (affective empathy) or to understand the emotions of another person (cognitive empathy). Empathy is most commonly measured by self-reported questionnaires, which record either responses to specific items or variously presented emotional scenarios (e.g. pictures, videotapes). Only recently have the questionnaires been adapted to measure both affective and cognitive empathy; much previous research, therefore, examines only one of the types of empathy.

There is a strong theoretical link between low empathy and offending (especially violent and sexual offending). Individuals are presumed to offend because they have a diminished capacity to share and/or understand the emotions of their victims. However, the empirical support for this theoretical relationship is not overwhelming. There is some evidence to suggest that offenders may have low empathy, but generally these studies have been of low methodological quality. As such it is not possible to rule out that other factors (e.g. low intelligence, low socioeconomic status) might account for the observed relationship between low empathy and offending. Furthermore, studies that would allow for the direction of the relationship between low empathy and offending to be established have not yet been undertaken. Low empathy may cause offending, but offending may just as plausibly result in low empathy.

Implications for practice

The overwhelming evidence for the impact of low intelligence and high impulsivity on offending suggests that these should be key targets for preventing offending and for intervening with established offenders. This is supported by the fact that pre-school enrichment programmes that target the thinking processes of 'at risk' children have proven to be some of the most cost-effective methods of crime prevention. Furthermore, a large number of the offending behaviour programmes that have proven most successful at reducing the reoffending of offenders target impulsivity and other cognitive skills. Empathy training is also often used as part of some offending behaviour programmes, especially those directed at violent and sexual offenders, but there is much less evidence to support their use. Substantial research, especially prospective longitudinal research (where empathy is assessed before offending), is required before empathy should be considered as salient a target for intervention as intelligence and impulsivity.

Darrick Jolliffe

Related entries

Juvenile delinquency; Intellectual assessment; Personality assessment (objective).

Key texts and sources

Farrington, D.P. (1998) 'Individual differences and offending', in M. Tonry (ed.) *The Handbook of Crime and Punishment*. New York, NY: Oxford University Press.

Jolliffe, D. and Farrington, D.P. (2004) 'Empathy and offending: a systematic review and meta-analysis', *Aggression and Violent Behavior*, 9: 441–76.

Lipsey, M.W. and Derzon, J.H. (1998) 'Predictors of violent and serious delinquency in adolescence and early adulthood: a synthesis of longitudinal research', in R. Loeber and D.P. Farrington (eds) *Serious and Violent Juvenile Offenders: Risk Factors and Successful Intervention*. Thousand Oaks, CA: Sage.

Lynam, D., Moffitt, T. and Stouthamer-Loeber, M. (1993) 'Explaining the relation between IQ and delinquency: class, race, test motivation, school failure or self-control?', *Journal of Abnormal Psychology*, 102: 187–96.

White, J.L., Moffitt, T.E., Caspi, A., Bartusch, D.J., Needles, D.J. and Stouthamer-Loeber, M. (1994) 'Measuring impulsivity and examining its relationship to delinquency', *Journal of Abnormal Psychology*, 103: 192–205.

INVESTIGATIVE PSYCHOLOGY

Investigative psychology is concerned with psychological input to the full range of issues that relate to the management, investigation and prosecution of crime. Its constituents can be derived from a consideration of the sequence of activities that constitute the investigative process. This runs from the point at which a crime is committed through to the bringing of a case to court.

David Canter coined the term 'investigative psychology' in 1990 to characterize the domain that covers all aspects of psychology that are relevant to the conduct of criminal or civil investigations. Its focus is on the ways in which criminal activities may be examined and understood in order for the detection of crime to be effective and for legal proceedings to be appropriate. As such it follows that psychological study contributes to three broad processes that are always present in any investigation: information gathering, inference and action.

More formally, then, investigative psychology is the systematic, scientific study of the following:

- Information (its retrieval, evaluation and utilization).
- Police actions and decisions (their improvement and support).
- The inferences that can be made about criminal activity (its development, differentiation and prediction).

The objective of investigative psychology, therefore, is improving criminal and civil investigations.

The first task in the investigative psychology process is the collection and evaluation of information derived from accounts of the crime. These accounts may include photographs or other records (such as bills paid or telephone calls made, possibly accessed through computer systems used by witnesses, victims or suspects). In addition there will be information from witnesses or the results of crime scene examinations. There will also be transcripts of interviews or reports from various experts. Further, there will be information in police and other records that may be drawn on to provide indications for action. Once the suspects have been identified, there is the potential for further information, gleaned either directly from interviews with them or indirectly through reports from others.

The major task of a police investigation is, therefore, typically the collection, assessment and utilization of a great variety of sources of information that provide accounts of crime. This is a task that can benefit considerably from the scientific study of human memory processes and other psychological studies of the reliability and validity of reports and their assessment. It also draws on techniques common in the behavioural sciences for distilling, summarizing and visualizing information.

The second task involves making the decisions and taking the related actions that will lead towards the arrest and conviction of the perpetrator. There has been remarkably little research into exactly what decisions are made during an investigation or into how those decisions are made. There is clearly a limited range of actions available to police officers, constrained as they are by the legal system within which they operate. From studies of human decision-making in other contexts, it is also apparent that there are likely to be many heuristic biases and other inefficiencies in the decision-making process. However, an awareness of these challenges to investigative decision-making is leading to the development of effective ways of overcoming them.

The third task (often referred to rather simplistically as 'offender profiling') is to derive inferences from the information available about the offender's characteristics that will assist the investigation. There is a growing body of research exploring the basis of these inferences. These studies have been characterized by Canter (1995) as attempts to solve the set of equations that link the actions that occur during the offence (including when and where it happened and to whom) to the characteristics of the offender (including the offender's criminal history, background and relationships to others). These are known as the A ➤ C equations (or the 'profiling equations'), where A is the actions related to the crime and C is the characteristics of typical perpertrators of such crimes. Studies of these equations have given rise to the identification of a number of aspects of criminal behaviour that are crucial to any models of inference for effective use in investigations. One important aspect of these models is that the variables on which they can draw are limited to those of use to police investigations. This implies that the A variables are restricted to those known prior to any suspect being identified. The C variables are limited to those on which the police can act. An offender's personality characteristics and detailed measures of his or her intelligence, attitudes and fantasies, therefore, are all of less use than information about where that person might be living or his or her criminal history or domestic circumstances.

All attempts to solve these equations are intended to help answer the following operational questions:

- What are the offender's salient characteristics that will help the investigators to identify and locate him or her?
- What searches of police records or other sources of information should be carried out to help identify the offender?
- Where, geographically, should searches for the offender be carried out?
- Which crimes are likely to have been committed by the same offender?
- Which suspects are most likely to have committed the crime in question?
- What sense can be made of the offence that will help to organize the legal case?

Deriving inferences to answer these questions is a complex matter. It requires managing issues of consistency and differentiation, together with development and change across a range of crimes that will vary in their degree of specialism. A number of investigative psychologists, therefore, have collaborated with police forces around the world to develop computer-based decision support systems.

Investigative psychology provides a holistic perspective on the investigation of crime, demonstrating that all aspects of the detective's work are open to scientific psychological examination. It helps police forces to to build psychological expertise into their computing capability, rather than just bringing in an expert when an investigation has reached a particularly difficult stage.

David Canter

Related entries

Police psychology; Police Service.

Key texts and sources

Ainsworth, P. (2001) *Offender Profiling and Crime Analysis.* Cullompton: Willan Publishing.
Canter, D. (1995a) 'Psychology of offender profiling', in R. Bull and D. Carson (eds) *Handbook of Psychology in Legal Contexts.* Chichester: Wiley.
Canter, D. (1995b) *Criminal Shadows.* London: HarperCollins.
Canter, D. (2005) *Mapping Murder.* London: Virgin Books.

J

JURY DECISION-MAKING

The right to trial by a jury of ordinary citizens (first developed in ancient Greece) was introduced into Britain by the Normans in the middle of the eleventh century. Trial by ordeal was abolished by the Pope in 1215 and, in the same year, Clause 39 of Magna Carta provided that 'No freeman shall be seized, or imprisoned, or disposed or outlawed, or in any way destroyed; nor will we condemn him, nor will we commit him to prison, excepting by the lawful judgement of his peers, or by the law of the land'.

In western common-law jurisdictions, qualification for jury service is usually 1) being on the electoral role; and/or 2) being a licensed driver; and/or 3) not coming under any of the categories of disqualified or ineligible persons detailed in statutory provisions. Those common law and civil law countries that have a jury system differ regarding various aspects of their jury system (such as, for example, how jurors are selected by the two sides and how far lawyers can question potential jurors). In addition, the size of the jury varies from country to country, often depending on whether it is a civil or criminal trial. Differences between jurisdictions mean that one should not unquestionably generalize findings about juror decision-making across jurisdictions.

The view that it is desirable to be tried by one's 'peers' is based on the argument that 1) it is good to be tried by a group of individuals who are representative of one's community; and 2) that 'representativeness' makes for impartial, objective, just and fair jury verdicts. The concept itself is problematic because 'trial by one's 'peers', 'representativeness' and 'impartiality' do not go together and, even if they did, they would not guarantee that a jury's verdict will be a fair one. Such arguments, however, are unlikely to be taken seriously by staunch supporters of the jury, especially, according to Cammack (1995: 407), in the USA where, historically, the jury has symbolized and embodied American democracy, and where the Supreme Court (in *Powers* v. *Ohio*) stated that 'jury service is second only to voting in the implementation of participatory government' (Cammack 1995: 483) and the right to an 'impartial jury' in criminal cases is explicitly guaranteed in the Sixth Amendment (p. 428). However, although on both sides of the Atlantic the jury has been a very controversial topic for decades and, furthermore, its use in criminal trials has been restricted, as has the requirement for a unanimous verdict (see Harman and Griffith 1979), and there have been many calls to reform it in one way or another, its existence for a long time to come is not in doubt.

Arguments in favour of the jury

Some of the main arguments in support of the jury are as follows:

- Jury service is an important civic experience: jurors discharge their duty with a strong sense of responsibility.
- A decision by a jury of one's peers is more acceptable to most defendants than the decision of a single judge.
- A jury is an antidote to tyranny. Twelve heads are better than one: unlike an experienced judge, a jury brings a fresh perception to each trial, and jurors make up in common sense and experience what they lack in professional knowledge and training.

- Jurors generally stick to the evidence and are not swayed by irrelevant considerations.
- It is not true that juries take too long to reach a verdict: jury deliberations iron out any undesirable idiosyncrasies of individual jurors.
- Unlike a judge, a jury can counter strict and unfair legal rules by deviating from them, motivated by its own social and ethical standards.
- A significant proportion of people who have attended for jury service have confidence in the jury system (for a more detailed discussion, see Kapardis 2003).

Arguments against the jury

Though not exhaustive, the following is a list of arguments that have been put forward against the jury:

- Trial by jury is not the cornerstone of the criminal justice system.
- Juries are not representative of the wider community – in some jurisdictions jury trial is almost extinct, and a jury does not give reasons, is not accountable for its verdict and deliberates in secret.
- A jury establishes no precedent.
- A significant number of jury trials end up in mistrials or there is a hung jury.
- Compared with a judge-alone trial, a jury trial is costly and time-consuming.
- Some jury verdicts reflect jurors' emotional involvement rather than rational decision-making.
- A jury can be interfered with and non-legal factors (such as inadmissible evidence and pre-trial publicity) impact on jury verdicts.
- Jury service can be a very traumatic experience.
- Jurors often lack the ability to understand and judge a legal case adequately and frequently cannot remember all the relevant facts of a case.
- Juries acquit too readily. Any form of *voir dire* (i.e. a trial within a trial to select jurors) is incompatible with both randomness and representativeness.

The arguments in favour of and against the jury make it clear that there are two conflicting views of what the function of the jury should be: 1) to return a 'correct verdict' by applying the law and on the basis of the facts before the jury; and 2) to go beyond the law and the facts of the case and to mediate 'between the law and community values' (Jackson 1996: 327). Indeed, jury verdicts can impact not only on individual defendants but also on a whole community – for example, at the end of the Rodney King trial in Los Angeles, the jury's verdict triggered riots.

Since the Chicago Jury Project of the 1950s (Kalven and Zeisel 1966; see below) stimulated renewed interest in the study of trial procedures and jury performances (Davis 1989), the jury has been a very popular research topic for psychologists, especially in the USA. For example, Devine *et al.* (2001) identified a total of 206 studies of jury decision-making from 1955 to 1999. There are very good reasons for the popularity of jury studies:

- The very nature of jury cases.
- The fact that the jury's task is clear.
- Jury studies appeal not only to cognitive psychologists interested in higher processes but also to psychologists in general.
- The symbolic importance and impact of jury decisions on ordinary people.

Comprehending evidence

Jackson (1996) reported the findings from an original study in Northern Ireland in which jurors who attended for jury service over a six-month period at Belfast Crown Court were asked to complete questionnaires regarding various aspects of jury service. Drawing on data from 237 questionnaires, it was found that, overall, jurors reported a higher level of comprehension than other trial participants - the judge, prosecution counsel, police witnesses, civilian witnesses, the accused and expert witnesses. Some 97 per cent of respondents said they understood the summing up and 84 per cent said they understood why they had been told to disregard some information.

Zander and Henderson (1994) reported that 90 per cent of the more than 8,000 Crown court jurors who took part in a national British study over a two-week period in 1992 for the Royal Commission on Criminal Justice were able to understand and remember the evidence in the 3,191 cases involved. Heuer and Penrod (1994: 536) surveyed 81 per cent of jurors in 160 trials and found that, as the amount of information in a case increased, the jurors admitted to greater difficulty in deciding the case. However, the finding from the Capital Jury Project that, while capital jurors could remember well the details about the defendant, they had difficulty comprehending and could barely recall the legal rules pertinent to their decision to impose the death penalty is rather more alarming (Luginbuhl and Howe 1995; Sarat 1995). It is therefore apparent that jurors' difficulties in understanding complex trial information could be overcome by helping them to cope with the demands placed by a trial on human information-processing abilities.

The jury foreperson

Jury studies in the USA indicate that the characteristics that predict foreperson election are high socio-economic status, being male, sitting at the end of the jury table and initiating discussion. Similarly in the UK, forepersons are more likely to be male, 40 years of age or older and in managerial, professional or intermediate occupations. However, Baldwin and McConville (1980) found no relationship between the social characteristics of forepersons and jury verdicts. The shadow jury research by McCabe and Purves (1974) similarly found that the foreperson did not seem unduly to influence jury members. The foreperson can, of course, have an effect on the outcome of the deliberation by directing the discussion, timing poll votes and influencing whether poll votes will be public or secret. The Spanish study by Arce (1995: 269) found that forepersons talked the most and, in hung juries, failed to control the deliberation, did not avoid destructive interventions, failed to be persuasive and did not inspire either authority or respect. More research, however, is needed on the foreperson to examine, for example, jury verdict and/or sentence severity as a function of the foreperson's group leadership style.

Jury deliberation

Most of the mock research into jury decision-making (see Levine 1992; Hastie 1993; Nietzel *et al.* 1999 for reviews) focuses on juror behaviour at the pre-deliberation stage in the belief that most jurors have already decided on a verdict before they retire to deliberate and that first-ballot majority verdict preferences reliably predict the final verdict. This belief can be traced back to Kalven and Zeisel's (1966) finding that, in nine out of ten juries, the deliberation task is concerned with convincing a minority of jurors to change their mind and embrace the verdict of the majority. This is referred to as Kalven and Zeisel's 'liberation hypothesis'. However, the relationship between the pre-deliberation distribution of juror preferences and jury verdict is not as simple as Kalven and Zeisel suggest. As already noted, the foreperson is another pertinent factor, and Hastie *et al.* (1983) reported that the verdict of one quarter of juries who were in a minority before deliberation ultimately managed to prevail.

We need, therefore, to distinguish between deliberations where jurors announce their verdict preferences before discussion begins (known as 'verdict driven' deliberations) and deliberations in which jurors' verdict preferences are expressed later in the deliberation process (known as 'evidence driven' deliberations). Sandys and Dillehay (1995) tested Kalven and Zeisel's 'liberation hypothesis' by asking ex-jurors what they did first, what they did upon retiring to deliberate, how much time they spent discussing the case before having their first ballot and, finally, what the outcome of the first ballot was. Sandys and Dillehay reported that, in support of Kalven and Zeisel, there is a significant relationship between first-ballot votes and final jury verdict; that in most of the trials concerned the juries spent an average of 45 minutes discussing the case before having their first ballot; and that in only 11 per cent of the trials the jurors had a ballot without any discussion taking place. They concluded that their results suggest that deliberation plays a more significant role in shaping the verdicts of real juries than was conjectured by Kalven and

Zeisel (1966) in their liberation hypothesis. The same view was expressed by Baldwin and McConville (1980) on the basis of their study.

If a jury is required to return a majority instead of a unanimous verdict, then the minority jurors will participate less and will be paid less attention by the rest of the jury. Taking a vote early in the deliberation will also speed up the process. However, jury deliberation will take longer if the jury is evidence rather than verdict driven (Hastie *et al.* 1983), but this will not necessarily result in a different verdict. Other studies of real juries have found that, the longer the retirement, the more likely it will lead to an acquittal (Baldwin and McConville 1980: 42). Osborne *et al.* (1986), however, found that, following deliberation, jurors shift to a severer decision if the jury is divided rather than in agreement. In this sense, therefore, the composition of a jury can be said to be related to its verdict.

Conclusions

The evidence discussed in this entry indicates that contradictory findings have been reported regarding jury competence and that 'scientific' jury selection, in itself a controversial practice, is not as simple and as successful in influencing trial outcome as some authors would have us believe. Inconsistent findings have been reported by experimental studies, on the one hand, and research into actual jurors on the other. Scepticism is therefore warranted when considering research findings about the relationship between juror characteristics and sentence, and juror/jury research should perhaps focus more on the interaction between juror and case characteristics. Finally, the empirical evidence casts doubt on the wisdom of having six-member juries, and the deliberation process seems to play a more significant role than was reported by Kalven and Zeisel's (1966) 'liberation hypothesis'.

Levine's (1992: 185) verdict on the American jury is that it is not representative of the public at large but does inject social values into the decision-making process. While juries find the law confusing at times and inevitably reflect the 'stains of the society', under the circumstances

juries are doing a reasonable job in deciding trials. Finally, Levine (1992) suggests that the jury 'is a good institution that could be better'.

Andreas Kapardis

Related entries

Courts; Criminal justice system; Legal profession.

Key texts and sources

Anderson, B.J., Snow, R.W. and Wells-Parker, E. (2000) 'Comparing the predictive validity of DUI risk screening instruments: development of validation standards', *Addiction*, 95: 915–29.

Gray, N.S., Fitzgerald, S., Taylor, J., MacCulloch, M.J. and Snowden, R.J. (2007) 'Predicting future reconviction in offenders with intellectual disabilities: the predictive efficacy of VRAG, PCL-SV and the HCR-20', *Psychological Assessment*, 19: 474–9.

Kline, P. (2000) *A Psychometrics Primer*. London: Free Association Books.

Walters, G.D. (2006) 'Risk-appraisal versus self-report in the prediction of criminal justice outcomes', *Criminal Justice and Behavior*, 33: 279–304.

JUVENILE DELINQUENCY

Juvenile delinquency covers a multitude of sins. As defined by the criminal law in England and Wales, it includes acts as diverse as theft, burglary, robbery, violence, vandalism, fraud, drug use and various kinds of sexual acts. However, because offenders are usually versatile rather than specialized, it is not unreasonable to analyse juvenile offenders as a group.

In England and Wales, juveniles are defined as offenders under the age of 18. The minimum age of criminal responsibility is 10. Many arrests of juveniles are followed by reprimands or final warnings rather than by appearances in the youth court. Final warnings are usually followed by community intervention programmes organized by youth offending teams, involving offenders and their families and designed to address the causes of offending.

Most research on juvenile offending is based on self-reports rather than official records. The advantages and disadvantages of official records and self-reports are to some extent complementary. In general, official records include the worst offenders and the worst offences, while self-reports include more of the normal range of delinquent activity. The worst offenders may be missing from samples interviewed in self-report studies. Officially recorded offences are only the 'tip of the iceberg'. Self-reports have the advantage of including undetected offences, but the disadvantages of concealment and forgetting. By normally accepted psychometric criteria of validity, self-reports are valid (for example, self-reported delinquency predicts later convictions among unconvicted persons).

The key issue is whether the same results are obtained with official records and self-reports. For example, if both methods show a link between parental supervision and delinquency, it is likely that supervision is related to delinquent behaviour (rather than to any biases in measurement). Generally, the worst offenders, according to self-reports (taking account of frequency and seriousness), tend also to be the worst offenders – according to official records – and the predictors and correlates of official and self-reported offending are very similar (Farrington 1992).

Prevalence

Juvenile offending is very common. For example, the 2005 Offending, Crime and Justice Survey (OCJS), conducted by the Home Office, found that 40 per cent of 16–17-year-old males reported committing at least one of 20 criminal offences in the previous 12 months, compared with 23 per cent of 16–17-year-old females (Wilson et al. 2006). According to the 2003 OCJS, 25 per cent of these males committed a property offence in the previous 12 months (compared with 10 per cent of females) and 30 per cent committed a violent offence in the previous 12 months (compared with 15 per cent of females).

Few offences are officially recorded. For example, according to the 2003 OCJS, only 7 per cent of males aged 10–17 had ever been arrested (compared with 3 per cent of females). This survey estimated that about 3,800,000 crimes were committed in England and Wales in 2002, compared with about 400,000 persons who were convicted or cautioned.

Changes with age

In general, the prevalence of offending increases to a peak in the teenage years and then decreases (see Criminal careers). There is also a change in the quality of offences. For example, the reasons given for offending up to the late teenage years are quite variable, including utilitarian ones (e.g. to obtain material goods or for revenge), for excitement or enjoyment (or to relieve boredom) or because people get angry (in the case of violent crimes). In contrast, from the age of 20 onwards, utilitarian motives become increasingly dominant.

Most offences up to the late teenage years are committed with others, whereas most offences from the age of 20 onwards are committed alone. This aggregate change is not caused by dropping-out processes or by group offenders desisting earlier than lone offenders. Instead, there is change in individuals – people change from group offending to lone offending as they get older. Burglary, robbery and theft from vehicles are especially likely to involve group offending. Generally, co-offenders are similar in age, sex and race to offenders and live close to the offenders' homes and to the locations of the offences. Juvenile offenders do not travel far to commit their offences. Co-offending relationships tend not to persist for very long – rarely more than one year.

Risk factors

Risk factors are defined as variables that predict a high probability of later offending. In order to establish risk factors, prospective longitudinal surveys are needed in which children are followed up into adulthood. For example, in the Cambridge Study in Delinquent Development (Farrington 2003a), 411 south London males were followed up from the age of 8 to the age of 48, and risk factors measured at the age of 8–10 were compared with juvenile convictions and self-reported offending between the ages of 10 and 16 (Farrington 1992). Among the most important childhood risk factors were high impulsiveness, low intelligence and low attainment, low family income, large family size, poor parental child-rearing, poor parental supervision, criminal parents and disrupted families.

In the Cambridge study, the strongest childhood predictor of later juvenile convictions was troublesome behaviour in the primary school, as rated by peers and teachers. This reflects the continuity in anti-social behaviour from childhood to adulthood. High daring (taking many risks), restlessness in class and poor concentration were also important predictors of official and self-reported delinquency. A combined measure of hyperactivity–impulsivity–attention deficit (HIA) predicted juvenile convictions independently of conduct problems at the age of 8–10, showing that HIA is a possible cause of delinquency rather than a measure of anti-social tendency. Low non-verbal IQ (measured by Raven's progressive matrices), low verbal IQ (vocabulary, word comprehension, verbal reasoning) and low school attainment were all highly correlated and all predicted later juvenile convictions and self-reported offending (see also Intelligence, impulsivity and empathy).

Many family factors measured at the age of 8–10 predicted juvenile official and self-reported offending. The strongest predictors were having a convicted parent or a delinquent sibling by the tenth birthday. Unlike most early precursors, a convicted parent was not particularly related to very early onset offending (age 10–13), but it did predict which juvenile offenders went on to become adult criminals. Large family size (four or more siblings) and low family income were also important predictors. Just as juvenile offenders tended to come from low-income families, they also tended to have unskilled manual jobs and an unstable job record at the age of 18.

In the Cambridge study, poor parental supervision and poor child-rearing (a combination of harsh and erratic parental discipline, cold and

rejecting parental attitudes and parental conflict) were important risk factors for juvenile official and self-reported delinquency. Poor child-rearing was related to early onset offending and was not characteristic of those first convicted in adulthood. Broken homes and early separations (lasting more than one month and not caused by death or hospitalization) also predicted juvenile convictions and self-reported delinquency (see also Family factors).

Having delinquent friends is also an important risk factor for delinquency. However, it is not clear whether 'birds of a feather flock together' or whether delinquent friends cause offending. Attending a high delinquency-rate school is also an important risk factor, but in the Cambridge study this primarily reflected selection effects (the most troublesome boys going to the worst schools). Living in an inner-city area characterized by physical deterioration, neighbourhood disorganization and high residential mobility is also important, but again it is unclear whether bad neighbourhoods cause offending or whether anti-social people disproportionately choose to live (or are allocated to live) in the worst neighbourhoods.

Correlates of delinquency

In the Cambridge study, the boys who were convicted up to the age of 18 were significantly more deviant than the non-offenders on almost every factor that was investigated at that age. The convicted delinquents drank more beer, got drunk more often and were more likely to say that drink made them violent. They smoked more cigarettes, they started smoking at an earlier age and they were more likely to be heavy gamblers. They were more likely to have been convicted for minor motoring offences, to have driven after drinking at least 10 units of alcohol (e.g. 5 pints of beer) and to have been injured in road accidents. The delinquents were more likely to have taken prohibited drugs, such as marijuana or LSD, although few of them had convictions for drug offences. They were also more likely to have had sexual intercourse, especially with a variety of different girls, and especially beginning at an early age, but they were less likely to use contraceptives. They were more likely to be living away from home and they tended not to get on well with their parents. They were also more likely to express aggressive and anti-establishment attitudes on a questionnaire (negative to police, school, rich people and civil servants).

Similar results were obtained in the 2005 OCJS. Offenders aged 10–15 tended to have been drunk at least once a month and to have taken drugs in the previous 12 months, tended to have been suspended or expelled from school, were more likely to approve of criminal acts and spent little or no time with their parents or guardians.

Delinquency (which is dominated by crimes of dishonesty) seems to be one element of a larger syndrome of anti-social behaviour that arises in childhood and usually persists into adulthood. In the Cambridge study, a scale of 'anti-social tendency' was developed at the age of 18, based on such factors as an unstable job record, heavy gambling, heavy smoking, drug use, drunk driving, sexual promiscuity, spending time hanging about on the street, anti-social group activity, violence and anti-establishment attitudes. The aim was to devise a scale that was not based on the types of acts (thefts and burglaries) that predominantly led to convictions, and it was found that the convicted males were usually anti-social in several other respects. For example, two-thirds (67 per cent) of those convicted up to the age of 18 had four or more of these anti-social features at that age, compared with only 15 per cent of the unconvicted males.

Implications for practice

A major implication for practice is that juvenile offending could be prevented by targeting key risk factors (see Farrington and Welsh 2007). Individual factors, such as high impulsiveness and low attainment, can be tackled using cognitive-behavioural skills training programmes and pre-school intellectual enrichment programmes. Family factors, such as poor supervision and erratic discipline, can be tackled using parent management training and home-visiting programmes for pregnant women. Cost-benefit analyses show that these kinds of programmes save much more money than they cost. Prevention is better than cure. It is more effective to fence off the top of the cliff than to have an ambulance at the bottom to deal with those who fall off.

David P. Farrington

Related entries

Criminal careers; Family factors; Intelligence, impulsivity and empathy.

Key texts and sources

Farrington, D.P. (1992) 'Juvenile delinquency', in J.C. Coleman (ed.) *The School Years.* London: Routledge.

Farrington, D.P. (2003a) 'Key results from the first 40 years of the Cambridge Study in Delinquent Development', in T.P. Thornberry and M.D. Krohn (eds) *Taking Stock of Delinquency: An Overview of Findings from Contemporary Longitudinal Studies.* New York, NY: Kluwer/Plenum.

Farrington, D.P. and Welsh, B.C. (2007) *Saving Children from a Life of Crime: Early Risk Factors and Effective Interventions.* Oxford: Oxford University Press.

Rutter, M., Giller, H. and Hagell, A. (1998) *Antisocial Behaviour by Young People.* Cambridge: Cambridge University Press.

Wilson, D., Sharp, C. and Patterson, A. (2006) *Young People and Crime: Findings from the 2005 Offending, Crime and Justice Survey.* London: Home Office (available online at www.home office.gov.uk/rds).

L

LEGAL PROFESSION

> The legal profession is the body of individuals who are qualified to practise law within the jurisdiction. In England and Wales there are essentially two types of lawyer that populate the profession: solicitors and barristers.

Lawyers must either have undertaken an undergraduate law degree or a one-year postgraduate diploma in law before commencing the practical components of their training. To become qualified, solicitors must complete a one-year Legal Practice Course before undertaking a two-year training period in practice with a firm. Barristers must undertake a one-year Bar Vocational Course. A further year of pupillage training entitles the barrister to practise independently thereafter.

The Inns of Court are responsible for the education of barristers and they oversee admission into the profession. The General Council of the Bar (the 'Bar Council') undertakes representation and provides services for members of the Bar. The Bar Standards Board, a part of the Bar Council, independently regulates standards of practice at the Bar in the public interest.

Solicitors work directly with their lay clients and provide legal advice and representation. Solicitors engage barristers for specialist legal advice in the preparation of legal pleadings and for the conduct of oral advocacy before the courts. Barristers, unlike solicitors, have full rights of audience to appear before any court in the jurisdiction. Solicitors have rights of audience but not for the high court, court of appeal or the House of Lords Judicial Committee.

They may, however, become certified solicitor advocates, subject to further training, and thus appear before the higher courts. Equally there are provisions for barristers to cross over and qualify as solicitors.

Solicitors are supervised, regulated and represented by the Law Society of England and Wales. The Law Society sets the standards for qualification, the rules of professional practice and disciplinary matters relating to compliance with those rules.

Legal executives form a third group of qualified lawyers who carry out work in particular areas of law, similar to that of a solicitor. Their training comprises less academic legal study. Legal executives are supervised and regulated by the Institute of Legal Executives.

Forensic psychologists may be called upon by solicitors or barristers to provide expert opinion in contemplation of litigation in a range of civil and criminal matters.

S. George Blom-Cooper

Related entries

Adversarial system; Courts; Criminal Justice System; Crown Prosecution Service (CPS).

Key texts and sources

Abel, R.L. (1989) T*he Legal Profession in England and Wales.* London: Blackwell (pp. 116, 127 and 243–9).

See also the following websites: http://www.barcouncil.org.uk; http://www.lawsociety.org.uk/home. law; and http://www.dca.gov.uk/consult/general/ rofa/annexb.htm.

MEDIUM SECURE UNITS (MSUs)

> Medium secure units (MSUs) provide 'care delivered in a hospital or healthcare NHS Trust aimed at providing a level of security suitable for public protection'. MSUs admit patients who represent a serious but not immediate risk to the public – patients considered a grave or immediate danger are held in high secure hospitals. MSUs do not form part of the prison system, even though MSU patients will often have been involved in court proceedings.

Medium secure units (MSUs) provide patients with an intensive level of psychiatric care in a secure environment, with sufficiently lengthy admissions to ensure that mental health problems are assessed and treated and that the patient's risks are assessed and managed or reduced through treatment. Some patients are transferred from prisons for a period of treatment and subsequently return to prison to complete their sentences. Those who are to return to the community or to a lower secure psychiatric service, on the other hand, usually progress through a programme of graduated community leaves to establish that they can be safely transferred. MSUs are staffed by multidisciplinary mental health teams consisting of consultant psychiatrists, psychiatric nurses, occupational therapists, psychologists, social workers and other professionals.

All MSUs have physical security features to contain patients safely within the building and its immediate grounds. Security is also maintained through procedural and relational factors. Procedural security refers to such practices as restricting or banning patients' access to certain items, searching patients and visitors, observation procedures and high staff to patient ratios. Relational security, which is often considered the most effective type of security, is based on having sufficient competent staff to provide good staff–patient relationships, to allow the accumulation of knowledge and understanding about the patients and to permit the continuous assessment of behaviour and mental state.

There are approximately 50 MSUs in England and Wales (in both the National Health Service and independent sectors) varying in size from 145 to 8–10-bed specialist units. Units have their own policies regarding acceptable patient groups. Commonly, admission policies are defined by gender or primary diagnosis. There are also specialist MSUs to address the needs of particular groups that are often excluded by other services (e.g. patients with a primary diagnosis of personality disorder). Some MSUs accept both males and females, although current best practice recommends single-sex units. Some 59 per cent of MSU patients have primary diagnoses of such psychotic conditions as schizophrenia (Meltzer and Tom 2000). Patients frequently have a concurrent diagnosis of substance misuse or personality disorder, and approximately 20 per cent of MSU patients have primary diagnoses of personality disorder.

The main sources of referrals to medium secure care are the prison or court system (approximately two thirds), special hospitals (high secure), National Health Service psychiatric hospitals and, infrequently, the community. Common reasons for referrals include the discovery of a mental health problem during judicial proceedings or in prison, a deterioration in mental state, aggressive behaviours in other settings and non-compliance with treatment. Most patients stay about two years (some up to four or five years), although many units – especially in the independent sector – have no specified maximum length of stay.

Julie Parker

Related entries

High security hospitals; National Health Service (NHS).

Key texts and sources

Department of Health and Ministry of Justice (2007) *Standards for Medium Secure Units.* London: Health Offender Partnerships, Department of Health.

Meltzer, D. and Tom, B. (2000) *Pathways into Medium Secure Psychiatric Provision in England and Wales.* Cambridge: Mental Healthcare Policy Research Group (available online at **www.phpc.cam.au.uk**).

Royal College of Psychiatrists (2007) *Supplementary Standards for Medium Secure Units.* London: Centre for Quality Improvement, Royal College of Psychiatrists.

See also the Royal College of Psychiatrists' website (**www.rcpych.ac.uk**).

MENTAL DISORDER INTERVENTIONS

The term 'mental disorder' has a general meaning in common parlance, a specific meaning in medical diagnoses and an additional meaning under the law. In common parlance 'mental' is taken to imply a disorder of the mind – an upset of health, an ailment or a deviation from the normal system or order. A similar broad stance is adopted in the Mental Health Act 2007, where mental disorder is described as 'any disorder or disability of mind.'

There are two principal classificatory systems that provide a structured framework within which to diagnose mental disorders. One is the *Diagnostic and Statistical Manual of Mental Disorders*, produced by the American Psychiatric Association (commonly referred to as the *DSM-IV*); the other is the *Classification of Mental and Behavioural Disorders*, produced by the World Health Organization (commonly referred to as the *ICD-10*). These systems offer a different classification and terminology but, in broad terms, they recognize a similar range of mental disorders.

It is acknowledged in the *DSM-IV* and, similarly, in the *ICD-10* that no definition of mental disorder adequately specifies precise boundaries. However, a definition must be attempted in order to demonstrate how decisions have been reached regarding the inclusion or exclusion of conditions as mental disorders. In the *DSM-IV*, mental disorder is conceptualized as a clinically significant behavioural or psychological syndrome or as a pattern that occurs in a person associated with distress (a painful symptom), disability (impairment in one or more important areas of functioning) or a significantly increased risk of suffering death, pain, disability or loss of freedom. In addition, this syndrome or pattern must not be merely an expectable response to a particular event (e.g. the death of a loved one). Whatever its original cause, it must currently be considered to be a manifestation of a behavioural, psychological or biological dysfunction in the person. Neither deviant behaviour (e.g. political, religious or sexual) nor conflicts primarily between the individual and society are mental disorders, unless the deviance or conflict is a symptom of a dysfunction.

The outcome of this difficulty in defining a mental disorder is that a vast range of conditions, ranging from learning disabilities, developmental difficulties, dementia, organic brain damage, psychosis, mood, anxiety, sleep difficulties and behaviours of various types to personality, may, according to the presenting symptoms, be classified as a mental disorder. A link, however, is recognized between the social circumstances and the condition in many mental disorders. To accommodate this diversity of conditions, a multi-axial approach has been developed. For example, in the *DSM-IV*, Axis I covers clinical syndromes and conditions; Axis II covers developmental and personality disorders; Axis III covers physical disorders; Axis IV covers the severity of psychosocial stressors;

and, finally, Axis V covers the global assessment of functioning.

A number of points should be considered in respect of mental disorder interventions. First, diagnoses are categorical: the individual either has the disorder or does not. Secondly, diagnoses are medical, and mental disorders are not discrete entities – they can overlap with each other and one individual may have several disorders. Thirdly, within a disorder (e.g. depression) the range and severity of symptoms can vary enormously. Fourthly, in the majority of disorders an underlying physiological cause may be hypothezised (e.g. an imbalance in neurotransmitters), but may not be measurable at the time. Finally, mental disorders have known prevalence rates in the general population but there may be different prevalence rates in forensic populations. Particular disorders, however, are not unique to offenders.

Interventions to assist patients who are suffering from mental disorders have historically included a wide range of approaches and they continue to do so today (for example, such, psychosurgical procedures as electroconvulsive therapy (ECT). While the full spectrum of psychological therapies is still utilized, the most prevalent intervention today is medication targeted at improving a hypothesized, but not directly measured, deficit in neurological functioning.

The effectiveness of such a broad spectrum of interventions can be measured in only the most general of terms. Indeed, some psychosurgical interventions have been discontinued due to inconsistent results and negative side-effects, and ECT remains a somewhat controversial treatment even though it does appear to produce a rapid and significant improvement in some of the most severely depressed patients. The repeated use of ECT, however, can lead to a loss of memory. Similarily, modern anti-psychotic medications produce very worthwhile reductions in primary symptoms, but some residual symptoms may remain and a variety of side-effects need to be monitored. The effectiveness of drug treatments generally varies greatly in relation to the particular disorder, the drug used, how the individual responds and situational pressures impinging on the individual at the time.

Interventions are often implemented in combination and are delivered by a multidisciplinary team, including psychologists. A severely depressed patient may, for example be given ECT, medication of different types and cognitive-behavioural therapy (see the websites of the National Institute for Clinical Excellence, the Cochrane Library, the Centre for Evidence Based Mental Health and Clinical Evidence (the *British Medical Journal*) for useful references about what does and does not work). Cognitive and cognitive-behavioural therapies are the psychological interventions that have the most powerful evidential support (e.g. in treating depression, anxiety, obsessional compulsive disorders, post-traumatic stress disorders, and personality disorders, to name but a few). It is, however, regrettable that, in spite of the evidence of their effectiveness, these psychological therapies are currently in very short supply in the National Health Service (NHS).

Mental disorders are seldom simply cured as a result of an intervention. In the majority of cases the usual outcome is that interventions produce an elimination or alleviation in symptomatology and assist individuals in coping more effectively with their everyday lives and with their vulnerability to relapse. Psychology has a particularly relevant role in improving the adaptive functioning of mentally disordered patients, and an alliance with psychiatry towards this objective is crucial.

Implications for practice

The implications for practice are perhaps best illustrated in forensic settings by the repeated claims that a large proportion of the offender population has mental health difficulties. While it is undoubtedly the case that the frequency of mental disorder is higher in offending populations relative to the general population, the proportion suffering from a serious mental disorder that would lead to treatment by the NHS remains low. Further, mental disorder is not a major cause of crime – such instances of this are rare but often attract media attention when they do occur. The real roots of criminal behaviour, for most offenders, lie in their deprived and conflictual social learning, not in their health.

Offending lifestyles are stressful, often associated with a lack of structure and are sometimes influenced by chronic substance misuse. Mental health difficulties can develop as a reaction to this type of lifestyle.

Psychologists should be wary of abandoning a rich psychological language comprising traits, states and continua and replacing this with the more categorical language of diagnosis. What is needed in the forensic field is a strong partnership between two independent professions – psychiatry and psychology – within which offenders who are unwell or who present with psychological difficulties are assessed as individuals regarding their views, motivation, suitability for different interventions, what drives their offending and the precipitants of their ill-health or psychological difficulty, if any. Psychiatrists would lead on some interventions; other interventions would be developed on a joint basis; and psychologists would lead on yet others. Similarly, some offenders would be recognized as rejecting either psychiatric or psychological support.

The most important implication, therefore, might be to leave psychiatric diagnosis and medical treatments to psychiatry. This is not easy in practice – first, because the term 'mental disorder' encompasses much that is psychological (e.g. personality); and, secondly, because a strong evidence base exists that indicates the effectiveness of psychological interventions (particularly cognitive and behavioural interventions) in treating many mental disorders and even some physical disorders. The real challenge for psychologists, therefore, is to deliver, on a far more extensive and reliable basis than is currently the case, those interventions that research has indicated to be the most effective. Psychologists working in forensic mental health need to be knowledgeable about what works in treating mental disorders, about risk assessment, risk management and interventions. The best results will be achieved in close partnership with psychiatry, where psychology does not lose its independence as a profession, its rich language or its preference for case formulation/conceptualization rather than diagnosis.

Finlay Graham and Graeme Richardson

Related entries

Applied psychology; Diagnosis of mental disorder; Forensic psychiatry.

Key texts and sources

American Psychiatric Association (1994) *Diagnostic and Statistical Manual of Mental Disorders (Fourth Edition) DSM-IV*. Washington, DC: American Psychiatric Association.

Gunn, J. and Taylor, P.J. (2001) *Forensic Psychiatry*. London: Butterworth Heinemann.

Tarrier, N., Wells, A. and Haddock, G. (eds) (1998) *Treating Complex Cases: The Cognitive Behavioural Therapy Approach*. Chichester: Wiley.

World Health Organization (1992) *The ICD-10 Classification of Mental and Behavioural Disorders (Clinical Descriptions and Diagnostic Guidelines)*. Geneva: World Health Organization.

See also the websites of the National Institute for Clinical Excellence (www.nice.org.uk), the Cochrane Library (www.cochrane.org), the Centre for Evidence Based Mental Health (www.cebmh.com) and Clinical Evidence (www.clinicalevidence.com).

META-ANALYSIS

A meta-analysis is a scientific method for integrating the empirical evidence on a specific topic in a systematic, representative and transparent manner by using quantitative techniques.

Meta-analysis is not a single method but a perspective with various techniques of measurement and statistical analysis (Cooper and Hedges 1994). These have been developed to overcome weaknesses in narrative literature reviews. In particular, meta-analyses should be less biased by the reviewers' personal preferences for specific methods, studies and findings. However, there is no dichotomy between meta-analyses and other methods of research synthesis (for example, antecedents have computed the proportion of significant findings ('vote counting') or mean correlations in a field). Since the late 1970s, meta-analyses have become widely applied in many disciplines, on many topics and in many types of studies (e.g. correlative or interventional). In forensic psychology, meta-analyses have been carried out, for example, on evaluations of offender rehabilitation, the prediction of recidivism, the effects of family and child-oriented crime prevention, the reliability of eyewitnesses, the accuracy in police line-up presentations, the validity of paraverbal indicators of deception and the effects of jury size.

Although meta-analyses differ in methodological details, they normally include the following procedures.

Precise definition of the respective topic

At the beginning of a meta-analysis, the research question has to be clearly described. This leads to criteria for the inclusion and exclusion of primary studies. For example, a meta-analysis on the effects of correctional treatment should formulate such eligibility criteria as the population of offenders, the modes of treatment, outcome criteria and the quality of the evaluation design required. Inclusion criteria can be more restrictive when there is a sufficiently large population of relevant primary studies.

Systematic search for primary studies

Based on the inclusion criteria, meta-analyses apply a systematic strategy to retrieve all eligible studies. This step contains a transparent process for searching literature databases, as well as relevant journals, previous review articles, primary studies and other sources of information. As a 'publication bias' favours positive findings, it is important to include not only published studies but also unpublished dissertations and research reports or information from websites. In a worldwide synthesis, the search procedure should not be restricted to English language publications only.

Coding of information on the single studies

All studies that fulfil the inclusion criteria are coded according to systematic categories. This refers to general study features (e.g. year and source of publication) and characteristics of the content. In a meta-analysis on offender treatment, for example, such categories address the characteristics of samples (e.g. sample size, age, offence history), interventions (e.g. mode of treatment, frequency of sessions, quality of programme delivery) and the measurement of outcomes (e.g. archival data, self-reports, length of follow-up). To secure reliability, coders need to be trained and inter-coder agreement needs to be assessed.

Evaluation of methodological quality

Although all studies need to meet the benchmark for eligibility, research designs may vary substantially. In evaluations of offender treatment, for example, control group studies may be randomized experiments or quasi-experiments with different levels of equivalence in control groups. Some meta-analyses apply general ratings of methodological quality, such as the Maryland Scale of Methodological Rigour (Sherman *et al.* 2002). Other approaches address not only internal/experimental validity but also issues of statistical, external, construct and descriptive validity (Lösel 2007).

Computation and integration of effect sizes

All reported outcomes of the primary studies are transferred into a comparable metric of effect size. Depending on the research question and the type of studies, one may use correlation coefficients, Cohen's *d* (mean differences between treatment and control group divided by pooled variances), odds ratios or other suitable indicators (Hedges and Olkin 1985). Effect sizes are computed for each measure of outcome in each primary study. However, when these are integrated to estimate the overall effect, studies with numerous outcome measures would be over-weighted. Therefore, many meta-analyses compute a study effect size (i.e. a mean of all effects within each primary study). These are then integrated with the other studies by computing a mean effect, its significance and confidence limits. Studies are weighted by their sample size, and a fixed or random model of integration may be applied depending on the diversity of outcomes across studies (Lipsey and Wilson 2001). To avoid an inappropriate impact of a few extreme findings, a sensitivity analysis should be carried out.

Analysis of relations between study characteristics and effect sizes

In addition to the estimation of an overall effect, meta-analyses aim to explain the differences in outcomes between studies. Typical moderators are characteristics of the studies' design (e.g. randomization), interventions (e.g. treatment mode), samples (e.g. offender risk level) and outcome measurement (e.g. length of follow-up). Moderator analyses require heterogeneity in the outcomes of single studies that is not due to sampling error. They bear the risk of fishing for significance in a pool of numerous variables. The detection of moderating effects is often complicated by confounded variables (Lipsey 2003). Hierarchical regression techniques with various moderators can help to disentangle some of these influences. However, there are basic limits to moderator analyses due to the small numbers of studies with specific characteristics.

Presentation of findings

All meta-analytic procedures and findings should be presented as transparently as possible. This includes information on the eligibility criteria, search processes, coding system and lists of studies included or excluded. As in single studies, meta-analyses require an appropriate interpretation of findings. This should be based on sound theoretical concepts and should avoid too much speculation about relatively weak moderator effects. The discussion should also address blind spots in the current research.

Meta-analyses can only be carried out if there are a sufficient number of similar studies on the respective topic. They also require a good description of the details of the primary studies that form the units of analysis. In principle, meta-analyses face the same problems of objectivity, reliability and validity as primary research. They also contain numerous decisions of the respective reviewers. For example, two meta-analyses on the same topic may differ in the definition of the research question, the eligibility criteria, the categories for coding, the statistical integration of outcome measures, the applied statistical models, the selection of moderators

and other procedures. Therefore, one should be aware that even a very thorough meta-analysis does not provide the one and only 'truth' about the evidence in a field. It is, therefore, meaningful to conduct and compare various research syntheses on the same topic. As with meta-analyses, such higher-order integrations should be carried out by independent researchers.

Friedrich Lösel

Related entries

Evidence based practice; Nothing Works; Offending behaviour interventions; What Works.

Key texts and sources

Cooper, H.M. and Hedges, L.V. (eds) (1994) *The Handbook of Research Synthesis.* New York, NY: Russell Sage Foundation.

Hedges, L.V. and Olkin, I. (1985) *Statistical Methods for Meta-analysis.* New York, NY: Academic Press.

Lipsey, M.W. (2003) 'Those confounded moderators in meta-analysis: good, bad, and ugly', *Annals of the American Academy of Political and Social Science*, 587: 69–81.

Lipsey, M.W. and Wilson, D.B. (2001) *Practical Meta-analysis.* Thousand Oaks, CA: Sage.

Lösel, F. (2007) 'Doing evaluation in criminology: balancing scientific and practical demands', in R.D. King and E. Wincup (eds) *Doing Research on Crime and Justice* (2nd edn). Oxford: Oxford University Press.

Sherman, L.W., Farrington, D.P., Welsh, B.C. and MacKenzie, D.L. (eds) (2002) *Evidence-based Crime Prevention.* New York, NY: Routledge.

MORAL REASONING

Moral reasoning (based in the cognitive-developmental tradition in psychology) refers to the way in which people reason about, and justify, their behaviour.

Jean Piaget was the first psychologist to consider moral reasoning in his research examining how young children understand the world around them (1932). Lawrence Kohlberg (1984) further developed this work into a theory of the development of moral reasoning, in which moral judgements are constructed through an individual's social experiences. This theory, therefore, focuses on the structure of moral reasoning (i.e. why a behaviour is right or wrong) rather than on the content of moral values (i.e. what is right or wrong).

Since Kohlberg first outlined his theory, one of the main areas that moral reasoning research has examined is offending behaviour and its association with the level and maturity of moral reasoning.

Moral reasoning theory

Kohlberg's theory comprised six stages of moral reasoning that individuals progress through, with each stage becoming more abstract and complex than the previous one. This progression is underpinned by developments in more general cognitive abilities, particularly social perspective-taking. Gibbs (2003) has revised Kohlberg's work, however, placing a greater emphasis on the role of perspective-taking in moral reasoning. This revision is a four-stage theory of 'sociomoral' reasoning that incorporates the first four stages of Kohlberg's theory:

- Stage 1 (unilateral and physicalistic): moral reasoning refers to figures of authority (e.g. parents) and the physical consequences of behaviour. Little or no perspective-taking ability is shown.
- Stage 2 (exchanging and instrumental): moral reasoning begins to include a basic understanding of social interactions. This tends to refer to cost/benefit deals, with the individual's own interests being paramount.
- Stage 3 (mutual and prosocial): moral reasoning shows an understanding of interpersonal relationships and the associated norms/expectations. Empathy and social perspective-taking inform reasoning. Appeals are also made to one's own conscience.
- Stage 4 (systemic and standard): moral reasoning shows an understanding of complex social systems, with references made to the requirements of society, basic rights and values, and character/integrity.

Stages 1 and 2 reflect immature moral reasoning, whereas Stages 3 and 4 reflect mature

moral reasoning. Gibbs et al. (1995: 44) also note that mature moral reasoning reflects 'the cognitive-structural norm for any culture', such as a society's formal laws and informal beliefs and values.

Gibbs (2003) also outlined how certain cognitive distortions may contribute to the use of moral reasoning from the immature stages to beyond early adolescence. Having an egocentric bias is proposed as the primary cognitive distortion. Egocentricity is a key aspect of reasoning at the immature moral reasoning stages, and is also characteristic of young children's reasoning. However, egocentricity usually decreases with age as social perspective-taking abilities improve. However, if this 'decentration' does not occur, individuals will not have the social perspective-taking skills required to progress to the mature stages of moral reasoning (Stages 3 and 4).

Gibbs (2003) then described three secondary cognitive distortions that are used to justify the behaviours that can result from having an egocentric bias:

- Assumption of the worst: a tendency to interpret ambiguous events/actions as hostile towards oneself.
- Blaming others: a tendency to avoid taking responsibility for oneself, for one's behaviour and for the consequences, preferring instead to blame other people or external events (e.g. being drunk).
- Mislabelling of one's behaviour/minimization of consequences: in order to reduce any negative feelings, such as regret or guilt.

Moral reasoning and offending

When moral reasoning theory is applied to offending as a specific behaviour, it is possible to justify offending at each of the stages:

- Stage 1: offending can be justified if punishment is avoided.
- Stage 2: offending can be justified if the benefits/rewards outweigh the risks/costs.
- Stage 3: offending can be justified if it helps maintain friendships or close relationships.
- Stage 4: offending can be justified if it is sanctioned by a social institution (e.g. religion) or helps to uphold society.

However, although offending can be justified at all four stages of moral reasoning, the conditions in which offending would be justified are more likely to occur at the less mature moral stages. A body of research now exists that has tested the prediction that offenders will have less mature moral reasoning than non-offenders (for a review, see Palmer 2003a), although studies have mostly used adolescent samples. An early review by Blasi (1980) of 15 studies reported an association between immature moral reasoning and offending in 10 of the studies. Nelson *et al.* (1990) conducted a meta-analytic review on 15 studies with adolescents (including some from the Blasi review). From this they concluded that the young offenders showed less mature moral reasoning than the young non-offenders. More recently, studies by Gregg and colleagues in the USA (1994) and Palmer and Hollin (1998) in the UK have shown similar results for male and female adolescents.

Turning to the cognitive distortions that may support developmental delay in moral reasoning (Gibbs 2003), egocentric thinking has often been shown among offenders (see Antonowicz 2005). Adolescent delinquents have been found to use cognitions similar to the secondary cognitive distortions to justify their offending and other anti-social behaviours (Liau *et al.* 1998).

Taken together, this body of research suggests that offending results from the persistence of immature moral reasoning beyond childhood, accompanied by an egocentric bias. If this results in offending behaviour, the self-serving secondary level of cognitive distortions allows individuals to justify their behaviours and to lessen any feelings of guilt or regret.

Implications for practice

While moral reasoning theory alone cannot offer a complete explanation for why people offend, the inclusion of moral reasoning in developmental models of offending offers a number of implications for intervention. First, prior to the development of offending, attempts can be made to facilitate the development of moral reasoning to the mature stages and to prevent the acquisition of associated cognitive distortions. Secondly, interventions with offenders can incorporate work to improve the maturity of their moral reasoning and to change cognitive distortions.

Work on moral reasoning is included in a number of general cognitive skills programmes for offenders. There are also some specific programmes that have an explicit moral reasoning component. One such programme is aggression replacement training (ART) (Goldstein *et al.* 1998) that was initially developed for use with aggressive youths and that has recently been adapted for other populations. As well as moral reasoning, ART includes social skills and anger management components that are run concurrently. Evaluations of programmes that target moral reasoning can be difficult to interpret, given that large shifts in moral reasoning are unlikely to be achieved in short interventions. Furthermore, the multifaceted nature of offending behaviour means that changes in moral reasoning alone may not be enough to bring about a long-term change in behaviour. Therefore, it is important to emphasize that these should be done while also providing comprehensive intervention packages that seek to address other factors associated with an individual's offending behaviour.

Emma J. Palmer

Related entries

Criminal careers; Family factors; Intelligence, impulsivity and empathy.

Key texts and sources

Gregg, V.R., Gibbs, J.C. and Basinger, K.S. (1994) 'Patterns of developmental delay in moral judgment by male and female delinquents', *Merrill-Palmer Quarterly*, 40: 538–53.

Nelson, J.R., Smith, D.J. and Dodd, J. (1990) 'The moral reasoning of juvenile delinquents: a meta-analysis', *Journal of Abnormal Child Psychology*, 18: 231–9.

Palmer, E.J. (2003a) 'An overview of the relationship between moral reasoning and offending', *Australian Psychologist*, 38: 165–74.

Palmer, E.J. (2005) 'The relationship between moral reasoning and aggression, and the implications for practice', *Psychology, Crime and Law*, 11: 353–61.

Palmer, E.J. and Hollin, C.R. (1998) 'A comparison of patterns of moral development in young offenders and non-offenders', *Legal and Criminological Psychology*, 3: 225–35.

MOTIVATIONAL INTERVIEWING (MI)

Motivational interviewing (MI) is a client-centred, goal-oriented therapeutic method to enhance readiness for change. MI helps people to explore and resolve ambivalence, to commit to change and to desist from harmful behaviours. It is a collaborative and respectful method, and research indicates it is a promising intervention.

Any behaviour change involves commitment and effort. On top of this, the criminal justice context presents particular challenges to those who assist offenders. For example:

- Offenders are often mandated and coerced into treatment, and the use of imposed 'sentence plans' is commonplace.
- Offenders may 'jump through the hoops' by participating in correctional programmes, but have little personal investment in the change process.
- The authoritarian setting and culture can be a barrier to collaboration. In prison, offenders may be open to the anti-social influence of their peers.
- Offenders are often labelled by the system (e.g. 'deviant', 'alcoholic').
- Well meaning practitioners and staff often use tactics of persuasion in an attempt to move the offender towards change ('why don't you just…', 'can't you see that…').
- Practitioners often face ethical dilemmas – for example, balancing the rights and needs of the offender with the need to protect the public.

Motivational interviewing (MI) can help with all these challenges. MI does not seek to correct thinking or to instil knowledge, insight, skills or even motivation itself. Instead it draws on Bem's self-perception theory that people tend to become more committed to that which they defend. MI draws out the offender's own values and motivations and explores how these may be used to change his or her behaviour. Rather than taking the expert role, the MI practitioner communicates 'You have what you need to make a change' rather than 'I have what you need'.

MI research indicates that a verbalized intention to change is particularly promising when combined with a specific plan for change. MI is therefore differentiated into two phases: the first is focused on increasing motivation for change and the second on consolidating commitment with a specific plan for change.

The MI practitioner actively listens to the offender's perspective and perceptions through skilful reflective listening. Yet MI is also consciously directive. The MI-adherent practitioner is equipped with a series of tools to evoke, strengthen and reinforce speech in the direction of change. The MI practitioner acknowledges and 'rolls with' any resistance to change. Research indicates that MI is particularly useful with clients who have a low readiness for change and who are angry or oppositional. This makes MI ideally suited to the forensic setting.

The following are some practical applications of the use of MI in forensic settings with offenders:

- To help offenders to take responsibility for changing dynamic risk factors and to desist from offending.
- To resolve ambivalence about whether to engage in treatment programmes and intervention services.
- As a prelude to group treatment programmes. MI enhances engagement and retention in treatment programmes and has been shown to enhance the effectiveness of programmes.
- Built into group treatment programmes, either as an entire motivational programme or at the front end of an offending behaviour programme.
- With offenders with drug and alcohol problems – particularly important where substance abuse is a criminogenic factor.
- In conjunction with assessment feedback (including risk assessment) to create a collaborative process.

In keeping with the cultural shift from moralistic, judgemental, punitive and demeaning methods of interacting with offenders, many have proposed the widespread use of MI methods across criminal justice systems (Mann *et al.* 2002).

There have been over 160 MI clinical trials. A recent meta-analysis of 72 trials across a wide range of target problems yielded a short-term between-group effect size of .77, decreasing to .30 at one-year follow-up (Hettema *et al.* 2005). While MI has been particularly well tested and found promising in addressing addictive behaviour change, outcomes across (and within) settings, populations and target problems are highly variable. In offender populations, outcomes have been equally variable. This has called into question 'treatment fidelity' (i.e. how well practitioners in the studies adhere to MI proficiency thresholds).

MI is not as easy to practise proficiently as people often assume. A successful MI practitioner understands the 'spirit' of MI and respects the offender's autonomy, as well as being skilful with MI's methods. A recent trial evaluated methods for learning MI using licensed substance-abuse professionals ($n = 140$). One finding was that clinician self-report of MI skilfulness was unrelated to proficiency levels in observed practice. A key finding was that there is little empirical reason to believe a one-shot training workshop is sufficient to establish enduring competence. At four months post-workshop, the workshop-only group were lagging at the proficiency levels of the untrained waiting-list group (Miller *et al.* in press). Ongoing support, such as systematic feedback and coaching, is needed for the acquisition and retention of proficiency. The challenge for the forensic setting is to ensure this support is in place post-workshop for practitioners with newfound skills.

Matthew Gaskell and Ruth Mann

Related entries

Anger and aggression assessment; Offending behaviour interventions.

Key texts and sources

Hettema, J., Steele, J. and Miller, W.R. (2005) 'Motivational interviewing', *Annual Review of Clinical Psychology*, 1: 91–111.
Mann, R.E., Ginsburg, J.I. and Weekes, J. (2002) 'Motivational interviewing with offenders', in M. McMurran (ed.) *Motivating Offenders to Change.* Chichester: Wiley.
McMurran, M. (ed.) (2002) *Motivating Offenders to Change: A Guide to Enhancing Engagement in Therapy.* Chichester: Wiley.
Miller, W.R. and Rollnick, S. (2002) *Motivational Interviewing: Preparing People for Change* (2nd edn). New York, NY: Guilford Press.
Miller, W.R., Yahne, C.E., Moyers, T.B., Martinez, J. and Pirritano, M. (in press) 'A randomised trial of methods to help clinicians learn motivational interviewing', *Journal of Consulting and Clinical Psychology*.

MULTI-AGENCY PUBLIC PROTECTION ARRANGEMENTS (MAPPAs)

Multi-agency public protection arrangements (MAPPAs) describe the risk assessment and management procedures carried out by the National Probation Service, the Police Service and the Prison Service to manage sexual and violent offenders.

The National Probation Service has worked with other agencies, such as the police, for many years. This relationship became statutory in the Criminal Justice and Court Services Act 2000 (ss. 67 and 68) when the Police and Probation Services were given responsibility for the joint risk assessment and management of sexual and serious violent offenders through the creation of multi-agency public protection panels (MAPPPs). This led to the introduction of formal multi-agency public protection arrangements (MAPPAs) in April 2001. MAPPAs have three 'responsible authorities' – the National Probation Service, the Police Service and the Prison Service. In addition, the Criminal Justice Act 2003 makes reference to the 'duty to co-operate'. This places responsibility on a number of other agencies (such as health authorities and National Health Service trusts, housing authorities and registered social landlords, social services departments, social security and employment services departments, youth offending teams, local education authorities and electronic monitoring providers) to assist MAPPAs by co-operation with the 'responsible authority.'

The function of MAPPAs as outlined in the initial MAPPA guidance of 2001 is to:

- share relevant information about targeted offenders;
- assess the level of risk and to recommend action to manage this risk: and
- monitor and review this plan periodically.

Home Office MAPPA guidance (National Probation Service 2007) recommends that certain types of offender should be considered under MAPPAs:

- *Category 1*: registered sex offenders (those offenders who have been convicted or cautioned of certain sexual offences since September 1997 under Part 1 of the Sex Offender Act 1997 or s. 327(2) of the Criminal Justice Act 2003).
- *Category 2*: violent and other sex offenders (those offenders who have received a sentence of 12 months or more).
- *Category 3*: other offenders (those not in Categories 1 or 2 but whose offending is considered by the responsible authority to pose a risk of serious harm to the public).

The offender is then managed according to the level of risk he or she poses as assessed using one of the approved risk-assessments. OASys (the Offender Assessment System) is used by the National Probation Service and the Prison Service. Risk Matrix 2000 is used by the National Probation Service, the Prison Service and the Police Service. ASSET is used by youth offending teams. Intelligence about offenders can be gathered from different agencies. The police have recently started using the ViSOR (Violent and Sex Offender Register), which was developed by the National Offender Management Service and the Police Service. It is intended that this information system will be available to the Prison Service and the National Probation Service in the near future. ViSOR contains information about offenders as well as photographs and details of distinguishing marks, such as tattoos.

There are three levels of management:

- *Level 1*: ordinary risk management (generally lead by a single agency).
- *Level 2*: local interagency risk management (where the active involvement of more than one agency is required but the case is not of sufficient complexity or seriousness to require management at Level 3).
- *Level 3*: multi-agency public protection panels (MAPPPs) ('the critical few' high or very high risk of harm, imminent and/or requiring special resource allocation/management at a senior level or likely to attract significant media interest).

Implications for practice

Despite the many advantages of a multi-agency approach, a situation of 'no risk' is impossible to achieve, but there are ways to improve practice. MAPPAs have to consider a variety of competing demands from differing viewpoints and agencies. When a MAPPA does not work, the outcome is very grave.

The success of MAPPAs is measured by the level of reoffending committed by those being managed by the process. The body that has therefore given the most feedback on the MAPPA process is HM Inspectorate of Probation. A report by the Chief Inspector, Andrew Bridges, about the Anthony Rice case was published in May 2006. In October 2005, Rice was convicted of the murder of Naomi Bryant when under the supervision of Hampshire Probation Area and a number of other agencies working jointly through a MAPPA.

The report outlined some of the ways in which the MAPPP process had failed in this case and it gave recommendations for practice. One of the principal findings was that 'The MAPPP handling the case allowed its attention to the public protection considerations of this case to be undermined by its human rights considerations' (HMIP 2006c). The report also criticized discontinuities in the case, such as changes in staff with lead responsibility for the offender. The report concluded that MAPPAs were most effective when staff adopted an 'investigative approach' (for example, ensuring that evidence cited in reports is available). In the Rice case some key assessments and information had been filed away. The report also advocated Kemshall's defensible decision-making model:

- All reasonable steps have been taken.
- Reliable assessment methods have been used.
- Information has been collected and thoroughly evaluated.
- Decisions have been recorded (and subsequently carried out).
- Policies and procedures have been followed.
- Practitioners and their managers have adopted an investigative approach and are proactive.

Other serious further offence reports (available from the inspectorate) provide useful guidance on practice improvement. These reports, however, are very high profile, and it is important to balance this against the achievements made by MAPPAs. In the financial year 2005–6, of a total of 13,783 offenders managed at Level 2 and Level 3, 61 (0.44 per cent) committed a serious further offence.

Kemshall et al. (2005) researched the efficacy of MAPPAs across the country and looked for improvements that had been made since Maguire et al.'s (2001) study on the introduction of MAPPAs. Kemshall et al. used a questionnaire and site visit methodology. Numerous recommendations were made regarding the improvement of MAPPP processes, management and administration. However, the study also noted that MAPPAs were now far more consistent nationally and that the tiered model had been adopted by all probation areas.

An issue highlighted by the report was the reticence of some mental health professionals to become involved in MAPPPs due to considerations about patient confidentiality and information sharing. The Royal College of Psychiatrists has issued guidelines for practitioners. Clearly, consideration must be given by the practitioner as to what information he or she chooses to share. Reference to their own professional bodies' codes of conduct and ethics should be made in these instances. The rights of the individual offender should also be weighed against the rights of potential victims.

The recent thematic report, *Putting Risk of Harm into Context* (HMIP et al. 2006), notes that psychologists have made an important, contribution to MAPPAs. It is important, for practitioners to maintain their professional identity as the value of a multi-agency approach is only fully realized when a range of opinions is shared.

Tania Tancred

Related entries

Cambridge Framework for Risk Assessment (CAMRA); National Probation Service (NPS); Public protection; Risk–needs assessment (Level of Service Inventory – LSI).

Key texts and sources

HM Inspectorate of Probation (2006c) *An Independent Review of a Serious Further Offence Case: Anthony Rice.* London: Home Office.

HM Inspectorate of Probation, HM Inspectorate of Constabulary and HM Inspectorate of Prisons (2006) *Thematic Inspection Report: Putting Risk of Harm into Context – a Joint Inspection on Public Protection. Inspection Findings 3/06.* London: Home Office.

Kemshall, H. (2003) 'The community management of high-risk offenders: a consideration of "best practice" – multi-agency public protection panel arrangements (MAPPPA)', *Prison Service Journal*, 146.

Kemshall, H., Mackenzie, G., Wood, J., Bailey, R. and Yates, J. (2005) *Strengthening Multi-agency Public Protection Arrangements. Home Office Development and Practice Report 45.* London: Home Office.

Maguire, M., Kemshall, H., Noaks, L. and Wincup, E. (2001) *Risk Management of Sexual and Violent Offenders: The Work of Public Protection Panels. Police Research Series 139.* London: Home Office.

National Probation Service (2007) *MAPPA Guidance: Multi-agency Public Protection Arrangements through Partnership.* London: Home Office.

MULTI-MODAL METHODS OF ASSESSMENT

Multi-modal methods of assessment refers to the plethora of available assessment tools and clinical skills at the disposal of applied psychologists for the purpose of assessing individuals across a range of modalities of functioning. These modalities include social, behavioural, interpersonal and cognitive functioning, in addition to clinical and actuarial measures of risk and directions for treatment.

Applied psychologists aim to synthesize information from various sources in order to develop a comprehensive impression of an individual and his or her psychological need. Psychological assessment tools are designed to aid the clinician in the gathering of this information and may be composed of static (historical) or dynamic (changing) assessment variables. In forensic and clinical psychology, the areas covered by this broad spectrum of assessment tools include risk of violence or sexual assault; psychological functioning (including personality, self-perception and global orientation); and the assessment of intellectual, cognitive, social and emotional factors.

Current debate centres on the argument between the accuracy of clinical versus actuarial methods of assessment – in particular, when assessing risk. A number of authors, however, have advocated the use of an 'all inclusive' approach when forensic psychologists are required to produce reports.

The wide range of structured, semi-structured and self-report assessment tools available covers general assessment areas and the majority of incidents of violent, sexual or other offending behaviours that psychologists are asked to report on. In order to choose the most appropriate assessment tools the psychologist should have a good understanding of what he or she is assessing and of what he or she hopes to achieve.

Graham John Evans

Related entries

Anger and aggression assessment; Family violence; Sexual offending: interventions.

Key texts and sources

Corcoran, M.H. and Cawood, J.S. (2003) *Violence Assessment and Intervention: The Practitioner's Handbook.* Boca Raton, FL: CRC Press.

Hollin, C.R. (2001) *Offender Assessment and Treatment.* New York, NY: Wiley.

Houston, J. (1998) *Making Sense with Offenders: Personal Constructs, Therapy and Change.* New York, NY: Wiley.

Laws, D.R. and Donohue, W. (1997) *Sexual Deviance: Theory, Assessment, and Treatment.* New York, NY: Guilford Press.

Quinsey, V.I., Harris, G.T., Rice, M.E. and Cormier, C.A. (1998) *Violent Offenders: Appraising and Managing Risk.* Washington, DC: American Psychological Association.

N

NACRO

Nacro (formerly the National Association for the Care and Resettlement of Offenders) is the largest voluntary agency in the UK working in the fields of crime reduction and offender resettlement. It is involved in a wide range of activities that support ex-offenders and it conducts lobbying work.

Nacro's Mental Health Unit was established in 1990 in an attempt to help tackle the difficulties faced by offenders with mental health problems. It also works with government agencies, statutory agencies and other organizations at a national, regional and local level to develop more effective ways to deal with mentally disordered offenders. It provides a range of services: an information and advice line for practitioners; policy development and consultancy services; and training. It also runs an annual conference on mental health and crime.

Nacro believes that responses to offenders with mental health problems should focus on their care and treatment rather than on punishment. To help bring about this change, Nacro campaigns for:

- more effective working partnerships between agencies;
- the development of specialist skills in the criminal justice system;
- better information sharing; and
- the education and training of staff so that they have the skills and encouragement they need to work with a group who can be difficult and unrewarding.

Jacqui Karn

Related entries

HM Prison Service; National Offender Management Service (NOMS); National Probation Service.

Key texts and sources

Nacro (2005a) *The Appropriate Adult and Vulnerable People: Working with Mentally Disordered Offenders and other Vulnerable Adults.* London: Nacro.

Nacro (2005b) *Working with Mentally Disordered Offenders: A Training Pack for Staff in Criminal Justice Agencies, Health and Social Care, and the Voluntary Sector* (CD-ROM). London: Nacro.

Nacro (2005c) *Multi-agency Partnership Working and the Delivery of Services to Mentally Disordered Offenders – Key Principles and Practice.* London: Nacro.

Nacro (2006) *Liaison and Diversion for Mentally Disordered Offenders.* London: Nacro.

See also Nacro's Mental Health Unit website (www.nacromentalhealth.org.uk).

NATIONAL HEALTH SERVICE (NHS)

The National Health Service (NHS) was set up on 5 July 1948 to provide healthcare for all citizens based on need, not the ability to pay. The NHS is managed by the Department of Health, which sets overall health policies and standards.

The National Health Service (NHS) was launched as an organization based around 14 regional hospital boards. Within this overall regional structure, the NHS was also split into these parts:

- Family doctors, dentists, opticians and pharmacists (primary care).

- Hospital services (secondary care).
- Local authority health services, including community nursing and health visiting (secondary care).

The NHS has developed and is currently changing the way it works to ensure there is more emphasis on a patient-centred health service. The NHS has strong working links with other organizations and services (in particular, with social care providers, the independent sector and the voluntary and community sector).

Primary care is the first point of contact most people have with the NHS. Primary care is mostly concerned with a patient's general healthcare needs. However, more specialist treatments are becoming available in such settings. Secondary care can be either planned specialist medical/surgery care or emergency care, which ordinarily takes place in an NHS hospital/day surgery.

Implications for practice

The *National Service Framework for Mental Health* (published in 1999) aims to improve the quality of the specialist mental healthcare patients receive, including the development of specialist community mental health teams that offer home treatment, early intervention to prevent a crisis occurring (e.g. assertive outreach teams and crisis resolution teams) and intensive support for people with the most complex needs (e.g. secure and forensic services).

The assessment and treatment of patients often involve a multidisciplinary team approach, and this can include psychological therapies, counselling, community and family support, occupational therapy and medical input. The team ordinarily comprises a consultant psychiatrist, a social worker, a chartered psychologist, an assistant psychologist, occupational therapy staff, nursing staff (often including community psychiatric nurses and other community support workers) and nursing assistants.

In secure and forensic services, assessment and treatment are aimed at helping prevent individuals who are suffering from a mental disorder that is currently associated with serious offending behaviour or potentially serious offending from offending further. Typically, offence types are of a violent or sexual nature,

which cause substantial physical or psychological harm to victims. Secure and forensic services therefore comprise many interlinked agencies that are all primarily working towards public protection and protection for the individual (e.g. the Prison Service, the National Probation Service, the Police Service, multi-agency public protection arrangements, courts and court diversion schemes, social services, substance misuse and learning disability services, the Home Office, special hospitals, local community mental health teams and acute and rehabilitation services, from both the private and voluntary sectors).

Sara Casado

Related entries

Care programme approach (CPA); Forensic psychiatry.

Key texts and sources

See the websites of the NHS (http://www.nhs.uk), the Department of Health (http://www.dh.gov.uk), the National Institute for Health and Clinical Excellence (http://www.nice.org.uk) and the National Institute for Mental Health in England (http://www.nimhe.csip.org.uk).

NATIONAL OFFENDER MANAGEMENT SERVICE (NOMS)

The National Offender Management Service (NOMS) is the system through which we commission and provide the highest quality correctional services and interventions in order to protect the public and reduce re-offending in England and Wales. NOMS started life in the Home Office but on 9 May 2007 it transferred to the Ministry of Justice (MoJ) and, from May 2008, a re-shaped NOMS is expected to be confirmed as an executive agency of the MoJ.

NOMS is made up of a number of organizations including HM Prison Service (with around 50,000 staff), contracted-out prisons, 42 local probation boards (with around 20,000 staff between them) and a number of private and third-sector suppliers. In 2006/07 spending by NOMS as a whole was around £4.3 billion.

NOMS was first set up in 2004 in response to Patrick Carter's report *Managing Offenders, Reducing Crime* (Carter 2003) and the Social Exclusion Unit report *Reducing Re-offending by Ex-prisoners* (Social Exclusion Unit 2002). Following a further report by Lord Carter published in December 2007 (*Securing the Future*), a re-shaped NOMS was created on 1 April 2008. It inherits the target to reduce re-offending by 5 per cent by 2008 working towards a reduction of 10 per cent by the end of the decade.

To achieve this, NOMS will continue to embed the Offender Management Model (OMM) based on having a single named offender manager for each offender responsible for ensuring the delivery of the sentence plan. The OMM was developed in 2004, published in 2005, updated in 2006 and was the subject of a strategic review in 2007. The model sets out the approach NOMS expects people managing individual offenders to deploy and it acts as the basis for the development of standards and performance measures that will apply to both community and custodial settings. The model describes, using a single language, a single end-to-end process which transcends the separate contributions of the main providers. Based upon a thorough assessment, an offender manager draws up a single sentence plan, in collaboration with the offender and providers of interventions. Resources and interventions are engaged using a brokerage approach. Personal supervision helps the offender to comply and co-operate. Different resources and styles are applied to different cases, producing a highly individualized service capable of adapting to the diverse needs, risks and circumstances of individual offenders. As of June 2007, the model applies to over 170,000 offenders on orders and licences in the community and to more than 11,000 offenders in custody.

To support offender management, NOMS operates the Offender Assessment System (OASys) and is taking steps to ensure this can be used electronically across prison and probation services. NOMS is also building a new electronic case management system, C-NOMIS, designed to eliminate many of the problems associated with the current paper-based processes. In December 2006 it began operating at HMP Albany as the first stage in going live.

Carter (2003) recommended moving to a commissioning system based on a purchaser/provider split. From April 2008, both commissioning and performance management across prison and probation services will be managed within the re-shaped NOMS. The intention is that placing both commissioning and performance management in a single organisation structure at both national and regional levels will further drive forward joined up offender management and deliver essential savings.

At present, design and organizational development work is underway to streamline the merged headquarters and begin to introduce the new role of Director of Offender Management (DOM) into the regions. The DOMs will be responsible for allocating resources across the region, commissioning services at local level and putting in place SLAs and contracts to incentivize high performance across prison and probation areas. The first DOMs have been appointed for Wales and the London region.

NOMS is responsible for developing and implementing a final model for probation trusts, which will replace the previous arrangement of 42 separate probation boards. The Offender Management Act 2007 allows for the dissolution of local probation boards, which have the statutory duty to deliver probation services and transfers that duty to the Secretary of State. The Act allows probation trusts to be established to contract with the Secretary of State. Six probation trusts have been created from 1 April 2008 (Dyfed Powys, South Wales, West Mercia, Leicestershire and Rutland, Merseyside and Humberside) and the experience of how these work during their first year of operation will help inform decisions on what comes next. Existing probation boards will continue to be managed through SLAs until they become probation trusts, from which point they will be managed under contract.

It is estimated that over half the resources required to reduce re-offending lie outside the criminal justice system. The National Reducing Re-offending Delivery Plan (NOMS 2005) sets out the key actions for different parts of Government to deliver. The plan identifies seven pathways out of offending: accommodation; education, training and employment; health; drugs and alcohol; finance, benefit and debt; children and families; and attitudes, thinking and behaviour. To monitor and drive progress, there exists an inter-Ministerial Board with a clear delivery plan and regional reducing re-offending boards bringing all the relevant partners together at the strategic regional level.

In order to go wider than Government NOMS has established three Reducing Re-offending Alliances. The Corporate Alliance is developing a network of businesses – public, private and voluntary sector – to help get more offenders into sustainable employment. The faith and voluntary and community sector alliance recognises and supports the huge amount of good work which is already done, much of it on a voluntary basis, to help support offenders and re-integrate them into the community. The third is the Civic Society Alliance focused on work with local authorities, local partners and local people to promote community re-integration.

This links strongly not only with proposals in the local government white paper (Communities and Local Government 2006), which emphasises the community leadership role of local authorities, but also with initiatives to embed reducing re-offending into the work of local partnerships and local area agreements.

Peter Kind

Related entries

HM Prison Service; National Probation Service (NPS).

Key texts and sources

Carter, P. (2003) *Managing Offenders, Reducing Crime: A New Approach.* London: Prime Minister's Strategy Unit, HM Treasury and Home Office.

Carter, P. (2007) *Securing the Future: Proposals for the Efficient and Sustainable Use of Custody in England and Wales.* London: Prime Minister's Strategy Unit, HM Treasury and Home Office.

Communities and Local Government (2006) *Strong and Prosperous Communities.* London: HMSO.

NOMS (2005) *The National Reducing Re-offending Delivery Plan.* London: Home Office.

NOMS (2006a) *The NOMS Offender Management Model 1.1.* London: Home Office.

Social Exclusion Unit (2002) *Reducing Re-offending by Ex-prisoners.* London: Office of the Deputy Prime Minister.

See also NOMS' website (**www.noms.justice.gov.uk**).

NATIONAL PROBATION SERVICE (NPS)

The National Probation Service (NPS) is the body that supervises offenders in the community, both those released from prison on licence and those sentenced by the courts to a community order. With the Prison Service it forms the National Offender Management Service.

The National Probation Service (NPS) is divided into 42 probation areas that share the same boundaries as their local police services. Probation areas receive their funding from the NPS and are managed by probation boards composed of members who represent their local communities. The service employs approximately 22,000 staff and, at any one time, is supervising some 200,000 offenders. In the past, probation was part of social services, with staff whose aim was to 'advise, assist and befriend' offenders. The modern service is a law-enforcement agency that works closely with the police and whose aim is public protection through the prevention of reoffending.

Probation staff supervise a wide range of offenders, from petty criminals to extremely dangerous sex and violent offenders who have been released from custody after coming to the end of their sentence. This latter group is managed by probation staff in conjunction with the Police and Prison Services under local multi-agency public protection arrangements. There are also special initiatives for prolific offenders and for offenders whose crimes are linked to drug and alcohol abuse.

At the heart of probation work is risk assessment to determine the likelihood of reoffending and the risk of harm an offender presents to the public and ways of managing that risk. To assist in this, the Probation and Prison Services have developed a joint assessment tool known as OASys, which assesses the level of risk, the criminogenic factors that have led to offending and the type of interventions likely to address these factors.

Probation staff prepare annually some 250,000 written pre-sentence reports for the courts. The report will propose a sentence but it is the court that makes the decision and passes the sentence. Offenders who are sentenced to a community order or suspended sentence order will have one or more of 12 requirements as part of their order. These include regular supervision by a probation officer, unpaid work (which can be between 40 and 300 hours in length, all to be completed within a year), drug or alcohol rehabilitation, mental health treatment and attendance at an offending behaviour programme. A suite of programmes, all of which have been nationally accredited, are available for sentencers. These can be delivered in a group or individual setting and they address such behaviour as general offending, domestic violence, sex offending, anger management, drug or alcohol abuse and drink-impaired driving.

Probation staff based in prisons assist with sentence planning and liaise with NPS staff in the areas. The service has a statutory duty to contact the victims of violent or sexual crimes where the offender has been sentenced to a year or more in prison. The NPS also manages 100 Home Office-approved premises that house offenders who pose a significant risk of harm.

Susan Lord

Related entries

Approved premises; Court duty officers (CPOs); National Management Service (NOMs).

Key texts and sources

See the NPS's website (**www.probation.homeoffice. gov.uk**).

NEUROPSYCHOLOGICAL ASSESSMENTS

Neuropsychological assessments look to assess a wide range of an individual's cognitive abilities, including how he or she receives information and commits it to memory, how he or she learns from this information and how he or she mentally organizes information, as well how the individual expresses him or herself.

Neuropsychological assessment evaluates a wide range of an individual's cognitive abilities. Traditionally, this has been considered in terms of intelligence measures, such as IQ (e.g. the WAIS III – Wechsler 1997). Such assessments were carried out to determine the extent of impairment to a particular skill after brain injury or neurological illness, in an attempt to identify the area of the brain that may have sustained damage. Neuropsychological assessment is now far advanced and refined, identifying much more about the subtleties of an individual's cognitive abilities and no longer restricted to an examination of a general IQ. It consists of more than psychological testing and is now coupled with a flexible and creative approach to determining an individual's difficulties and how these may be managed. More recently, neuropsychological assessment has been used to determine differential diagnosis, treatment planning, rehabilitation and use in legal proceedings.

Knowledge summary

As a result of the work of Halstead, Reitan and Goldstein in the USA, Rey in France and Luria in the then USSR, neuropsychological assessment had become a well defined discipline by the 1950s. The range of cognitive functioning that neuropsychological assessments can now assess, however, is varied and has developed substantially over the years. Although not exclusively, these include an individual's ability to reason and to express him or herself verbally, and his or her ability to respond to visual symbols and patterns, including novel-based learning through perceptual skills. It can also assess an individual's ability to process information given to him or her, examining a combination of motor speed, thinking speed, reaction time and ability to scan visually information quickly. All these can be assessed initially through an instrument such as the WAIS III (Wechsler 1997), with more specific assessments if difficulties arise, such as the Awareness of Social Inference Test (TASIT – McDonald *et al.* 2002) for a test of social perception or other tests from the Delis-Kaplan Executive Function System (D-KEFS – Delis *et al.* 2001), which include traditional assessments such as the STROOP test and other measures of an individual's executive functioning.

There is also an individual's working memory – sometimes referred to as 'attention'. This is a complex process that allows an individual to complete a variety of tasks. These include the holding and manipulation of information in the mind, responding to a problem, formulating a response or strategy, remaining focused on a task and having a good level of concentration. The WAIS III (Wechsler 1997) can look at the auditory aspects of working memory, with the Test of Everyday Attention (TEA – Robertson, *et al.* 1994) examining working memory in more detail.

Neuropsychological assessment also looks to explore an individual's executive functioning, of which working memory can be a part. This is an individual's ability to sustain his or her attention, to respond to abstract and hypothetical reasoning, to be able to develop and form concepts, to identify problems and to make successful efforts to manage these. It also looks at an individual's ability to monitor his or her own behaviour and social interactions to ensure appropriateness.

Implications for practice

The prevalence and type of cognitive deficits in offender populations are relatively under-researched. None the less, the application of detailed neuropsychological assessments can allow for a much greater consideration of how best to engage with clients who present with cognitive impairments. This is important when it is considered that, without such detailed neuro-psychological assessments, individuals with impairments can potentially be overlooked. Such impairments may not always be easily and readily observable. Alternatively, individuals may be labelled as demonstrating some other problematic behaviour, such as an un- willingness to engage in work or offering an impression of disinterest, rather than the consequences of their cognitive impairments. The use of neuropsychological assessments allows for a detailed summary of even subtle impairments that can have a significant impact on an individual's functioning. This would be a considerable move away from earlier assessments that focused only on very global cognitive abilities.

One of the most significant implications to derive from neuropsychological assessment is an appreciation of the impact of such cognitive difficulties and a consequent consideration of how to work with such individuals to maximize their abilities. This has led to greater attention being placed on how an individual may potentially behave, both during his or her offending and in assessment or intervention, and on the impact of his or her cognitive abilities on such behaviours. The appreciation and management of such difficulties help to maximize an individual's abilities to engage in forensic assessment or intervention.

For example, difficulties in working memory can lead to difficulties in retaining information and working out methods to solve problems, with consequent difficulties in planning and generating alternatives. In addition, cognitive impairments can also hinder a person in managing his or her emotions. Neuropsychological assessments can identify the reasons and motivations behind an individual's behaviour. In the example given, instead of simply seeing the individual as managing his or her emotions poorly, such behaviour might be assessed as the result of emotional dysregulation from brain injury and difficulty in the individual expressing him or herself when overwhelmed with information.

The recognition of the challenges that can arise from cognitive impairments has led to the development of methods to manage these. One such method is cognitive rehabilitation, which involves recognizing that an individual's behaviour, no matter how challenging, is a result of his or her cognitive impairments. Specific cognitive rehabilitation interventions include reinforcing, strengthening or re-establishing previously learnt patterns of behaviour or assisting the individual to adapt to his or her cognitive impairment, even though it may not be possible to modify it or to compensate for it. The approach aims to maximize an individual's relative strengths.

Carol A. Ireland

Related entries

Developmental disabilities in adults; Intellectual assessment.

Key texts and sources

Groth-Marnat, G. (2000) *Neuropsychological Assessment in Clinical Practice: A Guide Test Interpretation and Integration.* Chichester: Wiley.

Lezak, M.D., Howieson, D.B., Loring, D.W., Hannay, H.J. and Fischer, J.S. (2004) *Neuropsychological Assessment.* Oxford: Oxford University Press.

Seguin, J.R., Assaad, J., Nagin, D. and Tremblay, R.E. (2004) 'Cognitive-neuropsychological function in chronic physical aggression and hyperactivity', *Journal of Abnormal Psychology*, 13: 603–13.

Sohlberg, M.M. and Mateer, C.A. (2001) *Cognitive Rehabilitation: An Integrative Neuropsychological Approach.* London: Guilford Press.

Wood, R.L. and McMillan, T.M. (eds) (2001) *Neurobehavioural Disability and Social Handicap following Traumatic Brain Injury.* Hove: Psychology Press.

NOTHING WORKS

'Nothing Works' is a term based on an analysis conducted in the 1970s of 231 interventions with offenders undertaken between 1945 and 1967. This analysis concluded that, with a few and isolated exceptions, these interentions had no appreciable effect on criminal recidivism.

The term 'Nothing Works' initially derives from a paper by Martinson (1974), which summarized the findings of a report by Lipton *et al.*, that was itself published later, in 1975. In the report, the results of an analysis of 231 evaluations of interventions with offenders, undertaken between 1945 and 1967, were analysed. Martinson (1974: 25) concluded that '[w]ith few and isolated exceptions the rehabilitative efforts that have been reported so far have had no appreciable effect on recidivism'. This was widely interpreted as demonstrating that 'nothing works' in the rehabilitation of offenders. A US National Academy of Science panel concurred with this view when it reviewed the area (Sechrest *et al.* 1979), although by this time Martinson had tempered some of his earlier views. The term 'Nothing Works' was current at a time when public policy and opinion were moving the public away from rehabilitation and towards retribution or deterrence as justifications for the punishment of offenders.

Martinson's conclusions were not universally accepted, and it was suggested that the initial research was seriously flawed. First, it was argued that the methodology used was inadequate, with poor-quality data included in the analysis. Additionally, many of the interventions included in the analysis were very poorly implemented. Despite such concerns, the phrase 'nothing works' gained a wide currency in professional circles and among policymakers. This was followed by a reaction against this analysis, with the development of the similarly clichéd term 'What Works'.

Both terms represent a somewhat parochial view of intervention work with offenders, focused as it is on a narrow part of the available evidence base on psychological therapies (Crighton 2006b). Notions of evidence-based practice effectively subsume both narrow conceptions by addressing a range of individual and group-based interventions that may be effective in reducing levels of criminal behaviour, either singly or as part of a number of interventions co-ordinated into a broad 'programme'.

David A. Crighton

Related entries

Meta-analysis; Offending behaviour interventions; What Works.

Key texts and sources

Crighton, D.A. (2006b) 'Methodological issues in psychological research in prisons', in G.J. Towl (ed.) *Psychological Research in Prisons.* Oxford: Blackwell.

Lipton, D., Martinson, R. and Wilks, J. (1975) *The Effectiveness of Correctional Treatment: A Survey of Treatment Evaluation Studies.* New York, NY: Praeger.

Martinson, R. (1974) 'What works? Questions and answers about prison reform', *The Public Interest*, 35: 22–45.

Sechrest, L., White, S. and Brown, E. (1979) *The Rehabilitation of Criminal Offenders.* Washington, DC: National Academy of Sciences.

NUMBER NEEDED TO TREAT (NNT)

The number needed to treat (NNT) is a metric that combines the relative estimate of the treatment effect with the baseline risk. The NNT expresses the number of patients who would need to be treated with the experimental intervention to produce one more treatment outcome (beneficial or harmful) than would be expected in patients taking the control intervention.

The application of evidence from randomized clinical trials (RCTs) (and systematic reviews of RCTs) to clinical practice can be hampered by the fact that results are often expressed in a manner that is not clinically meaningful. There is good evidence that the way in which the results of, for example, RCTs are presented can influence the way those results are used in decision-making (Fahey *et al.* 1995). In general, measures of relative treatment effect (such as relative risk and odds ratio) tend to lead to a perception of larger treatment effects than measures of absolute treatment effect (such as risk difference). The rise of evidence-based practice,

with its emphasis on the explicit linking of research evidence to clinical practice decision-making, required intuitive and easy-to-understand measures of the effects of treatments that provided a clinically meaningful summary of the results of RCTs (Sackett *et al.* 1996).

Sackett *et al.* introduced the number needed to treat (NNT) – a metric that combines the relative estimate of the treatment effect with the baseline risk (Laupacis *et al.* 1988; Cook and Sackett 1995). The NNT expresses the number of patients who would need to be treated with the experimental intervention to produce one more treatment outcome (beneficial or harmful) than would be expected in patients taking the control intervention. From a clinical point of view, this gives an estimate of the power of the treatment. The NNT is simple to derive from trial reports that provide the event rates in each arm of the RCT – it is simply the reciprocal of the difference between the control event rate (CER) and the experimental event rate (EER):

$$NNT = \frac{1}{CER - EER}$$

The NNT is usually employed to indicate the number of patients needed to be treated to produce benefit (NNTB) but, obviously, it can also be employed to indicate the number of patients who need to be treated to cause harm (NNTH) – e.g. an adverse event such as a drug reaction. This latter is sometimes called the number needed to harm (NNH).

The clinical interpretation of the NNT needs to take into account the following:

• The amount of resource (cost, effort) that is required to deliver the intervention.
• The size of the likely benefit.
• The severity or importance of the outcome.

For most clinical interventions an NNT of somewhere between 1 and 10 would normally be considered to be clinically worthwhile – and this is the range in which many commonly used mental health interventions fall (e.g. SSRI in depression and cognitive therapy in depression). If the NNT is greater than 10, it would be seen to be a relatively small treatment effect, although it might still be worth having, depending on the factors above. For example, if 1,000 people with recent deliberate self-harm need to be given a leaflet to prevent one completed suicide, then this is likely to be worthwhile because even though the NNT is very high, a leaflet is cheap and suicide is a very important outcome.

Although the NNT is a useful summary for clinical use, it is a simplification and therefore has limitations. It certainly is not a replacement for a proper economic analysis, but it can be helpful to a clinician thinking about the potential power of the available treatments in a clinical situation. It is less useful for the patients themselves, who do not really want to know how many people would need to be treated to get one improved outcome but who are more interested in the likely risks and benefits in their own case. NNTs derived from systematic reviews can be misleading if the included trials vary in their lengths of follow-up and/or event rates (Smeeth *et al.* 1999).

John Geddes

Related entries

Evidence-based practice (EBP); Meta-analysis.

Key texts and sources

Cook, R.J. and Sackett, D.L. (1995) 'The number needed to treat: a clinically useful measure of treatment effect', *British Medical Journal*, 310: 452–4.

Fahey, T., Griffiths, S. and Peters, T.J. (1995) 'Evidence based purchasing: understanding results of clinical trials and systematic reviews', *British Medical Journal*, 311: 1056–9.

Laupacis, A., Sackett, D.L. and Roberts, R.S. (1988) 'An assessment of clinically useful measures of the consequences of treatment', *New England Journal of Medicine*, 318: 1728–33.

Sackett, D.L., Rosenberg, W.M., Gray, J.A., Haynes, R.B. and Richardson, W.S. (1996) 'Evidence based medicine: what it is and what it isn't', *British Medical Journal*, 312: 71–2.

Smeeth, L., Haines, A. and Ebrahim, S. (1999) 'Numbers needed to treat derived from meta-analyses – sometimes informative, usually misleading', *British Medical Journal*, 318: 1548–51.

O

OFFENDING BEHAVIOUR INTERVENTIONS

'Offending behaviour interventions' is a collective name for a range of psychologically based methods used in prearranged, structured formats with the objective of reducing criminal recidivism. The focus in such interventions is typically on identified intra-personal or interpersonal risk factors and on the direct analysis of offending behaviour itself, as opposed to education, employment or other socio-demographic variables, on the one hand, or therapeutic personality change on the other. This work is sometimes considered a prime example of the application of 'evidence-based practice' in criminal justice services.

Background

The rationale for the legal sanctioning of punishment is founded on the expectation that punishment serves a number of purposes, including retribution, incapacitation, deterrence and rehabilitation. There is a traditional, widely held assumption that formal legal sentencing – the imposition of penalties on those found guilty of crimes – will have an impact on their subsequent behaviour ('specific deterrence'). However, there are few indications of differential effects of various court sentences on the recidivism of either young or adult offenders. There is, therefore, an emerging consensus that the learning experiences that may be included in sentences are more likely 'active ingredients' in engendering long-term change.

Major reviews of sentencing outcomes reported in the 1970s concluded that there was little systematic evidence of positive effects from the 'treatment' of offenders, where this referred not only to the impact of court sentences but also to responsiveness to educational, vocational, psychotherapeutic or other types of interventions. Critics of these negative conclusions adduced findings from a number of studies in which positive effects had been found following the use of interventions that focused on psychological variables identified as mediating factors for criminal actions ('risk factors'; see below).

Since that period there has been a recurrent debate over whether or not offender treatment 'works' to reduce the frequency or severity of criminal conduct. Meta-analytic reviews of large numbers of outcome studies have sustained the viewpoint that interventions can be successful, but much remains to be learnt about the various factors that influence the consistency and the extent of this. Research findings support the use of structured, manualized interventions targeted on specific mediating 'risk factors' as the most promising formats in this respect.

Empirical base and 'risk factors'

Offending behaviour interventions are generally used in the context of 'tertiary prevention' – that is, in work with adjudicated offenders in penal settings (prisons, probation, youth justice). Interventions are typically used to address specific intermediate treatment 'targets' that are established as having an association with the occurrence of persistent offending and that have been shown to be susceptible to change by intervention efforts, with associated reductions in ensuing recidivism rates. Such targets have been defined as 'risk factors', and several approaches have been developed for the systematic assessment of them prior to the allocation of individuals to programmes.

Assessment is usually a two-stage process comprising an actuarial estimation or anchored judgement of levels of reoffending risk, followed by a broader appraisal of factors that have contributed to an individual's offence history. Typical individual risk factors include anti-social attitudes, regular contact with criminal associates, low levels of self-control of negative emotion, impulsivity, poor interpersonal skills, limited problem-solving skills and concomitant substance abuse.

Cognitive-behavioural orientation

Most offending behaviour interventions currently in use employ methods that are based on cognitive social learning theory. That is, they derive from the proposal that criminal behaviour is learnt, primarily through interaction with others, via socialization and other interpersonal influence processes (therefore mainly within families and in age-related peer groups in specific cultural contexts). This entails both direct behavioural learning by means of differential reinforcement, modelling habit formation and other process, and cognitive learning, skill acquisition, the development of problem-solving capacities and the evolution of attitudes and beliefs. There are conceptual parallels between these psychologically based processes (or the inhibition of them) and a number of models developed in sociological criminology, such as differential association, inner containment, general control and neutralization theories.

The remediation of the difficulties associated with offending behaviour is approached by focusing individuals' attention on the interactions between, and interdependence of, their thoughts, feelings and behaviour in offence-related situations. Participants examine past circumstances in which offences have occurred or where their behaviour has been problematic in other respects. They identify habitual or automatic sequences of thought and action, and they practise cognitive, emotional and behavioural alternatives to previously entrenched reaction patterns. Some interventions address offending behaviour more explicitly than others and involve a detailed analysis of crime events.

Most involve repeated practice in simulated re-enactments of social encounters, where possible supported by graduated practice to encourage the transfer of training.

Offending behaviour programmes

Most interventions of this type are organized in the form of programmes. This word has been used in a loose sense to refer to any officially dispensed criminal justice sanctioning process. However, in this context it refers to a structured, reproducible series of learning opportunities, usually supported by a specially designed manual, the training of selected staff and inter-connected methods for monitoring integrity and evaluating outcome. Programmes may be delivered on an individual basis but it is more common for them to be used with small groups (usually not exceeding 10 members), with defined sessions (typically lasting one to two hours) in a timetabled series, similar to an educational curriculum.

The development of such programmes has had considerable implications for practice in forensic psychology, and some criminal justice agencies now have available an extensive portfolio of offending behaviour programmes, with psychologists playing key roles with reference to offender assessment, staff training, intervention design, monitoring, evaluation, research and policy development. In the jurisdictions of several countries, the implementation of programmes has been subject to quality assurance and review procedures. This has led to the advent of accreditation systems, whereby programmes are required to meet a set of specific criteria prior to approval for their use, analogous to the validation procedures used for degree programmes in colleges and universities.

Diversity of programmes

There is now a large variety of programmatic interventions of this type. Some consist of as few as 10 sessions, while others may continue for as long as 120. They vary somewhat in their prescriptiveness (i.e. the extent to which the contents of sessions are dictated by the accompanying manual or allowance is made for tutors or session leaders to exercise discretion in terms of how the materials are applied). Various core methods from cognitive-behavioural therapies are employed in differing mixtures or balances according to programme objectives and the features of the target populations. Methods include anger management, self-control training, social problem-solving, social skills training, cognitive restructuring, moral reasoning training and motivational enhancement, among others. Given the complexity of the factors contributing to crime, most programmes are 'multi-modal' (i.e. they deploy a range of methods addressing a collection of outcome targets).

Specific, widely disseminated programmes now deployed in criminal justice services around the world include reasoning and rehabilitation (R&R), moral reconation therapy, aggression replacement training (ART), EQUIP, Think First, One-to-One, Controlling Anger and Learning to Manage it (CALM), enhanced thinking skills (ETS), self-risk management and multi-systemic therapy. Some of these exist in several different formats for use in different settings (e.g. custody vs. community). Some are available in modified forms to address diversity amongst participants with respect to age, gender and ethnicity. There are also a variety of specially devised substance abuse programmes. Using a wider definition, 'programmes' can also be taken to include therapeutic communities, mentoring, parent training interventions and a range of other frameworks.

In the Prison and Probation Services in the UK, programmes are conventionally divided into those that are 'generic' and those that are 'offence-specific'. In the former, participants may have committed a mixture of offence types, and the materials are designed to address a range of offences and allied problems. In the latter, although participants will almost certainly have been convicted of more than one kind of offence, the focus is on one type that all have committed (e.g. drink-driving, substance abuse, violence, domestic violence, sexual offending).

Outcomes

There is a substantial evidence base for the claim that it is possible to reduce rates of offender recidivism through the use of psychological intervention programmes. Numerous evaluative studies have been conducted in this field, and there are several meta-analytic reviews. The quality of such studies has often been regarded as weak since, in many instances, data are collected from applied service settings using quasi-experimental designs and with limited follow-up intervals. However, there are also well controlled trials using random allocation and with longer follow-up periods. Recent reviews have highlighted the need to consider contextual, organizational and implementation issues, alongside those of programme methods and contents *per se*.

There are controversies associated with the use of the interventions described here. There is, for example, a widespread perception that this approach locates all the causes of difficulties, and the only potential mechanisms of change, within individuals, and thereby neglects social conditions, structural factors and other external forces. Yet inside most programmes there is a considerable emphasis on the role of the environment as a causal influence, and on the mutual interplay between persons and their circumstances ('reciprocal determinism'). Offending behaviour interventions are entirely compatible with, and can be complementary to, the claim that offending behaviour should be addressed on a number of other levels – for example, through community-based inter- ventions or social support. Another common criticism is that programmes neglect individuality and impose homogeneity on participants ('one size fits all'). However, most programmes contain sufficient flexibility within the sessions to allow for individual exploration of issues and problems. Further, they are rarely seen as the sole option for attempting to secure behavioural change, and there is a growing recognition of the need for case management, or the involvement of significant others, to maximize and maintain the gains that are made.

James McGuire

Related entries

Motivational interviewing (MI); Nothing Works; What Works.

Key texts and sources

Hollin, C.R. and Palmer, E.J. (eds) (2006) *Offending Behaviour Programmes: Development, Application, and Controversies.* Chichester: Wiley.

McGuire, J. (ed.) (2002) *Offender Rehabilitation and Treatment: Effective Programmes and Policies to Reduce Re-offending.* Chichester: Wiley.

McGuire, J. (2004) *Understanding Psychology and Crime: Perspectives on Theory and Action.* Maidenhead: Open University Press/McGraw-Hill Education.

McMurran, M. and McGuire, J. (eds) (2005) *Social Problem-solving and Offending: Evidence, Evaluation and Evolution.* Chichester: Wiley.

Motiuk, L.L. and Serin, R.C. (eds) (2001) *Compendium 2000 on Effective Correctional Programming.* Ottawa: Correctional Service Canada.

P

PAROLE

Deriving from the French for 'word' or 'promise', parole can be defined generically as the discretionary and conditional early release of prisoners, whether serving determinate or indeterminate sentences, who then remain liable to recall to custody up to the conclusion of their licence period.

Any parole scheme has to determine the ambit of eligibility and the appropriate review machinery/procedures. Obvious tensions will be experienced regarding the minimum proportion of sentence to be spent incarcerated and the meaningfulness of the period of sentence served in the community (sometimes characterized as 'honesty' in sentencing). When the contemporary scheme in England and Wales (Scotland has separate but similar arrangements) was established in respect of fixed-term prisoners by the Criminal Justice Act 1967, parole was available to those serving less than a year, eligible for release after serving a third of their term. The catchment zone was narrowed by the Criminal Justice Act 1991 to those serving at least four years, eligible from the halfway point of sentence. Under the measures introduced by the Criminal Justice Act 2003, the focus has shifted to those attracting the Act's so-called 'dangerous offender' measures, targeting violent and sexual offenders who are deemed at point of sentence to pose a substantial risk of serious harm.

The review task – of initial release and on recall – is undertaken by an independent body, the Parole Board, whose decisions are based primarily on an evaluation of the risk to the public of the prisoner committing a further offence at a time that he or she would otherwise be in prison, taking account of any evidence of risk reduction since sentence and the potential rehabilitative benefits of supervision in the community. With lifers, the board has an important secondary function of recommending whether the prisoner is suitable for testing in an open prison.

The work of the board has developed in tandem with developments in intervention programmes, the availability and quality of professional risk assessment – static and dynamic, actuarial and clinical – and in oversight by the courts through applications for judicial review, particularly as informed by the European Convention on Human Rights in promoting fairness and due process. Prisoners now have full access to their dossiers, are able to seek legal representation, have gained greater right to an oral hearing rather than simply consideration on the papers and also receive reasoned decisions. It is now clearly established that a prisoner may not be refused release simply on the basis of his or her denial of guilt. Further, ultimate responsibility for decisions has shifted to a substantial degree away from ministerial control, acting on the board's advice, to direct authority exercised by the board.

Research interest has focused on the 'parole rate' (the proportion of eligible prisoners given parole – fluctuating around the 50 per cent mark but recently lowered following inquiries arising from notorious cases where parolees have murdered) and the parole failure rate (around 6.5 per cent being recalled on the basis of reoffending). There is modest evidence of a positive 'parole effect' – namely, that parolees outperform their predicted reconviction rate. While decision-making is properly centred on the individual subject, Hood and Shute (2000) established that board decisions about determinate prisoners could be predicted largely on the strength of seven key variables, including number of previous convictions of a sexual or violent nature, number of adjudications during sentence, prison security classification and probation officer recommendation.

Nigel Stone

Related entries

HM Prison Service; National Probation Service (NPS).

Key texts and sources

Arnott, H. and Creighton, C. (2006) *Parole Board Hearings: Law and Practice.* London: Legal Action Group.

Hood, R. and Shute, S. (2000) *The Parole System at Work: A Study of Risk-based Decision-making. Home Office Research Study* 202. London: Home Office.

Padfield, N. (in press) 'The role and functions of the Parole Board: perceptions of fairness.'

Padfield, N. and Liebling, A. (2000) *An Exploration of Decision-making at Discretionary Lifer Panels. Home Office Research Study* 213. London: Home Office.

See also the website of the Parole Board for England and Wales (**www.paroleboard.gov.uk**).

PERSONALITY AND CRIME

Most definitions of personality refer to regularities and consistencies in behaviour, thinking, perceiving and feeling that recur over time and across situations. They emphasize the integrated and organized nature of personality, not merely as a collection of traits but as a consistent, coherent and structured whole. Most models also incorporate some sense of hierarchy, with a small group of basic, latent traits around which lower-order dimensions of personality are organized. Traits are the most common dimension of personality used in the study of personality and crime.

There is no simple, fixed, objective definition of crime. As a social construct it may be defined from a normative perspective as an act that offends against a set of norms, such as a moral code. However, when considering the relationship between personality and crime, most investigators use more objective, legal definitions (for example, an act committed or omitted in violation of a law forbidding or commanding it and for which punishment is imposed on conviction).

Much of the research examining the relationship between personality and crime has focused on personality disorder, and the literature on 'normal' personality dimensions and crime is relatively meagre. Existing studies have tended to use diverse study designs, assessment instruments and outcome measures, and no systematic reviews or meta-analyses have been undertaken.

A small number of epidemiological follow-up studies have examined the relationship between 'normal' personality dimensions and indices of previous criminal behaviour. Evidence suggests that subjects with prior criminal arrest in the last 13 years score higher on scales of angry hostility, impulsiveness and excitement-seeking than those without prior arrest (e.g. Samuels *et al.* 2004). They scored lower on scales of trust, straightforwardness, compliance, modesty, dutifulness and deliberation. These associations were independent of demographic characteristics, alcohol or drug-use disorders and personality disorder dimensions. In a follow-up study of a birth cohort at 18 years, a composite measure of delinquency was negatively associated with the traditionalism and control scales and positively associated with the aggression scale of a modified version of the Multidimensional Personality Questionnaire (Kreuger *et al.* 1994). Those who abstained from delinquency were characterized by a preference for conventionality, planfulness, meek, non-aggressive behaviour and a non-assertive interpersonal style. Those at the opposite end of the distribution of delinquency were characterized by a preference for thrill-seeking, impulsivity, aggressive behaviour, a lack of sociability, feelings of alienation and a rejection of traditional values. In the same birth cohort, under-controlled temperament at 3 years of age predicted the number of health-risk behaviours at 21 years of age, including violent crime, but this effect became non-significant when personality traits at the age of 18 years were controlled for. The relationship between personality disorder symptoms and violent behaviour has also been investigated prospectively in an adolescent community sample. Paranoid personality disorder symptoms were associated with an increased risk of initiating physical fights; narcissistic personality disorder symptoms with an increased risk of being involved in arson or vandalism, with threatening to injure others, initiating physical fights and committing assault resulting in injury to others; and passive aggressive personality disorder symptoms with an increased risk of being involved in arson or vandalism, with threatening to injure others and initiating physical fights.

The relationship between personality and crime has also been explored in populations selected for criminal behaviour. In a retrospective study, violent offenders scored significantly higher on the hostility, depression, tension, psychopathic-deviate, impulsivity and aggression scales of the Special Hospital Assessment of Personality and Socialization than sexual or general offenders (Craig et al. 2006). Violent offenders were more likely to exhibit abnormal personality traits than sexual offenders and were characterized by psychopathic-deviate and aggressive traits, whereas sexual offenders were characterized by high introversion and lie scale scores. In a study looking at school-attending adolescents and institutionalized delinquent male adolescents, psychoticism, impulsivity and experience-seeking were positively correlated with anti-social behaviour (Romero et al. 2001). In the male group, disinhibition, psychoticism and experience-seeking were significant predictors of anti-social behaviour over a period of one year, whereas impulsivity and extraversion were more predictive in the female group. The evidence suggested that this relationship was not due to institutionalization, and those variables most closely related to anti-social behaviour in the non-institutionalized group were essentially the same as those in the institutionalized group.

Personality variables have been evaluated as potential factors in the relationship between specific mental disorders and crime. In a study that investigated the relationship between mental disorders and crime at the age of 21 years in a birth cohort, excessive threat perception accounted for 19 per cent of the association between marijuana dependence, alcohol dependence and violence (Arseneault et al. 2000). This cognitive personality style also accounted for 32 per cent of the association between schizophrenia spectrum disorders and violence. Evidence suggests that the relationship between particular mental disorders and violence may be mediated by different configurations across personality dimensions, such as impulse control, affect regulation, threatened egotism or narcissism and paranoid cognitive personal style.

Implications for practice

Although limited, the evidence linking personality and crime has a number of potentially significant practical implications. The assessment of 'normal' personality traits may help identify individuals at greater risk of criminal behaviour by providing information in addition to that provided by criteria for personality disorders. Indeed, some personality variables may prove to be useful predictors of changes in criminal behaviour over time, acting either as vulnerability factors or resilience factors. The extent to which particular personality dimensions mediate elevated rates of violence for particular types of mental disorder may be investigated further using objective personality measures. This may provide the basis for developing more specific interventions – for example, cognitive therapy or drug treatment that reduces threat perception and that in turn, may reduce violence in individuals with schizophrenia spectrum disorders.

Colin Campbell

Related entries

Attachment theory; Personality Assessment (objective); Personality Assessment (projective); Personality Disorder Assessment.

Key texts and sources

Arseneault, L., Moffitt, T.E., Caspi, A., Taylor, P.J. and Silva, P.A. (2000) 'Mental disorders and violence in a total birth cohort: results from the Dunedin study', *Archives of General Psychiatry*, 57: 979–86.

Craig, L.A., Browne, K.D., Beech, A. and Stringer, I. (2006) 'Differences in personality and risk in sex, violent and general offenders', *Criminal Behaviour and Mental Health*, 16: 183–94.

Kreuger, R.F., Schmutte, P.S., Caspi, A., Moffitt, T.E., Campbell, K. and Silva, P.A. (1994) 'Personality traits are associated with crime among men and women: evidence from a birth cohort', *Journal of Abnormal Psychology*, 103: 328–38.

Romero, E., Luengo, M.A. and Sobral, J. (2001) 'Personality and antisocial behaviour: study of temperamental dimensions', *Personality and Individual Differences*, 31: 329–48.

Samuels, J., Bienvenu, O.J., Cullen, B., Costa, P.T., Eaton, W.W. and Nestadt, G. (2004) 'Personality dimensions and criminal arrest', *Comprehensive Psychiatry*, 45: 275–80.

PERSONALITY ASSESSMENT (OBJECTIVE)

Objective personality assessments are used to establish the ways people think, feel and behave. Many such tests employ a standardized set of questions or items that have a limited choice of responses. Others use a structured interview format to collect the information necessary to score a set of items on a rating scale (e.g. The Hare Psychopathy Checklist). Many of the tests available evaluate specific disorders or problem areas (e.g. depression, anger and psychopathy).

Many of the most widely used objective personality assessments have a standardized set of questions or items that are presented to the respondent, who is provided with a limited choice of responses (e.g. agree/disagree). Other objective tests use a structured (or at least semi-structured) interview format to elicit the information necessary for the psychologist to score a set of defined items on a rating scale. There is a wide range of objective tests on offer, many of which evaluate specific disorders or problem areas (for example, depression, anger and psychopathy). Here, the most widely used tests that assess a range of both normal and abnormal personality traits are described.

The Personality Assessment Inventory (PAI) is a self-administered inventory of 344 items the respondents rate as 'totally false', 'slightly true', 'mainly true' or 'very true' of themselves. The test was developed in the early 1990s in the USA by Leslie Morey for use with adults aged 18 or above. It provides four validity scales, based on infrequency of response, inconsistency, and negative and positive impression management. Providing that the validity scales are within set tolerable limits, the test provides 11 clinical scales reflecting significant issues in common clinical practice (e.g. anxiety and alcohol problems) and 5 treatment considerations (e.g. suicide and treatment rejection). A computerized interpretation package is particularly useful in providing goodness of fit to comparison profiles of specific groups, such as spouse abusers, assault history, anti-social personality, rapists, etc. It also provides DSM-IV diagnostic considerations. Not surprisingly, the PAI has been widely used in forensic contexts to assist in risk decision-making (Edens *et al.* 2001).

The reliability data for the PAI show good stability over time, and its validity has been well established. It was designed to have general cross-cultural applicability and has been translated into a number of other languages, including Arabic and French.

The Minnesota Multiphasic Personality Inventory (MMPI-2) is an update of an over 60-year-old test that was probably the most widely used personality test in the world, having been translated into well over 100 different languages. The plethora of research using the MMPI is truly staggering, given that its critics would describe the original version as a time and culture-bound instrument based on a very small normative sample of mid-Western Americans in the 1940s. It was designed on the principle that the respondents' preferences and experiences were only important in so much as they reliably predicted behaviour and symptoms of personality pathology (for example, the item 'I used to like to play Drop the Handkerchief' has no inherent meaning other than its apparent ability to predict an aspect of personality).

The updated version has revised some of the item content and it has been re-normed on a broader section of the American populace. The revised test is a self-administered inventory of 567 items to be marked 'true' or 'false'. Scoring provides three validity indices (a lie scale, defensiveness and infrequency) as well as 10 major clinical scales and a variety of sub-scales. The major clinical scales were based on the ability of the items to discriminate between clinical and normal groups. Of particular interest to the forensic psychologist are the scales labelled 'psychopathic deviate' and 'hypomania', reflecting, respectively, a failure to accept social norms and impulsive overactive behaviour. There are a number of sub-scales that have been extracted and designed to identify specific problem areas, such as marital distress, anger, low self-esteem and alcoholism.

The NEO Personality Inventory – Revised (NEO PI-R) was specifically designed to measure normal personality characteristics as defined by the 'Big Five' theory. This theory, based on three decades of research concerning adjective checklists across a variety of cultures, posits that there are five essential traits of personality – namely, neuroticism, extraversion, openness, agreeableness and conscientiousness. The NEO PI-R measures an individual's position on these five personality continuums. Each of the five personality traits contains six facets, each of which can be described by a number of adjectives (for example, moody, irritable and excitable are all adjectives pertaining to the impulsiveness facet of the trait of neuroticism). The NEO PI-R is available as a self-report or an observer report set of 240 personal descriptions to be rated on a five-point scale from 'strongly disagree' through neutral to 'strongly agree'. There are male and female versions of the inventory in both self and observer formats. Internal consistency is acceptable, as is long-term test-retest stability. Of particular value to the forensic psychologist, there have been a number of successful attempts to map a variety

of personality disorders, including psychopathy, against personality patterns based on the NEO PI-R (Costa and Widiger 1993).

The Sixteen Personality Factor Questionnaire (16PF) was originally designed by Raymond Cattell in the 1940s. Now in its fifth edition, it is a self-administered inventory of 185 multiple-choice items designed to provide a comprehensive description of normal personality. Unlike most other inventories, the 16PF uses situational scenarios (for example, a format of 'When …, I usually … (do X or Y)') for the respondent to answer. Scoring provides three validity scales, an ability scale and 15 primary factor scales that can be variously combined to create five global scales readily identifiable as the 'Big Five' referred to above. Despite a much shorter format, the 16PF is reported as having good and similar levels of test-retest reliability as other longer inventories. Construct validity has been repeatedly established since its inception, the test having been developed on the basis of factor analysis.

All the above tests are available with computerized administration, scoring and interpretation packages. Computerized administration is often not feasible in many of the settings in which forensic psychologists work. Fortunately, computerized scoring and interpretation packages are available separately and enable a more comprehensive analysis and interpretation of the data than was previously available through hand scoring. The strength of most of the above personality assessment tools is the inclusion of validity indices that warn of attempts by the respondent to dissimulate or of respondent disabilities that might invalidate the results. The major limitation of all self-report inventories is the issue of the respondent's level of reading comprehension. While all the above tests state that they are designed for a reading level approximating that of 4–6 years of education, forensic psychologists work with a large number of clients who are functionally illiterate or whose concentration and attention are   compromised by drug abuse and other mental disorders. This limits the usefulness of self-report inventories in forensic settings. Regardless, all self-administered assessments should be treated with caution and the results seen as a set of hypotheses to be tested by other methods of assessment and by knowledge of the respondent's behaviour.

Gareth Hughes

Related entries

Personality and crime; Personality Assessment (projective).

Key texts and sources

Costa, P.T. and Widiger, T.A. (1993) *Personality Disorders and the Five-factor Model of Personality.* Washington, DC: APA.

Edens, J.F., Cruise, K.R. and Buffington-Vollum, J.K. (2001) 'Forensic and correctional applications of the Personality Assessment Inventory', *Behavioral Sciences and the Law*, 19: 519–43.

Hilsenroth, M.J. and Segal, D.L. (Editor-in-Chief, Leslie C. Morey) (2004) *Comprehensive Handbook of Psychological Assessment. Vol. 2: Personality Assessment.* Hoboken, NJ: Wiley.

PERSONALITY ASSESSMENT (PROJECTIVE)

Projective personality assessment methods are based on the assumption that the way in which a person perceives, interprets and responds to the test material or task is influenced by his or her psychological functioning, perception, memory and personality dynamics. The degree of projection involved in the process of response generation is thought to be indicated by the extent to which the test response is influenced by the person's unique personality dynamics or inner world.

Although Sigmund Freud originally used the concept 'projection' to describe a defence against anxiety, he later realized that projection is also applicable in the absence of anxiety and conflicts. He therefore described projection in a much broader sense, whereby all contemporary meaningful perception is predicated on, and organized by, memory traces of all previous perceptions (Bellak and Abrams 1997). Frank coined the term 'projective methods' in 1939, which was appropriate given the Zeitgeist of the first half of the twentieth century, during which time psychoanalysis became fashionable. Bellak, however, suggested the concept 'apppreciative distortion' for the process through which a person tends to distort what he or she perceives because of his or her own personality dynamics (this is the meaning of 'apperception' in the test known as the Thematic Apperception Test (TAT)). It follows, therefore, that, the more unstructured and ambiguous a test situation or stimulus, the more a person's response will be coloured, influenced, tinted and informed by memories, associations, previous experiences, inner wishes, needs, anxieties and conflicts.

Projective personality assessment tests can be used for different reasons, depending on the purpose for which they were designed (for example, cognitive development (Draw-a-person Test – DAP); interpersonal relationships (TAT); personality (Rorschach Inkblot Test); as a diagnosis tool (Sentence Completion Test for Depression – SCTD); and for neuropsychological impairment (Bender Gestalt)). They can also be categorized according to the nature of the task involved:

- Association techniques (Rorschach Inkblot Test, word association techniques).
- Completion techniques (Sentence Completion Test for Depression (SCTD)).
- Construction techniques, such as drawing and story telling (DAP, Kinetic-Family-Drawing Test (KFD), TAT).
- Copying techniques (Bender Gestalt).
- Forced choice or preference tasks (Szondi Test).
- Expression techniques (doll play, puppetry).

The one characteristic shared by all projective tests, however, is the relative unstructured nature of the task and/or the ambiguity of test stimuli. Projective methods are based on a few basic principles:

- They pose a problem-solving task. The person who is presented with an unstructured and/or ambiguous test situation is confronted with a problem-solving task whereby complex psychological operations are activated. How the task is approached and dealt with give an indication of that person's habitual problem-solving approach.

- A person's behaviour is an expression or reflection of his or her personality. The person's test response is a sample of his or her behaviour and therefore reveals aspects of that person's personality.
- How a person perceives and interprets his or her world depends on memory traces of previous perceptions and experiences.
- The over-elaborations, specific emphases, misinterpretations, distortions, and deviations from the stimulus field or instruction may contain the projective material.
- There is a continuity of personality. The basic psychological characteristics of a person that play a dominant role in determining his or her test response are relatively consistent across situations.

Summary of key knowledge

There is controversy concerning the reliability and validity of projective tests and methods, that has been the impetus for numerous research studies on the psychometric properties of these methods. The psychometric properties of projective methods, differ considerably, depending on 1) the nature of the test task and/or responses; 2) the scoring and/or interpretation system used; and 3) the extent to which the test responses are quantifiable and suitable for statistical calculations. For example, Exner developed a scoring system for the Rorschach test in order to overcome the psychometric inadequacies of other more subjective approaches. A wave of research studies have accumulated since the early 1970s, demonstrating that the Rorschach test possesses adequate psychometric properties, reliability and validity.

Projective tests, however, have become synonymous with a subjective assessment approach whereby practitioners' personalized interpretations of test protocols represent unsubstantiated statements and unfounded conclusions. Although most projective tests have objective scoring criteria, it is imperative that they are only used by clinicians who are adequately trained and experienced in the area of projective testing, as well as conversant with the theory, rationale, structure, current research, administration and interpretation of the specific test. Clinicians should therefore be familiar with the psychometric properties of the test, the purpose for which the test was designed and how to use it for the purpose it was designed.

Projective methods are regularly used in the USA and Europe, but it seems that there has been a general decrease in the use of projective methods over the past five years. This may be because of doubt cast over their use and because they require extensive and intensive training and are often time-consuming to administer, score and interpret.

Implications for practice

No single psychological test can responsibly be used in isolation and when projective methods are used, they should ideally be used as part of a test battery. The interpretation and conclusions should also be informed and substantiated by clinical and background information. Projective methods can be used responsibly when their limitations are kept in mind and when they are used for the purposes for which they were developed in the first place. The use of a projective method in isolation to draw a legal conclusion or to establish whether a historical event, such as child abuse, occurred is irresponsible and without foundations.

Methods that meet judicial requirements (such as the Rorschach test) are not only admissible at court hearings but expert testimonies prepared by proficient clinicians are also seldom rejected in either the USA or the UK. Projective tests can be administered to individuals, from pre-school to old age, in a group context and across cultures. The drawing methods, such as the DAP, are often less threatening and are an easy way to introduce personality assessment. They are especially useful in the case of children whose preferred medium of self-expression is often through drawing.

The clinician in a forensic context is often confronted with assessment issues, such as impression management, malingering, defensiveness and resistance. Clients are less likely to be able to influence the test results of such indirect methods as projective assessments because these methods are less transparent and their face validity is low. This characteristic of projective tests makes them uniquely suitable as an adjunct to other methods, such as interviews to obtain relevant data for personality assessment and treatment planning in forensic settings where intentional distortion is common.

Research has indicated that most, if not all, projective methods can be susceptible to aberrant response sets and are therefore 'fakable'. However, research has identified indicators on the SCTD and signs on the Rorschach test that may indicate malingering in the presence of external incentives to do so. Research has also found that participants were unable to reproduce the deficits of brain-injured patients on the Bender Gestalt test, which suggests that this test may be useful in the detection of malingering or neuropsychological impairment.

The Rorschach test has also been found to be especially useful in the assessment of sex offenders known to minimize psychological problems, and it is a sensitive instrument to differentiate between psychopathic and non-psychopathic anti-social personality disorder.

P.A. Botha

Related entries

Personality assessment (objective).

Key texts and sources

Bellak, L. and Abrams, D.M. (1997) *The Thematic Apperception Test, the Children's Apperception Test and the Senior Apperception Test in Clinical Use* (6th edn). Boston, MA: Allyn & Bacon.

Exner, J.E. (2003) *The Rorschach: A Comprehensive System. Volume 1: Basic Foundations* (4th edn). New York, NY: Wiley.

Gacono, C.B. (2000) *The Clinical and Forensic Assessment of Psychopathy: A Practitioner's Guide.* Mahwah, NJ: Erlbaum.

Pankratz, L. and Binder, L.M. (1997) 'Malingering on intellectual and neuropsychological measures', in R. Rogers (ed.) *Clinical Assessment of Malingering and Deception* (2nd edn). New York, NY: Guilford Press.

Schretlen, D.J. (1997) 'Dissimulation on the Rorschach and other projective measures', in R. Rogers (ed.) *Clinical Assessment of Malingering and Deception* (2nd edn). New York, NY: Guilford Press.

PERSONALITY DISORDER ASSESSMENT

Personality disorder assessment aims to establish whether a client meets the general criteria for a diagnosis of personality disorder, the diagnostic categories of the personality disorder the client meets and a quantitative measure of specific dysfunctional personality traits.

It is important to be clear about the purpose of a personality disorder assessment beforehand. In specialist personality disorder services, a thorough assessment and formulation of personality disorder are an essential first stage in the treatment process. In other settings the assessment of dysfunctional personality traits may be useful in the formulation of target behaviours and in tailoring an intervention to the needs of the client. In either case a diagnostic assessment linked to DSM-IV or ICD-10 personality disorder criteria will be of limited use in case formulation since these are empirically based, atheoretical constructs that provide little useful information in directing interventions. There is little evidence that specific personality disorder diagnoses predict treatment outcome, and the authors of DSM-IV note that the system is inadequate for the purpose. Dimensional, trait-based approaches to assessment can be used to measure change, tend to involve less pejorative language and can be used collaboratively with the client to help him or her to understand how his or her personality relates to his or her problems.

The most widely used trait-based measures are founded on the five-factor model (Costa and McCrae 1992). Evidence suggests that individual differences in personality disorder can be represented by four of these factors: emotional dysregulation (borderline), inhibited (schizoid avoidant), dissocial (psychopathic) and compulsive (obsessive-compulsive).

Structured personality assessments are preferable to unstructured clinical judgements because they are systematic, can correct the intuitive biases and counter-transference reactions of clinicians, and provide a more reliable measure of change. Given that interpersonal/relational dysfunctions are ubiquitous among people with a diagnosis of personality disorder, particular attention should be paid to process issues during the assessment. Any assessment of personality disorder should consider all the dimensions of personality: behavioural, cognitive, affective, interpersonal and self-concept.

Structured assessment tools for personality disorder can be divided into self-report diagnostic measures, such as the Millon Clinical Multi-axial Inventory-III (MCMI-III; Millon *et al.* 1997); structured diagnostic interviews, such as the International Personality Disorder Examination (IPDE; Loranger 1999); self-report trait measures, such as the Revised NEO Personality Inventory (NEO-PI-R; Costa and McCrae 1992); and structured interview measures of specific personality traits, such as the Psychopathy Checklist – Revised (PCL-R; Hare 2003).

Phil Wilmott

Related entries

Personality assessment (objective); Personality Assessment (projective)

Key texts and sources

Costa, P. and McCrae, R. (1992) *Revised NEO Personality Inventory (NEO-PI-R) and NEO Five-factor Inventory (NEO-FFI): Professional Manual.* Odessa, FL: Psychological Assessment Resources.

Hare, R. (2003) *Hare PCL-R* (2nd edn). Toronto: Multi-health Systems.

Loranger, A. (1999) *International Personality Disorder Examination Manual: DSM-IV Module.* Washington, DC: American Psychiatric Press.

Millon, T., Davis, R. and Millon, C. (1997) *MCMI-III Manual.* Minneapolis, MN: National Computer Systems.

Morey, L. (1991) *Personality Assessment Inventory.* Odessa, FL: Psychological Assessment Resources.

POLICE AND CRIMINAL EVIDENCE ACT 1984 (PACE)

The rights of suspects after arrest are contained in the Police and Criminal Evidence Act 1984 (PACE) and the PACE codes of practice. These provide the core framework of police powers and safeguards around stop and search, arrest, detention, investigation, identification and interviewing. PACE sets out to strike the right balance between the powers of the police and the rights and freedoms of the public. Maintaining that balance is a key area of PACE.

The latest versions of the Police and Criminal Evidence Act 1984 (PACE) codes of practice came into effect on 31 December 2005. The changes from the 2004 version reflect amendments to PACE in the Serious Organized Crime and Police Act 2005 and the Drugs Act 2005. A revised PACE Code C and a new PACE Code H came into effect on 24 July 2006.

The codes of practice include the following:

- *Code A*: governs the exercise by police officers of their powers of stop and search.
- *Code B*: relates to the searching of premises by police officers and the seizure of property found by police officers on people or in premises.
- *Code C*: deals with the detention, treatment and questioning of persons by police officers. This code is designed to ensure that all persons who are held in police custody are treated fairly and properly and in accordance with the law.
- *Code D*: deals with the procedure to be adopted by police officers for the identification of persons suspected to have been involved in a criminal offence, such as video identification or an identification parade.
- *Code E*: concerns the tape recording of interviews with suspects and the way in which the interview should be carried out.
- *Code F*: deals with the videotaping of suspects.

- *Code G*: concerns the powers of arrest under s. 24 of the Police and Criminal Evidence Act 1984 as amended by s. 110 of the Serious Organized Crime and Police Act 2005.
- *Code H*: sets out the requirements for the detention, treatment and questioning of suspects related to terrorism in police custody by police officers.

Deborah Hudspith

Related entries

Police Service.

Key texts and sources

Full details of PACE, the codes of practice and the PACE review are available online at http://police.homeoffice.gov.uk/operational policing/powers-pace-codes/pace-code-intro/.

POLICE PSYCHOLOGY

Numerous psychological theories and techniques are used to assist in policing. In criminal investigations, for example, psychological methods are employed when interviewing suspects, to assess witness credibility and to create psychological profiles. Psychological methods are also used to manage policing personnel (for example, in the treatment of post-traumatic stress disorder and in police officer recruitment).

Various branches of psychology (occupational, clinical, cognitive, social and forensic) have been drawn upon to address problems in the domains of police investigations, as well as to manage the personnel who work for the police. The early use of psychological knowledge involved the application of the Stanford Binet Intelligence scale in the USA to recruit police officers. The roles played by psychologists were consequently extended in a number of ways – for example, when post-traumatic stress disorders was first recognized, psychological

therapies were introduced to help alleviate it and, in the mid-1950s, psychological profiling emerged to help identify undetected serial murderers, such as Albert DiSalvo, the Boston strangler. Latterly, psychological concepts have been incorporated into police training, such as the interviewing of suspects and witness credibility assessment.

Psychology applied to policing

By policing is meant the procedures by which the police investigate crime, reassure the community and maintain public order. Psychology has contributed to an understanding of behaviour under these circumstances and has influenced police investigative techniques. Concepts from clinical, cognitive, environmental and social psychology may be most relevant here.

Eyewitness testimony

The accuracy of memory is critical if individuals are to be correctly identified as having committed a witnessed crime. Psychological research has been very influential in demonstrating that age, occupation, the presence of stress and prior beliefs may influence the accuracy of recall. The weapon focus effect (where people focus on one aspect, such as a gun in the crime they witnessed that interferes with their recall) and the flashbulb memory (in which stress or emotion is thought to heighten recall) have influenced police procedures in collecting eyewitness accounts and the credence placed on them.

Witness credibility

Increasingly, the police are drawing on psychological techniques (such as statement validity analysis) to determine the credibility of a witness – e.g. in child abuse and adult rape cases. Statement validity analysis is a procedure that applies content-based criteria and validity criteria to witness statements. These include such features as the presence of unusual details, self-correction or appropriate affect during the interview. These criteria are then analysed to make a probabilistic judgement that the statement is more likely to be true or false.

Interviewing

The cognitive interview technique was developed from memory research and was applied to the eliciting of more and accurate information from witnesses. The technique involves mentally reinstating the context of the event, asking witnesses to recall events in a different sequence, reporting all extraneous circumstances and recalling the event from a variety of participant perspectives. The cognitive interview has been used with sexual offences and child abuse and, more recently, it has been developed to assist in the recall of number plates.

Profiling

Offender profiling is a series of techniques whose aim is to identify an unknown perpetrator of a crime by analysing the crime scene and the nature of the offence in order to predict the characteristics of the likely offender. Profiles may try to link a series of crimes to determine if these are attributable to the same offender or may try to locate the offender's home or infer the offender's motive. Psychologists have drawn from clinical knowledge of known offenders, from notions of mental maps from environmental psychology and from the social psychology concepts of friendship patterns and networks to construct profiles.

Hostage negotiation

Sieges often, but not always, involve people suffering mental illness or disturbance, and psychological knowledge can be brought to bear on resolving the incident speedily and effectively. The clinical psychologist can help to monitor the mental state of the hostage taker, whether this is deteriorating and the impact this may have on subsequent behaviour. Often the psychological advice will be in the form of a risk assessment. This may be used to determine if a friend or relative's intervention might be timely and helpful.

Crowd control

Demonstrations, football and other sporting fixtures, mass protest and marches present the police with the potential for disorder. The police have drawn on social psychological processes to create public order policing tactics and strategies. Research has found that disorder at football fixtures tends to emerge when heavy-handed tactics are deployed that result in a collective social relationship being generated and fans sharing the perception of being subject to illegitimate police action. Low-level policing manages group-level dynamics to create a co-operative rather than conflictual, shared relationship between fans and the police.

Fear of crime and public reassurance

There is an increasing recognition that tackling the fear of crime and the perceived risk of victimization is a significant part of the policing function. It is, however, likely that young men are more often the victims of crime, yet older women are the more fearful of being victimized. The elements in the environment that signal the likelihood of crime being committed include such signifiers of disorder as litter, graffiti and evidence of drug taking. Community policing and crime prevention draw on psychological research to design campaigns and crime prevention initiatives.

Psychology applied to managing police personnel

The application of psychology to members of the police service draws on clinical, occupational and organization psychology and concerns staff well-being and the suitability of individuals to specific policing tasks.

Recruitment and selection

Psychological procedures are increasingly being used to recruit police personnel and are now often incorporated into assessment centres. Assessment may include personality measures, tests of cognitive abilities and role plays designed to measure such competencies as problem-solving, leadership, sensitivity towards ethnic minorities, gender issues and alternative sexual orientations. Work here involves the design and evaluation of appropriate exercises, and the application and scoring of personality and ability tests. Such procedures are also used to select personnel for specific police roles, such as firearms and undercover work, as well as for promotion to higher rank.

Fitness to practise

In the aftermath of such traumatic incidents as shootings, officers may be assessed to determine their fitness to resume their duties, as they may be suffering symptoms that will impair their job performance. These include difficulties in concentrating, turning up late for work, and loss of interest and motivation. Clinical assessments draw on a range of psychometric tests to provide an analysis of police officers' psychological state.

Stress management

Increasingly, the stress experienced by police personnel is recognized as an occupational hazard and may be the subject of intervention. Stress is taken to mean the overloading of a person's capacity to cope with the adverse impacts of his or her work (such as overload, fatigue after extended shift duties and oppressive management) or the operational consequences of shooting incidents or terrorist attacks. Symptoms of stress include depression, anxiety, substance abuse, hypertension and psychosomatic disorders. Interventions include group debriefing, one-to-one counselling and clinical assessments. Some police organizations also use employee assistance programmes or have occupational health units that monitor physical as well as mental health.

Leadership

The police is traditionally a command-and- control organization that has valued transactional leadership styles associated with men's preferred methods of completing tasks and focusing on short-term goals. The psychology of transformational leadership has influenced new models of policing management that are attempting to become more inclusive by recognizing the talents and preferences of women for a more transactional style of leadership that focuses on process and longer-term outcomes.

Conclusion

Psychology has been adapted for use by the police in their investigations or community interactions, or in the management of personnel (undertaken by the police themselves or by suitably qualified psychology practitioners). If the former, then principles and concepts are incorporated into training, and these influence procedure and practice. If the latter, then practitioner psychologists (such as forensic, clinical or occupational psychologists) should be appropriated from a recognized professional body. A cautionary note needs to be stated, however. Psychology's contribution to policing is often in the form of advice or assessment to aid in decision-making: the responsibility for managing an investigation lies with the senior investigating officer. Furthermore, selection and promotion advice does not pre-empt the organization's responsibility of care towards its personnel.

Jennifer Brown

Related entries

Applied Psychology; Forensic Psychology; Hostage Incidents; Investigative Psychology.

Key texts and sources

Ainsworth, P.B. (1995) *Psychology and Policing.* Chichester: Wiley.

Bailes, G. (2004) 'Sieges, the police… and a psychologist', *The Psychologist*, 17: 380–3.

Bartol, C.R. (1996) 'Police psychology: then, now and beyond', *Criminal Justice and Behaviour*, 23: 70–89.

Blau, T.H. (1994) *Psychological Services for Law Enforcement.* Chichester: Wiley.

Brown, J. (1998) 'Helping the police with their enquiries', *The Psychologist*, 11: 539–42.

Brown, J. (2002) 'Women as leaders? Catalyst for change', in R. Adlam and P. Villiers (eds) *Police Leadership in the 21st Century.* Winchester: Waterside Press.

Bull, R. and Horncastle, P. (1994) 'Evaluation of police recruit training involving psychology', *Psychology, Crime and Law*, 1: 143–9.

Canter, D. (1995a) 'Psychology of offender profiling', in R. Bull and D. Carson (eds) *Handbook of Psychology in Legal Contexts.* Chichester: Wiley.

Harrower, J. (1998) *Applying Psychology to Crime.* London: Hodder & Stoughton.

Milne, R. and Bull, R. (1999) *Investigative Interviewing.* Chichester: Wiley.

POLICE SERVICE

> The Police Services helps to reduce crime and, by the presence of police officers on the street, the fear of crime. All police forces aim to provide a safe environment in which to live and work. They play a crucial role in protecting the public from crime and anti-social behaviour; supporting victims and witnesses; and working with other agencies to reduce crime in the community.

In 2007, there were 43 police forces in England and Wales formed of more than 140,500 police officers, 14,000 volunteer special constables and 13,400 community support officers.

A police reform programme was initiated in 2001 that aimed to equip officers with the tools and knowledge necessary to meet the crime-fighting challenges they now face. The main priorities of the reform programme were to modernize the Police Service to meet the needs of the UK's changing population and to use cutting-edge techniques and technology in order to defeat ever more resourceful criminals. Now the programme focuses on improving neighbourhood policing and cutting bureaucracy. Significant progress has been made in the following areas:

- Since 1997, overall crime is down by 42 per cent – meaning 8.4 million fewer crimes a year.
- The risk of being a victim of crime is at a 25-year low.
- Investment in policing has increased by over a quarter since 1997.

Under the reform programme, the police will be equipped with the necessary skills for the twenty-first century:

- The service will be structured to enable it to provide effective neighbourhood policing and to address serious organized crime and terrorism.
- The way the police are held to account will be improved.
- The focus will be on improving police performance.

- Police bureaucracy will be reduced.
- Forces will be modernized.

The trust of the community is crucial to police officers being able to carry out their work effectively. A vital part of building up that trust is that the Police Service reflects the diversity of the society it serves and works together with the community to keep neighbourhoods safe.

Deborah Hudspith

Related entries

Investigative Psychology; Police and Criminal Evidence Act 1984 (PACE); Police Psychology.

Key texts and sources

See the Police Service's website (http://police. homeoffice.gov.uk/).

POLYGRAPHY

> The polygraph is colloquially known as a lie detector, but it does not in fact measure lies. Instead, it is an instrument that records physiological changes associated with activity in the autonomic nervous system – a part of the central nervous system, largely outside conscious control, that regulates the body's internal environment (for example, temperature, cardiovascular tone, gut activity).

At times of stress, the autonomic nervous systems responds by enhancing arousal and mobilizing resources in order to prepare the body for action. There is an increase in the supply of blood and oxygen to the muscles, heart and brain through a rise in heart and breathing rates, less important visceral activities, such as, digestion, are slowed, sweat glands become primed to dissipate heat generated by the rise in metabolism, and so on. Polygraphy is based on the notion that the act of deception produces a stress response in the automatic nervous system that is recorded by the polygraph instrument. Whether this stress is caused by the fear of deception, orientation to an issue of emotional salience and 'threat' to the individual, the increased cognitive processing required for deception or some other mechanism is unclear.

The polygraph gets its name from the original analogue instruments that were developed in the first part of the twentieth century in which blood pressure, pulse, respiration rate and electrodermal (i.e. sweat gland) activity were simultaneously recorded with pens that wrote on a moving sheet of paper – hence, 'many writings'. Modern polygraphs, although digitalized and computerized, still typically record these same measures.

The polygraph examination itself involves a pre-examination interview, an examinee's responses to a small number of questions that can be answered 'yes' or 'no' while attached to the instrument and a post-test 'debriefing' interview that takes place after the polygraph charts have been evaluated and the examiner has reached an opinion regarding whether or not the questions have been answered truthfully (although an inconclusive finding is also possible).

Because the physiological activity measured by the polygraph is not uniquely (or even always) associated with deception, and because of variation in technique, examiner experience and skill, there is ample opportunity for error when the polygraph is used to determine an individual's veracity. Just what this error rate is has been subject to much controversy, which has not on the whole been enlightened by the variable quality of research data that address it or the lack of a clear theoretical underpinning to the process itself. However, a definitive review undertaken by the National Academy of Sciences (National Research Council 2002) concluded that polygraph accuracy is probably in the region of 81–91 per cent, with the reviewers commenting: 'polygraph tests can discriminate lying from truth telling at rates well above chance, though well below perfection' (National Research Council 2002: 4).

Polygraphy is widely used in the USA as well as in many other countries. In the USA, practically all federal (including military) and numerous local law-enforcement agencies employ the polygraph in criminal investigations, in the pre-employment vetting of potential employees (although because of abuses the Employee Polygraph Protection Act 1988 outlawed this use by private sector employers) and in disciplinary proceedings. Polygraph evidence can be used in court, although with a few exceptions its admissibility must be determined on a case-by-case basis. Security agencies make similar use of polygraphy, in addition to vetting regularly for security breaches in those who work for them. In the USA (and to an extent in some other countries) there is also a large, mainly unregulated, number of private examiners who carry out tests ranging from criminal matters to checks on the fidelity of spouses and romantic partners. Increasingly, the polygraph is also being used in the treatment and supervision of offenders, particularly sex offenders.

The lack of standardization of polygraphy and the limited regulation of polygraph examiners are a frequent source of concern. Even among polygraph proponents there is disagreement about appropriate test types and applications, with the comparison question format (where responses to a number of questions distinct from the issue at hand are compared with responses to questions that relate specifically to that issue) and screening tests coming in for particular criticism. The National Academy of Sciences review, for example, argued that, for polygraphy to be viable, there should be an underlying base rate of deception of at least 10 per cent so that an acceptable balance between false positive and false negatives can be achieved – a threshold that is not reached in many screening settings, in particular.

Most supporters of polygraphy argue that, in spite of these issues, the utility of polygraphy in facilitating disclosures from examinees and in helping to build an overall picture of an individual's credibility outweighs its disadvantages, particularly when its results are not viewed in isolation but, instead, form part of a larger 'package' of information. In this respect, they note the importance of distinguishing between investigative and post-conviction applications of polygraphy, because the 'packages' of which they form part, and thus the consequences of error, differ greatly.

In terms of post-conviction applications, where polygraphy is intended to contribute to both treatment and supervision, proponents claim that polygraphy can be a useful tool in overcoming denial and in helping to monitor adherence to supervision conditions, especially with sex offenders. Research reports describe large increases in self-disclosures regarding past number and types of victims, types of offences, age of onset of sexually deviant behaviour, continued masturbation to deviant fantasies and engagement in so-called high-risk behaviours.

Polygraphy, however, remains controversial. Proponents argue that, when used by well trained examiners and in conjunction with other techniques, it can offer a useful adjunct in identifying those who attempt to deceive and in encouraging them to disclose information. Others distrust it on scientific and ethical grounds. But used cautiously and interpreted wisely, polygraphy would seem to have a role to play in a range of applications where credibility and truthful information are important.

Don Grubin

Related entries

Cognitive interviews; Detecting deception.

Key texts and sources

British Psychological Society (2004) *A Review of the Current Scientific Status and Fields of Application of Polygraphic Deception Detection: Final Report from the Working Party*. Leicester: BPS.

Grubin, D. and Madsen, L. (2005) 'Lie detection and the polygraph: a historical review', *British Journal of Forensic Psychiatry and Psychology*, 16: 357–69.

National Research Council (2002) *The Polygraph and Lie Detection: Committee to Review the Scientific Evidence on the Polygraph, Division of Behavioral and Social Sciences and Education*. Washington, DC: National Academies Press.

POST-TRAUMATIC STRESS DISORDER (PTSD)

Post-traumatic stress disorder (PTSD) is a diagnostic category used to describe a range of dysfunctional psychological responses to potentially traumatic events. It is defined by a requirement for exposure to one or more potentially traumatic events associated with feelings of intense fear, helplessness or horror, persistent re-experiencing and intense psychological distress at exposure to internal or external cues resembling the traumatic event.

The term 'post-traumatic stress disorder' (PTSD) was introduced in the third edition of the American Psychiatric Association's *Diagnostic and Statistical Manual of Mental Disorders* and was coined during the Vietnam conflict to describe a range of dysfunctional responses to coping with traumatic events (American Psychiatric Association 1980). It is in many respects similar to earlier concepts of trauma, such as 'shell shock' and 'combat fatigue' (Crighton and Towl 2008). The definition of PTSD includes a requirement for exposure to one or more potentially traumatic events, experiencing events involving actual or threatened death or serious injury, or a threat to the physical integrity of self or others. It involves a response of intense fear, helplessness or horror, with the event being persistently re-experienced in a recurrent, intrusive and distressing way, either in feelings or dreams. Individuals show intense psychological distress at exposure to internal or external cues resembling the traumatic event; physiological reactivity; persistent avoidance of associated stimuli; and a numbing of general responsiveness not present before the trauma. In order to meet the criteria for PTSD, the disturbance associated with the traumatic event needs to last more than one month and cause 'clinically significant distress or impairment' in social, occupational or other important areas of functioning.

Unlike some earlier notions of trauma, PTSD is construed in terms of a diathesis–stress model with an underlying vulnerability (diathesis), in turn 'triggered' by exposure to stressors (potentially traumatic events). Exposure to traumatic events theoretically places anyone at risk of developing PTSD. Initially, though, PTSD was reserved for extreme human experiences, such as participation in war or major civil disturbances. The diagnostic threshold for PTSD has steadily broadened to include a wide range of events with which traumatic responses might be associated. In turn this has been associated with an inflation of epidemiological estimates of prevalence over time. It has also led to suggestions of an additional diagnostic category of 'complex PTSD' (Herman 1997), which appears similar to the initial construction of PTSD.

The US National Comorbidity Survey (using DSM-IV criteria) has suggested a lifetime prevalence for PTSD of just under 8 per cent. Some groups in the population, however, appeared at markedly increased risk – groups including combat military personnel and police, corrections, fire and paramedical staff all appear at increased risk of PTSD (Kessler *et al.* 2005). Most people report strong initial reactions to potentially traumatic events, including initial feelings of being stunned, subjectively impaired memory and thinking, emotional lability and sleep disturbance. Reminders of the event are also often associated with visceral re-experiencing, negative affect and avoidance.

A number of individual characteristics have been associated with poorer long-term outcomes in response to traumatic events. These include attempts fully to suppress thoughts and feelings about the trauma. Such efforts seem to drain resources and also to increase rather than reduce levels of psychophysiological arousal. Multiple traumas or the experience of trauma early in development have also been associated with poorer prognosis. Other indicators include problems with self-care, affect regulation and changes to perceptions of personal agency and control. There is some evidence to suggest that poor adjustment is associated with selective attention to threats, which serves to confirm the perception of danger in the environment, habit-ual avoidance behaviour and negative responses from others. The best predictor of post-traumatic stress response is though the traumatic situation. The intensity and degree of threat to life experienced during the traumatic experience or experiences and the individual's peri-traumatic response to this appear most predictive of outcome accounting for the largest part of the variance seen in outcomes.

Cognitive-behavioural models of PTSD are based on the idea that conditioned emotional responses to traumatic events are primary in the development dysfunctional reactions. Following on from the peri-traumatic response, a wide range of cues may come to be associated with the event and, in turn, be capable of triggering a negative response. Where the traumatic event is a road-traffic accident, cues such as police and ambulance sirens may come to be associated and generate a stress response. This can become further generalized to include all loud noises, flashing lights and so on. A wide variety of stimuli are thus conditioned to produce responses, and these may become ever more easily accessible (hyper-accessibility) to memory. Emotional responses may be triggered by such memories and may result in defensive behaviours. In PTSD it is hypothesized that such defensive behaviours become routine and over-learnt, with two clear effects. One is that it becomes difficult for the person to show other behaviours, and the second is that this prevents sustained emotional processing of the trauma-related memory. Psychological 'scaring' associated with some of the most severe traumas appears to make a return to previous or normal functioning impossible. Examples here include some combat veterans, survivors of concentration camps or those who have experienced prolonged sexual or physical abuse.

Information-processing models of PTSD differ theoretically from cognitive-behavioural theories in a number of ways. They hypothesize that PTSD is closely related to other difficulties in managing anxiety. Such disorders are characterized by pathological information-processing biases developed early in life, with an excessive focus on some forms of information, such as threat cues. These biases, it is suggested, result in greater susceptibility to trauma in adulthood. This model provides a possible theoretical account of the links between experiences of childhood trauma (such as sexual and physical abuse) and problems in later life in developing adaptive responses to stress. The theoretical basis of information-processing models, however, has received only limited support from the evidence base.

A number of interventions have been used in relation to PTSD. Trauma-focused cognitive-behaviour therapy (CBT) is a modification of CBT designed to address trauma-related difficulties. There is emerging evidence suggesting that the use of these interventions performs better than waiting-list controls in reducing the likelihood of a PTSD diagnosis post-intervention ($k = 14$; $n = 716$; $RR = 0.47$, 95 per cent CI 0.37 to 0.59). There is also some evidence favouring trauma-focused CBT over waiting-list controls in terms of reduced severity of self-reported symptoms ($k = 8$; $n = 388$; SMD = -1.7, 95 per cent CI -2.21 to -1.18)($k = 13$; $n = 609$; SMD = -1.36, 95 per cent CI -1.88 to -0.84). There is also some evidence for reductions in self-reported depression ($k = 13$; $n = 585$; SMD = -1.2, 95% CI -1.65 to -0.75) and anxiety ($k = 10$; $n = 375$; SMD = -0.94; 95 per cent CI -1.16 to -0.72) (National Institute for Clinical Excellence 2005).

Eye movement desensitization and reprocessing (EMDR) is based on a theoretical information-processing model and postulates that dysfunctional intrusions, emotions and physical sensations experienced by trauma victims are due to the improper storage of the traumatic event in implicit memory. Intervention based on this model involves modifying the way individuals process information to help integrate the event adaptively within memory (Shapiro 2001). There is limited evidence favouring EMDR over waiting-list controls in terms of a lower likelihood of being diagnosed with PTSD post-intervention ($k = 5$; $n = 169$; $RR = 0.51$; 95 per cent CI 0.28 to 0.95). There is also limited evidence favouring EMDR over waiting list on reducing the severity of self-reported PTSD symptoms (self-report measures) ($k = 4$; $n = 116$; SMD = -1.1; 95 per cent CI -2.42 to 0.23). EMDR may reduce the severity of rated PTSD symptoms ($k = 4$; $n = 122$; SMD = -1.54,

95 per cent CI -1.96 to -1.12) and may reduce depression ($k = 4$; $n = 120$; SMD = -1.67, 95 per cent CI -2.1 to -1.25). Evidence favouring EMDR over waiting list on reducing anxiety symptoms is less clear ($k = 4$; $n = 116$; SMD = -1.18, 95 per cent CI -1.58 to -0.78).

Overall there are strongly contrasting reviews in relation to this intervention. The National Institute for Clinical Excellence (2005) review concluded that there was at present sufficient evidence to recommend continued use. Others have argued that the approach is weak in terms of its theoretical base and that the evidence base is inadequate to support such conclusions.

There is little evidence on adverse effects following from trauma-focused CBT and EMDR. There are some exceptions to this, and these have tended to focus on the negative effects of repeating exposure to the original trauma. There is evidence to suggest that the use of interventions in the form of post-incident psychological debriefings has adverse effects (Rose *et al.* 2002). It seems likely that such interventions serve to interfere with normal adaptation seen in most of those subject to traumatic events. In the case of long-term adjustment problems where normal recovery has not occurred, this is less evident, and it seems likely that the benefits of intervention generally outweigh the adverse effects.

David A. Crighton

Related entries

Hostage negotiation; Mental disorder interventions; Serious incidents in prisons.

Key texts and sources

Crighton, D.A. and Towl, G.J. (2008) *Psychology in Prisons* (2nd edn). Oxford: Blackwell.

Flouri, E. (2005) 'Post-traumatic stress disorder (PTSD): what we have learned and what we still have not found out', *Journal of Interpersonal Violence*, 20: 373–9.

National Institute for Clinical Excellence (2005) *Post-traumatic Stress Disorder: The Management of PTSD in Adults and Children in Primary and Secondary Care*. London: Gaskell (available online at **http://guidance.nice.org.uk/CG26/guidance/pdf/English**).

PREDICTIVE EFFICACY

> Predictive efficacy, more commonly reported as predictive validity (a form of criterion validity), is the extent to which a measure is able to predict, under ideal conditions, future behaviour or performance.

Predictive validity is usually derived from an analysis of large data sets that contain assessment information ('predictor variables') and a known outcome on the variable we are interested in being able to predict. The purpose of establishing predictive efficacy is to enable judgements to be made about the future behaviour or performance of an individual for whom only assessment information is known. For example, if we wished to predict the race time of an athlete (for whom we had no previous race-time information), we could base our prediction on measurements (ie. assessment information) that had been shown to be a good predictor of the race-time of others (e.g. height, weight, fitness and stamina). Needless to say, the more accurate the prediction is, the greater the assessment tool's predictive validity or efficacy.

Several areas of practice in the field of forensic psychology use the predictive utility of tools in order to aid decision-making in individual cases. These include risk assessment and the estimation of the likely benefit from treatment, to name just two.

Assessing predictive efficacy

A range of statistical methods can be used to judge the predictive efficacy of measures. These techniques are generally based on an analysis of large data sets, which are used to build a 'model' that can be used to make a prediction. A single data set or test of validity (or efficacy) is generally not considered sufficient, and so test users and developers usually accumulate a range of evidence over time in order to build a picture of the tool's performance. This process can be seen in the area of risk assessment where successive papers have addressed such issues, as

well as the use of risk assessment tools in different settings.

There is debate about the 'best' statistical approach to adopt when measuring a tool's predictive efficacy. Some of the most widely used approaches (the models and their associated statistics) are listed in Table 2.

What level of prediction is needed?

There are no easy rules of thumb for the level of predictive accuracy needed in forensic applications of prediction. For example, being able to predict at a level slightly better than chance may be considered worthwhile in some areas of practice whereas, for other applications, very high levels of accuracy are needed. Often such issues as the consequences of the errors and how the system views errors are important factors. Although indications for interpreting the statistic are available (e.g. for AUC, 0.9 would be considered excellent while 0.6 would be viewed as poor), in reality decisions about the usefulness of the measure need to be made at the local level. Such evaluations of a measure are likely to be based on what is being predicted, the increase the model offers above chance (or current practice, whichever is the better) and what the implications of incorrect judgements are.

Commonly used concepts

A number of key concepts/ideas are used in relation to prediction. These are summarized in Table 3, which also shows how these concepts are related. Good prediction models have high true positive and true negative rates and low false positive and false negative rates. Different analytic techniques report this information as errors, predictive values or in terms of specificity or sensitivity information.

Implications for practice

Before using a measure for prediction, questions need to be answered in order to understand the predictive efficacy of the instrument and its limitations. For example, are the criteria against

Table 2 Models for measuring predicitive efficacy

Model	Statistics	Comments
Regression (e.g. linear, multiple)	r^2 – amount of variance in the outcome variable accounted for by the predictor variables. Beta – the size of the increase or decrease produced in the outcome variable when the predictor variable is changed by one unit	Widely used and relatively easy to understand. Included in commonly used statistical packages
Discriminant function analysis	Table of classification – usually reported in percentages showing the overall correct classification rate and the true/error percentages	Widely used and relatively easy to understand. Included in commonly used statistical packages
Neural networks	Typically reported as classification information in percentages (of correct/error)	Allows model to be developed over time (and in real time) constantly to improve the accuracy of prediction. Less well used, fewer widely available packages
Receiver operator	Area under the curve (AUC) is the characteristic curves most widely used statistic. This measure can be interpreted as the probability that, when we pick randomly one positive and one negative case, the 'classifier' will assign a higher score to the positive example than to the negative	Widely used in medicine – arguments (e.g. REF) for using in risk assessment

Table 3 Some of the important concepts used in prediction

Predicted behaviour	Observed behaviour present	Observed behaviour absent	Sensitivity/specificity
Present	True positive	False positive (type I error)	Sensitivity (true positive/ true positive + false positive)
Absent	False negative (type II error)	True negative	Specificity (true negative/true negative + false negative)
Predictive value	Positive (true positive/true positive + false negative)	Negative (true negative/true negative + false positive)	

which the instrument has been validated clearly defined and relevant? In relation to risk, this would include what risk is predicted: reconviction for a violent crime of any severity; reconviction for serious violence; or engaging in minor or significant violence. Is this the same kind of risk we wish to make a decision about? Similarly, does the validation information generalize to the setting, individual or outcome we wish to use the tool for? In relation to treatment outcome, this would include: is the evidence from one prison applicable to another prison or a health setting? Does the individual 'fit' the profile of those who were part of the validation?

Is the treatment being offered the same in format, duration, delivery and approach?

Jason Davies

Related entries

Number needed to treat (NNT); Recidivism prediction; Risk Assessment.

Key texts and sources

Anderson, B.J, Snow, R.W. and Wells-Parker, E., (2000). Comparing the predictive validity of DUI risk screening instruments: development of validation standards. *Addiction.* 95(6), 915-929.

Gray, N.S., Fitzgerald, S. Taylor, J., MacCulloch, M.J. and Snowden, R.J. (2007). Predicting future reconviction in offenders with intellectual disabilites. The predictive efficacy of VRAG, PCL-SV and the HCR-20. *Psychological Assessment.* 19 (4), 474-479

Kline, P. (2000). *A Psychometrics Primer.* London: Free Association Books.

Walters, G.D. (2006). Risk-appraisal versus self-report in the prediction of criminal justice outcomes. *Criminal Justice and Behavior,* 33(3), 279–304.

PSYCHIATRIC DIAGNOSES

Psychiatric diagnoses are medical labels for manifestations of psychological abnormality. These labels are formally elaborated in classificatory frameworks (called 'psychiatric nosologies') developed by professional leaders, such as the *Diagnostic and Statistical Manual of Mental Disorders* of the American Psychiatric Association (1994) and *The ICD-10 Classification of Mental and Behavioural Disorders* developed by the World Health Organization (1992). These revisable frameworks offer lists of mental disorders that include varieties of mental illness, personality disorder and other forms of deviance (such as substance misuse).

Psychiatric diagnosis, like its equivalent in physical medicine, implies that a particular mental disorder has a particular root cause (aetiology), a specifiable outcome (prognosis) and a unique form of treatment (treatment specificity). Common criticisms of most psychiatric diagnoses are that little is properly understood about their aetiology, that prognosis is highly variable in patients with the same label and that treatments are used blunderbuss-fashion across diagnostic boundaries (for further details of the survival of psychiatric diagnosis, despite these criticisms, see, Pilgrim 2007). An interesting aspect of this survival is the ambivalence of psychologists: their discipline should emphasize formulation rather than diagnosis (dimensions not categories and context-specific understandings of experience and behaviour), yet many applied psychologists still retain a diagnostic approach to their work.

In ancient times Socrates suggested that madness and sanity had equal value. Positive aspects of mad rapture included prophesying (a 'manic art'), mystical initiations and rituals, poetic inspiration and the madness of lovers (Screech 1985). Hippocrates objected to speculation about the aetiology of madness and favoured instead close behavioural observation. For example, he opposed the common assumption of his time of mental abnormality being seated in the heart and diaphragm, or phren (hence such English terms as 'frenzy' and 'frenetic'). He argued that, with no direct evidence of causation, this assumption should be dropped in favour of simply observing and recording the patient's speech and action.

Although Hippocrates may have pleaded for close observation, the question still remained (as it does today) about whether this should be in relation to single symptoms or collections. For example, Galen adopted a single-symptom approach in Roman medicine, studying the separate conditions of sadness, excitement, confusion and memory loss.

Prior to the French Revolution, Pinel – following the strictures of Hippocrates on close observation – anticipated the more recent trend of basing the classification of mental illness on groups of symptoms and of suspending aetiological speculation or assertion. Pinel delineated such categories as mania with delirium, mania without delirium, melancholia, confusion and idiocy.

In the nineteenth century, German alienists began to categorize, and this empiricist approach to classification found its most noteworthy champion in Kraepelin (1883), who set the scene for the dominant paradigm in modern Western psychiatry, as characterized by three main features:

- Mental illnesses are separate, naturally occurring categories.
- These illnesses are a function of degeneracy – they are inherited conditions with a predictable, deteriorating course.
- Axiomatically and echoing Cullen – all symptoms of mental illness are caused by diseases of the brain or nervous system.

Although the Kraepelinian legacy has dominated psychiatric thought to date, in the twentieth century Adolf Meyer proposed an approach to psychiatric diagnosis that favoured dynamic holism, biographical uniqueness and continua rather than categories. Meyerian psychiatry is the basis of the 'biopsychosocial model' (Pilgrim 2002). While Meyer conceded the role of broad, inherited psychological tendencies, he saw mental disorders as reactions to peculiar biographical circumstances. His main question was not 'What is this patient's diagnosis?' but 'Why is this particular patient presenting with these particular problems at this time in his or her life?'

The 'anti-psychiatry' that subsequently developed in the 1960s saw psychiatric diagnosis as a problem, not as a solution. Szasz (1961) argued that minds, like economies, might only be sick in a metaphorical, not literal, sense. Consequently, he reasoned, the beneficiaries of socially constructed mental disorders are the psychiatric profession (whose role as a proper medical speciality is maintained) and those who are sane by common consent. Szasz did not deny that people were distressed or acted in perplexing or dysfunctional ways but, for him, these were problems of living, not symptoms of a medical condition.

Goffman (1961) pointed out that, in medical services, data are used to form a construct (a diagnosis) from two sources: the patient's communication (his or her actions and statements, called 'symptoms') and the patient's bodily state

(measurable bodily changes, called 'signs'). A problem for psychiatry, therefore, is that it relies far more than other branches of medicine on symptoms rather than signs.

Three positions about psychiatric knowledge now broadly exist.

- *Medical naturalism*: this position starts from the premise that current medical terminology describing mental abnormality is valid and has global and trans-historical applicability. Diagnoses such as 'schizophrenia' or 'depression' are taken to be labels for naturally occurring phenomena embodied in their sufferers. Here the object (mental disorder) is assumed to precede the subject (those using the term). Mental disorder is assumed to exist 'out there' and to be independent of its observers or diagnosticians. In other words, its factual status is deemed to be non-problematic.
- *Radical constructivism*: this inverts the first position and assumes instead that subject precedes object. Here the emphasis is on how diagnoses are context-specific human products. They are deemed to be socially negotiated outcomes that reflect the cognitive preferences and vested interests of the negotiators (in this case, and in modern times, the psychiatric profession is the most important, but not the only, group). In this view, mental disorder does not exist as an objective natural entity but is a by-product of psychiatric activity.
- *Critical realism*: critical realism is a bridge between the two previous positions in that external reality is deemed to precede the subject but is represented by shifting subjective or inter-subjective activity. The latter needs to be critically evaluated in order to identify the interests that are operating (thus it supports the radical constructivist position to an extent). Critical realists, however, concede the reality of some sort about mental abnormality (supporting to some extent the medical naturalists). Mental illness is not dismissed as being merely a by-product of professional activity, but it may be criticized for its poor conceptual validity.

A problem generated by the 'anti-psychiatric' critiques was that the legitimacy of physical disorders was seen as non-problematic. However, the grounds for querying the scientific merits of the diagnosis of a mental disorder can sometimes be applied to physical medicine: many diagnoses of 'true' physical pathology are vulnerable to such criticisms as a lack of aetiological and treatment specificity (for example, these criticisms can be made of inflammatory conditions, such as asthma and rheumatoid arthritis).

Thus the neat boundary that Szasz wished to retain between true and mythological pathology was not readily available. One political science reaction to this disputed boundary was to frame all illness as deviancy (Sedgwick 1982). Biomedicine, on the other hand, adapted a reductionist approach – all mental illnesses are simply brain diseases (Baker and Menken 2001).

While there is an overlap of epistemic features between mental and physical illness, mental illness is considered seperate from physical illness, for a number of reasons:

- Physical injuries and ailments happen to us, whereas we are mentally disordered. Mental disorder implicates the whole self, which thus becomes discreditable, though occasionally this negative attribution has also been a feature of physical conditions, such as sexually transmitted diseases, tuberculosis and cancer.
- The body is potentially understandable in physical terms, whereas human conduct can only be understood meaningfully via interpretive methods. Interpretation (hermeneutics) not biomedical science is required for the task (Ingleby 1980). Generally, measurable bodily signs confirm physical diagnoses, whereas mental disorders are overwhelmingly symptom-based diagnoses – they are about what people say and do.
- Coercion is applied much more frequently to the sufferer of one form of illness than the other. Mentally ill patients are deemed to lack cognitive capacity about their actions more often than physically ill patients.
- A final difference is that medicine itself rarely uses the term mental 'disease' (opting instead for the weaker and more subjectively based 'illness' notion). This implicitly concedes that the objective status of psychiatric diagnoses is open to question.

David Pilgrim

Related entries

Diagnosis of mental disorder; Forensic psychiatry; Mental disorder interventions.

Key texts and sources

American Psychiatric Association (1994) *Diagnostic and Statistical Manual of Mental Disorders.* Washington, DC: APA.

Baker, M. and Menken, M. (2001) 'Time to abandon mental illness', *British Medical Journal*, 322: 937.

Ingleby, D. (ed.) (1980) *Critical Psychiatry.* Harmondsworth: Penguin Books.

Kraepelin, E. (1883) *Compendium der Psychiatrie.* Leipzig.

Pilgrim, D. (2002) 'The biopsychosocial model in Anglo-American psychiatry: past, present and future?', *Journal of Mental Health*, 11: 585–94.

Pilgrim, D. (2007) 'The survival of psychiatric diagnosis', *Social Science and Medicine* (in press).

Screech, M.A. (1985) 'Good madness in Christendom', in W.F. Bynum *et al.* (eds) *The Anatomy of Madness: Essays in the History of Psychiatry. Volume I.* London: Tavistock.

Sedgwick, P. (1982) *PsychoPolitics.* London: Pluto Press.

Szasz, T.S. (1961) 'The use of naming and the origin of the myth of mental illness', *American Psychologist*, 16: 59–65.

World Health Organization (1992) *The ICD-10 Classification of Mental and Behavioural Disorders.* Geneva: WHO.

PUBLIC PROTECTION

The criminal justice system has, to some extent, always been influenced by the concept of public protection. However, since the 1990s England and Wales has seen a remarkable rise in 'the public protection machinery' (Nash 2006). One important reason for this was the release of some high-risk offenders into the community who subsequently reoffended, and the system's seeming inability to detect such potential danger, as in the case of Ian Huntley. Media coverage of such cases has added to this increased focus on public protection.

To understand the practicalities of public protection and its increased theoretical underpinnings in the criminal justice system, it is perhaps worthwhile to examine the key legislative changes that have occurred in recent years. The Criminal Justice Act 1991 was, in the main, concerned with the concept of proportionality in that sentence severity would be directly linked to the seriousness of the offence (Nash 2006b). However, the Act also laid out some exceptions, notably s. 1(2)(b), which referred to the potential danger to the public. Specifically, it allowed for the imposition of a custodial sentence (even if the offence did not merit custody) where 'only such a sentence would be adequate to protect the public from serious harm' (cited in Nash 2006b: 107). In addition, the Act also created voluntary judiciary powers to impose a custodial sentence longer than was commensurate on the basis of public protection. In the practical application of the Act, these new powers were infrequently applied by the judiciary.

In the mid-1990s the then Conservative government looked to some of America's legislation concerning public protection. The Crime Sentences Act 1997 subsequently implemented provisions for mandatory minimum penalties for a number of offences, which would later equate to the 'two strikes and you are out' policy for certain sexual and violent offences where the second incidence of such an offence would result in a mandatory life sentence. The offences covered included the following:

- Attempt, conspiracy, or incitement to murder.
- Offences under s. 4 of the Offences against the Person Act 1861 (soliciting murder).
- Manslaughter.
- Wounding or causing grievous bodily harm with intent.
- Rape or attempted rape.
- Intercourse with a girl under the age of 13.
- Possession of a firearm with intent to injure, or carrying a firearm with criminal intent.
- Robbery using a firearm or an imitation firearm (Nash 2006b: 111).

The Criminal Justice Act 2003 added to the public protection framework, introducing new sentences specifically concerned with the protection of the public. In addition to a life sentence, the judiciary now have two other sentences relating specifically to public protection – namely, the 'sentence for detention for public protection' and the 'extended sentence for public protection'. The Act also lists a total of 153 specified offences that are to be associated with potential dangerousness. A sentence for detention for public protection is to be imposed where the offender is convicted of a serious specified offence. The court sets a minimum term to be served before parole can be considered and, after release, the offender remains on licence for at least 10 years (Home Office 2005). The extended sentence for public protection is to be imposed when the offender is convicted of a specified offence. The sentence must be over 12 months but not longer than the maximum term for the offence in question. In addition, the court specifies a period of custody and an extension period where the offender remains on licence (Home Office 2005).

Another important legislative change in terms of the public protection framework is the Criminal Justice and Court Services Act 2000. This introduced a requirement for the National Probation Service and the Police Service to act jointly as the responsible authority and to implement arrangements for assessing and managing risks associated with sexual and violent offenders and other offenders who may pose a public protection risk (Kemshall *et al.* 2005). These arrangements came to be known as multi-agency public protection arrangements. They led to the setting up of multi-agency public protection panels to manage those offenders in the community who are assessed as high risk. The Criminal Justice Act 2003 further strengthened the arrangements by including the Prison Service as a responsible authority and by creating a 'duty to co-operate' for a range of other organizations, such as the National Health Service and social services (Kemshall *et al.* 2005).

Further legislative measures aimed at public protection and addressing specific offences can be seen in the Sex Offender Act 1997 and the Sexual Offences Act 2003. The first introduced the 'sex offender register', requiring sex offenders who meet certain criteria and who are to be released into the community to register with the police (Nash 2006). The Sexual Offences Act 2003 further tightened these provisions, such as requiring offenders to update their details with the police and provide identification aids, such as national security numbers and passports.

The public protection framework across England and Wales has expanded considerably over the past 10 years, largely driven by public outcry and legislative changes. Psychology staff have grown and developed to become key contributors to the public protection arena. Psychologists often report to multi-agency public protection panels and are involved in the risk assessments of offenders in custody and released into the community. Psychologists also provide reports to the Parole Board commenting on risk and public protection. Psychology staff in public sector prisons are also heavily involved in the delivery and management of structured groupwork interventions aimed at reducing reoffending, such as the Sex Offender Treatment Programme.

Derval Ambrose

Related entries

Multi-agency public protection arrangements (MAPPAs); Risk assessment; Violence risk assessment.

Key texts and sources

Home Office (2005) *Criminal Justice Act 2003 – New Sentences and the New Report Framework* (Probation Circular 18/2005). London: Home Office.

Kemshall, H., Mackenzie, G., Wood, J., Bailey, R. and Yates, J. (2005) *Strengthening Multi-agency Public Protection Arrangements (MAPPAs)*. London: Home Office.

Nash, M. (2006a) 'Everyone's watching: but is anyone listening?', *Prison Service Journal*, 165.

Nash, M. (2006b) *Public Protection and the Criminal Justice Process*. Oxford: Oxford University Press.

R

RECIDIVISM PREDICTION

Broadly speaking, recidivism is a lapse into previous patterns of criminal behaviour, measured by a range of indicators (such as absconding, parole/probation violation, reoffending and reconviction). It can also include behaviours that, while not illegal, are offence related – for example, a convicted child sexual abuser loitering outside a primary school (Falshaw et al. 2003).

Predicting recidivism requires actuarial or clinical assessment of the risk of a further offence being committed. Actuarial prediction relies on a calculation of the probability that an offender will reoffend. This is based on the average reoffending rate calculated from a sample of offenders who match an individual on factors associated with higher rates of reoffending. These factors are 'static' – i.e. historical and unchangeable (e.g. age, gender, criminal history and being a young male with a number of previous convictions are known risk factors for reoffending).

While more accurate than clinical judgement, actuarial risk prediction is not without limitations. For example, tools can only categorize risk for offenders falling into the group on which that procedure was tested. Moreover, actuarial measures do not identify which offenders will go on to reoffend, merely into which category an offender falls (e.g. high or low risk). Thus a risk prediction score of 65 per cent means that an average of 65 offenders out of every 100 presenting the same static factors as an offender given that score would probably reoffend. In addition, actuarial measures do not provide any indication of the risk of harm posed by an offender or how risk might be reduced.

In comparison, unstructured clinical approaches are based on interviews and observations concerning social, behavioural, environmental and personality factors related to previous offending. These are 'dynamic' as, unlike static factors, they are amenable to change (e.g. intimacy deficits, accommodation status, level of education, substance misuse), and assessment can help identify behavioural and environmental triggers for offending specific to individuals – i.e. factors that may increase (or indeed lessen) their risk. Clinical assessment, when accurate, is valuable in understanding behaviour and can assist in identifying appropriate treatment and management strategies designed to address dynamic risk factors (also known as 'criminogenic needs' as they affect the onset of offending behaviour, the persistence of offending over time and desistance from crime; Harper et al. 2005) and to reduce the risk of reoffending. The predictive validity of dynamic factors alone, however, is lower than that of static factors (although research indicates that their consideration can add substantial value when used alongside static assessment). Clinical approaches are also more open to bias than actuarial approaches and can be influenced by the assessor's opinion of the relative importance of different risk factors.

Given the limitations of using actuarial or clinical tools alone, the combination of both is widely accepted as the most reliable and useful method of risk (recidivism) prediction (e.g. Kemshall 2001). Beech et al. (2003) also advocate conducting a functional analysis of an offence in order to determine the motives for, and functions of, the offending behaviour.

A number of risk assessment instruments are available – some actuarial, some clinical and others a combination. The majority have been based on adult, non-psychopathic male populations, although some do exist for application to female, psychopathic and young offender populations. A number predict specific types of reoffending (e.g. sexual or violent); others are designed for general application. Not all, however, have been validated on UK populations.

Summary of key knowledge

In the UK, recidivism among adult offenders is usually measured by reconviction. The Home Office Offender Group Reconviction Scale 2 (OGRS2) uses static information, such as criminal history and demographic data, to predict the likelihood of an offender being reconvicted within two years of a community sentence or discharge from custody. An improved version of the tool (OGRS3) has recently been developed to address some of the limitations of the current version.

The prediction of reconviction is a key element of measuring progress in reducing reoffending in the UK. Observed reconviction rates are compared with predicted rates, based on a model that accounts for static risk factors. A reduction in reoffending rates is indicated by observed rates that are lower than the predicted rates. The latest adult reoffending results show reoffending rates within two years for adult offenders who started community penalties or were released from custody in the first quarter of 2004. The results show a 6.9 per cent reduction in reoffending when compared with the same period in 1997 and a reduction of 5.8 per cent when compared with 2000 (Home Office Statistical Bulletin 06/07).

Although using reconviction rates to measure recidivism is the best available measure, it is limited. For example, they do not take into account the severity and frequency of the offences committed and they are affected by changes in police and prosecution practice (Friendship et al. 2005). Reconviction rates also represent the narrowest interpretation of recidivism as they refer only to detected and successfully prosecuted offences. Reoffending is a wider interpretation that includes illegal behaviour not prosecuted/convicted, although even this is not as inclusive as interpretations that include offence-related behaviours.

In terms of assessment of the likelihood of general recidivism (i.e. for any offence), the tool used throughout the National Offender Management Service in England and Wales is the Offender Assessment System (OASys). The key aims of OASys include to assess how likely an offender is to be reconvicted; to identify offending-related needs; to assess risk of serious harm; and to assist with the management of that risk of harm. OASys considers both static risk factors (via OGRS2) and dynamic, and recent analysis has confirmed that drug misuse, criminal history and accommodation were the strongest predictors of reconviction (Moore et al. 2006).

The most commonly used tool in the UK for assessing specific risk of sexual and/or violent recidivism combines actuarial and clinical procedures (each can be used independently, although this is not advised). The Risk Matrix 2000 (RM2000, developed from the Structured Anchored Clinical Judgement; SACJ-Min) forms the actuarial element, and its three scales have been validated in the UK (although not on Internet offenders or men convicted of 'new' offences under the Sex Offences Act 2003). These scales predict sexual reoffending (RM2000/S), non-sexual violent reoffending (RM2000/V) and a combination of sexual and other violent reoffending (RM2000/C). RM2000 is used by the Police, Prison and Probation Services in the UK on offenders sentenced for violent or sexual offences. It has four risk categories (low, medium, high and very high) and has good predictive validity in the UK, with research identifying increasing reconviction rates corresponding to increasing risk (indicated by, for example, prior convictions for sexual offences against male and stranger victims).

The Structured Assessment of Risk and Need (SARN), which encompasses the RM2000, enables a structured clinical assessment of dynamic risk factors for sexual offenders. These are organized into four domains: sexual interests, offence-promoting thinking patterns, social and emotional functioning, and self-management. The results can be used to help develop and manage treatment and management plans for offenders. Such structured clinical tools ensure that a range of risk factors are addressed and so help reduce the bias inherent in clinical tools.

Similar combined actuarial and clinical tools for assessing the risk of sexual recidivism include the Sexual Violent Risk-20 (SVR-20) and the Risk of Sexual Violence Protocol (RSVP), which are used primarily in America. The STABLE 2000 (developed from the Sex Offender Needs Assessment Rating; SONAR) is also used, although this is predominantly a clinical tool to assess dynamic risk factors.

While RM2000 is the most commonly used actuarial tool in the UK for assessing static risk factors for sexual recidivism, the STATIC-99/02 (which superseded the Rapid Risk Assessment for Sex Offender Recidivism; RRASOR) tends to be predominant in the USA. For violent recidivism, the most widely used static actuarial tool is the Violence Risk Assessment Guide (VRAG). The Sex Offender Risk Assessment Guide (SORAG), an extension of the VRAG, is also used. While predominantly a static tool, it incorporates some clinical assessment of dynamic factors in relation to sexual and violent recidivism among sex offenders.

The primary clinical tool that considers dynamic risk factors for violent recidivism is the Historical Clinical Risk-20 (HCR-20). This considers historical elements but scores them according to professional judgement rather than an actuarial scoring scale. Other tools that incorporate both actuarial and dynamic factors in risk assessment for violent recidivism include the Spousal Assault Risk Assessment Guide (SARA) and the Violence Risk Scale (VRS). The Psychopathy Checklist-Revised (PCL-R), while primarily a tool to identify psychopathy among forensic patients rather than a risk assessment instrument, can be used to help measure psychopathy as a risk factor in predatory violence.

Implications for practice

Risk assessment underpins sentencing planning, resource allocation, the targeting of interventions designed to reduce reoffending and supervision. Thus it is central to the Offender Management Model (Home Office 2006b) adhered to in the UK and, in order for effective public protection, must be as accurate as possi-ble. However, it is important to acknowledge that the process is not an exact science and that no environment can be risk free. Accurate risk assessment aims to minimize over- or under-prediction of reoffending – in other words, to reduce the chance of Type I errors (i.e. 'false positives' or erroneously accepting that the offender is likely to reoffend) or Type II errors (i.e. 'false negatives' or failing to detect that the offender is likely to reoffend) occurring. Effective risk assessment is therefore a central component of predicting recidivism and a key element of the identification of criminogenic needs, which enables the appropriate targeting of treatment and management strategies.

For all those involved in the practice of offender management, from Parole Board release decisions to supervision and treatment, making a full and accurate assessment of risk is crucial to decision-making. It is important to remember that, as dynamic factors can be amenable to change, risk level can increase/decrease, so assessment should not be a one-off event and dynamic factors should be monitored to detect any possible imminent changes.

Jenny Cann and Gemma Harper

Related entries

Predictive efficacy; Reconviction studies; Risk assessment.

Key texts and sources

Andrews, D.A. and Bonta, J. (1998) *The Psychology of Criminal Conduct* (2nd edn). Cincinnati, OH: Anderson.

Beech, A.R., Fisher, D.D. and Thornton, D. (2003) 'Risk assessment of sex offenders', *Professional Psychology: Research and Practice*, 34: 339–52.

Hanson, R.K. and Morton-Bourgon, K. (2004) *Predictors of Sexual Recidivism: An Updated Meta-analysis. Public Safety and Emergency Preparedness Canada Report* 2004-02. Public Works and Government Service Canada.

Hollin, C.R. (ed.) (2004) *The Essential Handbook of Offender Assessment and Treatment.* Chichester: Wiley.

Risk Management Authority (2006) *Risk Assessment Tools Evaluation Directory (Version 1)*. RMA Scotland.

RECONVICTION STUDIES

> Reconviction studies examine the extent to which offenders have been convicted of one or more further offences after starting or completing a sentence (discharges, fines, community punishment, electronic monitoring, probation and custody) or a specific component of a sentence, such as a drug treatment programme.

It is tempting to assume that one can assess the extent to which any given sentence or intervention within a sentence has reduced reoffending by measuring offending before and after a sentence has been imposed. But that is an impractical plan, for a number of reasons. First, it assumes that nothing else has influenced the change. Secondly, it assumes that an offender would otherwise have maintained a steady rate of offending. Thirdly, it is clearly not reasonable to compare the impact of a two-year period in custody with two years on a community order from the day both sentences were imposed, as the periods 'at risk' of further offending differ. Fourthly, we cannot measure reoffending directly but must use proxies (such as rearrest and reconviction or self-reported offending), which all distort the underlying picture in some way. As a recent review of the effectiveness studies has noted, the main reason reconviction is most commonly used to assess effectiveness is because it is the most readily available measure.

In assessing the value of reconviction studies for practice, it is important to be aware of their pitfalls, including the following:

- Reconviction is not a direct measure of offending. Varying clear-up rates and subsequent decisions about processing by individual criminal justice personnel can affect whether an offence results in a conviction, whether a string of offences becomes one reconviction or many and the type of conviction an event becomes (e.g. an attempt to break in to a domestic dwelling may end up as a conviction for criminal damage or attempted burglary).
- Different studies count recidivism differently.

Some North American studies include rearrest and reimprisonment alongside reconviction. In the UK, each sentencing occasion is usually counted as a conviction rather than every offence, so a spate of offending over a short period may actually only be counted as one reconviction.

- Generally, even the best statistical modelling can only control for static criminal history variables as, until recently, this is all the information that has been easily available. Dynamic factors (such as a current drug problem) may both affect the likelihood that a particular sentence is imposed and the chances that a sentence will be effective.
- It is important to correct for pseudo-reconvictions, convictions which are recorded after the start of a sentence but which relate to offences committed before it began. Thus, they are not a measure of the current sentence's impact. Such corrections tend to be rather crude in studies based on data held on the Offender Index, which does not include date of offence, only date of conviction. The Police National Computer does contain date of offence, but studies using this are currently rare because it has been difficult to access it.
- Differences in the reconviction rates of particular sentences or programmes may indicate that they work (assuming other explanations can be discounted/controlled for), but they do not provide insight into why an intervention works or which parts of it work.

The likelihood that offenders will offend again once they have been dealt with by the criminal justice system is primarily determined by their characteristics (especially age and sex) and criminal history (e.g. age at first of offence, types of offending and previous sentences). Of course, these factors are also taken into account by sentencers when deciding which disposal to impose. This makes it is misleading to compare the 'raw' reconviction rates of different sentences. Home Office studies conducted in the 1990s therefore 'controlled' or adjusted for some of the key differences in those given different disposals and they allowed for pseudo-reconvictions. These studies concluded that there was no statistically significant difference in the effectiveness of custody and community penalties.

In theory, it is less problematic to use raw reconviction rates to track how a single sentence has performed over time. However, at the same time as the two-year reconviction rate for offenders released from prison in England and Wales was rising from 53 per cent in 1993 to 58 per cent in 2003, the courts were sending more and different people to prison and imposing longer sentences. This means that the rise may be an indication that the experience of going to prison is becoming less effective as a deterrent or a vehicle for rehabilitation. Equally, however, it could mean that sentencers are employing prison less effectively. For this reason the most recently published government statistics that are used to assess the effectiveness of prison and probation take account of changes in the characteristics of those receiving such sentences over time using statistical modelling. However, this exercise only compared community penalties with each other, not with custody. The authors believe that much of the difference in reconviction rates they did find reflects the fact that they could not control for a range of potentially important factors because they did not have information on them. For example, a severely drug-addicted offender is more likely to be sentenced to a drug treatment and testing order than a community punishment order, and this may well affect his or her reoffending, but data on this are not held centrally. The range of sentences available to the courts was changed by the Criminal Justice Act 2003. Most provisions were only implemented in 2005 and some have not yet been implemented. As a consequence, no reconviction studies have yet been published about the effectiveness of these sentences.

In assessing the effectiveness of a specific intervention, most studies consider the results of the 'treated' sample against those of a control group. While some studies have done this through random allocation, this is hard to arrange, and there are also ethical objections in some circumstances (e.g. it would clearly be unacceptable to decide to send someone to prison on the 'toss of a coin'). Studies in which the experimental group are matched on a few key characteristics with a control group are more common. One of the reasons that later British studies of the impact of cognitive-behavioural programmes in prison showed less impact than earlier ones is that the later ones used more closely matched comparison groups. Differences in implementation also contributed to the result, making it impossible to say whether the earlier evidence of success was mainly a consequence of better implementation or was mainly down to measurement error. Sometimes the sample acts as its own control when the offenders' actual reconvictions are compared with their 'expected' or 'predicted' rates (calculated using models based on the actions of similar offenders). This is a useful supplementary measure but a poor primary one as it predicts the likelihood of a group of offenders with a set of similar characteristics being reconvicted accurately, but it may not be true of a specific individual within the group.

Most of the recent reconviction studies of individual interventions, such as schemes to improve employability or drug treatment and cognitive-behavioural programmes, tend to show that they have only marginal effects, and even those effects are often short lived. In many of the recent reconviction studies, especially those delivered in a community setting, the degree of implementation failure was so great that it is possible to argue that the interventions were never properly tested. Also, it is possible that a 'yes/no' measure of reconviction in two years may be too crude to pick up important changes, such as longer gaps between offences and reductions in seriousness. The non-reconviction benefits of some interventions (such as improved health and functioning) may also make the interventions worthwhile. However, we know that most offenders have multiple problems, so it is also quite possible (and consistent with the findings of early 'What Works?' studies) that interventions which only target one issue are not enough to reduce reoffending. It has been suggested that more 'multi-modal' (holistic) interventions should be developed and assessed, but these are unlikely to report for several years.

This does not necessarily mean that reconviction studies are without value, as they may still result in net savings in offending. However, such studies sometimes fail to take account of the non-reconviction benefits such interventions may accrue.

Carol Hedderman

Related entries

Predictive efficacy; Recidivism prediction.

Key texts and sources

Harper, G. and Chitty, C. (eds) (2004) *The Impact of Corrections on Re-offending: A Review of 'What Works'. Home Office Research Study* 291. London: Home Office.

Hedderman, C. (2007) 'Past, present and future sentences: what do we know about their effectiveness?', in L.R. Gelsthorpe and R. Morgan (eds) *Handbook of Probation.* Cullompton: Willan Publishing.

Hollin, C.R. and Palmer, E.J. (2006) *Offending Behaviour Programmes: Development, Application and Controversies.* Chichester: Wiley.

Lloyd, C., Mair, G. and Hough, M. (1994) *Explaining Reconviction Rates: A Critical Analysis. Home Office Research Study* 136. London: Home Office.

REVOLVING DOORS

'Revolving doors' is an informal term that broadly refers to the process of entering, exiting and re-entering into a service, institution or organization.

'Revolving doors' is often used to refer to recidivism where offenders continue to come in to contact with the criminal justice system. It can also be used to refer to organizations that have a high workforce turnover. However, it is most notably used to refer to the phenomenon of mental health patients being rehospitalized after a period of time in the community – a phenomenon that came sharply into focus with the move away from the long-term institutionalization of people with a mental health diagnosis towards an increased emphasis on care in the community.

It was, however, the 1950s that saw the beginnings in the UK of a move away from the large-scale detention of people with mental health problems in asylums, initially influenced by advances in medical treatment (for example, the twentieth-century epidemic of the then termed 'general paralysis of the insane' – a late manifestation of syphilis that was eradicated through penicillin treatment; Abrahamson 2006). Other influences included the increased use of anti-psychotic medication and a recognition that the vast majority of mental health patients did not pose a risk to the community.

The Mental Health Act 1959 removed statutory controls from a large number of mental health patients and introduced a number of safeguards for those patients still subject to legal restrictions (Jewesbury and McCulloch 2002). The Mental Health Act 1983 retained a high proportion of these procedures. In addition, the Mental Health Act 1959 created a legal basis for local authorities to create residential alternatives to hospitals, to recruit mental welfare officers and to provide preventive services (Bartlett and Wright 1999). In 1961 the Minister of Health, Enoch Powell, announced the government's commitment to the eventual closure of the old mental hospitals (Jewesbury and McCulloch 2002). This trend continued through the 1960s and 1970s and beyond, with 'care in the community' becoming the preferred model.

In the early 1990s a joint review was commissioned by the Department of Health and the Home Office (the Reed Review) focusing on health and social services for mentally disordered offenders. This led to a number of implemented recommendations. One such recommendation saw the introduction of the Care Programme Approach, which was to be the basis of care for severely mentally ill people. Its main elements were:

- the systematic assessment of health and social care needs;
- an agreed care plan;
- allocation of a key worker; and
- regular review of the patient's progress (Jewesbury and McCulloch 2002: 51).

The Labour government's policy document, *Modernising Mental Health Services*, was published in 1998, following some highly publicized 'failings' in the mental health system in England and Wales, such as homicides committed by patients who had been released into the community from psychiatric care. This new policy emphasizes the relationship between active mental illness and violence, and it places the concept of public protection firmly on the agenda (Jewesbury and McCulloch 2002). Importantly the new approach introduced the idea of compulsory treatment in the community: the Mental

Health Act 1983 is currently under review, and one of the proposed revisions is concerned with compulsory treatment in the community.

Derval Ambrose

Related entries

Forensic psychiatry; Psychiatric diagnoses.

Key texts and sources

Abrahamson, D. (2006) 'History of care in the community', in A. Stephens and R. Walden (eds) *For the Sake of Humanity: Essays in Honour of Clemens N. Nathan.* Leiden and Boston, MA: Martinus Nijhoff.

Bartlett, P. and Wright, D. (eds) (1999) *Outside the Walls of the Asylum: The History of Care in the Community, 1750–2000.* London: Athlone Press.

Buchanan, A. (ed.) (2002) *Care of the Mentally Disordered Offender in the Community.* Oxford: Oxford University Press.

RISK ASSESSMENT

Risk assessment can be defined as the systematic collection of information to determine the degree to which harm (to self and others) is likely, at some future point in time.

A risk factor can be defined as an attribute, such as a habit (e.g. alcohol consumption), behaviour (e.g. aggression) or a personality trait, or exposure to some environmental, contextual, interpersonal or otherwise external hazard that leads to increased or greater risk. Risk assessment must be explicit and dynamic, and will normally be short term and take into account a balance of factors (hazards and protectors). The sources of information may be many and varied and might include standardized instruments, third-party information reports and purely idiosyncratic or idiographic detail. Much of the information from a full risk assessment will not fit easily in a mechanistic prediction model but may prove vital, none the less, in decision-making and in the planning of risk and care case management.

Prediction involves the assignment of a probability to a patient or offender and indexing the likelihood of that person committing harm to him or herself or others – e.g. suicide/self-harm or a violent offence (criminal or otherwise) in and/or outside hospital or other institutional setting. Typically, but not always, prediction is based on actuarial information organized according to some form of statistical model. This is a rather mechanistic approach to risk and has both advantages – in terms of standardization and apparent objectivity – and limitations – in terms of limited focus and contextual insensitivity (Monahan 1993; Clark 1999; Hammond and O'Rourke 2004).

Risk management inevitably involves the implementation of a set of values and principles that need to be properly integrated with a set of operational procedures and support systems. The successful management of a patient or client's risk will be based on sensitivity to the individual's needs (both dynamic and fixed), vulnerabilities and evolving behaviours. The fundamental purpose of these management procedures are risk reduction and the prevention of harmful behaviour, as well as the provision of safe, sound, supportive services. Effective risk management is crucial to the provision of safe and good-quality services and should be the main concern in any forensic service.

Risk assessment is at the very heart of professional practice in forensic services, and clinicians working in this speciality have three main areas of concern:

- Public safety.
- The functioning and future behaviour of the individual with whom they are working.
- The personal safety of themselves, their colleagues and of any users of or visitors to their services.

In the planning and development of a risk assessment strategy, it is useful to address the two discrete aspects of the process: assessment and management (defined above). The primary areas of risk relevant to the work of forensic specialists are, according to O'Rourke and Hammond (2005a), as follows:

- *Dangerousness*: the risk of causing harm or danger or encouraging/involving others in the causing of harm or injury to others.
- *Mental instability*: at risk to self or others because of a fluctuating and/or unpredictable mental health function, especially in relation to command hallucinations and other at-risk psychotic or disturbed phenomena.
- *Self-harm/suicide risk*: at risk of self-intentional injury or killing oneself, or of action/behaviours destructive to one's own safety or health.
- *Vulnerability*: at risk of, or exposed to, damage or harm through personal or external factors (e.g. naiveté, low insight, personal pressures, poverty, homelessness or other resource or capability deficits).

Implications for practice

The assessment and judgement of risk are thought to be improved by the use of structured risk assessment tools in the clinical process (Fuller and Cowan 1999; Litwack 2001; Hollin 2002; Gray *et al.* 2004). Some of the best known and most widely used tools in risk assessment in UK forensic contexts include the PCL-R (Hare 1991), the HCR-20 (Webster *et al.* 1995), RAMAS (O'Rourke and Hammond 2005b), the LSI-R (Andrews and Bonta 1994) and OASys. O'Rourke and Bailes (2006) provide a short description of each of these.

These tools vary in terms of design and content (e.g. mental disorder factors, or historical, clinical or other sources of risk factors), psychometric properties (validity, reliability and populations tested) and communication and administration (training or the skills required to use the measure). Robust risk assessment tools help professionals develop effective baselines. It must be borne in mind that arbitrary metrics are contrary to human rights. Safe practice dictates that forensic specialists should only use tools that are fit for purpose (valid, reliable, psychometrically robust) and that assist with professional judgement about risk, need and responsivity (O'Rourke and Hammond 2005).

Finally, partnership working is essential when it comes to effective risk management.

The link between adverse life conditions, offending and poor mental health is well established. People who pose a risk to themselves or to others often have a wide range of problems, including mental health or personality problems, substance misuse, legal or financial problems and, often, housing difficulties. Consequently, they will require a spectrum of services. High risk is most often (but not exclusively) associated with long-term need. Forensic professionals must be willing to work across services, as multi-agency communications and risk management are key to the ethically desirable and outcome-effective management of offenders.

Margaret O'Rourke

Related entries

Predictive efficacy; Recidivism prediction; Reconviction studies; Violence risk assessment.

Key texts and sources

Clark, D. (1999) 'Risk assessment in prisons and probation', *Forensic Update*, 1: 15–18.

Fuller, J. and Cowan, J. (1999) 'Risk assessment in a multi-disciplinary forensic setting: clinical judgement revisited', *Journal of Forensic Psychiatry*, 10: 276–89.

Gray, N., Snowden, R., Taylor, J. and MacCulloch, M. (2004) 'Relative efficacy of criminological, clinical and personality measures of future risk of offending in mentally disordered offenders,' *Journal of Consulting and Clinical Psychology*, 72: 523–30.

Hollin, C.R. (2002) 'Risk–needs assessment and allocation to offender programmes', in J. McGuire (ed.) *Offender Rehabilitation and Treatment: Effective Programmes and Policies to Reduce Reoffending*. Chichester: Wiley.

Litwack, T.R. (2001) 'Actuarial versus clinical assessment of dangerousness', *Psychology, Public Policy and Law*, 7: 409–43.

O'Rourke, M.M. and Bailes, G. (2006) *Risk Assessment and Management. Faculty of Forensic Clinical Psychology Occasional Paper*. Leicester: BPS.

RISK-NEEDS ASSESSMENT (LEVEL OF SERVICE INVENTORY - LSI)

Risk-needs assessment is an approach to the assessment and classification of offenders. It typically combines information about static risk factors (which cannot be changed by intervention – e.g. past criminal record) with dynamic risk factors or 'criminogenic needs' (which can, in principle, be changed – e.g. involvement with delinquent peers). Risk factors, appropriately weighted, are added together to produce a risk score.

The most widely used risk-needs assessment instrument is the Level of Service Inventory-Revised (LSI-R), a 54-item checklist developed originally in Canada and now in international use. Variants and derivatives include the LS/CMI (which incorporates a case management inventory) and the YLS/CMI for young offenders.

Evidence base

The LSI-R draws on a wide range of research on correlates of recidivism, and on a series of consultations and evaluative pilots with probation officers and correctional staff since the late 1970s. Much of this material is summarized in the user's manuals, and the theoretical basis lies in a broad social learning model of criminality, as set out in Andrews and Bonta (2003). There is strong evidence from several jurisdictions that the LSI-R predicts reconviction about as well as or better than other instruments. One of the larger reconviction studies, carried out in Britain (see Raynor 2007), has also shown dynamic predictive validity – in other words, offenders whose LSI-R scores increase during periods of supervision are shown to have an increased risk of reconviction, and offenders whose scores decrease have a decreased risk.

Research on using the LSI-R with women offenders and with minority ethnic groups has shown mixed results: the majority show a degree of validity, suggesting the broad applicability of the model. For women, there is evidence from Britain that risk can be over-predicted, and local reconviction studies are recommended to correct this. It is also now widely accepted that, although many dynamic risk factors are applicable to both men and women, some others are more gender-specific.

Implications for practice

The LSI-R has five main uses, if administered by competent and appropriately trained staff:

- It provides an estimated risk of further offending that can be used to inform decisions about the level of control over an offender that is needed to reduce or prevent reoffending.
- It provides information about dynamic risk factors that can be addressed by intervention, leading to better planned and individualized rehabilitation.
- It can provide information about the prevalence and distribution of needs in a population of offenders, to assist in service planning and policy.
- If readministered after appropriate intervals, it can assist in evaluation of the impact of services by monitoring changes in risk.
- It helps to identify cases where further detailed assessment (for example, of dangerousness or substance-abuse problems) is indicated.

Peter Raynor

Related entries

Cambridge Framework for Risk Assessment (CAMRA); Risk assessment.

Key texts and sources

Andrews, D.A. and Bonta, J.L. (1995) *The Level of Service Inventory – Revised (User's Manual)*. New York, NY and Toronto: Multi-health Systems.

Andrews, D.A. and Bonta, J.L. (2003) *The Psychology of Criminal Conduct* (3rd edn). Cincinnati, OH: Anderson.

Andrews, D.A. and Bonta, J.L. (2004) *The Level of Service/Case Management Inventory: An Offender Assessment System (User's Manual)*. New York, NY and Toronto: Multi-health Systems.

Bonta, J.L. (1996) 'Risk-needs assessment and treatment', in A.T. Harland (ed.) *Choosing Correctional Options That Work*. Thousand Oaks, CA: Sage.

Raynor, P. (2007) 'Risk and need assessment in British probation: the contribution of LSI-R', *Psychology, Crime and Law*, 13: 125–38.

S

SECURE TRAINING CENTRES (STCs)

Secure training centres (STCs) are purpose-built accommodation for young offenders, up to the age of 17, who are sentenced or remanded to custody by a court.

There are currently four secure training centres (STCs) in England: Hassockfield in Consett, Co. Durham, Oakhill in Milton Keynes, Beds, Rainsbrook in Rugby, Northants and Medway in Rochester, Kent. These STCs can accommodate 58–87 young people, who are known as trainees in the centre. Young people are ideally placed within a 50-mile radius from their home. However, this is not always possible. The Youth Justice Board sets out the Key Elements of Effective Practice, which guide STCs to work effectively towards specific goals.

Research has shown that young people who offend have multiple needs that must be identified and addressed in order to reduce their risk of reoffending. STCs promote a multidisciplinary approach where professionals from different backgrounds work together to form individualized plans for each young person so as to address specific needs.

STCs have a range of staff with a variety of backgrounds, including healthcare and social workers, psychologists, residental care staff, diversity staff, community programme workers, and alcohol and substance misuse staff, as well as all the other staff who support the centre. STC staff use a range of assessments to identify the needs of young people, the risk they present to themselves and others, and the likelihood of them reoffending. The assessments require STC staff to speak to the young person, their par-

ents/carers and other services that have worked with them to gather relevant information.

Education is a key focus, and the young people are provided with formal education 25 hours a week, 52 weeks of the year. Centres have been improving the range of education and vocational opportunities available to the trainees. There are qualified nurses on site at all times to provide primary healthcare. Doctors, dentists, psychiatrists, community psychiatric nurses and counsellors also visit centres to provide specialist services.

Trainees who have been sentenced receive tailored interventions as well as generic offending behaviour programmes focusing on their offending behaviour. Trainees who have been remanded receive programmes relating to citizenship.

Staff at STCs start to plan for the young person's resettlement into the community at their initial meeting, as reintergrating the young people successfully back into society, after the custodial element of the sentence, is of paramount importance. Staff will address accommodation, family relations, education, training and employment, as well as other issues. This work is usually organized by the young person's case manager in conjuction with the young offender team (YOT) and other community services.

Community programmes are explored with the young person to encourage him or her to learn new skills, such as fishing, painting and decorating, gardening, etc. A package of mobility or temporary release will also be formulated to aid successful reintergration into the community. Other interventions offer focus on restorative justice and reparation.

Prior to a young person being released, staff will liaise with the YOT and community agencies to make recommendations for further work in the community. STCs aim to help young people to develop as individuals by addressing their individual needs which, in turn, will help them stop reoffending.

Kay Cahill, Sharon Pearson
and Angela Donaghy

Related entries

HM Prison Service; Social services.

Key texts and sources

See the websites of the Youth Justice Board (www.yjb.gov.uk), the Home Office (www.homeoffice.gov.uk) and Crime Reduction (www.crimereduction.gov.uk).

SELF-INJURY ASSESSMENTS AND INTERVENTIONS

There has been some debate over the definition and classification of self-injury over the last few decades. One of the important consequences of this has been the establishment of the difference between self-injurious behaviour and suicidal behaviour (Walsh 2006). This is not to say that self-injurious behaviour cannot result in suicide, but the ending of life is not the intention of self-injury. It is also not to suggest that those who self-injure are not at increased risk of suicide. Crighton and Towl's (2000) proposal of placing self-injury at one end of a continuum of behaviour, with suicide at the other, is a helpful way of conceptualizing the risks.

The definition of self-injury used in this entry is as follows: 'Self-injury is intentional, self-effected, low-lethality bodily harm of a socially unacceptable nature, performed to reduce psychological distress' (Walsh 2006: 4).

The definition of self-injury given above and used in this entry, therefore, is intended to be non-judgemental and descriptive. The term 'self-effected' is a recognition that some individuals self-injure with the assistance of others, which is more common in adolescent populations (Walsh 2006). The use of the term 'low lethality' is to convey that the behaviour is not intended to pose a risk to life.

Walsh (2006) discusses the difference between suicide and self-injury exploring such issues as intent, level of physical damage and potential lethality, the frequency of the behaviour, multiple methods, the level of psychological pain and the constriction of cognition. Although there is not the space to explore this in detail here, it is nevertheless a helpful portrayal of some of the key differences between suicide and self-injury that will aid in a practitioner's assessment.

Assessment

In the assessment of self-injury it is useful to consider some of the demographics and key risk factors that have been explored in the research. Many researchers have noted that self-injury is more commonly observed among women, although men who self-injure tend to inflict more severe wounds (Babiker and Arnold 1997). However, in prison populations, there is a higher rate of self-injury among men than seen in the wider community (Babiker and Arnold 1997). In addition, self-injurious behaviour is more common in younger populations (mainly in the teens, 20s and 30s, and higher rates have been reported among lesbian and gay people, particularly young lesbians and gay men (Babiker and Arnold 1997).

A study in a prison setting exploring key differences between those who engage in self-injurious behaviour and those who attempt suicide reported that those who self-injure more commonly had a history of medium negative home life events and that the precipitating mood state was active (anger) (Snow 2006). In contrast, the people in the study who had attempted suicide had higher rates of negative home life experiences and were in more passive emotional states prior to the attempt (depression).

In prison populations there is evidence of higher rates of self-injury than in the community (Crighton and Towl 2000). Winkler (1992 cited in Crighton and Towl 2000) suggests that the rates of self-injury among young offenders are up to five times higher than adolescent self-injury rates reported in the community. However, it is not clear if this is a difference in detection rates or a difference in the characteristics of those who have been sentenced to prison (Crighton and Towl 2000). In prison populations there is also some evidence that self-injury rates are higher among white prisoners and among females in custody (Crighton and Towl 2000).

Walsh (2006) outlines a detailed biopsychosocial model for the assessment of self-injury that explores five interrelated dimensions: environmental, biological, cognitive, affective and behavioural. Walsh provides an account of aspects of the five dimensions that should be considered during assessment, such as a history of sexual abuse, low serotonin levels and a history of trauma. However, he goes on to suggest that assessment begins with the behavioural dimension. Assessment is based on the principles of behavioural analysis, examining the antecedents to the behaviour itself and the consequences of the behaviour (Kazdin 1994 cited in Walsh 2006).

Walsh (2006) also suggests that a useful information-collection tool is a self-injury log to establish the specifics of an individual's self-injurious behaviour. This log should record the frequency of the episodes; the nature and severity of the wounds; the extent of the physical damage; the particular body area targeted; the use of a tool (such as a knife); the pattern of the wounds; where the self-injury takes place; and what social context the self-injury takes place in. The assessment then moves on to explore the antecedents of the behaviour across the five dimensions discussed above. For example, some of the emotional antecedents might include a recent experience of loss, interpersonal conflict, frustration about personal needs not being met and social isolation (Walsh 2006). Biological antecedents may include such things as evidence of a reduced sensitivity to physical pain. The exploration of cognitive antecedents involves particular thoughts and beliefs that preceded and may trigger the event. Affective antecedents explore the emotions that precipitate the event, such as feelings of shame or

depression. Finally, behavioural antecedents include specific observable actions the person undertakes before the event (Walsh 2006). A thorough assessment of all five dimensions provides the practitioner with a detailed and individualized account of the risks and the behaviour. This can then be used to inform the most appropriate intervention for that person.

Interventions

There is a large range of interventions for people who self-injure. The empirical evidence for the effectiveness of interventions is still in its infancy, however. Linehan *et al.* (1991 cited in Walsh 2006) have reported that dialectical behaviour therapy is an effective intervention tool, and they detail a reduction in 'para-suicidal acts' during treatment with adult women with a diagnosis of borderline personality disorder. Linehan *et al.* applied behavioural and cognitive strategies in conjunction with strategies derived from the Buddhist idea of 'mindfulness', and validation and a non-judgemental approach underlie the intervention. However, Babiker and Arnold (1997) do not agree that the starting point of an intervention should be an assumption that self-injury is 'unacceptable' and debate that this is at odds with a non-judgemental approach.

One common intervention approach is that of replacement skills training. This is often used in conjunction with another form of intervention, such as cognitive therapy, psychotherapy or body image work. Replacement skills training explores with people alternative skills to manage their psychological pain or distress which should be at least as effective as the self-injurious behaviour itself in managing such pain or distress (Walsh 2006). Walsh (2006: 127–46) lists nine types of replacement skills:

- Negative replacement behaviours, such as applying ice packs to the area usually injured or marking the area with a red pen.
- Mindful breathing skills: using techniques to induce a state of being calm, relaxed and focused.
- Visualization techniques: involving identifying and imagining relaxing scenes that can aid the person to self-sooth.

- Physical exercise: engaging in a physical activity that can be easily accessed when experiencing distress, such as vigorous walking.
- Writing: such as keeping a daily journal.
- Artistic expression.
- Playing or listening to music.
- Communicating with others: identifying people in the the person's life whom it is safe for the client to discuss his or her urge to self-injure with in a focused and productive manner.
- Diversion techniques: identifying activities the person can apply temporarily to divert him or herself from engaging in self-injury.

Another intervention that is often used is cognitive therapy. This approach focuses on targeting the 'thoughts, assumptions, rules, attitudes and core beliefs that support the self injury' (Walsh 2006). The cognitions that precipitate the behaviour are seen to play a core role in both the onset of self-injury and the maintenance of the behaviour. Cognitive therapy looks to break down in detail the thought structure that supports the behaviour, and it aims to modify this structure as a way, in turn, to modify the behaviour. For example, a person may hold a core belief that he or she is 'a failure'. This may in turn inform particular attitudes, such as 'I deserve to feel the way I do'. This attitude may lead to a series of internal rules, such as the concept that self-injury is the most productive way to reduce the psychological pain that is being experienced (Walsh 2006).

Derval Ambrose

Related entries

Mental disorder interventions; Suicide.

Key texts and sources

Babiker, G. and Arnold, L. (1997) *The Language of Self-injury: Comprehending Self-mutilation.* Leicester: BPS.

Crighton, D. and Towl, G. (2000) 'Intentional self injury', in G. Towl *et al.* (eds) *Suicide in Prisons.* Leicester: BPS.

Snow, L. (2006) 'Psychological understanding of self-injury and attempted suicides in prisons', in G. Towl (ed.) *Psychological Research in Prisons.* Oxford: BPS/Blackwell.

Walsh, B. (2006) *Treating Self-injury: A Practical Guide.* New York, NY: Guilford Press.

SENTENCING

Sentencing decisions impact on the lives of many people and impose a great financial burden on the taxpayer. Sentencing, however, has been described as the 'cornerstone of the criminal justice system' (Sallmann and Willis 1984).

Disparities in sentencing

Despite the fact that a significant proportion of criminal cases decided by the courts are not serious and are processed routinely in the lower courts, the task of the sentencer is by no means an easy one, for a number of reasons. A very frequent complaint against sentencers concerns disparities – i.e. unjustifiable inconsistencies in sentencing cases that are not significantly different. Such disparities are often the grounds for appeal against a sentence by either the defendant's lawyer or the prosecuting authority, and disparities in sentencing in western common law countries have been a cause for concern since the nineteenth century (Kapardis 1985).

Variations in sentencing

On the basis of the research method used, studies of sentencing can be grouped under the following categories (see Kapardis 2003: 167–69 for details): 'crude comparison', 'random sample', matching by item, 'prediction', observational and experimental simulation. In studying sentencing, there is a need for a scale to measure penalty severity. Such a scale was reported in England by Kapardis and Farrington (1981: 113) who found significant consistency both within and between 168 magistrates (justices of the peace) from six different parts of England in their ranking of 12 different disposals across nine cases – in other words, the type of case did not seem to have much effect on their ranking of the severity of penalties.

It is a well established fact that a range of legally relevant case characteristics, both aggravating and mitigating, can impact on the choice of type of sentence and its severity. However, a number of non-legal factors also affect the sentencer's decision.

Extra-legal factors that influence sentencing decisions

When considering non-legal factors at the sentencing decision stage in criminal justice, it must be remembered that some of the same factors (e.g. stereotypes) influence decision-making at earlier stages in the criminal justice process.

Defendant's gender

Gender bias and the administration of criminal justice has been an issue of concern for a number of years now. Feminist authors have argued that the theoretical underpinnings of the law are, in many instances, biased in favour of men, and that the judiciary are guilty of sexism. In the context of sentencing, it has been argued that sexism operates to reinforce traditional gender roles and manifests itself in a paternalistic approach that aims to protect the social institution of the family (for example, the courts may be reluctant to fine female defendants because it would make their childcare responsibilities more difficult; (Gelsthorpe and Loucks 1997).

An examination of criminal statistics shows that the judiciary discriminate in favour of women and at the expense of men. However, caution is warranted in drawing conclusions on the basis of such statistics because of frequent differences between male and female defendants in terms of their offending, criminal records and social circumstances. With the exception of the study of the Cambridge Magistrates' Court by Farrington and Morris (1983), which found no gender differences when taking into account offence seriousness and previous convictions, other British studies of gender differences in sentencing by real sentencers (i.e. magistrates and judges) have reported that female defendants receive more lenient sentences (Kapardis 2003: 170–2). Wilczynski and Morris (1993) analysed data on 474 cases in which a child had been killed by a parent in England and found that female defendants were significantly more likely to be convicted of manslaughter rather than murder, to be dealt with on the basis of the defence of diminished responsibility, and to receive significantly more lenient sentences, especially non-custodial ones. The leniency of treatment

was especially evident for the women convicted of infanticide – none of them were incarcerated.

Wilczynski and Morris (1993: 35–6) concluded that labelling such women's killings as 'abnormal' behaviour contradicts sentencers' perceptions of women as 'inherently passive, gentle and tolerant ... nurturing, caring and altruistic', and that the idea that a woman 'must have been "mad" to kill her own child' results in lenient treatment by the courts. Studies of the importance of gender at the sentencing stage in the USA (which include a large proportion of experimental simulation studies of often low external validity) have reported contradictory findings. Considering also studies from Australia and New Zealand and taking the quality of the methodology used by the researchers into account (see Kapardis 1985, 2003), it can be concluded that a defendant's gender is an important factor in sentencing in many parts of the world.

Defendant's race

Research into race and sentencing has been reported in the USA, Canada, Australia and New Zealand – British researchers did not start looking into the possibility of racial discrimination at the sentencing stage until the late 1970s. However, since that time UK researchers have found that sentencing decisions are indeed influenced by a defendant's race. For example, Hood's (1992) study (in collaboration with Graca Cordovil), undertaken for the Commission of Racial Equality, analysed data on all cases (2,884 males and 433 females) tried in 1989 at five Crown court centres in the West Midlands. Taking into account 16 factors related to both the offences and the offenders' criminal records, Hood concluded that 7 per cent of the over-representation of black people among those imprisoned could be attributed to direct discrimination at the sentencing stage, and that discrimination against black people was much higher at Dudley, Warwick and Stafford Crown Courts. Racial discrimination by British magistrates has been reported by Gelsthorpe and Loucks (1997) to be attributable to magistrates being influenced by the defendant's demeanour in court, because they misinterpret the body language of black defendants as 'arrogance'.

As already noted, research into racial discrimination at the sentencing stage has a much longer history in the USA, where some jurisdictions provide for the death penalty for certain crimes. The weight of the evidence (see Kapardis 2003) supports the conclusion that racial discrimination in the use of capital punishment in the USA continues unabated, despite attempts by the Supreme Court to thwart it by providing guidelines (*see Furman* v. *Georgia*; *Gregg* v. *Georgia*).

Defendant's attractiveness

It is now widely accepted that the stereotype, 'what is attractive is good', exists across many cultures. 'Attractive' can refer to physical appearance or likeability, the appeal of an individual's personality, or both. Defendants are often advised by lawyers to look 'presentable' when appearing in court. However, an examination of both experimental studies and studies of real sentencers (Kapardis 2003) shows that the relationship between a defendant's attractiveness and sentencing severity remains unclear, due to contradictory findings.

The sentencer

There is a common belief that the sentence imposed on a defendant depends to a significant degree on who the individual sentencer is. It is also commonly known that lawyers indulge in 'magistrate/judge shopping' to get someone who is likely to be favourably disposed to their case. The importance of sentencer characteristics in understanding sentencing variations was emphasized by Everson (1919: 98) who concluded in his study of 28 magistrates' courts in New York that 'justice is a very personal thing, reflecting the temperament, the personality, the education, environment and personal traits of the magistrate'. On the basis of Kapardis' (1985, 2003) literature reviews, it can be concluded that, even though inconsistent findings have been reported regarding not only a sentencer's gender, religion, politics, and penal aims but also his or her sentencing decisions, the judiciary itself is a source of disparities.

Conclusions

The issue of disparity in sentencing is one of public concern and has attracted considerable research. The available empirical evidence shows that a defendant's gender and race are significant determinants of sentence, but inconsistent findings have been reported about the importance of a defendant's attractiveness. Similarly, sentencers themselves have been shown to be a source of disparity. Both legal and extra-legal factors impact on sentencing and contribute to disparities, leading to the conclusion that justice itself is not as effectively blindfolded as some conservative lawyers and judges would have us believe. One way in which psychologists can help to reduce sentencing disparities is by organizing sentencing exercises for the judiciary that help to sensitize them to the interaction of both legal and non-legal factors.

Andreas Kapardis

Related entries

Courts; Legal profession; Public protection; Sentencing Guidelines Council (SGC).

Key texts and sources

Everson, G. (1919) 'The human element in justice', *Journal of Criminal Law and Criminology*, 10: 90–9.

Farrington, D.P. and Morris, A. (1983) 'Sex, sentencing and reconviction', *British Journal of Criminology*, 23: 229–48.

Gelsthorpe, L. and Loucks, N. (1997) 'Magistrates' explanations of sentencing decisions', in C. Hedderman and L. Gelsthorpe (eds) *Understanding the Sentencing of Women. Home Office Research Study* 170. London: Home Office.

Hood, R. (1992) *Race and Sentencing: A Study in the Crown Court (a Report for the Commission for Racial Equality).* Oxford: Oxford University Press.

Kapardis, A. (1985) *Sentencing by English Magistrates as a Human Process.* Nicosia, Cyprus: Asselia Press.

Kapardis, A. (2003) *Psychology and Law.* Cambridge: Cambridge University Press.

Kapardis, A. and Farrington, D.P. (1981) 'An experimental study of sentencing by magistrates', *Law and Human Behavior*, 5: 107–21.

Sallmann, P. and Willis, J. (1984) *Criminal Justice in Australia.* Melbourne: Oxford University Press.

Wilczynski, A. and Morris, A. (1993) 'Parents who kill their children', *Criminal Law Review*, 31–6.

SENTENCING GUIDELINES COUNCIL (SGC)

The Sentencing Guidelines Council (SGC) issues guidelines designed to assist in the consistency of approach to the sentencing of criminal cases in England and Wales. Every court must have regard to a relevant guideline.

An offence guideline issued by the Sentencing Guidelines Council (SGC) sets out the key issues for a court and provides a starting point for sentence for a particular variant of the offence under consideration and a range within which the sentence for that type of offence will normally fall. Other guidelines, however, are more general in nature – for instance, dealing with the approach to assessing the seriousness of an offence, how to approach offences involving violence in a domestic context, how to apply a reduction in the sentence given for a guilty plea and how courts should approach new sentences as they are introduced.

Guidelines are prepared following a long process of consultation. Advice is prepared for the SGC by the Sentencing Advisory Panel, after wide-ranging consultation involving practitioners and the public. The council itself consults Parliament and government ministers. The council also issues regular newsletters, some containing general information, others containing detail about sentencing trends at both a national and local level.

Kevin McCormac

Related entries

Courts; Public protection; Sentencing.

Key texts and sources

See the SGC's website (**www.sentencing-guidelines. gov.uk**).

SERIOUS INCIDENTS IN PRISONS

Serious incidents that occur in prisons can disrupt the normal operation of an establishment and can cause potential risk to the safety of staff and prisoners and, in some cases, members of the public.

The serious incidents that can occur in prisons include assaults (by prisoners on members of staff or other prisoners), acts of concerted indiscipline (such as sit-down or rooftop protests), suicide attempts, fires and escape attempts. Prisons enact contingency plans in all these cases and, in doing so, they establish systems of management and communication to focus resources on the safe resolution of the incident. All serious incidents are investigated in detail and may result in charges being made for criminal behaviour or for infractions of the Prison Rules. Recommendations usually seek to reduce the risk of similar future incidents.

Of primary interest to psychologists are those serious incidents that occur over protracted time periods and that often involve negotiation. These include hostage incidents, rooftop protests and other 'sieges'. Typically, these incidents occur when prisoners act to achieve outcomes they cannot achieve through normal means (if at all). In other cases, the incidents occur without an apparent 'cause' or stimulus. In many, the stimulus is emotional – for example, when prisoners act to make a protest in a spontaneous way.

Hostage incidents are defined as occurring where a person is held and threatened by another person (or persons) to force the fulfilment of substantive demands on a third party (Lanceley 1999). In these incidents, substantive demands are the apparent goals of the prisoner, who is in the position of kidnapping a peer, a member of staff or another person, and where the safe release of the 'hostage' is traded for the demand. Examples of demands include immediate release, transfer to another establishment or contact with a specific person. Hostage incidents may be carefully planned by the perpetrator in order to maximize the influence to attempt to force the 'authorities' to comply rather than risk the safety of the hostage. Other incidents are less well organized and planned but still have the essential elements of kidnapping, with substantive demands being made in an attempt to 'trade'.

Other siege situations can occur that appear to be hostage incidents. These are usually spontaneous and are often characterized by emotional, destructive and chaotic behaviour. Prisoners may barricade themselves in an area (with or without others), may climb on to roofs (where it is dangerous for staff to intervene) or may hold another person under threat in an open area. Often, the perpetrators appear confused, self-defeating in their actions, emotional and unpredictable. They may make demands, but these may be apparently trivial or entirely unrealistic. Such incidents may be further complicated by the perpetrator's mental health problems.

Hostage incidents are relatively rare in prisons in England and Wales, particularly those involving members of staff. In the year to January 2007 there were 20 hostage incidents, one of which involved a member of staff. In the same time period there were over 53,000 other reported incidents (all types). In all protracted incidents, the prison's response is to deploy teams of specialist staff and to call on other agencies (such as the police, fire and ambulance services) to work in a co-ordinated way to bring the incident safely to an end and to return the prison to its normal state of operation.

Summary of key knowledge

The resolution of hostage and other siege incidents has largely been drawn from the analysis of the management of previous incidents. There are few opportunities for researchers to use experimental designs to test hypotheses about the most appropriate methods beyond detailed behaviour, such as that of trained negotiators or intervention staff. Many of the incidents that have yielded data for researchers have come from environments other than prisons. For example, most of the most detailed studies concern the management of terrorist incidents, such as plane hijacking (e.g. Wilson and Smith 1999).

The behaviour of perpetrators, negotiators, other staff, commanders and onlookers has been subject to detailed and structured analysis and has yielded important learning for practitioners. In particular, such studies have enabled the behaviour in incidents to be categorized and appropriate strategies to be constructed in order to manage the risks presented appropriately. The options to resolve an incident are, however, limited until a detailed analysis of the particular incident is available.

Implications for practice

At a basic level, it is fundamental to the safe operation of prison systems that hostage taking (and other siege behaviour) is known (by prisoners) to be ineffective in gaining any substantive demands. Hostage taking is not a new phenomenon and will, at times, be considered by prisoners to be a suitable method for forcing the authorities to comply with their demands, no matter how previous incidents concluded. Any hostage taking that resulted in escape from prison or other major concession, would, however, inevitably increase the frequency of these incidents. This is the fundamental basis of prison and police policies around the world with regard to the management of hostage incidents – i.e. to demonstrate that hostage taking 'does not work'.

The research findings that have enabled policies to be developed for prisons and the police broadly contain the following elements.

Time

Lanceley (1999) identifies time as being a key element in the management of serious incidents, for the following reasons:

- People in a crisis state change in a relatively short period of time and usually become more rational.
- As basic human needs increase, the perpetrator begins to realize that he or she must go through the negotiator to meet his or her needs. This increases the negotiator's influence and control over time.
- The gathering, collating and analysing of the information available takes time, but good decision-making requires accurate information.

- Time enables the negotiator to establish rapport with the perpetrator. This can enable a level of trust to develop that ensures the negotiator can persuade the perpetrator to release the hostage or end the siege.

Other benefits of time passing include the opportunity for the hostages to escape and changing dynamics in the siege situation, which can benefit a negotiated surrender and the safe resolution of an incident. An example of a human factor during a hostage incident is the so-called 'Stockholm syndrome', in which the captives empathize with, and may even come to support, the perpetrators of the incident.

There are also negative effects associated with the passage of time, and commanders and negotiators are trained to be vigilant for changing behaviour that may indicate risks associated with prolonged incidents.

Independent management decisions in an organized chain of command

Safe resolution requires an organized, consistent and disciplined approach by the authority dealing with the incident. For example, if staff were to attempt to intervene by force but failed to secure a safe resolution, it is extremely unlikely that a negotiator could then establish a level of trust in order to persuade the perpetrator to surrender. Similarly, untrained staff may offer solutions to the perpetrator that could either not be delivered or could risk the safety of others.

The Prison Service and all other agencies dealing with serious incidents train managers and staff to respond to emergencies in disciplined and organized ways. In prisons, managers will declare the establishment to be operating in 'command mode', where a command structure is established for the communicating of information, the issuing of instructions and the organization of resources. In some jurisdictions specialist staff are deployed purely as members of crisis intervention teams. Most of the methods employed by trained commanders, negotiators and other members of staff involved in the management of incidents are consistent across a wide range of agencies worldwide.

Use of intelligence

Research into the characteristics of incidents and their management (e.g. Wilson and Smith 1999) indicates that there are identifiable 'types' of serious incident and, further, that specific strategies can be identified to resolve them safely. Such research is commonly used to inform the training of commanders, whose decisions about strategy will be put into effect by trained staff during an incident.

Incident analysis

Prison and other authorities can now benefit from the findings of research into the specific aspects of behaviour during an incident. For example, Paul Taylor (1999) of the University of Liverpool has developed a sophisticated model to describe the verbal interactions between perpetrators and negotiators.

Such research informs the decisions about the likely conduct of the perpetrator and also enables the negotiator's effectiveness to be assessed. In reality, this information may assist in advising or coaching a negotiator, in agreeing a 'script' or set of negotiation tactics and in assessing progress to a safe resolution during a prolonged incident.

Safety and de-escalation

Incidents do not always end in a safe resolution, and some of the key learning about risk management has emerged from errors of judgement, a failure to maintain discipline, faulty intelligence or analysis, and inappropriate management strategies. An extreme example of this learning is the famous 1971 Attica Prison 'uprising' in New York State:

> On September 9 1971, a series of conflicts between prisoners and guards ended with a relatively minor incident, involving a guard disciplining two prisoners. This was the spark that set off the revolt which began when a group of inmates from D Block broke through a gate with a defective weld and taking over one of the four prison yards, with forty guards as hostages (http://libcom.org/history/1971-the-attica-prison-uprising/).

During the military assault that was ordered to bring the siege to an end, 31 prisoners and 9 members of staff were killed by gunfire. The personnel sent in to end the incident shot the prison officers.

Although this incident has many unique characteristics and was caused by a highly unusual set of conditions and circumstances, the fact that the intended 'rescue' resulted in such a number of fatalities indicated that improvements needed to be made in the planning and execution of such interventions. There is now a high level of expertise and experience available to the Prison Service and others in the management of many aspects of risk in the resolution of incidents, and learning from 'real' and simulated incidents has built up a sound knowledge base.

There are, of course, exceptions to the rule. Recently it has become apparent that many terrorist organizations have been able to develop tactics to which authorities struggle to respond. Most obviously here is the so-called 'suicide bomber' (e.g. '9/11' and the more recent attacks in London). In these instances, the normal responses of containment, negotiation and resolution are inadequate and inappropriate.

Negotiated resolutions

More positively, the expertise and training of negotiators have become increasingly sophisticated, and many organizations now use known methods to ensure that staff can be deployed to 'talk down' the perpetrators of many serious incidents. Trained negotiators can expertly buy time for commanders to attain and organize resources, and to establish strategies and contingency plans. Crucially, they create a psychological buffer for the decision-making members of the management team, enabling them to be protected from the emotional effects of the incident. In many incidents, trained negotiators are able to persuade the perpetrators to hand over weapons, to release the hostages and to surrender themselves to the authorities.

Similarly, knowledge and expertise in methods of intervention and rescue have also become more advanced. Trained staff are now capable of intervening safely in 'incidents at height' (i.e. on rooftops), are highly proficient at entering rooms at speed and can incapacitate an offender with remarkable accuracy, speed and relative safety.

Post-incident support and psychological effects

Following a serious incident, the official response of the Prison Service and other authorities may include criminal charges against the perpetrator (or charges against the Prison Rules), and subsequent criminal investigations, etc. There will be official investigation of the incident and its management in order to learn about future prevention and management.

In addition, a great deal is now known about the psychological impact of serious incidents on those directly involved (e.g. hostages) and also on members of staff and management. Usually, debriefing is available to enable staff to discuss the emotional impact of the incident and any further support that may be required. In many cases, the psychological impact of a serious incident is long lasting and seriously debilitating.

The role of the psychologist

The safe management of serious incidents is a disciplined team operation, with many individuals playing vital roles. Psychologists can be called to assist in a number of ways. Primarily this will involve an analysis of the psychology of the incident and its management. The psychologist may be asked to assist in the formulation of an appropriate negotiation strategy, to coach and support negotiators, to assist in the management of communication and to assess the perpetrators' characteristics. The role may include supporting the decision-making processes of commanders or ensuring that practicalities are attended to, such as the physical well-being of the staff in attendance.

Psychologists are also often involved in the post-incident arrangements, assessing, debriefing and supporting colleagues, attending and contributing to official debriefs, and assisting in investigations. In recent years, psychologists have been able to contribute to the learning about incidents and their management through research and practice. In this area of operational research there is a direct impact on the training of management and staff and a clear link to operational effectiveness in some of the most serious and demanding situations faced by prison authorities.

In summary, serious incidents in prisons vary widely in their characteristics, but sound operational experience and research from a wide variety of sources have combined to ensure that sound principles are applied in their management. Psychologists play their part in many aspects of incident management, including training, learning through research and assisting during incidents and in post-incident operations.

Graham Beck

Related entries

HM Prison Servce; Hostage negotiation; Post traumatic stress disorder (PTSD).

Key texts and sources

Lanceley, F.J. (1999) *On-scene Guide for Crisis Negotiators* (2nd edn).

Taylor, P. (1999) 'A cylindrical model of communication behaviour in crisis negotiations', *Human Communication Research*, 28.

Wilson, M.A. (2006) 'Terrorist behavior in hostage taking: policy issues and research directions', in J. Victoroff and S. Mednick (eds) *Psychology and Terrorism*. Amsterdam: IOS Press.

Wilson, M.A. and Smith, A. (1999) 'Roles and rules in terrorist hostage taking', in D. Canter and L. Alison (eds) *The Social Psychology of Crime: Groups, Teams, and Networks*. Aldershot: Dartmouth.

SEVERE MENTAL ILLNESS (SMI) (PSYCHOSIS)

The term 'severe mental illness' (SMI) is used to refer to several disorders, including schizophrenia, schizo-affective disorder, major depression, bipolar disorder and other non-drug and alcohol-related psychoses. These disorders usually onset in late adolescence or early adulthood, affect all domains of functioning and, in the great majority of cases, remain chronic throughout life.

Persons with severe mental illness (SMI) (Hodgins and Janson 2002) and, most particularly, those with schizophrenia and schizo-affective disorder, are at an increased risk, as compared with the general population, of committing non-violent crimes, are at a higher risk of committing violent crimes and are at an even higher risk of committing homicide (Hodgins and Janson 2002; Hodgins in press). This is a robust finding – it has been reported by several independent research groups working in industrialized and underdeveloped countries with distinct cultures and health, social service and criminal justice systems. Different cohorts and samples have been examined using various experimental designs, including prospective, longitudinal investigations on birth cohorts (Brennan *et al.* 2000) and population cohorts, follow-up studies comparing patients and their neighbours, random samples of incarcerated offenders (Fazel and Danesh 2002) and complete cohorts of homicide offenders (Erb *et al.* 2001). Much less is known about the prevalence of violent criminality among persons with major affective disorders than those with schizophrenia. The few existing studies suggest a weak relationship (Brennan *et al.* 2000).

The results of the studies reviewed above are remarkably consistent. They tell us four important facts about offending by persons with SMI. First, while the increase in the risks associated with SMI (that is, the odds ratios comparing crime rates among persons with SMI and persons in the general population) for non-violent and violent offending and for homicide reported in various studies is similar, the proportions of persons with SMI who offend differ across countries and time periods. For example, in a Swedish birth cohort, 14.6 per cent of the men and 6.3 per cent of the women with SMI were convicted for at least one violent crime before their thirtieth birthday. In a larger Danish birth cohort followed for 13 years longer, 11.3 per cent of the men and 2.8 per cent of the women with schizophrenia had at least one conviction for a violent crime (Brennan *et al.* 2000). In a more recent study of a large cohort of patients with schizophrenia in Denmark, 68 per cent had at least one conviction for a violent crime. A study of a series of cohorts of patients with schizophrenia in the state of Victoria, Australia, from 1975 to 1995 found that between 15 per cent and 25 per cent of the patients had at least one conviction for a violent crime. The proportions of people with SMI who commit crimes, therefore, vary by place and time period.

Secondly, while studies consistently report that the prevalence of SMI among incarcerated offenders exceeds the prevalence for gender and age-matched subjects in the general population, the proportions of inmates with SMI vary from country to country and from one time period to another, depending on the laws and policies that are in place concerning the diversion of persons with SMI from prisons (Hodgins and Côté 1995). Thirdly, whereas many more men than women with SMI commit crimes, SMI and, most particularly, schizophrenia, confers a greater risk for violent crime among women than among men (Brennan *et al.* 2000). Finally, while people with schizophrenia are responsible for approximately 10 times more homicides than people without schizophrenia (Erb *et al.* 2001), few offenders with SMI have committed homicides, and most have committed repeated assaults.

The prevalence of aggressive behaviour among persons with SMI

In concert with the evidence showing that persons with SMI, and most particularly those with schizophrenic disorders, are more likely than those without these disorders to commit violent crimes, there is a growing body of evidence on aggressive behaviour towards others by people with schizophrenia. In these studies aggressive behaviour is reported by patients, treatment staff and/or collateral informants using interview protocols that request information systematically on each type of physically aggressive behaviour (for example, hitting, slapping and biting) – first asking if the interviewee has been the victim of such behaviour and then if he or she has engaged in the behaviour. The information usually covers the six months prior to interview.

The prevalence of aggressive behaviour varies, depending on sample characteristics and the length of the study period. For example, in a British study of outpatients with psychosis, 20 per cent assaulted another person in a two-year period. In a US study of men with schizophrenic disorders admitted to psychiatric wards, 40.2 per cent had assaulted in the 10 weeks prior to admission. In another US study of patients with schizophrenia recruited into a recent trial of medications, 19.1 per cent had committed an assault in the previous six months. While rates vary from one study to another, they demonstrate that a significant minority of people with psychotic disorders, and most particularly with schizophrenia, present persistent aggressive behaviour.

Society's response to crime and aggressive behaviour by people with SMI

Despite this growing body of evidence, mental health policies fail to recognize that aggressive behaviour and violent criminality are problems for a proportion of persons with SMI, and most particularly for those with schizophrenia. For example, in the UK neither the National Service Framework for Mental Health (Department of Health 1999b) nor the National Institute of Clinical Excellence clinical guidelines for schizophrenia (Royal College of Psychiatrists and British Psychological Society 2003) take account of the evidence concerning the increased vulnerability associated with SMI for engaging in violent crime and assaultive behaviour.

While policy remains mute on the topic, health services in the UK and throughout Europe have responded to the situation by dramatically increasing the number of beds in forensic psychiatric hospitals and incarcerating large numbers of people with SMI in prisons. Most patients in forensic services are men with schizophrenia who have been in and out of general adult psychiatric services for many years while they were committing criminal offences. Mental healthcare for persons with SMI that is provided by general adult services does not address anti-social and criminal behaviour but, rather, focuses, almost exclusively, on providing medication to reduce psychotic symptoms.

Schizophrenic disorders and an increased risk of criminality and aggressive behaviour

Similar to offenders in the general population, offenders with schizophrenia constitute a population that is heterogeneous with respect to both criminal offending and the correlates of offending. Knowledge about the origins of criminal offending in the general population has exploded since investigations began to focus on subgroups defined by age of onset and persistence of anti-social behaviour. The available data suggest that a similar approach to the study of offenders with schizophrenia may prove useful for beginning to unravel the aetiology of both the violence and the schizophrenia, and for the development of effective treatment programmes.

A typology of offenders with schizophrenia

We have proposed a typology of offenders with schizophrenic disorders based on age of onset and persistence of anti-social behaviour. Type I, the early-start offenders, display conduct problems from a young age that escalate in severity and frequency as they grow up. These are active, persistent offenders from mid-adolescence through to at least middle age. They are non-compliant with treatment for their psychotic illness and, consequently, experience repeat acute episodes that usually require hospitalization. Once released, they fail to take medication and gradually develop more and more symptoms until readmission is required. This vicious cycle is further aggravated by their continual misuse of alcohol and illicit drugs. Several studies have shown, however, that it is the childhood pattern of conduct problems, and not the substance misuse, that is linked to criminality in adulthood. Rehabilitation programmes that have been shown to be effective with non-mentally ill offenders may be effective with this group of persons with schizophrenia. Trials of the Reasoning and Rehabilitation programme, for example, are currently ongoing.

A second type of offender with schizophrenia displays no anti-social behaviour prior to illness onset, but a stable pattern of aggressive behaviour thereafter. Some studies suggest that, among these Type II offenders, substance misuse is linked to aggressive behaviour towards others. There are programmes that have been shown to reduce substance misuse among people with schizophrenia effectively, but these are usually not provided by general adult psychiatric services. A third type of offender with schizophrenia displays no anti-social behaviour before illness onset or for many years thereafter, but then engages in very serious violence towards others. The available evidence suggests that these three types differ as to both aetiology and response to treatment.

Finally, while medication reduces the acute symptoms of psychosis, learning-based treatments are needed to educate afflicted persons about their illness and need for medication, to reduce high rates of co-morbid substance misuse and to increase life skills, interpersonal skills, cognitive performance and occupational skills.

Sheilagh Hodgins

Related entries

Diagnosis of mental disorder; Mental disorder interventions; Psychiatric diagnoses.

Key texts and sources

Brennan, A., Mednick, S.A. and Hodgins, S. (2000) 'Major mental disorders and criminal violence in a Danish birth cohort', *Archives of General Psychiatry*, 57: 494–500.

Erb, M., Hodgins, S., Freese, R., Müller-Isberner, R. and Jöckel, D. (2001) 'Homicide and schizophrenia: maybe treatment does have a preventive effect', *Criminal Behaviour and Mental Health*, 11: 6–26.

Fazel, S. and Danesh, J. (2002) 'Serious mental disorder in 23000 prisoners: a systematic review of 62 surveys', *Lancet*, 259: 545–50.

Hodgins, S. (in press) 'Criminality among persons with severe mental illness', in K. Soothill *et al.* (eds) *Handbook of Forensic Mental Health*. Cullompton: Willan Publishing.

Hodgins, S. and Janson, C.G. (2002) *Criminality and Violence among the Mentally Disordered: The Stockholm Metropolitan Project*. Cambridge: Cambridge University Press.

SEXUAL OFFENDING: INTERVENTIONS

Sexual offending covers a broad range of behaviours with variations across time and cultural settings. It is generally agreed to include sexual activity with children, with adults unable to give valid consent and sexual activity in the absence of consent.

Interventions to address sexual offending include a wide range of approaches designed with the explicit aim of reducing or preventing the occurrence or reoccurrence of such behaviours. These have included psychosocial and neurobiological approaches. A very powerful but infrequently and insufficiently highlighted characteristic of sexual offending are high levels of under-reporting and low levels of detection and conviction. This is a methodological challenge common to the evaluation of most interventions across criminal justice settings. Survey data suggest a large amount of unreported sexual offending. The vast majority of research into interventions with sexual offenders has focused on those convicted through the criminal courts, with a smaller number of studies of volunteers seeking interventions. This raises the risk of strong systematic biases in the evidence base. In reality, something is known about a subset of convicted sex offenders, but little is known about the larger group of perpetrators who are not subject to criminal convictions.

Two recent systematic reviews of the evidence base into interventions with sexual offenders have been undertaken in the UK (White *et al.* 1998; Kenworthy *et al.* 2004). The first of these reviews considered randomized trials using pharmacological, surgical and psychological interventions. Two subsequent reviews (reported in Kenworthy *et al.* 2004) looked at randomized studies of psychological interventions only. All three focused on adult offenders.

Good-quality evidence to support the efficacy of surgical interventions is largely absent (primarily castration in males). The use of pharmacological intervention in the form of the anti-libinal medroxyprogestrone combined with imaginal desensition has been compared with imaginal desensitization alone. Based on a small sample study of 31 sexual offenders, the use of medroxyprogestrone was not found to be more effective than imaginal desensitization alone (White *et al.* 1998).

A larger randomized study of 155 sexual offenders was also reviewed. This compared the use of psychological group therapy intervention, based on relapse prevention principles, with a no-intervention condition. No difference in terms of rates of sexual reoffending was reported between the intervention and no-intervention groups on follow-up. The intervention group was reported to show lower levels of non-sexual violent offending (White *et al.* 1998).

In a systematic review undertaken in the UK in 2004, non-randomized studies were also considered. In all 81, non-randomized studies were identified, of which 21 were assessed as meeting the basic minimum methodological standards for inclusion in the review, based on independent ratings by two assessors. Seven of these studies reported a statistically significant effect for the intervention group, four studies failed to report their data in a way that allowed evaluation and ten studies reported no statistically significant effect of intervention on the behaviour or attitudes of offenders (Kenworthy *et al.* 2004).

Meta-analyses have been used in this area, but the appropriateness of this method is contentious. One meta-analysis of parts of the evidence base suggested that failure to complete an intervention was a moderately good predictor of criminal recidivism (Lösel and Schmucker 2005). Importantly, more detailed analysis suggested that this was probably due to the effects of closer monitoring of those failing to complete interventions, rather than the efficacy of the interventions. In a separate 12-year follow-up of those who had volunteered for psychological interventions and those who had declined, no difference in reconviction rates was found. The pooling of evidence from non-randomized studies for meta-analysis has yielded evidence of some small positive effects. It is unclear to what extent this is due to biases in the publication of research in favour of reporting positive results.

The majority of the evidence base relating to qualitative research into interventions with sexual offenders is of poor quality. In reviewing this area in 2004, it was noted that four studies were assessed as meeting basic methodological criteria for 'soundness'. Three of these studies were process evaluations, and one compared two cognitive-behavioural groupwork interventions in prisons in England and Wales. Findings from these studies suggest that interactions in such interventions are complex. This was particularly noted in terms of the roles of 'victim' and 'victimizer', where many group members experienced both roles at differing times.

Two of the process studies looked at small samples of male incest offenders, focusing primarily on the experiences and views of psychological therapists and how these interacted with the intervention. A number of aspects seemed to be of high importance including frustration over mandatory legal requirements that interfer with intervention, desensitization resulting from repeated exposure to details of such offending and issues of counter-transference.

Comparable findings were reported in comparing groupwork across prisons in England and Wales. This study used semi-structured interviews and triangulation of data. The reported findings suggested that the use of reflective and self-critical practice tended to increase in relation to the practitioner's experience and length of training. Most surprisingly, perhaps, 30 per cent of those sampled defined sexual offenders in terms of having some form of biological abnormality.

To date there has been little or no good-quality research published in relation to mentally disordered sexual offenders suitable for inclusion in a systematic review. There has been a limited amount of research looking at interventions with learning-disabled sexual offenders. A review of this area found that there had been no randomized studies that met the basic criteria for methodological adequacy. At present there is no adequate evidence base for the effectiveness of interventions with these sexual offenders. As a result, practitioners need to base their practice on inadequate studies, to

extrapolate from the evidence base for non-mentally disordered offenders or contribute to the development of the evidence base (see Evidence-based practice (EBP)).

The current evidence base for psychological interventions with sexual offenders in prisons does not indicate statistically significant reductions in sexual offending. However, there is some evidence of reductions in the levels of violent offending when sexual and violent offences are combined for analysis. Approaches to work with sexual offenders have generally been weakly grounded in theory. Despite this, there have been a number of attempts to provide a theoretical basis for research and practice, often in the form of manual-based groupwork.

The current evidence base in relation to interventions with sexual offenders suggests there is a clear need to take stock of the research and to take on-board some of the findings from the existing evidence base, as well as undertaking adequate effectiveness research into this area. In recent years a small number of randomized studies of acceptable standard have been undertaken, and these have suggested that current interventions have no positive effect in reducing sexual reoffending. Some studies have found small reductions in violent offending among those completing interventions, suggesting some poorly understood effects. These may be positive effects or, alternatively, it may be that interventions are helping sexual offenders evade capture and/or use less violence in perpetrating sexual offences. Further research is necessary to clarify what the effects of different interventions are.

Non-randomized studies provide a mixed pattern of results. Methodological limitations of such studies add to the difficulty of interpretation. Some practitioners have suggested that the current lack of positive effects is due to current interventions not involving a sufficient amount of input and/or delivery failings on the part of groupworkers. Others have questioned the theoretical coherence of this position. Evidence to support such hypotheses is absent, and many such *post hoc* hypotheses could be generated.

The improving, though very limited, evidence base in relation to adult male sexual offenders makes clear that such interventions are still experimental. The evidence base in relation to women, young sexual offenders, children exhibiting sexual harmful behaviours and those with mental health problems is minimal and of generally poor quality.

Three main substantive implications can be derived from an assessment of the current evidence base. First, there is a need to treat any claims about best practice in such experimental interventions with sexual offenders with a high degree of circumspection. Secondly, there is a need to develop a broad range of evidence-based interventions. Thirdly, future evidence-based practice needs to be broadened to include the full range of perpetrators of sexual offences and sexual harmful behaviours, including both those within and outside the criminal justice system.

David A. Crighton

Related entries

Evidence based practice (EBP); Sexual abuse; Violent Offender and Sex Offender Register (ViSOR); Stalking.

Key texts and sources

Crighton, D. (2006a) 'Psychological research into sexual offenders', in G. Towl (ed.) *Psychological Research in Prisons*. Oxford: BPS/Blackwell.

Kenworthy, T., Adams, C.E., Bilby, C., Brooks-Gordon, B. and Fenton, M. (2004) 'Psychological interventions for those who have sexually offended or are at risk of offending', *Cochrane Database of Systematic Reviews*, 4: art. no. CD004858 (available online at www.Cochrane.org).

Lösel, F. and Schmucker, M. (2005) 'The effectiveness of treatment for sexual offenders: a comprehensive meta-analysis', *Journal of Experimental Criminology*, 1: 117–46.

White, P., Bradley, C., Ferriter, M. and Hatzipetrou, L. (1998) 'Management of people with disorders of sexual preference and for convicted sexual offenders', *Cochrane Database of Systematic Reviews*, 4: art. no. CD000251 (available online at www.Cochrane.org).

SOCIAL SERVICES

Social services are a range of public welfare services provided by local authority social services departments. The services provided are determined, to a large extent, by the 'powers' and 'duties' assigned to them through national government legislation. Broadly speaking, the key services provided by social services departments relate to children and families, mental health, physical and learning disabilities and the elderly.

Until now, children's social services have generally been provided jointly with services for adults, via social services departments in local authorities. However, structural changes in response to the Children Act 2004 meant that, from April 2006, education and social care services for children were brought together under a director of children's services in each local authority. Adult social services are now delivered via a director for adult services, who replaced the director of social services.

Services for children and families include the provision of family support services, child protection services and the accommodation of children who are unable to be cared for in their own families, including the provision of residential care, fostering and adoption. Specialist services are also provided for children with physical and learning disabilities, children with mental health needs and young people who have become involved in the criminal justice system. Childcare social workers, employed by local authorities, are often placed in multidisciplinary and multiagency teams, such as child and adolescent mental health teams and youth offending teams. The key legislation that sets out the powers and duties of local authorities in relation to children and families are; the Children Act 1989, the Children (Leaving Care) Act 2000, the Adoption and Children Act 2002 and the Children Act 2004.

Mental health services are provided by adult mental health social workers, most often working in multiagency community adult mental health teams or based in psychiatric hospitals.

The Mental Health Act 1983 requires the local authority to appoint approved social workers who have a duty to assess for hospital admissions under the Act within their area. The local authority, together with the health authority, also has a duty to provide aftercare for people who have been detained under the Act. The Care Programme Approach (DOH Circular 1990) directs the local authority to co-operate with health authorities to provide systematic arrangements for assessing and reviewing the health and social care needs of people referred to specialist psychiatric services. The Mental Health (Patients in the Community) Act 1995 extended this duty to the provision of formal aftercare under supervision ('supervised discharge') when there is considered to be a substantial risk of serious harm to the health or safety of the patient or the safety of others.

Local authorities provide a range of services to adults with physical and learning disabilities and the elderly. These services are determined by a range of legislation and statutes, most notably the National Assisstance Act 1948, the Chronically Sick and Disabled Persons Act 1970 and the NHS and Community Care Act 1990. In addition to the provision of services, local authorities also have a responsibility to register and inspect residential and community care services for both adults and children.

The organization and delivery of these services vary considerably between local authorities. For example, in childcare services some local authorities have separate teams providing child protection and family support services. Other local authorities have created initial intake teams that respond to all new requests for childcare services. Following an initial assessment of need, the child/family may be transferred to teams providing specific services – for example, family support or for looked-after children. Finding a suitable point of access to the social services required can therefore be quite complex. As a general guide, most social services departments will be divided into adult and childcare services and, within each, a 'duty' or 'intake' service will be provided to respond to all new inquiries or requests for services. A phone call to the duty or intake social worker in the geographical area of the potential service user should establish the appropriate point of access to the service needed.

It is worth noting that most social services are not universal and available to all but are subject to an assessment of need. Local authorities are reliant on money raised through local taxation and central government grants to provide social services and are, therefore, rarely able to meet all the need identified in their areas. Assessments, therefore, inevitably serve a gate-keeping role in rationing scarce resources and limiting demands made on the services. Many of the services provided are means treated and require a financial contribution from the service user.

Jackie Walton

Related entries

National Health Service (NHS); Public protection; Secure training centres (STCs).

Key texts and sources

Llewellyn, A. (2005) *Society Guardian NHS and Social Services Directory, 2005/6. Guardian Book Series.* London: Sage.

Thompson, N. and Thompson, S. (2007) *Understanding Social Care.* Lyme Regis: Russell House.

STALKING

The harassment behaviour known as stalking is notoriously difficult to define, principally because it often comprises the targeted repetition of behaviours that are ostensibly routine and harmless. Examples of common stalking behaviours include telephoning a target, walking past his or her house and physical approaches. There exist a variety of definitions but most incorporate the following elements: a pattern of unwanted pursuit, a credible threat and the induction of fear in the victim. The key component of stalking behaviour is its repetitive nature.

Although systematic research documenting the experiences of stalking victims only started as recently as the last few years of the twentieth century, good progress has been made. Many studies have revealed similar behavioural patterns among stalkers, and it is also certain that stalking often has significant negative emotional, physical, social and economic effects on the victim (see, e.g., Spitzberg and Cupach's 2006 meta-analysis of 175 studies). The majority of victims – around three quarters – will have had some form of prior acquaintance with their stalker, and a full half of all stalkers and victims will have shared a romantic relationship. Most studies have been conducted in English-speaking countries (i.e. the USA, Australia and the UK). A smaller number of studies have been carried out in continental European countries and elsewhere in non-western countries, including Japan and Iran. These have revealed that stalking is likely to be universal and that victims living in broadly ranging circumstances will share greatly similar victimization experiences.

Studies of community, student, forensic and clinical populations show that most victims of stalking are female and that most stalkers are male. There is some limited evidence, however, of under-reporting among male victims. Stalkers tend to be older (in their fourth decade of life) than most offenders, and both stalkers and their victims tend to be of higher socio-economic status than are the majority of victims of interpersonal crimes (see, e.g., Meloy 2007). Still, it is important to note that, among offenders, stalkers are a particularly heterogeneous subgroup, and this is evidenced by the relatively large number of typologies of stalkers that are available. These typologies tend to focus on three primary dimensions: 1) the underlying disorder, whether psychological, physiological or both; 2) the nature and context of any pre-existing stalker–victim relationship; and 3) the primary motivation, such as love or revenge (Spitzberg and Cupach, 2006). The various typologies have differing objectives and are based on very different samples, with the result that they are rarely comparable.

A categorization aimed at law enforcement was developed by Sheridan and Boon (2002). These authors suggested four subtypes of stalker based on cases reported to the police:

- Infatuation harassers who are motivated by a desire to fulfil fantasies of an idealized romantic relationship.
- Ex-partner stalkers who seek to regain power over or extract revenge upon their victim and who are likely to have exhibited controlling tendencies when the relationship was extant.
- Delusionally fixated stalkers who are mentally disordered and who may believe that they are in a relationship with a virtual stranger.
- Sadistic stalkers who are frequently psychopathic and who intend serious harm towards their victim.

Although most stalkers will engage in a shared central core of behaviours, motivational differences mean that individuals will pose very different levels of risk. Infatuation harassers, for instance, have poor social skills and intend no harm towards their targets, while sadistic stalkers will seek ultimately to control and remove all power from their victims.

Roughly speaking, around one third of stalkers will physically assault their victims. Researchers agree that the most violent stalkers tend to be ex-partners who do not have a history of mental illness. It is a robust finding from studies conducted on three continents that a majority of prior sexually intimate stalkers will assault their victims (see Meloy 2007). Injuries inflicted by stalkers can be life-threatening, and stalking is closely linked to a number of other crimes. Because it was only criminalized in recent years, with California leading the way in 1990 and England and Wales following in 1997, many criminal cases involving stalking were previously recorded as domestic violence, sexual assault, physical assault or murder. However, because of the chronic nature of stalking, with most cases persisting for more than six months, researchers are now concerned with the prediction of stalker violence (see, e.g., Rosenfeld and Lewis 2005). Another area of recent interest concerns cyber stalking – that is, stalking via the Internet and other technological innovations. A central debate concerns whether cyber stalking is a distinct subtype of this form of harassment or whether new technologies simply represent additional weapons in the arsenal of these highly prevalent and creative offenders.

Lorraine Sheridan

Related entries

Family violence; sexual offending interventions; Violent Offender and Sex Offender Register (ViSOR).

Key texts and sources

Meloy, J.R. (2007) 'Stalking: the state of the science', *Criminal Behavior and Mental Health*, 17: 1–7.

Rosenfeld, B. and Lewis, C. (2005) 'Assessing violence risk in stalking cases: a regression tree approach', *Law and Human Behavior*, 29: 343–57.

Sheridan, L. and Boon, J. (2002) 'Stalker typologies: implications for law enforcement', in J. Boon and L. Sheridan (eds) *Stalking and Psychosexual Obsession: Psychological Perspectives for Prevention, Policing and Treatment*. Chichester: Wiley.

Spitzberg, B.H. and Cupach, W.R. (2006) 'The state of the art of stalking: taking stock of the emerging literature', *Aggression and Violent Behavior*, 12: 64–86.

SUBSTANCE ABUSE/MISUSE

Substance misuse predominantly refers to the use of drugs or alcohol, which interferes with an individual's normal social functioning and physical and/or mental health and causes harm to the self and others, including anti-social and criminal behaviour.

Broader definitions of substance misuse than the one given above would include tobacco and solvents as well as drugs and alcohol because research suggests that young people are more likely to misuse tobacco, alcohol and cannabis than Class A drugs, such as cocaine or heroin. For forensic psychologists and practitioners working with offenders, however, drugs and alcohol will be the substances causing the most problematic behaviour. Poly-substance misuse refers to the abuse of both drugs and alcohol. Where appropriate, drugs and alcohol are discussed separately in this entry, but the term 'substance' is used to refer to both.

Drug misuse

Drug misuse may include both illegal and legal drugs, and some would argue that any use of illegal drugs is abuse. In the UK, 'problematic drug misuse' is the term often used to describe drug-misusing offenders. It involves excessive regular use (mainly Class A drugs) and dependency and poses significant health risks (Edmunds *et al.* 1999).

Drug misuse, offending behaviour and mental health

There are links between Class A drug misuse and certain types of offending behaviour – in particular, acquisitive crime – although whether these links are causative or correlative is debatable. Some research suggests that, if the drug misuse can be treated, then the criminal behaviour will reduce or desist. Two thirds of prisoners have used illegal drugs – almost twice the rate of the general population – and three fifths of prisoners have claimed their drug misuse was a problem (Social Exclusion Unit 2002). Prisoners reported crack, heroin and cannabis to be the most frequently (mis)used drugs prior to imprisonment (May 2005). A study of arrestees in custody suites in England found that 69 per cent tested positive for at least one drug, 29 per cent for opiates and 20 per cent for cocaine, including crack (Bennett 2000). It is widely recognized in the research that not all drug takers commit crime (Hough 1996).

Generally, the majority of 'problematic drug misusers' are male, and there is concern that services may not be able to meet adequately the different needs of female offenders with drug-misuse issues. Research suggests that these female offenders have a higher risk of mental ill-health than the general population and their male counterparts and have often experienced physical, sexual or emotional abuse, including domestic violence. There is some evidence to suggest that drug and alcohol misuse may be used by female offenders as a coping mechanism to deal with such traumas; others suggest the links are more complex and have not yet been fully explored.

Offenders with a drug or alcohol-misuse problem have a greater risk of mental ill-health than the general population – sometimes referred to as dual diagnosis (Department of Health 2002). Research suggests that those with a dual diagnosis are at an increased risk of relapse, suicide, more severe mental health problems and involvement in criminal behaviour, and that these risks increase for those with an added alcohol problem. Historically, individuals with a dual diagnosis have problems accessing help for either their drug or mental health problems, or both. The Department of Health (2002) set out a national framework for dual diagnosis services. This is mainly for those individuals with severe and enduring co-morbid mental health. Strathdee *et al.* (2002), however, note that less severe dual diagnosis problems have been given little attention.

There is an increasing evidence base that links cannabis use to the onset of some mental health disorders (Wittchen *et al.* 2007). Determining the onset and subsequent interaction of mental ill-health and drug misuse can be difficult to establish, and some suggest that drug misuse can exacerbate an underlying mental health issue (Crome 1996 cited in Abdulrahim 2001).

Drug misuse: treatments and interventions

Interventions that address drug misuse in offenders aim either to stop or to reduce significantly the drug-misusing behaviour. The UK (England and Wales) government's Drug Interventions Programme's key aim is also to stop or reduce the associated acquisitive offending behaviour. This is based on the links between Class A drug misuse and acquisitive offending behaviour.

Research has found the following treatment and interventions to be effective in reducing drug misuse and/or the associated offending behaviour: aftercare, therapeutic communities, cognitive-behavioural therapy, methadone prescription and arrest referral schemes. Interventions may be based in a prison, in the community or may involve residential rehabilitation. In a five-year follow-up study, drug taking and acquisitive crime had fallen by 25 per cent for those who had attended drug-treatment programmes (Gossop 2005). Research suggests that psychological interventions included as part of a substance misuser's treatment programme can have beneficial effects on their treatment outcomes.

Alcohol misuse

The World Health Organization has recognized several categories of alcohol misuse, which include hazardous, harmful and dependent drinking. The recommended levels of safe alcohol consumption are 14 units per week for women and 21 units per week for men. Binge drinking is included as misuse, which is more than 6 units per day for women and over 8 units per day for men.

Alcohol misuse and offending behaviour

There are strong links between alcohol misuse and anti-social and criminal behaviour – in particular violent behaviour, including domestic violence. A large proportion (62 per cent) of domestic violence cases involved alcohol consumption, and almost half those convicted were alcohol dependent (Gilchrist *et al.* 2003). A half of all violent crimes involve alcohol misuse (Prime Minister's Strategy Unit 2003). Those who abuse alcohol regularly are more likely to offend than people who do not (Matthews and Richardson 2005). Over one third of offenders under probation supervision are thought to have an alcohol problem and, for nearly a third, their violent behaviour was linked to their alcohol misuse (NOMS 2006b).

Alcohol misuse: treatments and interventions

There are a range of screening tools that can be used to determine alcohol misuse and the associated health and offending risks. The aims of treatment and interventions for alcohol misuse include improving the person's quality of life, drinking in moderation and abstinence (Raistrick *et al.* 2006). For offenders this should also include a reduction or cessation of the associated offending behaviour.

Research into the effectiveness of treatments has found the following to have benefits in reducing alcohol consumption and/or abstinence: the 12-step programme, cognitive-behavioural therapy, motivational enhancement therapy, brief interventions, relapse prevention and aftercare (Raistrick *et al.* 2006). Other interventions used include detoxification and medical treatments to address the physical harm caused. Treatment effectiveness can be affected by a number of factors, including the therapist, the individual's level of motivation, the severity of the alcohol problem and the individual's emotional state (Raistrick *et al.* 2006).

Alcohol treatment programmes for prisoners and offenders are less well developed than drug treatment programmes in the UK, and the evidence base is therefore less developed, according to some researchers. Prison-based programmes include the following (although the extent to which they are provided will vary in each prison): detoxification, structured counselling, assessment and screening, family therapy, educational awareness raising, Alcoholics Anonymous (AA), motivational-focused therapy, groupwork and links to community-based interventions for those leaving prison (HM Prison Service and Department of Health 2004).

Gossop *et al.* (2001) found that problematic alcohol consumption among drug-treatment clients in the UK did not reduce after the treatment. They suggest, therefore, that problematic alcohol consumption should also be addressed in drug-treatment programmes. While there are similarities in treatments and interventions used to address both alcohol and drug misuse, there are differences tailored towards the specific needs that different substance misuse brings. Poly-substance misuse may require specific tailored treatment to address both issues in parallel.

Researching substance misusers: a chaotic cohort

Many authors note the methodological difficulties of research involving self-report data, which rely on the memories of chaotic substance misusers. Some researchers are critical of findings in the substance misuse field where, for ethical reasons, control groups are often not included. Is it indeed ethical to exclude a group of individuals from treatment for the sake of research? More research is needed over longer follow-up periods to examine if gains made in the short term are maintained in the long-term, but

maintaining contact and keeping chaotic substance misusers engaged in research over longer periods of follow-up poses its own challenges.

The complex needs of substance-misusing offenders

A range of practitioners can provide substance misuse treatment and interventions. The degree of training required varies, depending on the type of intervention, the treatment, the setting and the country. Offenders who have substance misuse issues often require interventions that address much wider needs than those immediately associated with their substance misuse, such as help with mental health issues, debt/finance management and access to housing, education, training and employment opportunities (Social Exclusion Unit 2002). Treatment outcomes should therefore include those that go beyond the substance abuse and associated offending behaviour. Practitioners dealing with such offenders should therefore be aware of the need to work with other relevant agencies and practitioners in the field to maximize the positive outcomes for the individual.

Beverley Love

Related entries

Addictive behaviours; Homelessness and Crime.

Key texts and sources

Bennett, T. and Holloway, K. (2005) *Understanding Drugs, Alcohol and Crime.* Maidenhead: Open University Press.

Gossop, M., Marsden, J. and Stewart, D. (2001) *NTORS after Five Years: The National Treatment Outcome Research Study – Changes in Substance Use, Health and Criminal Behaviour during the Five Years after Intake.* London: National Addiction Centre.

Raistrick, D., Heather, N. and Godfrey, C. (2006) *Review of the Effectiveness of Treatment for Alcohol Problems.* London: National Treatment Agency for Substance Misuse.

SUICIDE

Suicide has been defined as an act with a fatal outcome, brought about by the deceased in the knowledge of a potentially fatal outcome with the purpose of bringing about change.

In the UK a coroner's verdict of suicide normally requires clear evidence of intent to die (for example, a suicide note). However, Prison Service statistics for deaths in custody are based on the more inclusive category of self-inflicted deaths (SIDs), including 'apparent suicides', in order to ensure that all possible suicides are counted and appropriately investigated. This difference in recording is very important when making comparisons with suicide rates for the general population or with deaths in custody in other countries (such as the USA, where a narrower definition is used). Rates of SID in prisons tend also to be inflated by being calculated as the number of deaths per annual average daily population, rather than against the total annual throughput of prisoners – a much larger figure since many prisoners are there for only a short time.

Notwithstanding these differences in recording, there seems little doubt that, in most countries, offenders have higher rates of suicide than the general population. In England and Wales suicide rates for male prisoners have tended to be approximately six times higher than for the male general population, although a study in 2001 comparing male prisoners with similar offenders in community settings found similar rates of suicide for the two samples, highlighting the general vulnerability of the offender population. A study of deaths of residents of approved premises (1998–2002) reported that 24 per cent of deaths were suicides and that 50 per cent were due to overdose, some of which may have been intentional. There is also evidence of high rates of suicide among convicted offenders in the year following release from prison – reported in one study as twice that of prisoners in custody. SIDs in custody differ from suicides in the community in that

hanging is the most common method of suicide in custody for both male and female prisoners, with relatively few deaths by overdose. Despite the relatively high rates of suicide among offenders, SIDs remain statistically rare events that are, therefore, difficult to predict. Assessing the impact of interventions on suicide rates requires a long-term analysis of trends, since suicides are rare and episodic and tend to occur in clusters.

Attempts to reduce the rates of SID in prisons have considered both individual vulnerability factors and aspects of the prison environment and regime. Individual vulnerability factors for suicide in the general population include mood disorders, treatment for mental illness (especially co-morbidity with alcohol or drugs misuse), impulsivity, aggression, hopelessness, cognitive rigidity and poor problem-solving. All these factors are more prevalent in offender populations than in the general population. For example, a national survey of prisoners in England and Wales (1998) reported that 40 per cent of male and 68 per cent of of female prisoners had a neurotic disorder, while 7 per cent of male and 15 per cent of female prisoners had a psychotic disorder. Prisoners are also more likely to report a history of self-harm or attempted suicide and other social problems linked to suicide risk, including family violence, abuse and being brought up in care. Designing screening for individual suicide risk on reception into custody is therefore difficult because of the low predictive power of standard risk factors. Nevertheless, screening for suicide risk in prisoners on reception has been introduced in England and Wales, Scotland and elsewhere. In Holland, the screening instrument is based on the following statistical predictors of suicide: previous suicide attempt, violent offence, misuse of hard drugs, previous psychiatric treatment and homelessness.

The ongoing assessment of risk also needs to take into account the person's experience of imprisonment and associated negative life events, including loss of social support and coping mechanisms, concerns about sentencing, problems related to detoxification and the fear of bullying or violence. Suicides in prison occur disproportionately during the first days of custody when the prisoner is adjusting to these experiences. Another consistent research finding is that most suicides occur when the prisoner is alone or in a single cell, with an increased opportunity to dwell on problems, less social support and less likelihood of the suicide attempt being detected. Countries where prisoners are accommodated predominantly in shared rooms or dormitories tend to have lower rates of suicide, although this arrangement may produce other problems. Psychological theories of suicide emphasize the importance of a sense of 'entrapment', caused by repeated experiences of humiliation combined with excessive rumination on problems and deficits in problem-solving ability. While this may apply to many offenders, those in custody are physically as well as psychologically 'trapped' in their environment.

The emphasis in several countries has been on developing and implementing care-planning systems, such as the Assessment, Care in Custody and Teamwork system in England and Wales, which incorporates assessments by trained assessors, flexible case reviews, multidisciplinary care planning and flexible, individualized patterns of observation. The introduction of this system in 2005 was followed by an apparent reduction in the rate of SIDs, although it is not possible to disaggregate the possible impact of this intervention from the impact of many other co-occurring changes, including improvements in drug treatment and improved staff training. Longer-term follow-up is required to establish whether the apparent downward trend is sustained.

At the organizational level, the prison culture and regime and the relationships between staff and prisoners have been examined in relation to suicide prevention. A study of the quality of life in selected local prisons (2001–4) found associations between prisoners' reported suicidal thoughts and three aspects of their experience of prison: their feelings of safety, the perceived fairness of the prison regime and the extent to which they felt the prison offered support for vulnerable prisoners. Prison-peer support initiatives have been developed in several countries and are generally welcomed by prisoners, although the evidence for an impact on suicide

rates is largely anecdotal. Staff training has been found to produce changes in staff attitudes and confidence in dealing with suicidal prisoners, particularly in Canadian studies. A multivariate analysis in 2003 of key prison regime characteristics reported a significant negative correlation between suicide rates and the amount of purposeful activity provided for prisoners, even when controlled for type of prison.

Another type of intervention is the attempt to reduce the opportunities and means to suicide. The Prison Service strategy in England and Wales since 2001 (and similarly in Scotland) has focused on improving general safety rather than removing personal items or clothing from individual prisoners, which prisoners tend to report as demeaning and stigmatizing. In practice this means designing cells with fewer potential ligature points, removing window bars, using ligature-free furniture and trying to create an environment that is both safe and normalizing. General research into the environmental control of behaviour suggests that this approach should have considerable value in preventing impulsive acts of suicide, particularly hanging, but a review of the introduction of safer cells was unable to evaluate fully their impact on suicide due to inconsistencies in the way the cells were allocated and used in different prisons.

In conclusion, much is known about the factors associated with suicides in prison, with less information about offenders in non-custodial settings or post-release. Obtaining empirical evidence of the effectiveness of interventions is fraught with difficulty, since randomized controlled trials are unlikely to be viable on ethical and practical grounds, and because most of the recommendations for practice are inferred from correlational data. Evaluating the impact of complex, multi-component suicide prevention programmes is particularly difficult. For example, a quasi-experimental design was used to evaluate the introduction of multiple improvements into selected local prisons, but positive changes also occurred in some control prisons as a result of shared learning and increased suicide awareness. There is a useful role for forensic psychologists in carrying out local evaluations of policy and practice.

Finally, it should be noted that suicides in custody can have a marked impact on staff and other prisoners, some of whom report symptoms of post-traumatic stress disorder. Recommendations from a small survey in prisons following a death are that staff should receive regular first-aid training, opportunities for peer support while remaining in the workplace and routine access to evidence-based clinical services if required.

Jo Borrill

Related entries

Cambridge Framework for Risk Assessment (CAMRA); Risk assessment; Self-injury assessments and interventions.

Key texts and sources

Blaauw, E. and Kerkhof, J.F.M. (2006) 'Screening prisoners for suicide risk', in G. Dear (ed.) *Preventing Suicide and Other Self-harm in Prison.* Basingstoke: Palgrave Macmillan.

Borrill, J. and Hall, J. (2006) 'Responding to a self-inflicted death in custody: support services and postvention', in G. Dear (ed.) *Preventing Suicide and Other Self-harm in Prison.* Basingstoke: Palgrave Macmillan.

Liebling, A. (2006) *The Role of the Prison Environment in Prison Suicide and Prisoner Distress.*

Paton, J. and Jenkins, R. (2005) 'Suicide and suicide attempts in prisons', in K. Hawton (ed.) *Prevention and Treatment of Suicidal Behaviour – from Science to Practice.* Oxford: Oxford University Press.

VICTIM SUPPORT

Victim Support is the national charity for crime victims, witnesses, their families and friends. It is an independent voluntary organization working alongside the criminal justice system, government and other organizations nationally and in local communities.

Victim Support consists of a network of affiliated charities across England and Wales (sister organizations work in Scotland and Northern Ireland), although it hopes to move to a single charity soon. Under the government's code of practice for victims of crime, the police have a duty to refer all victims to Victim Support (with exceptions for less serious crimes). For 'sensitive' crimes, such as murder, serious sexual assault and domestic violence, the active consent of the victim to referral is required. In addition, any victim of crime can refer him or herself, whether or not he or she has reported the crime to the police.

Services to victims are predominantly provided by trained volunteers supervised by paid staff. Victims are offered emotional support, tailored to the victim's individual needs, and/or information, advice and advocacy (for example, with other criminal justice agencies or insurance companies). In particular, there is assistance offered in relation to applications for criminal injuries compensation. Although Victim Support offers a generic service to all victims, it has volunteers trained to work with all types of serious crime. In addition, it refers those needing more specialist assistance, such as counselling, to the appropriate agencies.

Victim Support also provides a Witness Service in every criminal court in England and Wales. This is an impartial service offered to both prosecution and defence witnesses to alleviate the stress of giving evidence in court.

Victim Support has lobbied successfully to improve the rights of victims of crime – indeed, the creation of the *Victims' Code of Practice* was a response to many of its agenda issues. Unlike some other victims' organizations, it never comments on the appropriateness of any individual sentencing decisions, being concerned more with improving the treatment of victims, not just by other criminal justice agencies but also by agencies such as health and housing.

Mark Harris

Related entries

Children and Families Court Advisory and Support Services (CAFCAS); Courts; Criminal Justice System; Public protection.

Key texts and sources

See the website of Victim Support (**www.victim support.org.uk**).

VIOLENCE RISK ASSESSMENT

In general, risk assessment is the process of understanding a hazard – violence, sexual violence, suicide and so on – in order to prevent it from occurring. More specifically, risk assessment is an estimation of risk potential based on an understanding of the presence and relevance of certain conditions that are regarded as either risk factors or protective factors.

A risk assessment should result in a risk formulation – a working model of how the most relevant risk and protective factors interact with one another over time to create changes in risk. Risk management follows from risk formulation and is the action taken to control and, ultimately, to reduce risk, through regularly reviewed treatment interventions, supervision practices, client monitoring and victim safety planning. Risk management involves measures that serve to reduce the relevance of risk factors as well as to increase and develop the role of protective factors. Therefore, the purpose of risk assessment is to inform risk management. An assessment of risk that is not followed by a risk management plan may constitute unethical practice.

Violence risk assessment is an essential component of the work of psychologists employed in forensic settings. Practitioners tasked with undertaking violence risk assessments are required to work with clients to understand the nature of any future violent act they may commit, its potential impact on victims, how soon the violent act could occur and how likely it is to occur. The definition of violence underpinning this activity is that violence is any actual, attempted or threatened physical harm that is deliberate (as opposed to accidental) and nonconsenting. Therefore, an assessment of violence risk is not limited just to the risk of actual physical harm. Understanding a client's risk of future violence is based on an understanding of that person's lifetime history of actual, attempted or threatened acts of violence – the client's past is used to understand the nature of his or her potential for violence in the future. A comprehensive assessment like this requires time as well as sound knowledge of the relevant research on violence and its antecedents. So, practitioners undertaking these assessments should be qualified forensic practitioners (or appropriately supervised while in training), as well experienced in working with individuals who are violent.

Most research on violence risk has focused on individual rather than situational risk factors. Thus, there is an abundance of research on the role of such factors as mental illness, psychopathy and substance use problems in relation to violence potential. While protective factors are acknowledged as important, far less research has examined their role in mediating the impact of risk factors. However, recent research does suggest that clients with a history of violence may be less likely to be violent in the future when protective factors, such as social support, a stable lifestyle, effective treatment and employment, are present. The absence of factors, such as drug or alcohol dependence, untreated or treatment-resistant mental illness or early trauma, is also regarded as positive and protective.

Practice issues

An assessment of risk may be carried out in one of three different ways. First, practitioners may make unstructured judgements about the risk potential of a client that are based only on that practitioner's experience of working with similar clients and his or her knowledge of the client him or herself. Unstructured judgements about risk are no longer regarded as good or even acceptable practice because they involve inconsistent decision-making that is empirically unfounded and difficult to justify and challenge. Secondly, actuarial risk assessment involves estimating the likelihood that a client will be violent during a specified period of time following the assessment. This form of risk assessment practice is based on the findings of studies that have tried to identify the collection of variables most strongly associated with violent reoffending. Therefore, the emphasis of actuarial approaches is on violence prediction. Thirdly, structured professional judgement is an alternative approach to risk decision-making in which the practitioner makes a clinical judgement about the relevance of a range of violence risk factors to a client's risk potential. The task of such approaches to risk assessment is to formulate individual risk with a view to developing a risk management plan. Therefore, the emphasis of structured professional judgement approaches is on violence prevention. Forensic practitioners most frequently use actuarial and structured professional judgement approaches to violence risk assessment. Generally, practitioners choose the approach that is most suitable to the requirements of the assessment, often using the two approaches in tandem.

There is a range of violence risk assessment guides or tools that exemplify the actuarial and structured professional judgement approaches. An example of an actuarial risk assessment tool is the Violence Risk Appraisal Guise (VRAG). The VRAG was developed in Canada on a sample of over 600 male patients of a high-secure forensic psychiatric hospital. It consists of 12 items or risk factors, each of them weighted in terms of their contribution towards a prediction of violence risk. The most heavily weighted risk factor in this scheme is a client's score on the Psychopathy Checklist-Revised – a higher level of psychopathy is associated with a greater potential for violence in the future. Other risk factors include age (young age is associated with higher risk), personality disorder diagnosis, alcohol problems, problems at elementary school and so on. A client is rated on each of the VRAG items, and a total score is obtained that reflects the extent to which each risk factor is present in that individual. This total score is then compared with data provided by the VRAG authors in which ranges of total scores are paired with percentages that represent the number of men in the validation sample who had such scores and who were known to have reoffended violently over a seven-year follow-up period. The outcome of the VRAG assessment, therefore, is an estimation of how similar the client is to a group of men with a comparable range of risk factors whose rate of reoffending is known. Thus, if the client being assessed is comparable to a subset of the validation sample who reoffended at a very high rate, the practitioner carrying out the assessment has good grounds for recommending the most stringent risk management plans.

The VRAG is the most common example of an actuarial risk assessment tool where violence risk is the focus. Other examples of actuarial tools are the Classification of Violence Risk (COVR), which can be used with men and women to estimate violence potential following discharge from civil psychiatric hospitals, and the Offenders Group Reconviction Scale (second version; OGRS-2), which estimates general as well as violence risk potential in released prisoners over a two-year follow-up period.

An example of a tool exemplifying the structured professional judgement approach is the HCR-20. H stands for historical – the first 10 items cover aspects of the client's history of violence, social functioning and mental health. C stands for clinical – the next five items in the HCR-20 cover current clinical issues. R stands for risk management – the last five items cover requirements relevant to managing risk of violence. The task of the practitioner is to compare the client against each of the 20 HCR-20 items and to make a clinical judgement about the relevance of each of those that are present to the individual's risk of violence in the future. For example, psychopathy is a risk factor in the HCR-20 as it is in the VRAG but, in the HCR-20, the practitioner is required to think through why and how psychopathic personality traits could relate to a future violent incident. Relevant risk factors are then woven together into a risk formulation that uses scenario planning to try to identify the nature of future violence, its impact, frequency and imminence, as well as its likelihood. Risk management plans are then derived, covering treatment needs, supervision requirements, monitoring guidelines and victim safety planning, all based on the risk formulation. The HCR-20 requires a sophisticated level of clinical skill and it is often time-consuming to complete. While it is a very popular tool, its use is limited because of the scale of effort required to complete it.

Other examples of tools exemplifying the structured professional judgement approach to violence risk assessment are the Violence Risk Scale (VRS), which examines risk of violence emphasizing motivation to engage in treatment and risk management, the Spousal Assault Risk Assessment Guide (SARA), which examines risk of domestic violence, and the Structured Assessment of Violence Risk in Youth (SAVRY), which supports violence risk assessment in young people aged between 12 and 18 years. As with the HCR-20, the SARA and the SAVRY are suitable for use with women and young girls. There is also the Early Assessment of Risk List for Boys (EARL-20B) and the Early Assessment of Risk List for Girls (EARL-21G), which are suitable for use with children under 12. The

Short-term Assessment of Risk and Treatability (START) is a relatively new instrument that supports risk assessment over very short periods of time (days, weeks) as opposed to the typical assessment time frame of the other instruments listed, which is months up to a year or so, after which a reassessment is required.

The collaboration of the client in an assessment of violence risk is highly desirable, and all efforts should be made to engage the client in this process. However, many clients are understandably anxious about risk assessments and may refuse to participate because they are afraid of the consequences for them of doing so. In such circumstances, and where a risk assessment is in the public interest, a more limited assessment of violence risk can be carried out on file information alone in addition to consultation with relevant others (e.g. the personal officer of a prisoner or the named nurse of a forensic psychiatric patient).

Conclusions

Practice in violence risk assessment has improved greatly in the last 20 or so years due to the development of tools that structure the assessment process and ground it in empirical research into violence. Actuarial and structured clinical approaches differ in their emphasis – prediction vs. prevention – and have hitherto largely been seen as competitors rather than as alternative approaches to assessment that offer a means of evaluating quite different information about violence potential. More recently, interest has increased among practitioners and researchers in improving the links between risk assessment and risk management. However, much work still needs to be done in this area before we are able reliably to measure what it is we have prevented. In the meantime, practitioners are recommended to select one or more violence risk assessment tools on the basis of the needs of their client and the requirements of the situation in which he or she is to be placed and managed. If risk management is the objective, structured professional judgement tools will offer more guidance than actuarial tools.

Caroline Logan

Related entries

Cambridge Framework for Risk Assessment (CAMRA); Parole; Risk assessment; Risk–needs assessment (Level of Service Inventory – LSI).

Key texts and sources

Douglas, K.S., Yeomans, M. and Boer, D.P. (2005) 'Comparative validity analysis of multiple measures of violence risk in criminal offenders', *Criminal Justice and Behavior*, 32: 479–510.
Hart, S.D., Michie, C. and Cooke, D.J. (2007) 'The precision of actuarial risk assessment instruments: evaluating the "margins of error" of group versus individual predictions of violence', *British Journal of Psychiatry*, 190(S49): s61–s66.
O'Rourke, M., Bailes, G. and Davies, J. (2006) *Risk Assessment and Management. Occasional Briefing Paper 4.* Leicester: BPS.
Whittington, R., Barr, W., Brown, A., Leitner, M., Logan, C. and Nathan, T. (in press) 'Best practice in managing risk: principles and evidence for best practice in the assessment and management of risk to self and others (National Mental Health Risk Management Programme).'
See the Risk Management Authority's website (www.RMAscotland.gov.uk) for information about risk assessment tools (in the *Risk Assessment Tools Evaluation Directory* or *RATED*) and for standards and guidelines on both risk assessment and risk management planning.

VIOLENT OFFENDER AND SEX OFFENDER REGISTER (VISOR)

The Violent Offender and Sex Offender Register (ViSOR) was developed by the Police Information Technology Organization and is now managed by its successor organization, the National Policing Improvement Agency. It is a centralized application and data store of information and intelligence on offenders and other persons who pose a risk of serious harm to the public.

Part 2 of the Sexual Offences Act 2003 provides for notification requirements on offenders who receive convictions or cautions for certain sexual offences. These notification requirements are often known as the 'sex offender's register'. They are intended to ensure that the police are kept informed of the whereabouts of sex offenders. They help the Police and Probation Services to manage the risks posed by such offenders and also help in the detection of sexual crime. The notification requirements were originally introduced through the Sex Offenders Act 1997, which came into force on 1 September 1997. They were repealed and re-enacted with considerable amendment by the Sexual Offences Act 2003.

The Criminal Justice and Court Services Act 2000 established the statutory framework for interagency co-operation in assessing and managing violent offenders and sex offenders. These are known as the multi-agency public protection arrangements (MAPPAs). These provisions were repealed and re-enacted by the Criminal Justice Act 2003.

The principal purpose of the Violent Offender and Sex Offender Register (ViSOR) is to facilitate the work of MAPPAs by co-operative working and information sharing between the three 'responsible authorities' (the Police, Probation and Prison Services) in their joint management of individuals posing a risk of serious harm to the public. A sec-ondary purpose is to assist in the identification of potential suspects following a crime of a violent or sexual nature. ViSOR facilitates this through its powerful search engine, which allows officers to retrieve records based on criteria relating to any information or intelligence stored on the system.

Mark Jones

Related entries

Multi Agency Public Protection Arrangements (MAPPA); Public protection; Sexual abuse; Sexual offending: interventions.

Key texts and sources

Home Office (2004) *MAPPA Guidance.* London: Home Office.

See the Office of Public Sector Information's website for the texts of the Criminal Justice Act 2003 (**http://www.opsi.gov.uk/acts/acts2003/20030044. htm**) and the Sexual Offences Act 2003 (**http://www.opsi.gov.uk/acts/acts2003/20030042. htm**).

See also the National Policing Improvement Agency's website (**www.npia.police.uk**).

WHAT WORKS

A firm definition of 'What Works' is elusive as this is an everyday, colloquial term used in a specialized sense in forensic psychology and allied areas. It refers mainly to an accumulated body of evidence regarding the outcomes of psychologically based and other interventions with offenders, particularly where they are focused on the reduction of criminal recidivism. This closely parallels similar debates that have taken place concerning the outcomes of psychological therapies in mental health services.

The use of the phrase 'What Works' is normally attributed to a specific source: a journal paper written by Robert Martinson (1974) which questioned whether there was any convincing evidence of the beneficial effects of psychotherapy, education, training or other concerted efforts in reducing the subsequent reoffending of those who participated. Martinson's conclusions that the research relevant to this question was of fairly poor quality and that treatment had failed effectively ended an era characterized as one of optimism regarding the possibility of rehabilitating offenders. Perceived as having instituted an ensuing era of 'Nothing Works', he is widely regarded as having been highly influential in the progressively increasing punitiveness of criminal justice in North America, the UK and elsewhere from the late 1970s onwards. This is almost certainly a simplistic analysis: economic and political factors were such that this change of direction might well have occurred in any case, and other publications that appeared contemporaneously drew broadly similar conclusions.

In challenging this position, several other researchers published rejoinders, marshalling positive evidence that Martinson had neglected (e.g. Gendreau and Ross 1980). In the period since then, and particularly with the advent of meta-analytic reviews of research outcomes, there has been a steadily accumulating knowledge base regarding effective approaches to working with persistent offenders and reducing the frequency and seriousness of their crimes. By late 2006 there were 60 published meta-analytic reviews of different segments of this field of research (McGuire in press), alongside other studies that highlighted risk factors for criminal involvement, thereby contributing to the construction and consolidation of theory in this area.

Accumulated knowledge and practical implications

Gradually, a consensus has emerged to the effect that there are numerous findings showing generally that offender recidivism can be reduced. More specifically, there are indications regarding how that can be achieved with respect to various combinations of types of offence, offender characteristics, intervention methods, patterns of delivery and sentencing contexts. (Hence 'What Works' is often issued as a statement rather than posed as a question.) One key element in this has been the Risk–Needs–Responsivity (RNR) model of Andrews and his colleagues (Andrews *et al.* 2006). Another has been the emergence of structured programmes for addressing risk factors, thereby having an impact on the likelihood of reoffending (Hollin and Palmer 2006).

From the late 1990s onwards, 'What Works' was also used to refer to a series of changes in policy and practice in a number of jurisdictions, most notably the UK, whereby there was large-scale, government-initiated dissemination of intervention programmes designed to reduce recidivism. This has been only partially successful and has led to extensive debates regarding the reasons for the respective successes and failures. There is widespread agreement that far more research is required, with a particular need to improve understanding of how to implement lessons from research in criminal justice services.

James McGuire

Related entries

Criminology; Meta-analysis; Moral reasoning; Nothing Works.

Key texts and sources

Andrews, D.A., Bonta, J. and Wormith, J.S. (2006) 'The recent past and near future of risk and/or need assessment', *Crime and Delinquency*, 52: 7–27.

Gendreau, P. and Ross, R.R. (1980) 'Effective correctional treatment: bibliotherapy for cynics', in R.R. Ross and P. Gendreau (eds) *Effective Correctional Treatment*. Toronto: Butterworths.

Hollin, C.R. and Palmer, E.J. (2006) (eds) *Offending Behaviour Programmes: Development, Application, and Controversies*. Chichester: Wiley.

Martinson, R. (1974) 'What works? Questions and answers about prison reform', *The Public Interest*, 10: 22–54.

McGuire, J. (in press) 'What's the point of sentencing? Psychological aspects of crime and punishment', in G. Davies *et al.* (eds) *Forensic Psychology*. Chichester: Wiley.

Appendix I

ABBREVIATIONS

The following list includes not only abbreviations used in this Dictionary but also many others found in common use in forensic psychology and forensic psychology-related documentation.

16PF	Sixteen Personality Factor Questionnaire
AA	Alcoholics Anonymous
ACCT	assessment, care in custody and teamwork
ACMD	Advisory Council on the Misuse of Drugs
AIDS	acquired immune deficiency syndrome
APA	American Psychological Association
ARO	alcohol-related offending
ART	aggression replacement training
ASB	anti-social behaviour
ASBO	anti-social behaviour order
ASW	approved social worker
AUC	area under the (ROC) curve
BASW	British Association of Social Workers
BCS	British Crime Survey
BEST	behaviour and educational support team
BME	black and minority ethnic
BPS	British Psychological Society
BVC	Bar Vocational Course
CAFCASS	Children and Family Court Advisory and Support Service
CALM	Controlling Anger and Learning to Manage It
CAMRA	Cambridge Framework for Risk Assessment
CARATS	Counselling, Assessment, Referral, Advice, Throughcare Service
CBCA	content-based credibility analysis
CBT	cognitive-behavioural therapy/treatment
C Ct	Crown court
CCTV	closed-circuit television
CD	conduct disorder
CDATE	Correctional Drug Abuse Treatment Effectiveness
CDO	court duty officer
CI	cognitive interview
CJS	criminal justice system
C of E	Council of Europe

COVR	Classification of Violence Risk
CPA	care programme approach
CPD	continuing professional development
CPN	community psychiatric nurse
CPR	Civil Procedure Rule
CPS	Crown Prosecution Service
CPsychol	chartered psychologist
C & R	control and restraint
CRASBO	criminal anti-social behaviour order
CSDD	Cambridge Study in Delinquent Development
CV	criterion variable(s)
DAP	Draw-a-person (test)
DAT	Draw-a-tree (test)
DCLP	Division of Criminological and Legal Psychology
DCSF	Department for Children, Schools and Families
DD	developmental disability
DFP	Division of Forensic Psychology
DIP	director of inmate programmes/drug intervention programme
DIPC	Direct and Indirect Prison Behaviour Checklist
D-KEFS	Delis–Kaplan Executive Function System
DMM	Dynamic-maturational Model
DofEE	Department of Education and Employment
DoH	Department of Health
DPAS	Drug Prevention Advisory Service
DPP	Director of Public Prosecutions
DRR	drug rehabilitation requirement
DSM-III-R	Diagnostic and Statistical Manual of Mental Disorders (third edition, revised)
DSM-IV-R	Diagnostic and Statistical Manual of Mental Disorders (fourth edition, revised)
DSPD	dangerous and severe personality disorder
DSS	Department of Social Security
DTO	detention and training order/drug treatment order
DTTO	drug treatment and testing order
EARL-20B	Early Assessment of Risk List for Boys
EARL-21G	Early Assessment of Risk List for Girls
EBP	evidence-based practice
EC	European Commission/European Community
ECHR	European Convention on Human Rights
ECT	electroconvulsive therapy
ECtHR	European Court of Human Rights
EEG	electroencephalogram
EMDR	eye movement desensitization and reprocessing
ETS	enhanced thinking skills
FDR	fast delivery report
fMRI	functional magnetic resonance imaging

HCR-20	Historical Clinical Risk – 20
HIA	hyperactivity–impulsivity–attention
HIT	high-intensity training
HIV	human immuno-deficiency virus
HMCIC	Her Majesty's Chief Inspector of Constabulary
HMCIP	Her Majesty's Chief Inspector of Prisons
HMIC	Her Majesty's Inspectorate of Constabulary
HMIP	Her Majesty's Inspectorate of Prisons/Probation
HMP	Her Majesty's prison
HMPS	Her Majesty's Prison Service
HMYOI	Her Majesty's young offender institution
HO	Home Office
HPC	Health Professions Council
HTP	House–tree–person (test)
ICD	International Classification of Diseases
ILEX	Institute of Legal Executives
IPDE	International Personality Disorder Examination
IPP	imprisonment for public protection/indefinite (sentence for) public protection
IQ	intelligence quotient
IT	information technology/intermediate treatment
KEEPs	Key Elements of Effective Practice
K-F-D	Kinetic family drawing (test)
LEA	local education authority
LGBT	lesbian, gay, bisexual, transgender
LPC	Legal Practice Course
LSI	Level of Service Inventory
LSI-R	Level of Service Inventory – Revised
MAPPA	multi-agency public protection arrangement
MAPPP	multi-agency public protection panel
MARAC	multi-agency risk assessment conference
MCMI-III	Millon Clinical Multi-axial Inventory – III
MCTC	Military Corrective Training Centre
MDO	mentally disordered offender
MDT	multi-disciplinary team/mandatory drug testing
MI	motivational interviewing
MMPI-2	Minnesota Multiphasic Personality Inventory
MPA	minor physical anomaly
MRI	magnetic resonance imaging
MSE	mental state examination
MSU	medium secure unit
Nacro	National Association for the Care and Resettlement of Offenders
NAPO	National Association of Probation Officers
NAS-PI	Novaco Anger Scale and Provocation Inventory
NAVSS	National Association of Victim Support Schemes

NDNAD	National DNA Database
NEO PI-R	NEO Personality Inventory – Revised
NHS	National Health Service
NICE	National Institute of Clinical Excellence
NNH	number needed to harm
NNT	number needed to treat
NNTB	number needed to treat to (produce) benefit
NNTH	number needed to treat to (cause) harm
NOMIS	National Offender Management Information System
NOMM	National Offender Management Model
NOMS	National Offender Management Service
NPIA	National Policing Improvement Agency
NPS	National Probation Service
NSF	National Service Framework
NTORS	National Treatment Outcome Research Study
OASys	Offender Assessment System
OB	offending behaviour
OBP	offending behaviour programme
OBPU	Offending Behaviour Programmes Unit
OCJS	Offending, Crime and Justice Survey
ODPM	Office of the Deputy Prime Minister
OGRS-2	Offender Group Reconviction Scale (second version)
PACE	Police and Criminal Evidence Act 1984
PAI	Personality Assessment Inventory
PCC	physical control in care
PCL-R	Psychopathy Checklist – Revised
PCT	primary care trust
PD	personality disorder
PDO	potentially dangerous offender
PEI	post-event information
PET	positron emission tomography
PITO	Police Information Technology Organization
PNC	Police National Computer
PPOs	prolific and other priority offenders
PSE	Present State Examination
PTSD	post-traumatic stress disorder
RAAP	RAMAS Anger Assessment Profile
RATED	Risk Assessment Tools Evaluation Directory
RCS	Rorschach
RCT	randomized clinical trial/randomized controlled trial
RDS	Research, Development and Statistics (Directorate)
RM2000	Risk Matrix 2000
RNR	risk–needs–responsivity
ROM	regional offender manager
ROR	risk of reoffending
R & R	Reasoning and Rehabilitation

RRASOR	Rapid Risk Assessment for Sex Offender Recidivism
RSVP	Risk of Sexual Violence Protocol
SACJ-Min	Structured Anchored Clinical Judgement
SARA	Spousal Assault Risk Assessment (guide)
SARN	Structured Assessment of Risk and Need
SAVRY	Structured Assessment of Violence Risk in Youth
Sch. 1	Schedule 1 offence/offender
SCID-II	Structured Interview for the DSM-IV
SCTD	Sentence Completion Test for Depression
SDR	standard delivery report
SEU	Social Exclusion Unit
SFO	Serious Fraud Office/serious further offence
SGC	Sentencing Guidelines Council
SID	self-inflicted death
SMI	severe mental illness
SOA	Sexual Offences Act 2003
SOCA	Serious and Organized Crime Agency
SOCAP	Serious Organized Crime and Police Act 2005
SONAR	Sex Offender Needs Assessment Rating
SORAG	Sex Offender Risk Assessment Guide
SOTP	Sex Offender Treatment Programme
START	Short-term Assessment of Risk and Treatability
STAXI	State Trait Anger Expression Inventory
STC	secure training centre
SV	statement validity (analysis)
SVR-20	Sexual Violent Risk – 20
TASIT	Awareness of Social Inference Test
TAT	Thematic Apperception Test
TC	therapeutic community
TEA	Test of Everyday Attention
VDT	voluntary drug testing
ViSOR	Violent Offender and Sex Offender Register
VIW	vulnerable and intimidated witness
VLO	victim liaison officer
VRAG	Violence Risk Assessment Guide
VRS	Violence Risk Scale
VSS	Victim Support Services
WHO	World Health Organization
YOI	young offender institution
YOT	youth offending team

References

Abdulrahim, D. (2001) *Substance Misuse and Mental Health Co-morbidity (Dual Diagnosis) Standards for Mental Health Services*. London: HAS.

Abel, R.L. (1989) *The Legal Profession in England and Wales*. London: Blackwell.

Abrahamson, D. (2006) 'History of care in the community', in A. Stephens and R. Walden (eds) *For the Sake of Humanity: Essays in Honour of Clemens N. Nathan*. Leiden and Boston, MA: Martinus Nijhoff.

Ainsworth, M., Blehar, M., Waters, E. and Wall, S. (1978) Patterns of Attachment. Hillsdale, NJ: Erlbaum.

Ainsworth, P.B. (2001) *Offender Profiling and Crime Analysis*. Cullompton: Willan Publishing.

Ainsworth, P.B. (1995) *Psychology and Policing*. Chichester: Wiley.

Ajzen, I. (1985) 'From intentions to actions: a theory of planned behaviour', in J. Kuhl and J. Beckman (eds) *Action-control: From Cognition to Behaviour*. Heidelberg: Springer.

Ajzen, I. (1988) *Attitudes, Personality and Behaviour*. Chicago, IL: Dorsey Press.

American Psychiatric Association (1980) *Diagnostic and Statistical Manual of Mental Disorders* (3rd edn). Washington, DC: APA.

American Psychiatric Association (1994) *Diagnostic and Statistical Manual of Mental Disorders* (4th edn) *DSM-IV*. Washington, DC: American Psychiatric Association.

American Psychiatric Association (2000) *Diagnostic and Statistical Manual of Mental Disorders* (4th edn). Washington, DC: American Psychiatric Association.

Anderson, B.J., Snow, R.W. and Wells-Parker, E. (2000) 'Comparing the predictive validity of DUI risk screening instruments: development of validation standards', *Addiction*, 95: 915–29.

Andrews, D.A. and Bonta, J.L. (1994) *The Psychology of Criminal Conduct*. Cincinnati, OH: Anderson.

Andrews, D.A. and Bonta, J.L. (1995) *The Level of Service Inventory – Revised (User's Manual)*. New York, NY and Toronto: Multi-health Systems.

Andrews, D.A. and Bonta, J.L. (1998) *The Psychology of Criminal Conduct* (2nd edn). Cincinnati, OH: Anderson.

Andrews, D.A. and Bonta, J.L. (2003) *The Psychology of Criminal Conduct* (3rd edn). Cincinnati, OH: Anderson.

Andrews, D.A. and Bonta, J.L. (2004) *The Level of Service/Case Management Inventory: An Offender Assessment System (User's Manual)*. New York, NY and Toronto: Multi-health Systems.

Andrews, D.A., Bonta, J.L. and Wormith, J.S. (2006) 'The recent past and near future of risk and/or need assessment', *Crime and Delinquency*, 52: 7–27.

Andrews, J.A. (ed.) (1982) *Human Rights in Criminal Procedure: A Comparative Study*. The Hague: Martinus Nijhoff.

Antonowicz, D.H. (2005) 'The reasoning and rehabilitation program: outcome evaluations with offenders', in M. McMurran and J. McGuire (eds) *Social Problem-solving and Offending: Evidence, Evaluation and Evolution*. Chichester: Wiley.

Arce, R. (1995) 'Evidence evaluation in jury decision making', in R. Bull and D. Carson (eds) *Handbook of Psychology in Legal Contexts*. Chichester: Wiley.

Archbold (ed. J. Richardson) (2006) *Criminal Pleading, Evidence and Practice.* London: Sweet & Maxwell.

Arnott, H. and Creighton, C. (2006) *Parole Board Hearings: Law and Practice.* London: Legal Action Group.

Arrigo, B. and Shipley, S.L. (2005) *Introduction to Forensic Psychology: Issues and Controversies in Law, Law Enforcement and Corrections* (2nd edn). New York, NY: Elsevier Academic Press.

Arseneault, L., Moffitt, T.E., Caspi, A., Taylor, P.J. and Silva, P.A. (2000) 'Mental disorders and violence in a total birth cohort: results from the Dunedin study', *Archives of General Psychiatry*, 57: 979–86.

Arthur, R. (2007) *Family Life and Youth Offending.* London: Routledge.

Ascione, F.R. and Arkow, P. (1999) *Child Abuse, Domestic Violence and Animal Abuse: Linking the Circles of Compassion for Prevention and Intervention.* West Lafayette, IN: Purdue University Press.

Ashman, L. and Duggan, L. (2002) 'Interventions for learning disabled sex offenders', *Cochrane Database of Systematic Reviews*, 2: art. no. CD003682 (available online at **www.Cochrane.org**).

Averill, J.R. (1982) *Anger and Aggression: An Essay on Emotion.* New York, NY: Springer-Verlag.

Babiker, G. and Arnold, L. (1997) *The Language of Self-injury: Comprehending Self-mutilation.* Leicester: BPS.

Badenoch, D. and Heneghan, C. (2005) *Evidence-based Medicine Toolkit.* London: BMJ Books.

Bailes, G. (2004) 'Sieges, the police… and a psychologist', *The Psychologist*, 17: 380–3.

Baker, M. and Menken, M. (2001) 'Time to abandon mental illness', *British Medical Journal*, 322: 937–8.

Baldry, E., McDonnell, D., Maplestone, P. and Peeters, M. (2003) *Ex-prisoners and Accommodation: What Bearing do Different Forms of Housing have on Social Reintegration?* Melbourne: Australian Housing and Urban Research Institute (available online at **www.ahuri.edu.au/general/search/**).

Baldwin, J. and McConville, M. (1980) 'Juries, foreman and verdicts', *British Journal of Criminology*, 20: 35–44.

Bartlett, P. and Wright, D. (eds) (1999) *Outside the Walls of the Asylum: The History of Care in the Community, 1750–2000.* London: Athlone Press.

Bartol, C.R. (1996) 'Police psychology: then, now and beyond', *Criminal Justice and Behaviour*, 23: 70–89.

Beck, F. and Godin, W. (1951) *Russian Purge and the Extraction of Confession.* New York, NY: Viking Press.

Beech, A.R., Fisher, D.D. and Thornton, D. (2003) 'Risk assessment of sex offenders', *Professional Psychology: Research and Practice*, 34: 339–52.

Bellak, L. and Abrams, D.M. (1997) *The Thematic Apperception Test, the Children's Apperception Test and the Senior Apperception Test in Clinical Use* (6th edn). Boston, MA: Allyn & Bacon.

Bem, D.J. (1966) 'Inducing belief in false confessions', *Journal of Personality and Social Psychology*, 3: 707–10.

Benjafield, J. (1992) *Cognition.* Englewood Cliffs, NJ: Prentice Hall.

Bennett, T. (2000) *Drugs and Crime: The Results of the Second Developmental Stage of the NEW-ADAM Programme. Home Office Research Study* 205. London: Home Office.

Bennett, T. and Holloway, K. (2005) *Understanding Drugs, Alcohol and Crime.* Maidenhead: Open University Press.

Blaauw, E. and Kerkhof, J.F.M. (2006) 'Screening prisoners for suicide risk', in G. Dear (ed.) *Preventing Suicide and Other Self-harm in Prison.* Basingstoke: Palgrave Macmillan.

Blackburn, R. (1996) 'What is forensic psychology?', *Legal and Criminological Psychology*, 1: 3–16.

Blasi, A. (1980) 'Bridging moral cognition and moral action: a critical review of the literature', *Psychological Bulletin*, 88: 1–45.

Blau, T.H. (1994) *Psychological Services for Law Enforcement*. Chichester: Wiley.

Blom-Cooper, L. (ed.) (2006) *Experts in the Civil Courts*. Oxford: Expert Witness Institute/Oxford University Press.

Blom-Cooper, L., Brown, M., Dolan, R. and Murphy, E. (1992) *Report of the Committee of Inquiry into Complaints about Ashworth Hospital*. London: HMSO.

Blumstein, A., Cohen, J., Roth, J.A. and Visher, C.A. (1988) *Criminal Careers and 'Career Criminals'* (2 vols). Washington, DC: National Academy Press.

Bond, C.F. and DePaulo, B.M. (2006) 'Accuracy of deception judgements', *Personality and Social Psychology Review*, 10: 214–34.

Bond, C.F., Solon, M. and Harper, P. (1997) *The Expert Witness in Court*. Crayford: Shaw & Sons.

Bonta, J.L. (1996) 'Risk–needs assessment and treatment', in A.T. Harland (ed.) *Choosing Correctional Options That Work*. Thousand Oaks, CA: Sage.

Borrill, J. and Hall, J. (2006) 'Responding to a self-inflicted death in custody: support services and postvention', in G. Dear (ed.) *Preventing Suicide and Other Self-harm in Prison*. Basingstoke: Palgrave Macmillan.

Bottoms, A., Rex, S. and Robinson, G. (eds) (2004) *Alternatives to Prison: Options for an Insecure Society*. Cullompton: Willan Publishing.

Bowlby, J. (1969/1982) *Attachment and Loss. Vol. 1. Attachment*. New York, NY: Basic Books.

Bowlby, J. (1973) *Attachment and Loss. Vol. 2. Separation*. New York, NY: Basic Books.

Bowlby, J. (1980) *Attachment and Loss. Vol. 3. Loss*. New York, NY: Basic Books.

BPS (1997) *Ethical Guidelines in Forensic Psychology*. Leicester: BPS.

BPS (2004) *A Review of the Current Scientific Status and Fields of Application of Polygraphic Deception Detection: Final Report from the Working Party*. Leicester: BPS.

BPS (2005) *Subject Benchmarks for Applied Psychology*. Leicester: BPS.

BPS (2006a) *The British Psychological Society: Ethics and Code of Conduct*. Leicester: BPS (available online at **http://www.bps.org.uk/document-download-area/document-download$.cfm?file_uuid=5084A882-1143-DFD0-7E6C-F1938A65C242&ext=pdf**).

BPS (2006b) *DECP Booklet: Educational and Child Psychologists within Communities*. Leicester: BPS.

Brennan, A., Mednick, S.A. and Hodgins, S. (2000) 'Major mental disorders and criminal violence in a Danish birth cohort', *Archives of General Psychiatry*, 57: 494–500.

Brown, J. (1998) 'Helping the police with their enquiries', *The Psychologist*, 11: 539–42.

Brown, J. (2002) 'Women as leaders? Catalyst for change', in R. Adlam and P. Villiers (eds) *Police Leadership in the 21st Century*. Winchester: Waterside Press.

Browne, K.D., Hanks, H., Stratton, P. and Hamilton, C.E. (2002) *The Early Prediction and Prevention of Child Abuse: A Handbook*. Chichester: Wiley.

Browne, K.D. and Herbert, M. (1997) *Preventing Family Violence*. Chichester: Wiley.

Buchanan, A. (ed.) (2002) *Care of the Mentally Disordered Offender in the Community*. Oxford: Oxford University Press.

Bull, R. and Horncastle, P. (1994) 'Evaluation of police recruit training involving psychology', *Psychology, Crime and Law*, 1: 143–9.

Butterworth, B. (2005) 'The development of arithmetical abilities', *Journal of Child Psychology and Psychiatry*, 46: 3–18.

Cammack, M. (1995) 'In search of the post-positivist jury', *Indiana Law Journal*, 70: 405–89.

Canter, D. (1995a) 'Psychology of offender profiling', in R. Bull and D. Carson (eds) *Handbook of Psychology in Legal Contexts*. Chichester: Wiley.

Canter, D. (1995b) *Criminal Shadows*. London: HarperCollins.

Canter, D. (2005) *Mapping Murder*. London: Virgin Books.

Carlen, P. (1996) *Jigsaw: A Political Criminology of Youth Homelessness*. Buckingham: Open University Press.

Carter, P. (2003) *Managing Offenders, Reducing Crime: A New Approach*. London: Prime Minister's Strategy Unit, HM Treasury and Home Office.

Carter, P. (2007) *Securing the Future: Proposals for the Efficient and Sustainable Use of Custody in England and Wales*. London: Prime Minister's Strategy Unit, HM Treasury and Home Office.

Carver, C.S., Scheier, M.F. and Weintraub, J.K. (1989) 'Assessing coping strategies: a theoretically based approach', *Journal of Personality and Social Psychology*, 56: 267–83.

Ceci, S.J., Crossman, A.M., Scullin, M., Gilstrap, L. and Huffman, M.L. (2002) 'Children's suggestibility research: implications for the courtroom and the forensic interview', in H.L. Westcott *et al.* (eds) *Children's Testimony: A Handbook of Psychological Research and Forensic Practice*. Chichester: Wiley.

Clark, D. (1999) 'Risk assessment in prisons and probation', *Forensic Update*, 1: 15–18.

Coleman, C. and Norris, C. (2000) *Introducing Criminology*. Cullompton: Willan Publishing.

Communities and Local Government (2006) *Strong and Prosperous Communities*. London: HMSO.

Conner, M. and Norman, P. (2007) *Predicting Health Behaviour* (2nd edn). Buckingham: Open University Press.

Conti, R.P. (1999) 'The psychology of false confessions', *Journal of Credibility Assessment and Witness Psychology*, 2: 14–36.

Cook, R.J. and Sackett, D.L. (1995) 'The number needed to treat: a clinically useful measure of treatment effect', *British Medical Journal*, 310: 452–4.

Cooper, H.M. and Hedges, L.V. (eds) (1994) *The Handbook of Research Synthesis*. New York, NY: Russell Sage Foundation.

Corcoran, M.H. and Cawood, J.S. (2003) *Violence Assessment and Intervention: The Practitioner's Handbook*. Boca Raton, FL: CRC Press.

Corey, M. and Corey, G. (2002) *Groups: Process and Practice*. Pacific Grove, CA: Brooks/Cole.

Costa, P. and McCrae, R. (1992) *Revised NEO Personality Inventory (NEO-PI-R) and NEO Five-factor Inventory (NEO-FFI): Professional Manual*. Odessa, FL: Psychological Assessment Resources.

Costa, P.T. and Widiger, T.A. (1993) *Personality Disorders and the Five-factor Model of Personality*. Washington, DC: APA.

Costanzo, M. and Leo, R.A. (2007) 'Research and expert testimony on interrogations and confessions', in D. Krauss and K. Pezdek (eds) *Expert Psychological Testimony in the Courts*. Mahwah, NJ: Erlbaum.

Council of Europe (1986) *Violence in the Family. Recommendation No R(85) 4, adopted by the Committee of the Council of Europe on 26 March 1985 and Explanatory Memorandum*. Strasbourg: Council of Europe.

Courtney, J. and Rose, J. (2004) 'The effectiveness of treatment for male sex offenders with learning disabilities: a review of the literature', *Journal of Sexual Aggression*, 10: 215–36.

Craig, L.A., Browne, K.D., Beech, A. and Stringer, I. (2006) 'Differences in personality and risk in sex, violent and general offenders', *Criminal Behaviour and Mental Health*, 16: 183–94.

Crighton, D.A. (2006a) 'Psychological research into sexual offenders', in G.J. Towl (ed.) *Psychological Research in Prisons*. Oxford: BPS/Blackwell.

Crighton, D.A. (2006b) 'Methodological issues in psychological research in prisons', in G.J. Towl (ed.) *Psychological Research in Prisons*. Oxford: Blackwell.

Crighton, D.A. and Towl, G.J. (2000) 'Intentional self injury', in G.J. Towl *et al.* (eds) *Suicide in Prisons.* Leicester: BPS.

Crighton, D.A. and Towl, G.J. (2008) *Psychology in Prisons* (2nd edn). Oxford: Blackwell.

Crittenden, P.M. (1999) 'Danger and development: the organization of self-protective strategies', in J.I. Vondra and D. Barnett (eds) *Atypical Attachment in Infancy and Early Childhood among Children at Developmental Risk. Monographs of the Society for Research on Child Development.* Ann Arbor, MI: Society for Research on Child Development.

Crittenden, P.M. (2002) 'Attachment theory, information processing, and psychiatric disorder', *World Journal of Psychiatry*, 1: 72–5.

Crittenden, P.M. (2006a) 'A dynamic-maturational model of attachment', *Australian and New Zealand Journal of Family Therapy*, 27: 105–15.

Crittenden, P.M. (2006b) 'Why do inadequate parents do what they do?', in O. Mayseless (ed.) *Parenting Representations: Theory, Research, and Clinical Implications.* Cambridge: Cambridge University Press.

Davey, G., Albery, I.P., Chandler, C., Field, A., Jones, D., Messer, D., Moore, S. and Sterling, C. (2004) *Complete Psychology.* London: Hodder & Stoughton.

Davies, M., Croall, H. and Tyrer, J. (2005) *Criminal Justice: An Introduction to the Criminal Justice System of England and Wales* (3rd edn). Harlow: Longman.

Davis, J. (1989) 'Psychology and law: the last 15 years', *Journal of Applied Social Psychology*, 19: 199–230.

Delis, D.C., Kaplan, E. and Kramer, J.H. (2001) *Hit or Miss? Insight into Executive Functions: Delis–Kaplan Executive Functions System.* San Antonio, TX: Psychological Corporation.

Department of Health (1990) *The Care Programme Approach for People with a Mental Illness Referred to the Specialist Psychiatric Services. Joint Health/Social Services Circular* HC (90) 23/LASSM90 11. London: Department of Health.

Department of Health (1994) *Report of the Working Group on High Security and Related Psychiatric Provision* (the Reed Report). London: Department of Health.

Department of Health (1996) *An Audit Pack for Monitoring the Care Programme Approach.* London: Department of Health.

Department of Health (1998) *Modernising Mental Health Services: Safe, Sound and Supportive.* London: Department of Health.

Department of Health (1999a) *Effective Care Co-ordination in Mental Health Services: Modernising the Care Programme Approach – a Policy Booklet.* London: Department of Health.

Department of Health (1999b) *The National Service Framework for Mental Health.* London: Department of Health.

Department of Health (2001) *Treatment Choice in Psychological Therapies and Counselling: Evidence-based Clinical Practice Guideline.* London: Department of Health.

Department of Health (2002) *Mental Health Policy Implementation Guide: Dual Diagnosis Good Practice Guide. Department of Health Publication* 27767. London: Department of Health.

Department of Health (2003) *Personality Disorder: No Longer a Diagnosis of Exclusion.* London: Department of Health.

Department of Health (2004a) *The National Service Framework – Five Years On.* London: Department of Health.

Department of Health (2004b) *Organising and Delivering Psychological Therapies: July 2004.* London: Department of Health.

Department of Health (2006a) *Choosing Health: Supporting the Physical Needs of People with Severe Mental Illness – Commissioning Framework.* London: Department of Health.

Department of Health (2006b) *Our Health, Our Care, Our Say: A New Direction for Community Services.* London: Department of Health.

Department of Health (2006c) *Reviewing the Care Programme Approach*. London: Department of Health.

Department of Health (2008) *Refocusing the Care Programme Approach*. London: Department of Health.

Department of Health and Home Office (1992) *Review of Mental Health and Social Services for Mentally Disordered Offenders and Others Requiring Similar Services. Vol. 1. Final Summary Report* (Cm 2088). London: HMSO.

Department of Health and Ministry of Justice (2007) *Standards for Medium Secure Units*. London: Health Offender Partnerships, Department of Health.

DePaulo, B.M., Kashy, D.A., Kirkendol, S.E., Wyer, M.M. and Epstein, J.A. (1996) 'Lying in everyday life', *Journal of Personality and Social Psychology*, 70: 979–95.

Devine, D.J., Clayton, L.D., Dunford, B.B. and Seying, R.P. (2001) 'Jury decision making: 45 years of deliberating groups', *Psychology, Public Policy and Law*, 7: 622–727.

Devlin, P. (1959) *The Enforcement of Morals* (reprinted as *Morals and the Criminal Law*, ed. R.M. Baird and S.E. Rosenbaum 1988). Loughton: Prometheus Books.

DfEE (2000) *Educational Psychology Services (England): Current Role, Good Practice and Future Directions*. London: HMSO.

DfES (2003) *Every Child Matters* (Cm 5860). London: HMSO.

DfES (2006) *A Review of the Functions and Contribution of Educational Psychologists in England and Wales in the Light of Every Child Matters* (RR792). London: HMSO.

DiClemente, C.C. and Prochaska, J.O. (1985) 'Stages of change profiles in out-patient alcoholism treatment', *Journal of Substance Abuse*, 2: 217–35.

Dobash, R.E., Dobash, R.P., Cavanagh, K. and Lewis, R. (2000) *Changing Violent Men*. Beverley Hills, CA: Sage.

Douglas, K.S., Yeomans, M. and Boer, D.P. (2005) 'Comparative validity analysis of multiple measures of violence risk in criminal offenders', *Criminal Justice and Behavior*, 32: 479–510.

Doyle, M. and Dolan, M. (2006) 'Evaluating the validity of anger regulation problems, interpersonal style, and disturbed mental state for predicting inpatient violence', *Behavioural Sciences and the Law*, 24: 783–98.

Eckhardt, C., Norlander, B. and Deffenbacher, J. (2004) 'The assessment of anger and hostility: a critical review', *Aggression and Violent Behavior*, 9: 17–43.

Edens, J.F., Cruise, K.R. and Buffington-Vollum, J.K. (2001) 'Forensic and correctional applications of the Personality Assessment Inventory', *Behavioral Sciences and the Law*, 19: 519–43.

Edmunds, M., Hough, M., Turnbull, P.J. and May, T. (1999) *Doing Justice to Treatment: Referring Offenders to Drug Services. DPAS Paper* 2. London: Home Office.

Engel, G.L. (1977) 'The need for a new medical model: a challenge for biomedicine', *Science*, 196: 129–35.

Engel, G.L. (1980) 'The clinical application of the biopsychosocial model', *American Journal of Psychiatry*, 137: 535–44.

Erb, M., Hodgins, S., Freese, R., Müller-Isberner, R. and Jöckel, D. (2001) 'Homicide and schizophrenia: maybe treatment does have a preventive effect', *Criminal Behaviour and Mental Health*, 11: 6–26.

Everson, G. (1919) 'The human element in justice', *Journal of Criminal Law and Criminology*, 10: 90–9.

Exner, J.E. (2003) *The Rorschach: A Comprehensive System. Volume 1: Basic Foundations* (4th edn). New York, NY: Wiley.

Fahey, T., Griffiths, S. and Peters, T.J. (1995) 'Evidence based purchasing: understanding results of clinical trials and systematic reviews', *British Medical Journal*, 311: 1056–9.

Fallon, P., Bluglass, R., Edwards, B. and Daniels, G. (1999) *Report of the Committee of Inquiry into the Personality Disorder Unit, Ashworth Special Hospital. Vol. 1.* London: HMSO.

Falshaw, L., Bates, A., Patel, V., Corbett, C. and Friendship, C. (2003) 'Assessing reconviction, re-offending and recidivism in a sample of UK sexual offenders', *Legal and Criminological Psychology*, 8: 207–15.

Farrington, D.P. (1992) 'Juvenile delinquency', in J.C. Coleman (ed.) *The School Years*. London: Routledge.

Farrington, D.P. (1993) 'Understanding and preventing bullying', in M. Tonry (ed.) *Crime and Justice: A Review of Research.* Chicago, IL: University of Chicago Press.

Farrington, D.P. (1997) 'Human development and criminal careers', in M. Maguire *et al.* (eds) *The Oxford Handbook of Criminology* (2nd edn). Oxford: Oxford University Press.

Farrington, D.P. (1998) 'Individual differences and offending', in M. Tonry (ed.) *The Handbook of Crime and Punishment.* New York, NY: Oxford University Press.

Farrington, D.P. (1999) '21 years of the DCLP', *Forensic Update*, 56: 21–37.

Farrington, D.P. (2002) 'Families and crime', in J.Q. Wilson and J. Petersilia (eds) *Crime: Public Policies for Crime Control* (2nd edn). Oakland, CA: Institute for Contemporary Studies Press.

Farrington, D.P. (2003a) 'Foreword', in G.J. Towl (ed.) *Psychology in Prisons*. Oxford: BPS/Blackwell.

Farrington, D.P. (2003b) 'Key results from the first 40 years of the Cambridge Study in Delinquent Development', in T.P. Thornberry and M.D. Krohn (eds) *Taking Stock of Delinquency: An Overview of Findings from Contemporary Longitudinal Studies.* New York, NY: Kluwer/Plenum.

Farrington, D.P., Coid, J.W., Harnett, L., Jolliffe, D., Soteriou, N., Turner, R. and West, D.J. (2006) *Criminal Careers up to Age 50 and Life Success up to Age 48: New Findings from the Cambridge Study in Delinquent Development. Home Office Research Study* 299. London: Home Office (available online at **www.homeoffice.gov.uk/rds**).

Farrington, D.P., Ditchfield, J., Hancock, G., Howard, P., Jolliffe, D., Livingston, M. and Painter, K. (2002) *Evaluation of Two Intensive Regimes for Young Offenders. Home Office Research Study* 239. London: Home Office.

Farrington, D.P. and Morris, A. (1983) 'Sex, sentencing and reconviction', *British Journal of Criminology*, 23: 229–48.

Farrington, D.P. and Welsh, B.C. (2007) *Saving Children from a Life of Crime: Early Risk Factors and Effective Interventions.* Oxford: Oxford University Press.

Fazel, S. and Danesh, J. (2002) 'Serious mental disorder in 23000 prisoners: a systematic review of 62 surveys', *Lancet*, 259: 545–50.

Fisher, R.P. and Geiselman, R.E. (1992) *Memory Enhancing Techniques for Investigative Interviewing: The Cognitive Interview.* Springfield, IL: Charles C. Thomas.

Fisher, R.P., Geiselman, R.E. and Amador, M. (1989) 'Field test of the cognitive interview: enhancing the recollection of actual victims and witnesses of crime', *Journal of Applied Psychology*, 74: 722–7.

Flanagan, D.P. and Harrison, P.L. (2005) *Contemporary Intellectual Assessment: Theories, Tests, and Issues.* New York, NY: Guilford Press.

Flouri, E. (2005) 'Post-traumatic stress disorder (PTSD): what we have learned and what we still have not found out', *Journal of Interpersonal Violence*, 20: 373–9.

Flynn, J. (2007) *What is Intelligence? Beyond the Flynn Effect.* Cambridge: Cambridge University Press.

Friendship, C., Street, R., Cann, J. and Harper, G. (2005) 'Introduction: the policy context and assessing the evidence', in G. Harper and C. Chitty (eds) *The Impact of Corrections on Re-offending: A Review of 'What Works'. Home Office Research Study* 291. London: Home Office.

Fuller, J. and Cowan, J. (1999) 'Risk assessment in a multi-disciplinary forensic setting: clinical judgement revisited', *Journal of Forensic Psychiatry*, 10: 276–89.

Gacono, C.B. (2000) *The Clinical and Forensic Assessment of Psychopathy: A Practitioner's Guide.* Mahwah, NJ: Erlbaum.

Garland, D. (1985) *Punishment and Welfare: A History of Penal Strategies.* Aldershot: Gower.

Garland, D. (1994) 'Of crimes and criminals: the development of criminology in Britain', in M. Maguire *et al.* (eds) *The Oxford Handbook of Criminology.* Oxford: Oxford University Press.

Garland, D. (1997) 'The punitive society: penology, criminology, and the history of the present', *Edinburgh Law Review*, 1: 1–20.

Gelsthorpe, L. and Loucks, N. (1997) 'Magistrates' explanations of sentencing decisions', in C. Hedderman and L. Gelsthorpe (eds) *Understanding the Sentencing of Women. Home Office Research Study* 170. London: Home Office.

Gendreau, P. and Ross, R.R. (1980) 'Effective correctional treatment: bibliotherapy for cynics', in R.R. Ross and P. Gendreau (eds) *Effective Correctional Treatment.* Toronto: Butterworths.

George, R. (1991) 'A field evaluation of the cognitive interview.' Unpublished masters thesis, Polytechnic of East London.

Gibbs, J.C. (2003) *Moral Development and Reality: Beyond the Theories of Kohlberg and Hoffman.* Thousand Oaks, CA: Sage.

Gibbs, J.C., Potter, G.B. and Goldstein, A.P. (1995) *The EQUIP Program: Teaching Youth to Think and Act Responsibly through a Peer-helping Approach.* Champaign, IL: Research Press.

Gibson, B. and Cavadino, P. (2002) *Introduction to the Criminal Justice Process.* Winchester: Waterside Press.

Gilchrist, E., Johnson, R., Takriti, R., Western, S., Beech, A. and Kebbell, M. (2003) *Domestic Violence Offenders: Characteristics and Offending Related Needs. Home Office Research Findings* 217. London: Home Office.

Glaziou, P., Vandenbroucke, J. and Chalmers, I. (2004) 'Assessing the quality of research', *British Medical Journal*, 328: 39–41.

Goffman, E. (1961) *Asylums: Essays on the Social Situation of Mental Patients and Other Inmates.* New York, NY: Doubleday.

Goldstein, A.P., Glick, B. and Gibbs, J.C. (1998) *Aggression Replacement Training* (2nd edn). Champaign, IL: Research Press.

Goring, C. (1913) *The English Convict.* London: HMSO.

Gossop, M. (2005) *Drug Misuse Treatment and Reductions in Crime: Findings from the National Treatment Outcome Research Study (NTORS). Research Briefing* 8. London: NHS/National Treatment Agency for Substance Misuse.

Gossop, M., Marsden, J. and Stewart, D. (2001) *NTORS after Five Years: The National Treatment Outcome Research Study – Changes in Substance Use, Health and Criminal Behaviour during the Five Years after Intake.* London: National Addiction Centre.

Gould, R.A., Ball, S., Kaspi, S.P., Otto, M.W., Pollack, M.H., Shekhar, A. and Fava, M. (1996) 'Prevalence and correlates of anger attacks: a two site study', *Journal of Affective Disorders*, 39: 31–8.

Gray, N.S., Fitzgerald, S., Taylor, J., MacCulloch, M.J. and Snowden, R.J. (2007) 'Predicting future reconviction in offenders with intellectual disabilities: the predictive efficacy of VRAG, PCL-SV and the HCR-20', *Psychological Assessment*, 19: 474–9.

Gray, N.S., Snowden, R.J., Taylor, J. and MacCulloch, M.J. (2004) 'Relative efficacy of criminological, clinical and personality measures of future risk of offending in mentally disordered offenders,' *Journal of Consulting and Clinical Psychology*, 72: 523–30.

Gregg, V.R., Gibbs, J.C. and Basinger, K.S. (1994) 'Patterns of developmental delay in moral judgment by male and female delinquents', *Merrill-Palmer Quarterly*, 40: 538–53.

Gregory, R.J. (1998) *Foundations of Intellectual Assessment*. Boston, MA: Allyn & Bacon.

Groth-Marnat, G. (2000) *Neuropsychological Assessment in Clinical Practice: A Guide Test Interpretation and Integration*. Chichester: Wiley.

Grubin, D. and Madsen, L. (2005) 'Lie detection and the polygraph: a historical review', *British Journal of Forensic Psychiatry and Psychology*, 16: 357–69.

Guardian (2006) 'Justice at last: killer pleads guilty in Britain's first double jeopardy trial', 12 September.

Gudjonsson, G. (1992) *The Psychology of Interrogations, Confessions and Testimony*. Chichester: Wiley.

Gudjonsson, G. (2003) *The Psychology of Interrogations and Confessions: A Handbook*. Chichester: Wiley.

Gudjonsson, G. and Sigurdsson, J.F. (1994) 'How frequently do false confessions occur? An empirical study among prison inmates', *Psychology, Crime and Law*, 1: 21–61.

Gudjonsson, G., Sigurdsson, J.F. and Asgeirsdottir, B.B. (2007) 'Custodial interrogation: what are the background factors associated with claims of false confession to police?', *Journal of Forensic Psychiatry and Psychology*, 18: 266–75.

Gunn, J. and Taylor, P.J. (1993) *Forensic Psychiatry: Clinical, Legal and Ethical Issues*. London: Butterworth-Heinemann.

Gunn, J. and Taylor, P.J. (2001) *Forensic Psychiatry*. London: Butterworth Heinemann.

Hagan, J. and McCarthy, B. (1997) *Mean Streets: Youth Crime and Homelessness*. Cambridge: Cambridge University Press.

Hammond, S.M. and O'Rourke, M.M. (2004) 'Developing a psychometric model of risk', *Issues in Forensic Psychology*, 5: 100–14.

Hampson, M. (2005) *CPA Views of Consultant Psychiatrists, 15 Years On*. London: Royal College of Psychiatrists.

Hanson, R.K. and Morton-Bourgon, K. (2004) *Predictors of Sexual Recidivism: An Updated Meta-analysis. Public Safety and Emergency Preparedness Canada Report* 2004-02. Ottawa: Public Works and Government Service Canada.

Hare, R. (1991) *Manual for the Hare Psychopathy Checklist Revisited*. Toronto: Multi-health Systems.

Hare, R. (2003) *Hare PCL-R* (2nd edn). Toronto: Multi-health Systems.

Harman, H. and Griffith, J. (1979) *Justice Deserted: The Subversion of the Jury*. London: National Council for Civil Liberties.

Harper, G. and Chitty, C. (eds) (2004) *The Impact of Corrections on Re-offending: A Review of 'What Works'. Home Office Research Study* 291. London: Home Office.

Harper, G., Man, L., Taylor, S. and Niven, S. (2005) 'Factors associated with offending', in G. Harper and C. Chitty (eds) *The Impact of Corrections on Re-offending: A Review of 'What Works'. Home Office Research Study* 291. London: Home Office.

Harrower, J. (1998) *Applying Psychology to Crime*. London: Hodder & Stoughton.

Hart, H.L.A. (1963) *Law, Liberty and Morality* (reprinted 1968). Oxford: Oxford University Press.

Hart, S.D., Michie, C. and Cooke, D.J. (2007) 'The precision of actuarial risk assessment instruments: evaluating the "margins of error" of group versus individual predictions of violence', *British Journal of Psychiatry*, 190(S49): s61–s66.

Hastie, R. (ed.) (1993) *Inside the Juror: The Psychology of Juror Decision Making*. Cambridge: Cambridge University Press.

Hastie, R., Penrod, S.D. and Pennington, N. (1983) *Inside the Jury*. Cambridge, MA: Harvard University Press.

Haves, R. (2004) 'Introduction to evidence-based practices', in C.E. Stout and R. Haves (eds) *Evidence-based Practice: Methods, Models and Tools for Mental Health Professionals.* Hoboken, NJ: Wiley.

Hedderman, C. (2007) 'Past, present and future sentences: what do we know about their effectiveness?', in L.R. Gelsthorpe and R. Morgan (eds) *Handbook of Probation.* Cullompton: Willan Publishing.

Hedges, L.V. and Olkin, I. (1985) *Statistical Methods for Meta-analysis.* New York, NY: Academic Press.

Herman, J.L. (1997) *Trauma and Recovery: The Aftermath of Violence from Domestic Abuse to Political Terror.* New York, NY: Basic Books.

Hettema, J., Steele, J. and Miller, W.R. (2005) 'Motivational interviewing', *Annual Review of Clinical Psychology,* 1: 91–111.

Heuer, L. and Penrod, S. (1994a) 'Juror note taking and question asking during trials: a national field experiment', *Law and Human Behaviour,* 13: 409–30.

Heuer, L. and Penrod, S. (1994b) 'Trial complexity: its meaning and effects', *Law and Human Behaviour,* 18: 29–51.

Hilsenroth, M.J. and Segal, D.L. (Editor-in-Chief, Leslie C. Morey) (2004) *Comprehensive Handbook of Psychological Assessment. Vol. 2: Personality Assessment.* Hoboken, NJ: Wiley.

HM Inspectorate of Prisons (2005a) *Annual Report, 2003–2004.* London: HMSO.

HM Inspectorate of Prisons (2005b) *IRC Expectations: Criteria for Assessing the Conditions for and Treatment of Immigration Detainees.* London: HMSO.

HM Inspectorate of Prisons (2005c) *Juvenile Expectations: Criteria for Assessing the Conditions for and Treatment of Children and Young People in Custody.* London: HMSO.

HM Inspectorate of Prisons (2006a) *Annual Report, 2004–2005.* London: HMSO.

HM Inspectorate of Prisons (2006b) *Expectations: Criteria for Assessing the Conditions in Prisons and the Treatment of Prisoners.* London: HMSO.

HM Inspectorate of Probation (2006c) *An Independent Review of a Serious Further Offence Case: Anthony Rice.* London: Home Office.

HM Inspectorate of Probation, HM Inspectorate of Constabulary and HM Inspectorate of Prisons (2006) *Thematic Inspection Report: Putting Risk of Harm into Context – a Joint Inspection on Public Protection. Inspection Findings* 3/06. London: Home Office.

HM Prison Service and Department of Health (2004) *Alcohol Treatment/Interventions: Good Practice Guide.* London: Drugs Strategy Unit.

Hodgins, S. (2008) 'Criminality among persons with severe mental illness', in K. Soothill *et al.* (eds) *Handbook of Forensic Mental Health.* Cullompton: Willan Publishing.

Hodgins, S. and Côté, G. (1995) 'Major mental disorder among Canadian penitentiary inmates', in L. Stewart *et al.* (eds) *Clinical Criminology: Toward Effective Correctional Treatment.* Toronto: Solliciteur général et Service correctionnel du Canada.

Hodgins, S. and Janson, C.G. (2002) *Criminality and Violence among the Mentally Disordered: The Stockholm Metropolitan Project.* Cambridge: Cambridge University Press.

Hollin, C.R. (2001) *Offender Assessment and Treatment.* New York, NY: Wiley.

Hollin, C.R. (2002) 'Risk–needs assessment and allocation to offender programmes', in J. McGuire (ed.) *Offender Rehabilitation and Treatment: Effective Programmes and Policies to Reduce Re-offending.* Chichester: Wiley.

Hollin, C.R. (ed.) (2004) *The Essential Handbook of Offender Assessment and Treatment.* Chichester: Wiley.

Hollin, C.R. and Palmer, E.J. (eds) (2006) *Offending Behaviour Programmes: Development, Application, and Controversies.* Chichester: Wiley.

Home Office (2002) *Achieving Best Evidence in Criminal Proceedings: Guidance for Vulnerable or Intimidated Witnesses, including Children.* London: Home Office Communications Directorate (available online at **http://www.cps.gov.uk/publications/prosecution/ bestevidencevol1.html**).

Home Office (2004) *MAPPA Guidance.* London: Home Office.

Home Office (2005) *Criminal Justice Act 2003 – New Sentences and the New Report Framework* (Probation Circular 18/2005). London: Home Office.

Home Office (2006a) *Crime in England and Wales, 2005/06.* London: Home Office (available online at **http://www.homeoffice.gov.uk/rds/pdfs06/ hosb1206.pdf**).

Home Office (2006b) *The NOMS Offender Management Model.* London: Home Office.

Home Office (2006c) *Crime Statistics: An Independent Review carried out for the Secretary of State for the Home Department.* London: Home Office.

Home Office (2007a) *Crime in England and Wales, 2005/06. Supplementary Volume 1.* London: Home Office (available online at **http://www.homeoffice.gov.uk/rds/pdfs07/ hosb0207.pdf**).

Home Office (2007b) *Crime in England and Wales, 2005/06. Supplementary Volume 2.* London: Home Office (available online at **http://www.homeoffice.gov.uk/rds/pdfs07/ hosb1007.pdf**).

Home Office (2007c) *Re-offending of Adults: Results from the 2004 Cohort. Home Office Statistical Bulletin* 06/07. London: Home Office.

Home Office (2007d) *Home Office Response to the Smith Review of Crime Statistics.* London: Home Office.

Hood, R. (1992) *Race and Sentencing: A Study in the Crown Court (a Report for the Commission for Racial Equality).* Oxford: Oxford University Press.

Hood, R. and Shute, S. (2000) *The Parole System at Work: A Study of Risk-based Decision-making. Home Office Research Study* 202. London: Home Office.

Hough, M. (1996) *Drugs Misuse and the Criminal Justice System: A Review of the Literature. DPI Paper* 15. London: Home Office.

Houston, J. (1998) *Making Sense with Offenders: Personal Constructs, Therapy and Change.* New York, NY: Wiley.

Howard, P. (2006) *The Offender Assessment System: An Evaluation of the Second Pilot. Home Office Findings* 278. London: Home Office.

Ingleby, D. (ed.) (1980) *Critical Psychiatry.* Harmondsworth: Penguin Books.

Ireland, J.L. (2000) 'Bullying among prisoners: a review of research', *Aggression and Violent Behaviour: A Review Journal,* 5: 201–15.

Ireland, J.L. (2002) *Bullying among Prisoners: Evidence, Research and Intervention Strategies.* Hove: Brunner-Routledge.

Ireland, J.L. (ed.) (2005) *Bullying among Prisoners: Innovations in Theory and Research.* Cullompton: Willan Publishing.

Ireland, J.L. and Ireland, C.A. (2003) 'How do offenders define bullying? A study of adult, young and juvenile male offenders', *Legal and Criminological Psychology,* 8: 159–73.

Jackson, J. (1996) 'Juror decision-making in the trial process', in G. Davis *et al.* (eds) *Psychology, Law and Criminal Justice.* Berlin: de Gruyter.

Jewesbury, I. and McCulloch, A. (2002) 'Public policy and mentally disordered offenders in the UK', in A. Buchanan (ed.) *Care of the Mentally Disordered Offender in the Community.* Oxford: Oxford University Press.

Johnson, J.G., Cohen, P., Smailes, E., Kasen, S., Oldham, J.M., Skodol, A.E. and Brook, J.S. (2000) 'Adolescent personality disorders associated with violence and criminal behavior during adolescence and early adulthood', *American Journal of Psychiatry,* 157: 1406–12.

Jolliffe, D. and Farrington, D.P. (2004) 'Empathy and offending: a systematic review and meta-analysis', *Aggression and Violent Behavior*, 9: 441–76.

Kalven, H. and Zeisel, H. (1966) *The American Jury*. Chicago, IL: University of Chicago Press.

Kapardis, A. (1985) *Sentencing by English Magistrates as a Human Process*. Nicosia, Cyprus: Asselia Press.

Kapardis, A. (2003) *Psychology and Law*. Cambridge: Cambridge University Press.

Kapardis, A. and Farrington, D.P. (1981) 'An experimental study of sentencing by magistrates', *Law and Human Behavior*, 5: 107–21.

Kassin, S.M. (1997) 'The psychology of confession of evidence', *American Psychologist*, 52: 221–33.

Kavale, K.A. and Forness, S.R. (2000) 'What definitions of learning disability say and don't say: a critical analysis', *Journal of Learning Disabilities*, 33: 239–56.

Kemshall, H. (2001) *Risk Assessment and Management of Known Sexual and Violent Offenders: A Review of Current Issues*. Police Research Series Paper 140. London: Home Office.

Kemshall, H. (2003) 'The community management of high-risk offenders: a consideration of "best practice" – multi-agency public protection panel arrangements (MAPPPA)', *Prison Service Journal*, 146: 1.

Kemshall, H., Mackenzie, G., Wood, J., Bailey, R. and Yates, J. (2005) *Strengthening Multi-agency Public Protection Arrangements*. Home Office Development and Practice Report 45. London: Home Office.

Kenworthy, T., Adams, C.E., Bilby, C., Brooks-Gordon, B. and Fenton, M. (2004) 'Psychological interventions for those who have sexually offended or are at risk of offending', *Cochrane Database of Systematic Reviews*, 4: art. no. CD004858 (available online at **www.Cochrane.org**).

Kessler, R.C., Chiu, W.T., Demler, O. and Walters, E.E. (2005) 'Prevalence, severity, and comorbidity of 12-month DSM-IV disorders in the National Comorbidity Survey Replication', *Archives of General Psychiatry*, 62: 617–27.

Kilkelly, V. (1999) *The Child and the European Convention on Human Rights*. Aldershot: Ashgate.

Kline, P. (2000) *A Psychometrics Primer*. London: Free Association Books.

Kohlberg, L. (1984) *Essays on Moral Development: The Psychology of Moral Development*. San Francisco, CA: Harper & Row.

Kraepelin, E. (1883) *Compendium der Psychiatrie*. Leipzig.

Kreuger, R.F., Schmutte, P.S., Caspi, A., Moffitt, T.E., Campbell, K. and Silva, P.A. (1994) 'Personality traits are associated with crime among men and women: evidence from a birth cohort', *Journal of Abnormal Psychology*, 103: 328–38.

Lanceley, F.J. (1999) *On-scene Guide for Crisis Negotiators*. Boca Raton, FL: CRC Press.

Lanceley, F.J. (2003) *On-scene Guide for Crisis Negotiations* (2nd edn). Boca Raton, FL: CRC Press.

Langan, J. and Lindow, V. (2004) *Living with Risk: Mental Health Service User Involvement in Risk Assessment and Management*. London: Policy Press.

Laupacis, A., Sackett, D.L. and Roberts, R.S. (1988) 'An assessment of clinically useful measures of the consequences of treatment', *New England Journal of Medicine*, 318: 1728–33.

Laws, D.R. and Donohue, W. (1997) *Sexual Deviance: Theory, Assessment, and Treatment*. New York, NY: Guilford Press.

Levine, J.P. (1992) *Juries and Politics*. Pacific Grove, CA: Brooks/Cole Publishing.

Lezak, M.D. (1995) *Neuropsychological Assessment* (3rd edn). Oxford: Oxford University Press.

Lezak, M.D., Howieson, D.B., Loring, D.W., Hannay, H.J. and Fischer, J.S. (2004) *Neuropsychological Assessment*. Oxford: Oxford University Press.

Liau, A.K., Barriga, A.Q. and Gibbs, J.C. (1998) 'Relations between self-serving cognitive distortions and overt vs. covert antisocial behavior in adolescents', *Aggressive Behavior*, 24: 335–46.

Liebling, A. (2006) *The Role of the Prison Environment in Prison Suicide and Prisoner Distress.* Basingstoke: Palgrave-Macmillan.

Lindsay, W.R., Hogue, T., Taylor, J.L., Steptoe, L., Mooney, P., O'Brien, G., Johnston, S. and Smith, A.H.W. (in press) 'Risk assessment in offenders with intellectual disability: a comparison across three levels of security', *International Journal of Offender Therapy and Comparative Criminology.*

Lindsay, W.R. and Taylor, J.L. (2005) 'A selective review of research on offenders with developmental disabilities: assessment and treatment', *Clinical Psychology and Psychotherapy,* 12: 201–14.

Lindsay, W.R., Taylor, J.L. and Sturmey, P. (eds) (2004) *Offenders with Developmental Disabilities.* Chichester: Wiley.

Lipsey, M.W. (2003) 'Those confounded moderators in meta-analysis: good, bad, and ugly', *Annals of the American Academy of Political and Social Science,* 587: 69–81.

Lipsey, M.W. and Derzon, J.H. (1998) 'Predictors of violent and serious delinquency in adolescence and early adulthood: a synthesis of longitudinal research', in R. Loeber and D.P. Farrington (eds) *Serious and Violent Juvenile Offenders: Risk Factors and Successful Intervention.* Thousand Oaks, CA: Sage.

Lipsey, M.W. and Wilson, D.B. (2001) *Practical Meta-analysis.* Thousand Oaks, CA: Sage.

Lipton, D., Martinson, R. and Wilks, J. (1975) *The Effectiveness of Correctional Treatment: A Survey of Treatment Evaluation Studies.* New York, NY: Praeger.

Lipton, D.S., Pearson, F.S., Cleland, C.M. and Yee, D. (2002a) 'The effects of therapeutic communities and milieu therapy on recidivism', in J. McGuire (ed.) *Offender Rehabilitation and Treatment: Effective Programmes and Policies to Reduce Re-offending.* Chichester: Wiley.

Lipton, D.S., Pearson, F.S., Cleland, C.M. and Yee, D. (2002b) 'The effectiveness of cognitive-behavioural treatment methods on offender recidivism', in J. McGuire (ed.) *Offender Rehabilitation and Treatment: Effective Programmes and Policies to Reduce Re-offending.* Chichester: Wiley.

Litwack, T.R. (2001) 'Actuarial versus clinical assessment of dangerousness', *Psychology, Public Policy and Law,* 7: 409–43.

Llewellyn, A. (2005) *Society Guardian NHS and Social Services Directory, 2005/6. Guardian Book Series.* London: Sage.

Lloyd, C., Mair, G. and Hough, M. (1994) *Explaining Reconviction Rates: A Critical Analysis. Home Office Research Study* 136. London: Home Office.

Lloyd-Bostock, S. (1989) *Law in Practice.* Chicago, IL: Lyceum.

Loftus, E.F. and Palmer, J.C. (1974) 'Reconstruction of automobile destruction: an example of the interaction between language and memory', *Journal of Verbal Learning and Verbal Behavior,* 13: 585–9.

Lombroso, C. (2006) *Criminal Man* (trans. M. Gibson and N.H. Rafter). Durham, NC: Duke University Press (originally published in 1876).

London Deanery (2007) *Forensic Psychiatry* (available online at **www.londondeanery.ac.uk/careers/career-guide/forensic-psychiatry**).

Loranger, A. (1999) *International Personality Disorder Examination Manual: DSM-IV Module.* Washington, DC: American Psychiatric Press.

Lösel, F. (2007) 'Doing evaluation in criminology: balancing scientific and practical demands', in R.D. King and E. Wincup (eds) *Doing Research on Crime and Justice* (2nd edn). Oxford: Oxford University Press.

Lösel, F. and Schmucker, M. (2005) 'The effectiveness of treatment for sexual offenders: a comprehensive meta-analysis', *Journal of Experimental Criminology,* 1: 117–46.

Luginbuhl, J. and Howe, J. (1995) 'Discretion in capital sentencing: guided or misguided?', *Indiana Law Journal*, 70: 1161–85.

Lynam, D., Moffitt, T. and Stouthamer-Loeber, M. (1993) 'Explaining the relation between IQ and delinquency: class, race, test motivation, school failure or self-control?', *Journal of Abnormal Psychology*, 102: 187–96.

Macpherson, Sir W. (1999) *The Stephen Lawrence Inquiry: Report of an Inquiry by Sir William Macpherson of Cluny* (Cm 4262-1). London: HMSO.

Magid, D. (2001) 'Deceptive police interrogation practices: how far is too far?', *Michigan Law Review*, 99: 1168–210.

Maguire, M., Kemshall, H., Noaks, L. and Wincup, E. (2001) *Risk Management of Sexual and Violent Offenders: The Work of Public Protection Panels. Police Research Series* 139. London: Home Office.

Mair, G. (ed.) (2004) *What Matters in Probation?* Cullompton: Willan Publishing.

Management Advisory Service (1989) *Review of Clinical Psychology Services*. London: MAS.

Mann, R.E., Ginsburg, J.I. and Weekes, J. (2002) 'Motivational interviewing with offenders', in M. McMurran (ed.) *Motivating Offenders to Change*. Chichester: Wiley.

Mann, S., Vrij, A. and Bull, R. (2002) 'Suspects, lies and videotape: an analysis of authentic high-stakes liars', *Law and Human Behavior*, 26: 365–76.

Mann, S., Vrij, A. and Bull, R. (2004) 'Detecting true lies: police officers' ability to detect suspects' lies', *Journal of Applied Psychology*, 89: 137–49.

Martinson, R. (1974) 'What works? Questions and answers about prison reform', *The Public Interest*, 10: 22–54.

Matarazzo, J.D. (1980) 'Behavioural health and behavioural medicine: frontiers for a new health psychology', *American Psychologist*, 35: 807–17.

Matthews, S. and Richardson, A. (2005) *Findings from the 2003 Offending, Crime and Justice Survey: Alcohol-related Crime and Disorder. Home Office Research Findings* 261. London: Home Office.

May, C. (2005) *The CARAT Drug Service in Prisons – Findings from the Research Database. Home Office Research Findings* 262. London: Home Office.

McCabe, S. and Purves, R. (1974) *The Jury at Work*. Oxford: Blackwell.

McCann, J. (1998) 'A conceptual framework for identifying various types of confessions', *Behavioral Sciences and the Law*, 16: 441–53.

McDonald, S., Flanagan, S. and Rollins, J. (2002) *The Awareness of Social Inference Test*. Bury St Edmunds: Thames Valley Test Company.

McGuire, J. (ed.) (2002) *Offender Rehabilitation and Treatment: Effective Programmes and Policies to Reduce Reoffending. Wiley Series in Forensic Clinical Psychology*. Chichester: Wiley.

McGuire, J. (2004) *Understanding Psychology and Crime: Perspectives on Theory and Action*. Maidenhead: Open University Press/McGraw-Hill Education.

McGuire, J. (in press) 'What's the point of sentencing? Psychological aspects of crime and punishment', in G. Davies *et al.* (eds) *Forensic Psychology*. Chichester: Wiley.

McMurran, M. (2000) 'Offenders with drink and drug problems', in C.R. Hollin (ed.) *Handbook of Offender Assessment and Treatment*. Chichester: Wiley.

McMurran, M. (ed.) (2002) *Motivating Offenders to Change: A Guide to Enhancing Engagement in Therapy*. Chichester: Wiley.

McMurran, M. and McGuire, J. (eds) (2005) *Social Problem-solving and Offending: Evidence, Evaluation and Evolution*. Chichester: Wiley.

Meloy, J.R. (2007) 'Stalking: the state of the science', *Criminal Behavior and Mental Health*, 17: 1–7.

Meltzer, D. and Tom, B. (2000) *Pathways into Medium Secure Psychiatric Provision in England and Wales*. Cambridge: Mental Healthcare Policy Research Group (available online at **www.phpc.cam.au.uk**).

Miller, W.R. and Rollnick, S. (2002) *Motivational Interviewing: Preparing People for Change* (2nd edn). New York, NY: Guilford Press.

Miller, W.R., Yahne, C.E., Moyers, T.B., Martinez, J. and Pirritano, M. (in press) 'A randomised trial of methods to help clinicians learn motivational interviewing', *Journal of Consulting and Clinical Psychology*.

Millon, T., Davis, R. and Millon, C. (1997) *MCMI-III Manual*. Minneapolis, MN: National Computer Systems.

Milne, R. and Bull, R. (1999) *Investigative Interviewing*. Chichester: Wiley.

Milne, S. (2004) *It All Comes Down to Stress...and that Value Word...: A View of the Causes of Sickness Absence in the Prison Service from the Perspective of its Staff* (internal report).

Ministry of Justice (1998) *Civil Procedure Rules, Part 35: Experts and Assessors*. London: Ministry of Justice.

Ministry of Justice (2005a) *Criminal Procedure Rules, Part 33: Expert Evidence*. London: Ministry of Justice.

Ministry of Justice (2005b) *Civil Justice Council Protocol for the Instruction of Experts to give Evidence in Civil Claims*. London: Ministry of Justice.

Moffitt, T.E., Caspi, A., Harrington, H. and Milne, B.J. (2002) 'Males on the life-course-persistent and adolescence-limited antisocial pathways: follow-up at age 26 years', *Developmental Psychopathology*, 14: 179–207.

Monahan, J. (1993) 'Limiting therapist exposure to Tarasoff liability: guidelines for risk containment', *American Psychologist*, 48: 242–50.

Moody, J.W., Blanton, J.E. and Cheney, P.H. (1998) 'A theoretically grounded approach to assist memory recall during information requirements determination', *Journal of Management Information Systems*, 15: 79–98.

Moore, R., Howard, P. and Burns, M. (2006) 'The further development of OASys: realising the potential of the Offender Assessment System', *Prison Service Journal*, 167: 36–42.

Morey, L. (1991) *Personality Assessment Inventory*. Odessa, FL: Psychological Assessment Resources.

Morrison, N. (2001) 'Group cognitive therapy: treatment of choice or suboptimal option?', *Behavioural and Cognitive Psychotherapy*, 29: 311–32.

Motiuk, L.L. and Serin, R.C. (eds) (2001) *Compendium 2000 on Effective Correctional Programming*. Ottawa: Correctional Service Canada.

Nacro (2005a) *The Appropriate Adult and Vulnerable People: Working with Mentally Disordered Offenders and other Vulnerable Adults*. London: Nacro.

Nacro (2005b) *Working with Mentally Disordered Offenders: A Training Pack for Staff in Criminal Justice Agencies, Health and Social Care, and the Voluntary Sector* (CD-ROM). London: Nacro.

Nacro (2005c) *Multi-agency Partnership Working and the Delivery of Services to Mentally Disordered Offenders – Key Principles and Practice*. London: Nacro.

Nacro (2006) *Liaison and Diversion for Mentally Disordered Offenders*. London: Nacro.

Nash, M. (2006a) 'Everyone's watching: but is anyone listening?', *Prison Service Journal*, 165: 14–18.

Nash, M. (2006b) *Public Protection and the Criminal Justice Process*. Oxford: Oxford University Press.

National Institute for Clinical Excellence (2005) *Post-traumatic Stress Disorder: The Management of PTSD in Adults and Children in Primary and Secondary Care*. London: Gaskell (available online at **http://guidance.nice.org.uk/CG26/guidance/pdf/English**).

National Probation Service (2007) *MAPPA Guidance: Multi-agency Public Protection Arrangements through Partnership*. London: Home Office (available online at **http://www.probation.homeoffice.gov.uk/files/pdf/MAPPA%20Guidance%202007%20v2.0.pdf**).

National Research Council (2002) *The Polygraph and Lie Detection: Committee to Review the Scientific Evidence on the Polygraph, Division of Behavioral and Social Sciences and Education.* Washington, DC: National Academies Press.

Needs, A. and Towl, G. (2004) *Applying Psychology to Forensic Practice.* Oxford: BPS/Blackwell.

Nelson, J.R., Smith, D.J. and Dodd, J. (1990) 'The moral reasoning of juvenile delinquents: a meta-analysis', *Journal of Abnormal Child Psychology,* 18: 231–9.

Newburn, T. and Rock, P. (2006) *Living in Fear: Violence and Victimisation in the Lives of Single Homeless People.* London: Crisis.

Nietzel, M.T., McCarthy, D.M. and Kery, M. (1999) 'Juries: the current state of the empirical literature', in R. Roesch *et al.* (eds) *Psychology and Law: The State of the Discipline.* New York, NY: Kluwer Academic/Plenum Publishers.

NOMS (2005) *The National Reducing Re-offending Delivery Plan.* London: Home Office.

NOMS (2006a) *The NOMS Offender Management Model 1.1.* London: Home Office.

NOMS (2006b) *Working with Alcohol Misusing Offenders – a Strategy for Delivery.* London: Home Office.

Novaco, R.W. (2000) 'Anger', in A.E. Kazdin (ed.) *Encyclopedia of Psychology.* Washington, DC: American Psychological Association and Oxford University Press.

Novaco, R.W. (2003) *The Novaco Anger Scale and Provocation Inventory (NAS-PI).* Los Angeles, CA: Western Psychological Services.

Novaco, R.W. (2007) 'Anger dysregulation: its assessment and treatment', in T.A. Cavell and K.T. Malcolm (eds) *Anger, Aggression, and Interventions for Interpersonal Violence.* Mahwah, NJ: Erlbaum.

Novaco, R.W. and Taylor, J.L. (2004) 'Assessment of anger and aggression in male offenders with developmental disabilities', *Psychological Assessment,* 16: 42–50.

Office of the Deputy Prime Minister (2004) *Mental Health and Social Exclusion: Social Exclusion Unit Report.* London: Office of the Deputy Prime Minister.

Ogden, J. (2004) *Health Psychology: A Textbook* (3rd edn). Buckingham: Open University Press.

Olweus, D. (1978) *Aggression in Schools: Bullies and Whipping Boys.* Washington, DC: Hemisphere.

Ormerod, D. (ed.) (2005) *Smith and Hogan's Criminal Law* (11th edn). London: LexisNexis.

O'Rourke, M.M. and Bailes, G. (2006) *Risk Assessment and Management. Occasional Briefing Paper 4.* Leicester: BPS.

O'Rourke, M.M. and Hammond, S.M. (2000) *RAMAS Anger Assessment Profile: Professional Manual.* London: RAMAS Foundation (available online at **www.ramas.co.uk**).

O'Rourke, M.M. and Hammond, S.M. (2005a) 'Risk need and responsivity: working from effective baselines.' Paper presented at the Home Office conference, 'The treatment and management of dangerous and severe personality disordered offenders', York.

O'Rourke, M.M. and Hammond, S.M. (2005b) *Risk Assessment Management and Audit Systems Professional Manual.* London: RAMAS.

O'Rourke, M.M. and Titley, K. (1999) *Examination of the Liaison Psychiatric Service.* Surrey: NHS.

O'Rourke, M.M., Van der Watt, D. and Picardo, M. (2001) *Domestic Violence: A Practitioner's Handbook.* London: NHS.

Osborne, Y.H., Rappaport, N.B. and Meyer, R.G. (1986) 'An investigation of persuasion and sentencing severity with mock juries', *Behavioural Science and the Law,* 4: 339–49.

Ost, J. (2006) 'Recovered memories', in T. Williamson (ed.) *Investigative Interviewing: Rights, Research, Regulation.* Cullompton: Willan Publishing.

Otto, R.K. and Heilbrun, K. (2002) 'The practice of forensic psychology: a look to the future in the light of the past', *American Psychologist,* 57: 5–18.

Padfield, N. (in press) 'The role and functions of the Parole Board: perceptions of fairness.'

Padfield, N. and Liebling, A. (2000) *An Exploration of Decision-making at Discretionary Lifer Panels. Home Office Research Study* 213. London: Home Office.

Palmer, E.J. (2003a) 'An overview of the relationship between moral reasoning and offending', *Australian Psychologist*, 38: 165–74.

Palmer, E.J. (2003b) *Offending Behaviour: Moral Reasoning, Criminal Conduct and the Rehabilitation of Offenders.* Cullompton: Willan Publishing.

Palmer, E.J. (2005) 'The relationship between moral reasoning and aggression, and the implications for practice', *Psychology, Crime and Law*, 11: 353–61.

Palmer, E.J. and Hollin, C.R. (1998) 'A comparison of patterns of moral development in young offenders and non-offenders', *Legal and Criminological Psychology*, 3: 225–35.

Pankratz, L. and Binder, L.M. (1997) 'Malingering on intellectual and neuropsychological measures', in R. Rogers (ed.) *Clinical Assessment of Malingering and Deception* (2nd edn). New York, NY: Guilford Press.

Paton, J. and Jenkins, R. (2005) 'Suicide and suicide attempts in prisons', in K. Hawton (ed.) *Prevention and Treatment of Suicidal Behaviour – from Science to Practice.* Oxford: Oxford University Press.

Patrick, C.J. (ed.) (2006) *Handbook of Psychopathy.* New York, NY: Guilford Press.

Pennington, B.F. (2006) 'From single to multiple deficit models of developmental disorders', *Cognition*, 101: 385–413.

Petersen, M.L. and Farrington, D.P. (2007) 'Cruelty to animals and violence to people?', *Victims and Offenders*, 2: 21–43.

Piaget, J. (1932) *The Moral Judgment of the Child.* London: Routledge & Kegan Paul.

Pilgrim, D. (2002) 'The biopsychosocial model in Anglo-American psychiatry: past, present and future?', *Journal of Mental Health*, 11: 585–94.

Pilgrim, D. (2007) 'The survival of psychiatric diagnosis', *Social Science and Medicine* (in press).

Pinheiro, P.S. (2006) *World Report on Violence against Children (United Nations Secretary-General's Study on Violence against Children).* New York, NY: United Nations.

Piquero, A.R., Farrington, D.P. and Blumstein, A. (2007) *Key Issues in Criminal Career Research: New Analyses of the Cambridge Study in Delinquent Development.* Cambridge: Cambridge University Press.

Porporino, F.J., Robinson, D., Millson, B. and Weekes, J.R. (2002) 'An outcome evaluation of prison-based treatment programming for substance users', *Substance Use and Misuse*, 37: 1047–77.

Powell, M., Fisher, R. and Wright, M. (2005) 'Investigative interviewing', in N. Brewer and K.D. Williams (eds) *Psychology and Law: An Empirical Perspective.* New York, NY: Guilford Press.

Prime Minister's Strategy Unit (2003) *Interim Analytical Report.* London: Cabinet Office.

Quinsey, V.L. (2004) 'Risk assessment and management in community settings', in W.R. Lindsay *et al.* (eds) *Offenders with Developmental Disabilities.* Chichester: Wiley.

Quinsey, V.L., Harris, G.T., Rice, M.E. and Gromier, C.A. (1998) *Violent Offenders: Appraising and Managing Risk.* Washington, DC: APA.

Radelet, M.L., Bedau, H.A. and Putnam, C.E. (1992) *In Spite of Innocence.* Boston, MA: Northeastern University.

Raine, A. (2002) 'The biological basis of crime', in J.Q. Wilson and J. Petersilia (eds) *Crime: Public Policies for Crime Control.* Oakland, CA: ICS Press.

Raistrick, D., Heather, N. and Godfrey, C. (2006) *Review of the Effectiveness of Treatment for Alcohol Problems.* London: National Treatment Agency for Substance Misuse (available online at **www.nta.nhs.uk**).

Raynor, P. (2007) 'Risk and need assessment in British probation: the contribution of LSI-R', *Psychology, Crime and Law*, 13: 125–38.

Raynor, P. and Robinson, G. (2005) *Rehabilitation, Crime and Justice*. London: Palgrave Macmillan.

Reik, T. (1959) *The Compulsion to Confess*. New York, NY: Farrar, Strauss & Cudahy.

Rice, M. and Brooks, G. (2004) *Developmental Dyslexia in Adults: A Research Review*. London: National Research and Development Centre for Adult Literacy and Numeracy.

Risk Management Authority (2006) *Risk Assessment Tools Evaluation Directory (Version 1)*. Edinburgh: RMA Scotland.

Robertson, I.H., Ward, T., Ridgeway, V. and Nimmo-Smith, I. (1994) *The Test of Everyday Attention Manual*. Bury St Edmunds: Thames Valley Test Company.

Romero, E., Luengo, M.A. and Sobral, J. (2001) 'Personality and antisocial behaviour: study of temperamental dimensions', *Personality and Individual Differences*, 31: 329–48.

Rose, S., Bisson, J., Churchill, R. and Wessely, S. (2002) 'Psychological debriefing for preventing post traumatic stress disorder (PTSD)', *Cochrane Database of Systematic Reviews*, 2: art. no. CD000560 (available online at **www.Cochrane.org**).

Rosenfeld, B. and Lewis, C. (2005) 'Assessing violence risk in stalking cases: a regression tree approach', *Law and Human Behavior*, 29: 343–57.

Rosner, R. (2003) *Principles and Practice of Forensic Psychiatry* (2nd edn). London: Hodder.

Royal College of Psychiatrists (2007) *Supplementary Standards for Medium Secure Units*. London: Centre for Quality Improvement, Royal College of Psychiatrists.

Royal College of Psychiatrists and British Psychological Society (2003) *Schizophrenia Core Interventions in the Treatment and Management of Schizophrenia in Primary and Secondary Care*. London: National Institute of Clinical Excellence.

Rutter, M., Giller, H. and Hagell, A. (1998) *Antisocial Behaviour by Young People*. Cambridge: Cambridge University Press.

Sackett, D.L., Rosenberg, W.M., Gray, J.A., Haynes, R.B. and Richardson, W.S. (1996) 'Evidence based medicine: what it is and what it isn't', *British Medical Journal*, 312: 71–2.

Safer Services (1999) *National Confidential Inquiry into Suicide and Homicide by People with Mental Illness*. Manchester: Safer Services.

Sainsbury Centre for Mental Health/Mental Health Act Commission (2005) *Back on Track: CPA Care Planning for Service Users who are Repeatedly Detained under the Mental Health Act*. London: Sainsbury Centre.

Sallmann, P. and Willis, J. (1984) *Criminal Justice in Australia*. Melbourne: Oxford University Press.

Sampson, R.J. and Laub, J.H. (2006) *Developmental Criminology and its Discontents: Trajectories of Crime from Childhood to Old Age. Annals of the American Academy of Political and Social Science Series*. Newbury Park, CA: Sage.

Samuels, J., Bienvenu, O.J., Cullen, B., Costa, P.T., Eaton, W.W. and Nestadt, G. (2004) 'Personality dimensions and criminal arrest', *Comprehensive Psychiatry*, 45: 275–80.

Sandys, M. and Dillehay, R.C. (1995) 'First-ballot votes, predeliberation dispositions, and final verdicts in jury trials', *Law and Human Behaviour*, 19: 175–95.

Sarat, A. (1995) 'Violence, representation and responsibility in capital trials: the view from the jury', *Indiana Law Journal*, 70: 1103–39.

Schachter, S. and Singer, J.R. (1962) 'Cognitive, social and physiological determinants of emotional state', *Psychological Review*, 69: 379–99.

Schein, E.H. (1956) 'The Chinese indoctrination program for prisoners of war', *Psychiatry*, 19: 149–72.

Schretlen, D.J. (1997) 'Dissimulation on the Rorschach and other projective measures', in R. Rogers (ed.) *Clinical Assessment of Malingering and Deception* (2nd edn). New York, NY: Guilford Press.

Scottish Executive (2002) *Review of Educational Psychology Services in Scotland.* Edinburgh: Scottish Executive.

Screech, M.A. (1985) 'Good madness in Christendom', in W.F. Bynum *et al.* (eds) *The Anatomy of Madness: Essays in the History of Psychiatry. Volume I.* London: Tavistock.

Sechrest, L., White, S. and Brown, E. (1979) *The Rehabilitation of Criminal Offenders.* Washington, DC: National Academy of Sciences.

Sedgwick, P. (1982) *PsychoPolitics.* London: Pluto Press.

Seguin, J.R., Assaad, J., Nagin, D. and Tremblay, R.E. (2004) 'Cognitive-neuropsychological function in chronic physical aggression and hyperactivity', *Journal of Abnormal Psychology*, 13: 603–13.

Shapiro, F. (2001) *Eye Movement Desensitization and Reprocessing: Basic Principles, Protocols, and Procedures* (2nd edn). New York, NY: Guilford Press.

Sharma, A. (2006) *Are Human Rights Western?* Oxford: Oxford University Press.

Shelter (2007) *Barred from Housing: A Discussion of the Barriers Faced by Prisoners in Accessing Accommodation on Release.* London: Shelter (available online at **www.shelter.org.uk**).

Sheridan, L. and Boon, J. (2002) 'Stalker typologies: implications for law enforcement', in J. Boon and L. Sheridan (eds) *Stalking and Psychosexual Obsession: Psychological Perspectives for Prevention, Policing and Treatment.* Chichester: Wiley.

Sherman, L.W., Farrington, D.P., Welsh, B.C. and MacKenzie, D.L. (eds) (2002) *Evidence-based Crime Prevention.* New York, NY: Routledge.

Silva, J.A. (2007) 'The relevance of neuroscience to forensic psychiatry', *Journal of the American Academy of Psychiatry and the Law*, 35: 6–9.

Simons, R.L., Simons, L.G. and Wallace, L.E. (2004) *Families, Delinquency and Crime.* Los Angeles, CA: Roxbury.

Smeeth, L., Haines, A. and Ebrahim, S. (1999) 'Numbers needed to treat derived from meta-analyses – sometimes informative, usually misleading', *British Medical Journal*, 318: 1548–51.

Smeets, T., Jelicic, M., Peters, M.J.V., Candel, I., Horselenberg, R. and Merckelbach, H. (2006) '"Of course I remember seeing that film" – how ambiguous questions generate crashing memories', *Applied Cognitive Psychology*, 20: 779–89.

Snow, L. (2006) 'Psychological understanding of self-injury and attempted suicides in prisons', in G. Towl (ed.) *Psychological Research in Prisons.* Oxford: BPS/Blackwell.

Social Exclusion Unit (2002) *Reducing Re-offending by Ex-prisoners.* London: Office of the Deputy Prime Minister.

Sohlberg, M.M. and Mateer, C.A. (2001) *Cognitive Rehabilitation: An Integrative Neuropsychological Approach.* London: Guilford Press.

Spencer, R.J. (ed.) (1989) *Jackson's Machinery of Justice in England.* Cambridge: Cambridge University Press.

Spielberger, C.D., Jacobs, G.A., Russell, S. and Crane, R.S. (1983) 'Assessment of anger: the State-Trait Anger Scale', in J.N. Butcher and C.D. Spielberger (eds) *Advances in Personality Assessment. Vol. 2.* Hillsdale, NJ: Erlbaum.

Spitzberg, B.H. and Cupach, W.R. (2006) 'The state of the art of stalking: taking stock of the emerging literature', *Aggression and Violent Behavior*, 12: 64–86.

Strathdee, G., Manning, V., Best, D., Keaney, F., Bhui, K., Witton, J., Wall, S., McGillivary, L., Marsden, J., Johnson, F., Piek, C. and Wilson-Jones, C. (2002) *Dual Diagnosis in a Primary Care Group (PCG).* London: National Treatment Agency for Substance Misuse.

Szasz, T.S. (1961) 'The use of naming and the origin of the myth of mental illness', *American Psychologist*, 16: 59–65.

Tarling, R. (1993) *Analysing Offending: Data, Models and Interpretations*. London: HMSO.

Tarrier, N., Wells, A. and Haddock, G. (eds) (1998) *Treating Complex Cases: The Cognitive Behavioural Therapy Approach*. Chichester: Wiley.

Taylor, J.L. (2002) 'A review of assessment and treatment of anger and aggression in offenders with intellectual disability', *Journal of Intellectual Disability Research*, 46 (suppl. 1): 57–73.

Taylor, P. (1999) 'A cylindrical model of communication behaviour in crisis negotiations', *Human Communication Research*, 28(1): 7–48.

Thomas-Peter, B.A. (2006) 'The modern context of psychology in corrections: influences, limitations and values of "what works"', in G.J. Towl (ed.) *Psychological Research in Prisons*. Oxford: BPS/Blackwell.

Thompson, N. and Thompson, S. (2007) *Understanding Social Care*. Lyme Regis: Russell House.

Tilt, R., Perry, B. and Martin, C. *et al.* (2000) *Report of the Review of Security at the High Security Hospitals*. London: Department of Health.

Towl, G.J. (1999) 'Notes from the chair', *Forensic Update*, 59: 4–5.

Towl, G.J. (2004) 'Applied psychological services in HM Prison Service', in A. Needs and G.J. Towl (eds) *Applying Psychology to Forensic Practice*. Oxford: BPS/Blackwell.

Towl, G.J. (ed.) (2006) *Psychological Research in Prisons*. Oxford: Blackwell.

Towl, G.J. and Crighton, D.A. (1996) *The Handbook of Psychology for Forensic Practitioners*. London: Routledge.

Towl, G.J. and Crighton, D.A. (2000) 'Risk assessment and management', in G.J. Towl *et al.* (eds) *Suicide in Prisons*. Leicester: BPS.

Tucker, M. and Oei, T.P.S. (2007) 'Is group more cost effective than individual cognitive behavioural therapy? The evidence is not solid yet', *Behavioural and Cognitive Psychotherapy*, 35: 77–91.

United Nations (1983) *Human Rights: A Compilation of International Instruments*. New York, NY: United Nations.

Vellutino, F.R., Fletcher, J.M., Snowling, M.J. and Scanlon, D.M. (2004) 'Specific reading disability (dyslexia): what have we learned in the past four decades?', *Journal of Child Psychology and Psychiatry*, 45: 2–40.

Vinogradov, S. and Yalom, I. (1994) 'Group therapy', in R. Hales *et al.* (eds) *The American Psychiatric Press Textbook of Psychiatry* (2nd edn). Washington, DC: American Psychiatric Press.

Vrij, A. (2002) 'Deception in children: a literature review and implications for children's testimony', in H.L. Westcott *et al.* (eds) *Children's Testimony: A Handbook of Psychological Research and Forensic Practice*. Chichester: Wiley.

Vrij, A. (2008) *Detecting Lies and Deceit: Pitfalls and Opportunities*. Chichester: Wiley.

Walker, J. (2001) *Control and the Psychology of Health: Theory, Measurement and Application*. Buckingham: Open University Press.

Walsh, A. and Ellis, L. (2007) *Criminology: An Interdisciplinary Approach*. Thousand Oaks, CA: Sage.

Walsh, B. (2006) *Treating Self-injury: A Practical Guide*. New York, NY: Guilford Press.

Walters, G.D. (2006) 'Risk-appraisal versus self-report in the prediction of criminal justice outcomes', *Criminal Justice and Behavior*, 33: 279–304.

Webster, C.D., Eaves, D., Douglas, K.S. and Wintrup, A. (1995) *The HCR-20: The Assessment of Dangerousness and Risk*. Vancouver: Simon Fraser University and British Colombia Forensic Psychiatric Services Commission.

Wechsler, D. (1997) *WAIS-III Manual*. New York, NY: Psychological Corporation.

Weekes, J.R., Moser, A.E. and Langevin, C.M. (1998) 'Assessing substance abusing offenders for treatment', in E.J. Latessa (ed.) *What Works – Strategic Solutions: The International Community Corrections Association Examines Substance Abuse*. Arlington, VA: Kirby Lithographic Co.

Westcott, H.L. (2006) 'Child witness testimony: what do we know and where are we going?', *Child and Family Law Quarterly*, 18: 175–90.

White, J.L., Moffitt, T.E., Caspi, A., Bartusch, D.J., Needles, D.J. and Stouthamer-Loeber, M. (1994) 'Measuring impulsivity and examining its relationship to delinquency', *Journal of Abnormal Psychology*, 103: 192–205.

White, P., Bradley, C., Ferriter, M. and Hatzipetrou, L. (1998) 'Management of people with disorders of sexual preference and for convicted sexual offenders', *Cochrane Database of Systematic Reviews*, 4: art. no. CD000251 (available online at **www.Cochrane.org**).

Whittington, R., Barr, W., Brown, A., Leitner, M., Logan, C. and Nathan, T. (in press) 'Best practice in managing risk: principles and evidence for best practice in the assessment and management of risk to self and others (National Mental Health Risk Management Programme).'

Whitton, E. (1998) *The Cartel: Lawyers and their Nine Magic Tricks.* Glebe, NSW: Herwick.

Whitton, E. (2003) '21 reasons you won't get justice from the adversarial court system' (available online at **http://www.onlineopinion.com.au/view.asp?article=268**).

Wilczynski, A. and Morris, A. (1993) 'Parents who kill their children', *Criminal Law Review*, 31–6.

Williams, V. (2007) *Civil Procedure Handbook, 2007/2008* (rev. edn). Oxford: Oxford University Press.

Wilson, D.B. and MacKenzie, D.L. (2006) 'Boot camps', in B.C. Welsh and D.P. Farrington (eds) *Preventing Crime: What Works for Children, Offenders, Victims and Places.* Dordrecht: Springer.

Wilson, D.B., Sharp, C. and Patterson, A. (2006) *Young People and Crime: Findings from the 2005 Offending, Crime and Justice Survey.* London: Home Office (available online at **www.homeoffice.gov.uk/rds**).

Wilson, M.A. (2006) 'Terrorist behavior in hostage taking: policy issues and research directions', in J. Victoroff and S. Mednick (eds) *Psychology and Terrorism.* Amsterdam: IOS Press.

Wilson, M.A. and Smith, A. (1999) 'Roles and rules in terrorist hostage taking', in D. Canter and L. Alison (eds) *The Social Psychology of Crime: Groups, Teams, and Networks.* Aldershot: Dartmouth.

Wilson, P. and Norris, G. (2003) 'Relationship between criminal behaviour and mental illness in young adults: conduct disorder, cruelty to animals and young adult serious violence', *Psychiatry, Psychology and Law*, 10: 239–43.

Wittchen, U.H., Fröhlich, C., Behrendt, S., Günther, A., Rehm, J., Zimmermann, P., Lieb, R. and Perkonigg, A. (2007) 'Cannabis use and cannabis use disorders and their relationship to mental disorders: a 10-year prospective longitudinal community study in adolescents', *Drug and Alcohol Dependence*, 88: 60–70.

Wolfgang, M.E. (1973) *Patterns in Criminal Homicide.* Glen Ridge, NJ: Patterson Smith.

Wood, R.L. and McMillan, T.M. (eds) (2001) *Neurobehavioural Disability and Social Handicap following Traumatic Brain Injury.* Hove: Psychology Press.

World Health Organization (1992) *The ICD-10 Classification of Mental and Behavioural Disorders (Clinical Descriptions and Diagnostic Guidelines).* Geneva: World Health Organization.

World Health Organization (2002) *World Report on Violence and Health.* Geneva: WHO.

Worrall, A. and Hoy, C. (2005) *Punishment in the Community: Managing Offenders, Making Choices.* Cullompton: Willan Publishing.

Wrightman, L. and Kassin, S.M. (1993) *Confessions in the Courtroom.* London: Sage.

Zander, M. and Henderson, P. (1994) 'The Crown court study: Royal Commission on Criminal Justice Study No. 19', *Research Bulletin*, 35: 46–8.

Index

Note: Words represented in **bold italic** indicate main dictionary entries.